MEDIA EVENTS IN A GLOBAL AGE

We live in an age where the media are intensely global and profoundly changed by digitalization. Not only do many media events have audiences who access them online, but additionally digital media flows are generating new ways in which media events can emerge. In times of increasingly differentiated media technologies and fragmented media landscapes, the "eventization" of the media is increasingly important for the marketing and everyday appreciation of popular media texts.

The chapters in this collection are organized into six thematically linked sections:

- Media Events Rethought
- The History and Future of the Media Event
- Media Events in the Frame of Contemporary Social and Cultural Media Theory
- Media Events and Everyday Identities
- Media Events and Global Politics
- Media Events and Cultural Contexts

Events covered include *Celebrity Big Brother*, 9/11, the Iraq War and World Youth Day 2005 to give readers an understanding of the major debates in this increasingly high-profile area of media and cultural research.

Contributors: Göran Bolin, Nick Couldry, Peter Csigo, Daniel Dayan, Florian Deffner, Udo Göttlich, Andreas Hepp, Stewart M. Hoover, Elihu Katz, Douglas Kellner, Veronika Krönert, Friedrich Krotz, Lisa Leung, Tamar Liebes, Joost van Loon, Roy Panagiotopoulou, Nancy K. Rivenburgh, Eric W. Rothenbuhler, Agnieszka Stepinska, Ingrid Volkmer, Norbert Wildermuth, Jürgen Wilke..

Nick Couldry is Professor of Media and Communications at Goldsmiths, University of London, and director of its Centre for the Study of Global Media and Democracy. Previous publications include *The Place of Media Power* (2000), *Media Rituals* (2003), and *Media Consumption and Public Engagement: Beyond the Presumption of Attention* (2007).

Andreas Hepp is Professor of Communications and Head of the Institute for Media, Communication and Information (IMKI) at the University of Bremen, Germany. Recent publications in English include the co-edited volume *Connectivity, Networks and Flows: Conceptualizing Contemporary Communications* (2008).

Friedrich Krotz is Professor of Social Communication and Head of the Research Centre "Communication and Digital Media" at the University of Erfurt, Germany. He is the editor of *Communications: The European Journal of Communication Research*.

COMEDIA
Series Editor: David Morley

MEDIA EVENTS IN A GLOBAL AGE

*Edited by Nick Couldry, Andreas Hepp
and Friedrich Krotz*

Routledge
Taylor & Francis Group

LONDON AND NEW YORK

First published 2010
by Routledge
2 Park Square, Milton Park, Abingdon, Oxon OX14 4RN

Simultaneously published in the USA and Canada
by Routledge
270 Madison Ave, New York, NY 10016

Routledge is an imprint of the Taylor & Francis Group, an informa business

Typeset in Garamond 3 by
Keystroke, Tettenhall, Wolverhampton
Printed and bound in Great Britain by
TJ International Ltd, Padstow, Cornwall

British Library Cataloguing in Publication Data
A catalogue record for this book is available
from the British Library

Library of Congress Cataloging in Publication Data
Media events in a global age / edited by Nick Couldry, Andreas
Hepp and Friedrich Krotz.
p. cm. – (Comedia)
1. Mass media–Social aspects. 2. Mass media and culture.
3. Mass media and globalization. 4. Mass media–Influence.
I. Couldry, Nick. II. Hepp, Andreas. III. Krotz, Friedrich.
P94.6.M4255 2009
302.23–dc22
2009016086

ISBN10: 0–415–47710–7 (hbk)
ISBN10: 0–415–47711–5 (pbk)
ISBN10: 0–203–87260–6 (ebk)

ISBN13: 978–0–415–47710–9 (hbk)
ISBN13: 978–0–415–47711–6 (pbk)
ISBN13: 978–0–203–87260–4 (ebk)

CONTENTS

CONTENTS

CONTENTS

LIST OF ILLUSTRATIONS

Figures

Tables

CONTRIBUTORS

Göran Bolin is Professor of Media and Communication Studies, Södertörn University, Sweden.

Nick Couldry is Professor of Media and Communications and Director of the Centre for the Study of Global Media and Democracy, Goldsmiths, University of London, UK.

Peter Csigo is Researcher in Cultural Studies, Budapest University of Technology, Hungary.

Daniel Dayan is Directeur de Recherche at the Centre National de la Recherche Scientifique, Paris, a fellow of the Marcel Mauss Institute (Ecole des Hautes Etudes en Sciences Sociales), and Hans Speier visiting Professor of Sociology at The New School for Social Research, New York.

Florian Deffner is a PhD student in Media and Communications at University of Melbourne, Australia.

Udo Göttlich is Senior Researcher in Sociology, University of Duisburg-Essen, Germany.

Andreas Hepp is Professor of Communication and Head of the Institute for Media, Communication and Information (IMKI), University of Bremen, Germany.

Stewart M. Hoover is Professor of Media Studies, Professor Adjoint of Religious Studies and Director of the Center for Media, Religion, and Culture, University of Colorado at Boulder, USA.

Elihu Katz is Distinguished Trustee Professor of Communication at The Annenberg School for Communication, University of Pennsylvania, USA, and Emeritus Professor in the Departments of Sociology and of Communication and Journalism at The Hebrew University of Jerusalem, Israel.

Douglas Kellner is Professor of the Philosophy of Education, University of California, Los Angeles, USA.

Veronika Krönert is Researcher in Media and Communication at the Institute for Media, Communication and Information (IMKI), University of Bremen, Germany.

Friedrich Krotz is Professor of Social Communication, University of Erfurt, Germany.

Lisa Leung is Lecturer in Cultural Studies, University of Lingnan, Hong Kong/China.

Tamar Liebes is Professor of Communication at The Hebrew University of Jerusalem, Israel.

Joost van Loon is Professor of Media Analysis, Nottingham Trent University, UK.

Roy Panagiotopoulou is Professor of Sociology, University of Athens, Greece.

Nancy K. Rivenburgh is Associate Professor of International Communication, University of Washington, USA.

Eric W. Rothenbuhler is Professor of Communication, Texas A&M University, USA.

Agnieszka Stepinska is Assistant Professor in Political Science and Journalism, University of Adam Mickiewicz, Poznan, Poland.

Ingrid Volkmer is Associate Professor of Media and Communications, University of Melbourne, Australia.

Norbert Wildermuth is Associate Professor of Media Studies, University of Odense, Denmark.

Jürgen Wilke is Professor of Communication Research, University of Mainz, Germany.

ACKNOWLEDGMENTS

The editors and the publishers gratefully acknowledge the permissions granted to reproduce the copyright material in this book. The two chapters are listed as they appear in the book.

Dayan, D. (2008) "Beyond Media Events: Disenchantment, Derailment, Disruption", in D. Dayan and M.E. Price (eds) *Owning the Olympics: Narratives of the New China*, Ann Arbor: Michigan University Press, 391–401.

Katz, E. and Liebes, T. (2007) " 'No More Peace!': How Disaster, Terror and War Have Upstaged Media Events", *International Journal of Communication*, 1: 157–66. Available HTTP: <http://ijoc.org>.

1

INTRODUCTION
Media events in globalized media cultures

Andreas Hepp and Nick Couldry

The interest in exceptional forms of media communication may be traced back to the beginning of interdisciplinary media and communication research; for example, Hadley Cantril's (1940) study on the panic caused by Orson Welles' radio play *The Invasion from Mars* (written with the assistance of Hazel Gaudet and Herta Herzog). We find early research on outstanding ceremonial events in broadcasting (cf. Lang and Lang 1969 [1952]; Shils and Young 1956; Chaney 1983). Other authors, more cynically, such as Daniel Boorstin (1963), complained about an increasing number of "pseudo events" in media communication. However, in their 1970s and 1980s work, culminating in the path-breaking book of 1992, it was Daniel Dayan and Elihu Katz who brought this hitherto somewhat neglected discussion to a new stage, drawing our attention to certain phenomena which they called "media events."

In this introductory chapter we want to consider this intervention carefully, in its full theoretical context, in order to establish the basis for researching media events today as an important aspect of power processes in a "global age" (Albrow 1996; Beck 2005). In doing so we want to reflect on the academic discussion that started from Daniel Dayan and Elihu Katz's book *Media Events*, and resulted in a rethinking and extension of the original concept. While we find highly important arguments in the original discussion, we need to update our understanding of contemporary media events within an analysis of globalized media cultures. Through these reflections we come – at least that is our endeavor – to a core definition of media events in a global age, that can offer an orientating frame not only for the different chapters in this book but also for future research.

Media events: an intervention

From today's perspective we can understand the book *Media Events: The Live Broadcasting of History* and its preceding articles and chapters[1] by Daniel Dayan and Elihu Katz as an intervention in media and communication studies in at least a double sense: *theoretically,* it brought together the traditions of social science's mass communication research with semiotics-influenced media and cultural studies, trying to capture a new phenomenon of broadcasting; *methodologically,* it broke with the notion that a focus on the "average" – the "ordinary" viewer, the "normal" program or the "regular" production – is the only or necessary approach to studying media communication in present cultures and societies. In contrast, and making a highly innovative link to anthropological research, Dayan and Katz argued strongly for the relevance of "single," "outstanding" ritual ceremonies in media communication: the media event.

Daniel Dayan and Elihu Katz's intervention was made through a highly nuanced understanding of the phenomena of media events. In short, they defined media events, metaphorically, as "high holidays of mass communication" (Dayan and Katz 1992: 1),[2] or more concretely as a "genre" of media communication that may be defined on syntactic, semantic and pragmatic levels (Dayan and Katz 1992: 9–14). On the *syntactic level,* media events are "interruptions of routine"; they monopolize media communication across different channels and programs, and are broadcast live, pre-planned and organized outside the media. On the *semantic level,* media events are staged as "historic" occasions with ceremonial reverence and the message of reconciliation. On the *pragmatic level*, media events enthrall very large audiences who view them in a festive style. The main point of these criteria is that each as a single attribute may also be found in other forms of media communication; however, when they come together, they constitute the distinctive "genre" of media events.

Drawing on Max Weber's three ideal types of authority (rational-legal, traditional and charismatic: Weber 1972: 124) Daniel Dayan and Elihu Katz distinguish three basic "scripts" of media events. First, the "contest" (like the Olympics) developed as a cyclical media event, taking place under agreed rules in an arena, stadium, forum or studio, person by person, marked by the drama of "who will win?" and presented in a non-partisan way to a judging audience, organized around *rational-legal* authority, and focused on the present. Second, the "conquest" (like the televising of the first steps on the moon) which operates as a single media event, lying beyond any rules at the frontiers and limits of social space, with a hero acting against norms, belief or nature, marked by the drama of "will the hero succeed?" and presented in a bardic way to a witnessing audience, organized around *charismatic* authority focused on the future. Third, the "coronation" (including in this category the funeral) which is not a fixed but recurrent media event, taking place based on traditions in public spaces, marked by the drama of "will the ritual succeed?" and presented in a reverent way to an audience renewing the contract with the center, confirming *traditional* authority, focused on the past. The idea is that within this frame of three basic "scripts" all different media events can be analyzed, something Dayan and Katz go on to do focusing on the production and negotiation of media events, their performance in media coverage and their celebration by the audiences.

If we look at this intervention from today's perspective we may characterize it as an approach to *ritual media events* (Hepp 2004a: 326–32): the main argument for studying media events may be seen in their ritual character, and their role in the integration of societies. In this sense the approach to media events outlined by Daniel Dayan and Elihu Katz may be understood as an attempt to describe important "mediated rituals" (Rothenbuhler 1998: 79); that is, "ritual celebrations" that "may play the role of periodic social gather-ings for the celebration of society as discussed by Durkheim" (Rothenbuhler 1998: 79). Thus Dayan and Katz's approach is marked by a "neo-Durkheimian" (Couldry 2003: 61) perspective in the way media events are researched as occasions "where television makes possible an extraordinary shared experience of watching events at society's 'centre' " (Couldry 2003: 61). Dayan and Katz formulate this, linking to Edward Shils (1975), when they write that the origin of media events "is not in the secular routines of the media but in the 'sacred centre' (Shils 1975) that endows them with the authority to preempt our time and attention" (Dayan and Katz 1992: 32). On this reading, media events *as a form of ritual* become a force of social integration:

> during the liminal moments [of media events], totality and simul-taneity are unbound, organizers and broadcasters resonate together; competing channels merge into one; viewers present themselves at the same time and in every place. All eyes are fixed on the ceremonial centre, through which each nuclear cell is connected to all the rest. Social integration of the highest order is thus achieved via mass communication.
>
> (Dayan and Katz 1992: 15)

Thus in Dayan and Katz's account, the relevance of media events depends on their character as one of the most important institutions "integrating" the highly dispersed members of national societies – and maybe also beyond. We return later to some potential problems with this formulation.

Approaching media events: rethinking and extending

If we want to appreciate the reception of this ritual approach to media events, we first of all have to consider its origin more carefully. Our reference to the number of articles and chapters by Dayan and Katz published in the 1980s and early 1990s already indicates that the book *Media Events* was the outcome of a longer research process, beginning shortly after Anwar el-Sadat's journey to Jerusalem in 1977 (cf. Dayan and Katz 1992: 295). In this process, from 1980 to 1984 Daniel Dayan and Elihu Katz held a number of seminars at the Hebrew University of Jerusalem and the Annenberg School, University of Southern California, Los Angeles. At these seminars, a number of students participated who are nowadays well known in the field of media and communication research; among others Tamar Liebes, Eric Rothenbuhler, Barbie Zelizer and Gabriel Weimann. These seminars not only influenced Dayan and Katz's approach to media events,[3] the work of the young scholars at that time offered a thoroughgoing assessment of the original approach. This may be demonstrated from the work of Eric Rothenbuhler, Barbie Zelizer and Gabriel Weimann.

While taking the general approach of Dayan and Katz, Eric Rothenbuhler (1985; 1988) investigates the audience of the media event of the 1984 Olympics based on a representative telephone survey, asking whether the Olympics qualified as a celebration of a coherent set of values, beliefs and symbols through the formation of a special public around the media event. The idea was to examine how far the media event may be understood as a celebration of the "civil religion" of American society. Perhaps the most striking point of this early empirical work is that while Rothenbuhler does not avoid the frame of standardized mass communication research or the analytical frame of the integrative character of ritual media events, his interpretation of his data already indicates the potentially contradictory character of the supposed "integrative function" of media events. He highlights the inconsistency of media events when arguing (albeit in relation to Parsons) that "both the games and the values they celebrated were diffuse phenomena throughout American society" (Rothenbuhler 1985: 200f.). This intense discussion was continued in the doctoral dissertation of Barbie Zelizer, and developed in her book *Covering the Body: Kennedy Assassination, the Media and the Shaping of Collective Memory*. Taking the Kennedy assassination, Zelizer (1993) does not merely investigate the Kennedy funeral as a ritual media event (in Dayan and Katz's sense, a form of "coronation"), but the Kennedy assassination and resulting media coverage in its entirety. In this way, she demonstrates how far such media coverage is intended as performances by the media or by other social actors who have an interest in *constructing* reality in specific and perhaps conflicting ways, in order to establish certain discursive positions and to maintain power. Within such a power analysis, we find an emergent critique of media events as a genre.

An additional assessment may be seen in the early work of Gabriel Weimann (1987; 1990), who was interested in researching media coverage of terrorism within the frame of media events research. Very early on he insisted on an understanding of "mass-mediated terrorism" as a further scenario of media events he called "coercions," meeting many of the criteria of ritual media events but in a conflict-orientated way where rules are not affirmed but contested (cf. Weimann and Winn 1994: 108). Implicit here was a critique of

Dayan and Katz's typification (conquest, contest and coronation) of media events which seems to have no space for such a conflictual process.

We will organize these early moments in the development of the media events approach into three main points of wider importance which structure the discussion that follows: a critique of a certain reading of the ritual perspective on media events, a critique of the core definition of media events as genres, and finally a critique of the narrowness of the three typical scenarios of media events (cf. Hepp and Krotz 2008: 266–7). Let us now discuss each in turn.

1 *Ritual perspective*: Dayan and Katz defined media events as rituals of mediated communicative integration and their considerations are often marked by a neo-Durkheimian perspective focusing on the question of possible (national) order, although their argument may also be developed in other ways. The problematic assumption which needs to be isolated here is the consideration that "rituals are significant because they 'hold society together' and do so by affirming a common set of values" (Couldry 2003: 65): critiques of that assumption may be traced back to the early debate on media events, although such critiques were not always remembered when the "media events" concept came to be more broadly popularized by other writers. The problem with the account of media events if understood from within such a perspective lies in the implicit understanding of societies as being stable and marked by a shared set of values – an assumption that is highly doubtful when we consider contemporary fragmented "late" or "post"-modern societies, and has perhaps always been doubtful. This problem is magnified when we move beyond a national perspective – the implicit frame of Daniel Dayan and Elihu Katz's original argument – to a global perspective. When we do so, the suggestion of media events as rituals of affirmed values becomes additionally misleading as the variety of media events-based representations increases (cf. Hepp 2004a: 332–40): when we consider examples such as the Olympics it is obvious that they are mediated very differently, depending on the region and nation where one lives.

Overcoming the problems of this neo-Durkheimian reading of "media events" would mean not assuming an integrative role of ritual media events but investigating them as "media rituals" (Couldry 2003) in a different sense; that is, as forms of media communication that *construct* the "myth of the mediated centre." In such a perspective, media events are forms of communication that articulate the power-related, hegemonic imagination of the media as the center of present societies, as the expression of the important incidents within that society. Such an approach can allow considerable flexibility over the implications for value consensus (or otherwise) of both media events and indeed (see Bell 1992) for ritual itself. Therefore, a critical approach to media events should move these processes of construction themselves into the foreground of our analysis.

2 *Defining media events as genres*: Already in his review of Dayan and Katz's book, Paddy Scannell (1995: 153) had argued that the reverent and priestly style of presenting media events was not necessarily given (or at most could be seen as part of a specific historical style). Scannell (1999; 2002) himself has worked rather with a basic distinction between happenings (things that happen to us such as an earthquake or a plane crash) and events (things that we make happen), and researches media events in their historical context as mediatized performances, an approach which overlaps with writers such as Roger Silverstone (1999: 68–77). In relation to Diana's funeral Roger Silverstone argues as follows:

> The Diana funeral provides, in an exaggerated but triumphant way, an example of the way in which the blurring of audience and performer takes place on a public stage, both in the media and beyond its reach (though, of course, never completely beyond its reach). It also takes place on a stage, as a result of its mediation, which removes it from the realm of the personal and transforms each moment into a fragment of a national or even global event. We might want, as a consequence, to think about it quite differently. To think of its participation in the funeral not as a shared and committing moment, but as a performance without responsibility; a sharing of private grief without public mourning.
>
> (Silverstone 1999: 75)

From another direction, John Fiske outlines a different understanding of media events, emphasizing that a distinction between "media events" and "real events" is not appropriate for present-day, mediatized cultures: "The term *media event* is an indication that in a postmodern world we can no longer rely on a stable relationship or clear distinction between 'real' event and its mediated representation" (Fiske 1994: 2, emphasis in original). Leaving aside the problematic claim that all of "us" have shifted into a "postmodern world," there is an interesting point here. While there are events beyond the media in local settings, Fiske insists that only translocally mediated events (that is, events whose significance is transmitted across borders) gain a broader socio-cultural relevance in contemporary societies. But these events are the articulation of competing cultural discourses. In this sense a media event is for him a " 'discursive event' . . ., not a discourse *about* an event" (Fiske 1994: 2, emphasis in original).

Related trajectories may also be found in the work by Douglas Kellner, using the concept of the "media spectacle" (Kellner 2003). Referring back to Guy Debord's (1983) *Society of the Spectacle* rather than anthropological theory, Kellner describes spectacles as a regular phenomenon of consumer societies that is of broad significance:

Media spectacles are organized around "the consumption of images, commodities" as part of the vast institutional and technical apparatus of contemporary capitalism, [and] all the means and methods power employs, outside of direct force, to relegate subjects passive to societal manipulation and to obscure the nature and effects of capitalism's power and deprivations.

(Best and Kellner 1997: 4)

Within the critical analysis of Kellner, most contemporary spectacles appear as mediatized phenomena, which is why he also uses the expression "spectacular media events" (Kellner 2004: 1).

Based on reflections like these, Simon Cottle (2008) has recently tried to extend the concept of media events into a more general approach to "mediatized rituals." In his definition, mediatized rituals "are those exceptional and performative media phenomena that serve to sustain and/or mobilize collective sentiments and solidarities on the basis of symbolization and a subjunctive orientation to what should or ought to be" (Cottle 2006: 415). Within such a frame, ritual media events in the sense of Dayan and Katz may be ranked as "celebratory media events," alongside "moral panics" (Cohen 1972), "conflicted media events" (Fiske 1994), "media disasters" (Liebes 1998), "media scandals" (Lull 1997) and "mediatized public crises" (Alexander and Jacobs 1998). While this approach seems at first instructive, integrating different "media-event-like" phenomena into one super-category, it falls short conceptually owing to its thin use of the concept of the ritual (Couldry and Rothenbuhler 2007). In addition, Cottle's concept of mediatization seems to be undertheorized (cf. Krotz 2008; Lundby 2009). However, Cottle's argument at least opens up an important point about how we describe the wider spectrum of which media events (properly understood) form a part.

3 *The narrow typification of media events*: We can see here a certain pattern where many colleagues who contributed to Dayan and Katz's developing work highlighted the narrowness of how the "scenarios" of media events were originally typified. We can understand the research by Tamar Liebes on "disaster marathons" (Liebes 1998: 71) as an argument in this direction. Liebes conceptualizes them in the tradition of ritual media events, understanding "disasters marathons" as a "genre" (Liebes 1998: 72) that shares a high number of characteristics with media events, including its monopolistic character and its interruption of the everyday banal. The main difference is that the "celebration of disasters" (Liebes 1998: 73) is not in that form pre-planned and is marked more by an overtaking of the public domain by oppositional forces (not hegemonic ones). Thus while Tamar Liebes accepts – as does Gabriel Weimann – the basic definition of Dayan and Katz, she argues for a broader understanding that also reflects disasters as a certain "scenario." This point was not only taken up by Elihu Katz himself in a joint publication

(cf. Katz and Liebes 2007; and Chapter 3, this volume), but it also connects to a varying degree with other research on media events focusing, for example, on terrorism (Nossek 2008), on war (Wark 1994) or on political unification (Krotz 2000) as media events.

We can understand such arguments for extending the typification of ritual media events into three scenarios in a further direction, the direction of "conflict orientated media events": there are a number of outstanding forms of media communication that to a varying degree may be described using such an approach to ritual media events.

However, once we consider extended definitions of the "media event" genre, we also need to make another extension that takes account of consumer and celebrity cultures. Coming from completely different research traditions we find a number of studies that focus on such forms of "eventization" (Hepp 2004b) in this area of media. Considering different forms of "popular media events" (Hepp and Vogelgesang 2003) such as outstanding reality TV events or film events, we see similarities to the concept of ritual media events but also differences. Thus *popular media events* break with the everyday but in a much more routine way; they do not monopolize the media coverage in total, but in a certain segment ("tabloid," "boulevard"); they do not happen "live" but in a continuous development (quite often also of marketing and branding); they are mostly organized by the media themselves not just as pre-planned but as completely commercialized; they are less celebratory and more pleasure-oriented; often they polarize and generate the attention of certain "cultural segments" (e.g. scenes, youth cultures) where popular media events have an outstanding role (see Göttlich, Chapter 12, this volume).

In such a frame we can understand, for example, *Big Brother* not just as a reality TV format but as a kind of popular media event, transgressing the boundaries of single TV coverage (cf. Scannell 2002; Bignell 2005). Or we can grasp how certain celebrities are constructed by the use of certain popular media events (cf. Turner 2004). Taking examples like these, we can see that an approach to contemporary media events must also integrate these phenomena that are more closely related to the staging and marketing of the popular (cf. Puijk 1999). While not being "ritual" in the sense of Dayan and Katz, these events nevertheless contribute strongly to processes of constructing the "mediated centre" (Couldry 2003; 2008) in contemporary cultures and societies.

To sum up thus far, the outlined – albeit preliminary[4] – selection of studies and reflections demonstrate through their critique the relevance of the intervention made by Daniel Dayan and Elihu Katz: media events are highly important contemporary phenomena. However, we have to rethink and extend the original approach towards ritual media events if we want to analyze their importance. Such a rethinking and extension are reinforced once we consider media events as aspects not only of national cultures and societies but of an increasingly globalized world.

Media events in a global age: thickenings of globalized media cultures

If we want to extend our reflections on conceptualizing media events to questions concerning the globalization of media communication, it is worth referring to Daniel Dayan's chapter here. In the context of an analysis of the staging of the Olympics in China 2008 he discusses the original approach to ritualized media events once more, indicating an interesting shift of emphasis.[5] Dayan argues that many aspects of the original work have to be seen in their historical context of national broadcasting. However, there are four major features within the original analysis which are still relevant; that is: (1) "emphasis" (the omnipresence of the transmitted events), (2) "performativity" (their constructing character, creating actively realities), (3) "loyalty" (the acceptance of the definition of the event as proposed by the organizers) and (4) "shared experience" (construction and reconstruction of a "we" in their reception) (see Dayan, Chapter 2, this volume). In our perspective, these four criteria are a good starting point for defining a general frame for researching media events; however, they have to be contextualized in a more general understanding of contemporary globalized media cultures.

When speaking about "media cultures" specifically we include all cultures whose *primary resources* of meaning are accessible through technology-based media. By this we do not want to say that everything is mediated technically within these cultures, but within media cultures "the media" are constructed as the main mediators of "the center." From this point of view, all media cultures have to be theorized as translocal phenomena, inasmuch as media make translocal communicative connections possible (Hepp 2008). They are not "placed" at a defined locality, but are articulated through "disembedded" communicative processes, while still being related to a greater or lesser number of localities within or beyond particular national or regional boundaries.[6] That said, we can understand media cultures as articulated by a connectivity of communication processes that may be based around a relatively centralized power structure (as with traditional mass media) or marked by a more multi-centered power structure (as many hope for the Internet). They may be larger or smaller in terms of the contents and interests that are focused together. We need to allow also for "media cultures" which are highly generalized; for example, the various ways in which the celebrity/audience relationship is worked through in different media/political territories (a point to which we will return below).

Describing media cultures in this sense as translocal phenomena, we also draw on a specific understanding of culture. Some time ago, Jan Nederveen Pieterse (1995) divided the principal understandings of culture into two: a territorial and a translocal one. The essence of his arguments is that territorial concepts of culture are inward looking, endogenous, focused on organicity, authenticity and identity, whereas translocal concepts of culture are outward looking, exogenous, focused on hybridity, translation and identification.

9

Based on our arguments it seems helpful to us to understand cultures in general in a translocal frame: all present cultures are more or less hybrid, and have to translate, change their identities and so on. In contrast to this, what is problematic for a general territorial conceptualization of culture is that it refers to a container-thinking of nation states that is not appropriate in times of globalization. Within this concept, cultures are *from the beginning* interpreted as national cultures of territorial states: no other template or model is considered (for critique, see Beck 2000; Robins 2006; Hepp 2009). More helpful than such territorial bordering is to suggest that cultures – as the sum of the classificatory systems and discursive formations on which the production of meaning draws (see Hall 1997: 222) – transgress the local without being necessarily focused on territoriality as a reference point of their meaning articulation. In this sense, cultures are a kind of "thickening" (Löfgren 2001; cf. Hepp and Couldry 2009) of translocal processes for the articulation of meaning. Such a theorization opens the possibility of understanding territorialization, and deterritorialization, as contested practices through which specific cultures are articulated in their particularity – by the media and beyond (García Canclini 1995; 2001; Tomlinson 1999).

David Morley's metaphor of the "home territory" (Morley 2000) is, at this point, important in a dual sense. On the one hand, it shows the specificity of national media cultures. It is possible to describe national media cultures whose translocal communicative thickening has been territorialized in such a way that national frontiers are the main borders of many communicative networks and flows. The process of thickening the national imagined community is territorially bound. On the other hand, Morley's metaphor of the home territory shows us quite clearly that this territoriality of the media-influenced home no longer exists in a pure form. In a time of globalization, communicative connectivity is becoming more and more deterritorialized. With the distribution of media products across different national borders and the emergence of the Internet, global communicative connectivity grows, making the thickenings of national "media cultures" relative and overlapping. One must contextualize such national "media events" as part of different media networks.

This understanding of globalized media cultures makes it also possible to come to a general frame for understanding media events in the "global age." Our reflections up to this point make clear that there are limits to understanding media events on a global scale as the genre of integrative ritual they were originally thought to be. However, if with Daniel Dayan we understand "emphasis," "performativity," "loyalty" and "shared experience" as the "core" of the original definition, we can bring this together with our understanding of media cultures as resulting from specific "thickenings" of meaning that have links of varying strength with specific territories.

The idea of *emphasis* – the omnipresence of the transmitted events – may be brought together with our argument about their thickening. If we regard media events in a global age not as phenomena that refer to a territorialized national media culture but – with 9/11, the Olympics or comparable "mega-events" (Roche 2000) in mind – as transcultural phenomena, it makes sense to understand them as thickenings of media communication, produced not only by the mass media (television, radio) but also by the Internet and other digital media, covering different forms of "mediated quasi-interaction" (e.g. www, blog-journalism) and "mediated interaction" (e.g. chats, online discussions) of the event.[7] In such a frame the original idea of the "monopolizing" aspect of media events seems to be much more a *situative* (and so not necessarily complete or total) thickening of media communication: at particular moments we find intensive processes of communication under way across very different media products and communicative forms.

Taking the aspect of *performativity* – the constructive character of media events – we have to link this in a global frame to struggles for power and influence in and between media cultures. Relating media events to questions of performativity reminds us that they are power-related articulations, produced with a large amount of resources and fulfilled with certain interests in mind. But when we consider outstanding media events in their transcultural character it becomes obvious that this performativity cannot be related to just *one* power center. Especially if we consider conflict-orientated media events such as terror attacks, war or the always in part politically driven Olympics we reach an understanding of the variety of interest groups and power discourses related to the performance of these events. Reflecting power is a key aspect of performativity, and a one-dimensional analysis at this point falls short.

If we consider questions of *loyalty* – the acceptance of the definition of the event as proposed by the organizers – in the frame of globalized media cultures, we must be careful: up to a certain point we can detect an invocation of loyalty within the definitions of the event organizers. Turning again to the case of disasters, a media event may be marked transculturally by the refutation of original definitions or their disputation. However, another point becomes important: namely that beyond all discursive struggle and dissent media events in their transcultural extension also have something that we might call a thematic core. To take 9/11 as an example, we can argue that, while the representation – and also the meaning – of this media event varied across different media cultures in its thematic core, the iconographic images of the twin towers destroyed by the terror attack worked as the unifying focus of the diversity of discourses gathered within the situative thickening of this event.

As a last criterion, Dayan named *shared experience*; that is, the construction and reconstruction of a "we" in the reception of media events. Again, we hesitate at this point when we consider media events in a global context. It seems highly unlikely that a "global we" in a media event might exist; or at least only very few media events like mediatized natural disasters can

11

be taken as a reference point for diverse discourses in this direction (cf. Volkmer 2006; Kyriakidou 2008). Rather, we would argue, media events in a global-transcultural frame open the space for the construction and reconstruction of many different constructions of a common "we," and of many varied national, ethnic, religious, subcultural and other voicings of that "we," all relating to how the main cultural thickenings within a media event are appropriated locally.

If we try to condense these different considerations into an – albeit fairly general – definition of media events in a global age we can formulate the following: *media events are certain situated, thickened, centering performances of mediated communication that are focused on a specific thematic core, cross different media products and reach a wide and diverse multiplicity of audiences and participants.*

A major aspect of this definition is the expression "centering performances." By this we mean various typical forms of communicative action – called "scenarios" in the original approach of Dayan and Katz and leading to their idea of media events as "genres" – through which a centering is articulated in two senses: first, the thematic core of the media event is "central" to the event's narratives; second, this core is constructed in relation to the "center" of a certain social entity ("a society," "a deterritorial community," "the world").[8] Hence, media events are closely related to processes of constructing the "mediated center." As a consequence they are in general power-related and so must be analyzed critically, that is, in terms of *how* they are constructed *as centering*. In this context we must consider to what extent media events are intended – by the media or by other social actors who have interests in constructing reality in specific, perhaps conflicting ways – to establish certain discursive positions and to maintain those actors' power.

However, the kinds of performances by which this centering construction is articulated vary in relation to the thematic core of a media event. This is the reason why we are confronted today by both "ritual media events" and their scenarios as described in the original approach of Dayan and Katz, by "conflictual media events" like mediatized terror attacks, disasters or wars, and also by "popular media events" of celebrity culture. Therefore, any typification of a certain set of media events – something that is undertaken across the volume's different chapters – is only a snapshot of media's event-based centering power at a certain time and therefore can only be understood as preliminary.

This brings us to our main point about researching media events. Because of their diversity, the "integrative" moment of media events is, instead of being something that may be assumed in advance as characteristic, something uncertain that must be investigated from one case to another. We always have to research critically the interrelation between the "centering" performances of media events on the one hand and the everyday appropriation of them by audiences and populations on the other. Exactly this appropriation may also be a "bypassing" or "reinterpretation" of the centering which the original model of media events saw prioritized. Therefore, in the case of media events too, the construction of a "mediated center" remains an uncertain and contested process, however totalizing the *claims* that such a construction involves.

The volume: an overview

In all, the chapters in this volume present across their diversity the relevance of media events in contemporary globalized media cultures, structured in six parts: Part I rethinks the classical media events approach; Part II focuses on the history and future of media events, Part III on media events in present social and cultural theory, Part IV on the status of media events for everyday identities, Part V on media events in global politics, and Part VI on media events in different cultural contexts. Reflecting this diversity, the volume closes with a retrospective concluding chapter.

Part I, Media Events Rethought, includes chapters by the authors who started this debate through their 1992 book *Media Events: The Live Broadcasting of History*. In his chapter "Beyond media events" – first published 2008 in the book *Owning the Olympics: Narratives of the New China*, co-edited with Monroe Price (pp. 391–401) – Daniel Dayan takes the original approach as a starting point to argue for a further development of a theory of media events. This seems necessary not because the basic assumptions of this publication were wrong but because media events themselves have changed in the global age. Elihu Katz and Tamar Liebes also revise the original approach to media events in their chapter " 'No more peace!': How disaster, terror and war have upstaged media events" (originally published in *International Journal of Communication*, 1, 2007: 157–66). They argue for a rise of disruptive events such as disaster, terror and war, and believe that cynicism, disenchantment and segmentation are undermining attention to ceremonial events, while the mobility and ubiquity of television technology, together with the downgrading of scheduled programming, provide ready access to disruption.

Such a contextualization of the original approach is extended in the three chapters comprising Part II, The History and Future of the Media Event. Jürgen Wilke compares in Chapter 4, "Historical perspectives on media events," the Lisbon earthquake in 1755 and the Tsunami catastrophe in 2004. Combining these analyses with a sophisticated theoretical approach, he makes clear the necessity of a historical perspective on media events. Chapter 5, "From media events to ritual to communicative form" by Eric Rothenbuhler, starts by revisiting the original idea of media events, understanding it as a radical opening of mass communication research to sociological theory, anthropology, and interdisciplinary humanities, and contextualizes this approach in contemporary analyses of communicative form. Another important perspective is brought in by Douglas Kellner in Chapter 6, "Media spectacle and media events: some critical reflections." He connects the tradition of researching "media events" to his own separate and well-known critique

(Kellner 2003) of the regular reliance on spectacle within contemporary cultures and societies.

While Part II opens the discussion on media events to questions of change, Part III focuses on Media Events in the Frame of Contemporary Social and Cultural Theory. It opens with Chapter 7, "Creating a national holiday: media events and symbolic power" by Friedrich Krotz. Within this, Krotz, referring to Pierre Bourdieu, argues that ritual media events may be seen as the announced investment of symbolic capital by the institution which organizes the event. In Chapter 8, Joost van Loon rethinks in "Modalities of mediation" the category of the media event in the light of a philosophically grounded phenomenology that draws on Heidegger's philosophy of being and the reconceptualization of the space of the "social" as part of a rethinking of the work of technology within Actor Network Theory. Finally, Göran Bolin, in Chapter 9, "Media events, Eurovision and societal centers," takes the example of the Eurovision Song Contest as a starting point to investigate media events within the frame of the critique of a "myth of the mediated center." In doing so he moves towards a more Habermasian critique of media events.

Researching contemporary media events also has a high relevance for under-standing everyday processes of meaning articulation. This is demonstrated by the chapters in Part IV, Media Events and Everyday Identities. This section is opened by Peter Csigo in Chapter 10, "Permanent turbulence and reparatory work: a dramaturgical approach to late modern television," in which he revisits Dayan and Katz's approach in the light of the everyday, coming to the conclusion that whether or not a society is "held together" in late modernity depends less on broadcast-like, macro-level integration than on people's dispersed micro-performances in which they enact utopian discourses of civil society in reaction to aestheticized affective impulses. In Chapter 11, "Media events and gendered identities in South Asia – Miss World going 'Deshi'," Norbert Wildermuth takes the popular media event of the annual Miss World nomination in India as an example to demonstrate how media events have been drawn into a broader ideological struggle about notions of gender and national identity in South Asia. Chapter 12, "Media event culture and lifestyle management" by Udo Göttlich, then discusses media events' influence on identity management in contemporary media and everyday culture.

Part V, Media Events and Global Politics, brings a perspective into the foreground that focuses on questions of political communication. Chapter 13 by Nancy Rivenburgh, "In pursuit of a global image: media events as political communication," researches the relevance of hosting political events to gain prestige and favorable opinion via international media representations. In Chapter 14, "9/11 and the transformation of globalized media events" Agnieszka Stepinska discusses one of the most prominent political media events of the last decade: the 9/11 attacks and related changes in contemporary public spheres. The section is completed by Ingrid Volkmer and Florian Deffner, who in Chapter 15, "Eventspheres as discursive forms: (re-)negotiating the 'mediated center' in new network cultures," investigate the articulation of new, so-called transcultural "event-spheres" in today's globalized political communications.

In Part VI, Media Events and Cultural Contexts, the relevance of media events in important cultural fields of the present is discussed. The section opens with Chapter 16, "Sports events: the Olympics in Greece" by Roy Panagiotopoulou, reflecting on the example of the Olympic games as characteristic of an "eventization" of the field of sport and therefore the promotion of a diversity of national images. Lisa Leung in Chapter 17, "Performing global 'news': indigenizing WTO as media event," researches the eventization of (social movement) politics, and how this is based on notions of "professionalism," "ethics," and "media globalization" and media's practice of representing such notions in the recent history of Hong Kong. In Chapter 18, "Religious media events: the Catholic 'World Youth Day' as an example of the mediatization and individualization of religion," Andreas Hepp and Veronika Krönert deal with a hybrid religious media event as the manifestation of current changes in the field of religion.

Finally, the volume concludes with a chapter by Stewart Hoover, reviewing the arguments put forward in the book and reflecting the relevance of media events for contemporary cultural transformations. In all, we hope that these different chapters make clear the continued relevance of ritual and popular media events in today's globalized media cultures and provide a point of departure for future empirical research and theoretical reflection within media and cultural studies and media anthropology. The debate that Dayan and Katz started remains, as they say, "to be continued."

Acknowledgments

This chapter reflects the long-lasting discussion on "media events" in which we have been involved individually and then together since 2000, culminating in the conference "Media Events, Globalization and Cultural Change," organized by the Media Sociology Section of the German Communication Association (DGPuK) and the Mediated Communication, Public Opinion, and Society Section of the International Association for Media and Communication Research (IAMCR) and held in July 2007 at the University of Bremen, Germany. We wish to thank all participants at this conference for stimulating discussions, which resulted in a constructive atmosphere for further developing media events research. Other papers presented at the conference were published in special issues of *Communications: The European Journal of Communication Research*, vols 33(3) (2008) and 34(1) (2009), edited by Andreas Hepp and Friedrich Krotz.

At the Bremen conference and afterwards we received important feedback from a number of colleagues whom we would like to thank personally, especially Daniel Dayan, Ronald Hitzler, Eric Rothenbuhler, Waldemar

Vogelgesang and Ingrid Volkmer. Eric Rothenbuhler also provided helpful comments on an earlier draft of this chapter. Pia Rauball has supported us in carefully preparing this book for publication. In addition, we gratefully acknowledge David Morley as editor of the Comedia series for his feedback on the volume and our Introduction as well as Natalie Foster, Charlie Wood and Sarah Hamilton from Routledge for all of their engagement with this project.

Finally, we wish to thank the editors of the *International Journal of Communication* for consenting to the reprinting of "'No More Peace!'" by Elihu Katz and Tamar Liebes (first published in edition 1(1) 2007), and The University of Michigan Press for consenting to the reprinting of "Beyond Media Events" by Daniel Dayan (first published *Owning the Olympics: Narratives of the New China*, Daniel Dayan and Monroe Price (eds), (2008): 391–401).

Notes

1 Cf. Dayan and Katz 1995; Katz and Dayan 1985; Katz et al. 1981.
2 This is also the title of the French version of the book; cf. Dayan and Katz 1996.
3 For example, Dayan and Katz (1988: 183) credit Eric Rothenbuhler for "making explicit the connection between Durkheim's moral ceremonies and media events".
4 Other important contributions are, for example, Maurice Roche's (2000) analysis of "mega-events" as globalized forms of media events, Göran Bolin's (2006) historical contextual contextualization of contemporary media events and Roel Puijk's (2000) and Knut Lundby's (1997) analyses of the religious dimensions of media events.
5 One impetus for our Bremen conference was the debate (Religion and Media Conference, July 2006, Sigtuna, Sweden) between Daniel Dayan and Nick Couldry about the latter's critique of the original media events model, which brought out the common ground between their then current positions.
6 It is important however not to confuse two questions: the degree to which a locality is translocally connected through communication and the degree to which people living in that locality live their life within the physical space of that locality. The latter can never be reduced to zero, since as physical beings we must all reside somewhere.
7 Cf. Thompson (1995: 85) for the distinction of these forms of communication.
8 That said, we must also bear in mind the variety of the geographical scales on which media events operate, whether regional or national (with some being aimed at particular population sectors) or indeed global.

References

Albrow, M. (1996) *The Global Age*, Cambridge: Polity Press.
Alexander, J.C. and Jacobs, R.N. (1998) "Mass Communication, Ritual and Civil Society", in T. Liebes and J. Curran (eds) *Media, Ritual and Identity*, London: Routledge, 23–41.
Beck, U. (2000) *What is Globalization?*, translated by Patrick Camiller, London: Blackwell.

—— (2005) *Power in the Global Age: A New Global Political Economy*, London: Polity Press.

Bell, Catherine (1992) *Ritual Theory, Ritual Practice*, New York: Oxford University Press.

Best, S. and Kellner, D. (1997) *Debord and the Postmodern Turn: New Stages of the Spectacle*. Available HTTP: <http://www.gseis.ucla.edu/faculty/kellner/essays/debordpostmodernturn.pdf> (accessed 17 September 2008).

Bignell, J. (2005) *Big Brother: Reality TV in the Twenty-First-century*, Basingstoke: Palgrave Macmillan.

Bolin, G. (2006) "Visions of Europe. Cultural Technologies of Nation States", *International Journal of Cultural Studies*, 9, 2: 189–206.

Boorstin, D.J. (1963) *The Image, or, What Happened to the American Dream*, Harmondsworth: Penguin.

Cantril, H. (1940/1952) *The Invasion from Mars. A Study in the Psychology of Panic*, New York: Princeton University Press.

Chaney, David (1983) "A Symbolic Mirror of Ourselves: Civic Ritual in Mass Society", *Media Culture & Society*, 5, 2: 119–136.

Cohen, S. (1972) *Folk Devils and Moral Panics: The Creation of the Mods and Rockers*, London: MacGibbon and Kee.

Cottle, S. (2006) "Mediatized Rituals: Beyond Manufacturing Consent", *Media, Culture and Society*, 28, 3: 411–32.

—— (2008) " 'Mediatized Rituals': A Reply to Couldry and Rothenbuhler", *Media, Culture and Society*, 30, 1: 135–40.

Couldry, N. (2003) *Media Rituals: A Critical Approach*, London: Routledge.

—— (2008) " 'The Media': A Crisis of Appearances", inaugural lecture as Professor of Media and Communications at Goldsmiths, University of London. Available HTTP: <http://www.goldsmiths.ac.uk/media-communications/staff/couldry-inaugural-lecture.pdf> (accessed 6 May 2008).

Couldry, N. and Rothenbuhler, E.W. (2007) "Simon Cottle on Mediatized Rituals: A Response", *Media, Culture and Society*, 29, 4: 691–5.

Dayan, D. (2008) "Beyond Media Events: Disenchantment, Derailment, Disruption", in D. Dayan and M.E. Price (eds) *Owning the Olympics: Narratives of the New China*, Ann Arbor, MI: Michigan University Press, 391–401.

Dayan, D. and Katz, E. (1988) "Articulating Consensus: The Ritual and Rhetoric of Media Events", in J.C. Alexander (ed.) *Durkheimian Sociology: Cultural Studies*, Cambridge: Cambridge University Press, 161–86.

—— (1992) *Media Events: The Live Broadcasting of History*, Cambridge, MA: Harvard University Press.

—— (1995) "Political Ceremony and Instant History", in A. Smith (ed.) *Television. An International History*, Oxford: Oxford University Press, 169–88.

—— (1996) *La Télévision Cérémonielle*, Paris: Presses Universitaires de France.

Debord, G. (1983) *Society of the Spectacle*, Detroit: Black and Red.

Fiske, J. (1994) *Media Matters. Everyday Culture and Political Change*, Minneapolis: Minnesota University Press.

García Canclini, N. (1995) *Hybrid Cultures. Strategies for Entering and Leaving Modernity*, Minneapolis: Minnesota University Press.

—— (2001) *Consumers and Citizens. Globalization and Multicultural Conflicts*, Minneapolis: Minnesota University Press.

Hall, S. (1997) "The Centrality of Culture: Notes on the Cultural Revolutions of

Our Time", in K. Thompson (ed.) *Media and Cultural Regulation,* London: Sage, 207–38.

Hepp, A. (2004a) *Netzwerke der Medien. Medienkulturen und Globalisierung,* Wiesbaden: VS.

—— (2004b) "Radio and Popular Culture in Germany. Radio Culture between Comedy and Eventization", in A. Crisell (ed.) *More Than a Music Box. Radio in a Multi Media World,* New York: Berghan Press, 189–212.

—— (2008) "Translocal Media Cultures: Networks of the Media and Globalisation", in A. Hepp, F. Krotz, S. Moores and C. Winter (eds) *Connectivity, Networks and Flows. Conceptualizing Contemporary Communications,* Cresskill, NJ: Hampton Press, 33–58.

—— (2009) "Transculturality as a Perspective: Researching Media Cultures Comparatively", *Qualitative Social Research (FQS),* 10 (1), Art. 26. Available HTTP: <http://nbn-resolving.de/urn:nbn:de:0114-fqs0901267> (accessed 10 January 2009).

Hepp, A. and Couldry, N. (2009) "What Should Comparative Media Research be Comparing? Towards a Transcultural Approach to 'Media Cultures' ", in D.K. Thussu (ed.) *Globalising Media Studies,* London: Routledge, 32–47.

Hepp, A. and Krotz, F. (2008) "Media Events, Globalization and Cultural Change: An Introduction to the Special Issue", *Communications: The European Journal of Communication Research,* 33: 265–73.

Hepp, A. and Vogelgesang, W. (eds) (2003) *Populäre Events: Medienevents, Spielevents und Spaßevents,* Opladen: Leske + Budrich.

Katz, E. and Dayan, D. (1985) "Media Events: On the Experience of Not Being There", *Religion,* 15: 305–14.

Katz, E. and Liebes, T. (2007) " 'No More Peace!': How Disaster, Terror and War Have Upstaged Media Events", *International Journal of Communication,* 1: 157–66.

Katz, E., Dayan, D. and Motyl, P. (1981) "In Defence of Media Events", in R.W. Haigh, G. Gerbner and R.B. Byrne (eds) *Communication in the Twenty-first Century,* New York: Wiley, 43–59.

Kellner, D. (2003) *Media Spectacle,* London: Routledge.

—— (2004) "9/11, Spectacles of Terror, and Media Manipulation: A Critique of Jihadist and Bush Media Politics", *Critical Discourse Studies,* 1, 1: 41–64. Available HTTP: <http://www.gseis.ucla.edu/faculty/kellner/essays/911terrorspectacle media.pdf> (accessed 1 December 2008).

Krotz, F. (2000) "The German Unification 1990 as a Media Event and its Development Until Today", paper presented at the IAMCR Annual Conference, Singapore.

—— (2008) "Media Connectivity. Concepts, Conditions, and Consequences", in A. Hepp, F. Krotz, S. Moores and C. Winter (eds) *Network, Connectivity and Flow. Conceptualising Contemporary Communications,* New York: Hampton Press, 13–31.

Kyriakidou, M. (2008) "Rethinking Media Events in the Context of a Global Public Sphere: Exploring the Audience of Global Disasters in Greece", *Communications: The European Journal of Communication Research,* 33, 3: 273–91.

Lang, K. and Lang, G. (1969) [1952] "The Unique Perspective of Television and its Effect: A Pilot Study", in W. Schramm (ed.) *Studies in Mass Communication* 2nd edition, Urbana: University of Illinois Press, 544–560.

Liebes, T. (1998) "Television Disaster Marathons: A Danger of Democratic

Processes?", in T. Liebes and J. Curran (eds) *Media, Ritual and Identity,* London: Routledge, 71–84.

Löfgren, O. (2001) "The Nation as Home or Motel? Metaphors of Media and Belonging", *Sosiologisk Årbok,* 1–34.

Lull, J. (1997) *Media Scandals: Morality and Desire in the Popular Culture Marketplace,* Oxford: Polity Press.

Lundby, K. (1997) "The Web of Collective Representations", in S.M. Hoover and K. Lundby (eds) *Rethinking Media, Religion and Culture,* New Delhi: Sage, 146–64.

—— (ed.) (2009) *Mediatization: Concept, Changes, Consequences,* New York: Peter Lang.

Morley, D. (2000) *Home Territories.* London: Routledge.

Nederveen Pieterse, J. (1995) "Globalization as Hybridization", in M. Featherstone, S. Lash and R. Robertson (eds) *Global Modernities,* London: Sage, 45–68.

Nossek, H. (2008) " 'News Media' – Media Events: Terrorist Acts as Media Events", *Communications: The European Journal of Communication Research,* 33: 313–30.

Puijk, R. (1999) "When the Nation Stops: Media Event's Place in Popular Culture", in W. Gozdog (ed.) *Aspects of Audiovisual Culture in Norway and Poland,* Kraków: Jagiellonian University Press, 25–41.

—— (2000) "A Global Event? Coverage of the 1994 Lillehammer Olympic Games", *International Review for the Sociology of Sport,* 35, 3: 309–30.

Robins, K. (2006) "The Challenge of Transcultural Diversities: Final Report of the Transversal Study on the Theme of Cultural Policy and Cultural Diversity", in K. Robins (ed.) *The Challenge of Transcultural Diversities,* Strasbourg: Council of Europe, 7–48.

Roche, M. (2000) *Mega-events and Modernity. Olympics and Expos in the Growth of Global Culture,* London: Routledge.

Rothenbuhler, E.W. (1985) *Media Events, Civil Religion, and Social Solidarity: The Living Room Celebration of the Olympic Games,* doctoral dissertation, University of Southern California.

—— (1988) "The Living Room Celebration of the Olympic Games", *Journal of Communication,* 38, 3: 61–81.

—— (1998) *Ritual Communication: From Everyday Conversation to Mediated Ceremony,* Thousand Oaks, CA: Sage.

Scannell, P. (1995) "Review Essay: Media Events", *Media, Culture and Society,* 17, 1: 151–7.

—— (1999) "The Death of Diana and the Meaning of Media Events", *Review of Media, Information and Society,* 4: 27–50.

—— (2002) "Big Brother as Television Event", *Television and New Media,* 3, 3: 271–82.

Shils, E. (1975) *Centre and Periphery,* Chicago, IL: Chicago University Press.

Shils, E. and Young, M. (1956) "The Meaning of the Coronation", *Sociological Review,* 1: 63–82.

Silverstone, R. (1999) *Why Study the Media?,* London: Sage.

Thompson, J.B. (1995) *The Media and Modernity. A Social Theory of the Media,* Cambridge: Cambridge University Press.

Tomlinson, J. (1999) *Globalization and Culture,* Oxford: Polity Press.

Turner, G. (2004) *Celebrity,* London: Sage.

Volkmer, I. (2006) "Globalization, Generational Entelechies, and the Global Public Space", in I. Volkmer (ed.) *News in Public Memory: An International Study of Media Memories Across Generations,* New York: Peter Lang, 251–68.

Wark, M. (1994) *Virtual Geographies: Living with Global Media Events*, Bloomington: Indiana University Press.

Weber, M. (1972) *Wirtschaft und Gesellschaft. Grundriss der verstehenden Soziologie*, Tübingen: Mohr Verlag.

Weimann, G. (1987) "Media Events: The Case of International Terrorism", *Journal of Broadcasting and Electronic Media*, 31, 1: 21–39.

—— (1990) "Redefinition of Image: The Impact of Mass-Mediated Terrorism", *International Journal of Public Opinion Research*, 2, 1: 21–39.

Weimann, G. and Winn, C. (1994) *The Theatre of Terror. Mass Media and International Terrorism*, New York: Longman.

Zelizer, B. (1993) *Covering the Body: Kennedy Assassination, the Media and the Shaping of Collective Memory*, Chicago, IL: Chicago University Press.

Part I

MEDIA EVENTS
RETHOUGHT

2

BEYOND MEDIA EVENTS

Disenchantment, derailment, disruption

Daniel Dayan

The Olympics exemplify a class of occurrences that are not only pre-planned and heralded long in advance, but also inscribed on calendars. The issue is not whether or not they will take place. We know they will. And since the "what" of the event is already known, the "how" becomes the important issue. Given the predictable nature of the Olympic formula, the Olympics tend to be no longer envisaged as "events-on-their-own" (as expressive actions, or as gestures). They are not seen as messages but as media. They are used as blank slates, as empty stages available for all sorts of new dramaturgies besides their own. The Olympics thus become palimpsests, scrolls that have been written upon, scraped almost clean, and written upon again.

The Olympics have a discontinuous existence made up of long intervals and episodic re-enactments. They are an unusual form of "repertory" events. As in repertory theater, each enactment means to be different. Yet the play or event must be recognizable from repeat to repeat, from episode to episode. This might lead to a "freezing" of the event. Short of freezing the event, the organizers try to control its performance.

In the case of the Olympics, two models of episodic re-enactments come to mind. The first model is religious. The Olympic "religion" is dominated by an almost mystical entity: the Olympic "spirit," a doctrine that, like all dogmas, calls for a hermeneutic approach. A body of specialized literature is devoted to identifying, contextualizing, and updating this "spirit" in reference to the pronouncements of the institution's entrepreneurial prophet, Pierre de Coubertin. Conducted in the name of this doctrinal belief, the orthodoxy of the Games generates a whole bureaucracy of semantic gestures, symbolic displays, and ritual manifestations. Like the Vatican bureaucracy, the IOC bureaucracy seems ferociously attached to detail, and the Olympics are not open to un-negotiated change.

Originally published in: D. Dayan and M.E. Price (eds) *Owning the Olympics: Narratives of the New China*, Ann Arbor, MI: Michigan University Press, 391–401.

Yet, unlike the Church, the IOC cannot rely on threats of excommunication. Attempts by the IOC to impose a given reading of the Olympics involve, therefore, another dimension. This second dimension is legalistic. A given script is handed over and must be implemented. Variability is accepted but only within limits. Implementation is governed by contract. In this regard, the IOC is not very different from the Dutch television company, Endemol, whose reality television shows – including the universally imitated *Big Brother* – are franchised into formats meant to encourage successful reproduction. Like Endemol, the Olympics offer "probabilistic" dramaturgies: ready-to-implement situational plots. Delivered to very different sets of actors and countries, these dramaturgies are meant to function independently of cultural contexts and specific outcomes. In the case of the Olympics, as in the case of Endemol (and, of course, in the case of many other serials as well), the dramaturgies are submitted to managerial rationalization. One could describe them as "taylorized" or "bureaucratic."

In 1992, Elihu Katz and I wrote *Media Events: The Live Broadcasting of History* about those great occasions – mostly occasions of state – that are televised as they take place and transfix a nation or the world. We called these events – which include epic contests of politics and sports, charismatic missions, and the rites of passage of the great – Contests, Conquests, and Coronations. In so doing, we were seeking to identify a narrative genre that employed the unique potential of the electronic media to command attention universally and simultaneously in order to tell a primordial story about current affairs. These were events, we argued, that in effect placed a halo over the television set, thus transforming the viewing experience. Fifteen years have now passed since *Media Events* was first published. The world has changed. We have learned from experience and from the many who have commented on our writings. This chapter on the Beijing Olympics provides an opportunity to revisit several aspects of our joint approach to the phenomena of modern communications. For example, in our book, we focused on three story forms, or "scripts," that constitute the main narrative possibilities within the genre of Contests, Conquests, and Coronations. We argued that these three story forms are dramatic embodiments of Weber's (1946) three types of authority: rationality, charisma, and tradition. This volume opens the possibility of additional themes that are less tied to celebration and that reflect new tensions in the world, including what Tamar Liebes (1998) calls "disaster marathons" and what James Carey (1998) describes as television rituals of "shame" and "degradation."

When we wrote *Media Events*, we found that the fact that the events were pre-planned – announced and advertised in advance – was significant, as advance notice gives time for negotiation, but also for anticipation and preparation on the part of both broadcasters and audiences. These broadcast events were generally presented with reverence and ceremony. In the past, journalists who presided over them suspended their normally critical stance and treated their subject with respect, even awe. Even when these programs addressed conflict – as they often did – they frequently celebrated not conflict but reconciliation. On our reading, media events were generally ceremonial efforts to redress conflict or restore order or, more rarely, to institute change. They called for a cessation of hostilities, at least for a moment, very much in keeping with the ancient Greek tradition of an Olympic truce. Here, too, there have been great changes. Each of us has been contemplating whether there is a retreat from the genres of media events, as we described them, and an increase in the live broadcasting of disruptive events of disaster, terror, and armed conflict.

In our book we also discussed how media events preview the future of media technology. We suggested that when radio became a medium of segmentation – subdividing audiences by age and education – broadcast television replaced it as the medium of national integration. But that too has changed, as so many have recognized. Beijing is not the first Olympics to take place in this fundamentally altered television environment, but it is clearly a theater for seeing the implications of new distribution methods. As new media technology multiplies the number of channels, television has become a medium of segmentation, and television-as-we-knew-it continues to disappear. It is not yet clear whether any medium has replaced or will replace it; if anything, the newest technologies, like mobile, further increase this segmentation. In 1992 we wrote that "the nation-state itself may be on the way out, its boundaries out of sync with the new media technology. Media events may then create and integrate communities larger than nations. Indeed, the genre of media events may itself be seen as a response to the integrative needs of national and, increasingly, international communities and organizations." Beijing seems to be a laboratory for these and related ideas.

The moments that Elihu Katz and I characterized as "Media Events" offered a powerful contrast to ordinary news. Media Events, as we defined them, invite their audiences to stop being spectators and to become witnesses or participants of a television performance. Rephrasing in a slightly different vocabulary the characteristics explored in the original volume, I would hold that the concept of Media Events includes the following four major features:

- insistence and emphasis
- an explicitly "performative," gestural dimension
- loyalty to the event's self-definition
- access to a shared viewing experience.

The first feature, emphasis, is manifested through the omnipresence of the transmitted events; the length of broadcasts that disrupt organized schedules without being themselves disrupted; the live dimension of these broadcasts; and the repetition of certain shots in seemingly endless loops. Performativity means that Media Events have nothing to do with balance, neutrality, or

25

objectivity. They are not accounts but gestures: gestures that actively create realities. Loyalty consists in accepting the definition of the event as proposed by the organizers. It means that the proposed dramaturgy is not questioned but substantially endorsed and relayed. Finally, Media Events provide not only knowledge or information but also a shared experience. This participatory function leads to formats that rely on narrative continuity, visual proximity, and shared temporality. Media Events, in our original formulation, were about the construction or reconstruction of "we."

The Beijing Olympics exemplify in many other ways the established sense of media events, as defined in the analytical framework we sought to forward in 1992. Audiences recognize Media Events as an invitation—even a command—to stop their daily routines. If festive viewing is to ordinary viewing what holidays are to the everyday, these events are among the highest holy days of mass communication. In keeping with this insight, our original project attempted to bring the anthropology of ceremony (Durkheim 1915; Handelman 1990; Levi-Strauss 1963; Turner 1985) to bear on the process of mass communication. In this way, we defined the corpus of events in terms of three categories inspired by linguistics—syntactics, semantics, and pragmatics. We showed that a media event, as a contemporary form of ceremony, deals reverently with sacred matters (semantics), interrupts the flow of daily life (syntactics), and involves the response (pragmatics) of a committed audience.

Because the Beijing Olympics is taking place in a different world from the one in which *Media Events* was first published, it is useful to reprise the three categories as a means of marking the contrast. To better understand the nature and some of the consequences of the changes I will briefly explore the semantics of conflictualization, the syntactics of banalization, and the pragmatics of disenchantment. All are characteristics of today's media events and ways of differentiating today's "media events" from the Media Events in the grand sense we implied in 1992.

In terms of semantics, an ideological sea change has taken place. In 1992, what had particular resonance was the end of conflicts, the waning of feuds, the rise of gestures that seemed to lessen the possibility of war. This mood was later captured in the title of Francis Fukuyama's book *The End of History and the Last Man* (1992). On the eve of the Beijing Olympics, the themes that resonate globally are significantly more somber than those of the late 1980s and 1990s. After a long eclipse, Foucault's "order of supplices" seems to be back, lending its macabre accoutrements to televised ordeals, punishments, and tortures. Numerous events are in keeping with, and indeed extend, James Carey's emphasis on stigmatization and shaming. War rituals multiply. Agon is back, where the dramaturgy of "contest" succeeded in civilizing the brutality of conflict. Media events have stopped being "irenic." Their semantics is no longer dominated by the theme of a reduction of conflict through mediation and resolution of differences. Rather, they could be characterized by Gregory Bateson's notion of "schismogenesis" (1935), that process through which one provokes irremediable hostility, fosters divides, and installs and perpetuates schisms.

In terms of syntactics, there is also a significant change. The format of media events has been dismantled into discrete elements, many of which have migrated toward other genres. As a result of this dissemination, the rhetoric of media events no longer stands out as radically distinct. Take the notion of an event that is automatically guaranteed a monopoly of attention, a characteristic imputed to the royal weddings, coronations, and moon walks of an earlier day. This kind of exclusive focusing on one event at any given time is now becoming almost impossible. Instead, there is a "field" of events in which different candidates compete with each other for privileged status, with the help of entrepreneurial journalists. Social and political polarization and its effect on media means that it is harder to achieve a broad consensus about the importance of particular events. News and media events are no longer starkly differentiated entities but exist rather on a continuum. This banalization of the format leads to the emergence of an intermediate zone characterized by the proliferation of what I would call "almost" media events.

Finally, the pragmatics of media events has also changed. One of the characteristics of classical Media Events was the way in which such events seemed capable of transforming the home into a public space by inviting spectators to assemble into actual viewing communities. The power of those events resided, first and foremost, in the rare realization of the full potential of electronic media technology. Students of media effects know that at most times and places this potential of radio and television is restricted by society. In principle, radio and television are capable of reaching everybody simultaneously and directly; their message, in other words, can be total, immediate, and unmediated. But this condition hardly ever obtains. Messages are multiple; audiences are selective; social networks intervene; diffusion takes time. In the case of media events, however, these intervening mechanisms are suspended. Interpersonal networks and diffusion processes are active before and after the event, mobilizing attention to the event and fostering intensive hermeneutic attempts to identify its meaning. But during the liminal moments we described in 1992, totality and simultaneity were unbound; organizers and broadcasters resonated together; competing channels merged into one; viewers gathered at the same time and in every place. All eyes were fixed on the ceremonial center, through which each nuclear cell was connected to all the rest. Social integration of the highest order was thus achieved via mass communication (Kornhauser 1959).

Since the 1990s, entertainment genres such as reality TV have called for a similar transformation of the home into a communal, public space while media events themselves have offered less of a communal experience. One may watch the Olympics in a living room or even in a stadium, but in both cases, the ubiquitous cell phone is a constant invitation to disengage from the surrounding community. Reliance on new media has reintroduced

27

individualized reception, and this in turn has led to what seems to me to be one of the most significant differences in context: it is not merely the notion of a shared social experience that wanes, it is the very notion of "communitas." What characterized great Media Events was a kind of agreed conspiracy among organizer, broadcaster, and audience: a tacit decision to suspend disbelief, repress cynicism, and enter a "subjunctive" mode of culture. It is this machinery of suspension that is now at risk.

The resonance of media events used to be associated with what Victor Turner called the "as if" or subjunctive modes of culture. Even when an event was perceived as "mere spectacle," authors like John MacAloon (1984) believed in a process through which it would ultimately transcend this status and become truly festive and participatory. But a noticeable change of mood has taken place at the level of reception. Media events produce cynical behaviors. They foster rather than suspend disbelief. Spectators and publics act like Clausewitzian strategists. While they do so, they are themselves being negotiated, acquired, or stolen. Media events still mobilize huge audiences, but they have lost a large part of their enchantment. Bureaucratically managed, they are an exploited resource within a political economy of collective attention. Their magic is dissipating. They have become strategic venues.

These changes in the character of media events have at least two implications. The first implication is theoretical. By virtue of their explicitly "performative" nature, media events are an excellent starting point for understanding the status of news images. Yet the visual "performatives" at play in media events are not to be opposed to some "normal" – that is, devoid of performatives – status of television news images. Quite the contrary. While media events display a spectacular performative dimension, a performative dimension characterizes news as well. Indeed, excluding those systems of unmanned video surveillance (whose function involves neither watching nor showing anything, but retroactively retrieving the recorded traces of past occurrences), television never offers images that are merely informative, images that are enunciatively neutral.

Yet this does not mean that the two performances – news and media events – are or should be identical. They call for a distinct set of rules and for different grammars. And the nature of these grammars brings us to the second implication, a political one. It concerns the quest for proximity that characterizes media events, and almost specializes them in the construction of what I have suggested is a collective "we." In the case of Media Events, the process of "we" construction is perfectly explicit. This process is what the event is about: it is heralded, discussed, negotiated in advance. The construction of a "we" becomes much less explicit for events in which the sharing of an experience is imposed by a merely journalistic decision. In this case, the construction of a "we" (insufficiently heralded, negotiated, or discussed) intervenes before and/or without any sort of debate. News quietly turns into rituals. When this transformation takes place on a daily basis, when we attend a constant banalization of the format, the very multiplication of "almost" media events leads to the emergence of a "gray" zone, inhabited by images that are neither Media Events nor news.

Any event can be turned into a media event through an addition of specific features. The same event can be given more or less space, more or less attention. The same incident can be summed up in a few shots, or treated as a continuous narrative. It can be told retrospectively or transmitted live. It can be shown once or repeated in a continuous loop. Events, and their producers, contend with each other for being awarded the largest amount of features. In today's "gray zone," where there is a blurring of the limits between media events and news, each event can be treated as a news item and as a media event at once. Each situation can be simultaneously addressed through different formats, lending itself to a whole array of discursive statements. Such statements enter in dialogue or debate with each other. Rather than being spoken by a single, monolithic voice – the voice of the nation – any event becomes part of a conversation involving competing versions of the same event, some of them local, some foreign. This conversation enacts a new model of public affairs in which the centrality of events seems to have dethroned that of newscasts (Csigo 2007). Instead of dominant media organizing and conferring a hierarchy on the multiplicity of events, dominant events now serve as the contested ground for a multiplicity of media voices.

Following Daniel Hallin (1986), Michael Schudson (2006) proposes a strong distinction between two exclusive modes of functioning of the public sphere. One corresponds to the normal regime of a democratic society. It is the "sphere of legitimate controversy." The other corresponds to exceptional moments, such as wars, crises, and periods of redefinition of identity. It is a sphere dominated by consensus and complemented by a mirroring sphere, the sphere of deviance. One sphere is meant to allow deliberation and debate. The other sphere is meant to stifle it in the name of some higher general interest.

I would suggest that one sphere is characterized by the normal, critical, informative functioning of news while the other is characterized by a situation where all news items tend to be treated as if they were media events. Schudson points to the danger of allowing the sphere of consensus/deviance to persist beyond moments of acute crisis, of allowing it to take over functions that are normally performed in the sphere of debate. This – I believe – is the danger involved in the undue generalization of a media event model to all news forms, in the rampant progression of the gray zone.

Disenchantment and the loss of the "we"

These issues are obviously relevant to the Beijing Olympics and the contested territory of media events. Events compete with each other for the conquest of public attention. All aspire to the privilege of being on all media at once. In this competition, there will be not only efforts by the organizers of an event to persuade but efforts by many to shape the pattern of that persuasion. Any media event happens because it is willed by some entity, but every media event is also offered as a "public" event. This dual status entails a series of tensions. Such tensions are first of all a matter of production versus reception. From the point of view of spectators, it is clear that the producers of an event have no right to claim ownership over its meaning. The event's meaning depends on producers' own responses and interpretations. But there are other tensions as well: between the ratified performers of a given event and other would-be performers; between the "bona fide" definition of the event and alternative definitions of the same event; between the core of the event and the crowd of parasitic manifestations that proliferates around it, as so many doppelgangers or satellites, as discussed in Price's chapter in this volume.

In the contest for ownership, media events lend themselves to a rich grammar of appropriations. They fall prey to entities that are neither their organizers nor their publics. They may be subverted (denounced), diverted (derailed), or perverted (hijacked). They may be used as Trojan horses or placed under the threat of a sword of Damocles. These multiple tensions and the calculated moves of various public actors interested in the exploitation of the event's charisma ask the question of "legitimate ownership" and undue appropriation. Can anyone own a public event?

This legalistic question is in a way typical of today's media events. It is one of the main questions raised by the Beijing Olympics and by the general transformation undergone by the Games. The Olympics, meant to propose a normative enactment, have become a provider of collective attention on a grand scale. For the IOC, international power consists in brokering such attention. For political publics, the Olympics provide an opportunity of harnessing that attention to the benefit of neglected agendas. For national organizers, the Games offer the prospect of a rite of passage into a certain "elite" of nations. For advertisers, this attention is available in serendipitous quantities. For spectators, they are a spectacle or entertainment. What about those who embody that attention? What about the public and the spectators? Is it cynicism or communitas, skepticism or suspension of disbelief?

In each case what seems at risk is a certain form of "enchantment." Of course disenchantment is not a particularly new development. John MacAloon's classical analysis of the Olympic experience (1984) is centrally concerned with this disenchantment, a disenchantment it does acknowledge but transforms into a mere prelude to the real experience of the Games. Thus a complex initiation process takes the spectators of the Olympics through a succession of steps, or frames. The Olympic experience is framed as spectacle, festival, ritual, and finally as access to truth. MacAloon's process starts with skepticism (spectacle) and ends with belief (truth). Is this progression still conceivable today? Is there any room for an Olympic experience framed as an access to some truth? Or should we rewrite MacAloon's sequence in a style inspired by Baudrillard: "spectacle, festival, ritual, and finally: . . . simulacrum?"

References

Bateson, G. (1935) "Culture Contact and Schismogenesis", MAN 35, article 199, republished in G. Bateson (1972) (ed.) *Steps to an Ecology of Mind*, New York: Ballantine Books.

Carey, J. (1998) "Political Ritual on Television. Episodes in the History of Shame Degradation and Excommunication", in T. Liebes and J. Curran (eds) *Media, Ritual and Identity*, London: Routledge, 42–70.

Csigo, P. (2007) "Ritualizing and Mediating 'Ordinary' Reality in the Era of 'Event Television' ", paper presented at the conference on Media Events, Globalization, and Culture Change at the University of Bremen, Germany, 5–7 July.

Dayan, D. (2006) "Terrorisme, Performance, Représentation: notes sur un genre discursif contemporain", in D. Dayan (ed.) *La Terreur Spectacle*, Paris-INA: De Boeck.

Dayan, D. and Katz E. (1992) *Media Events: The Live Broadcasting of History*, Cambridge, MA: Harvard University Press.

Durkheim, E. (1915) *The Elementary Forms of the Religious Life: A Study in Religious Sociology*, translated by J. W. Swain, London: Allen & Unwin.

Fukuyama, F. (1992) *The End of History and the Last Man*, New York: Free Press.

Hallin, D. (1986) *The Uncensored War: The Media and Vietnam*, New York: Oxford University Press.

Handelman, D. (1990) *Models and Mirrors: Towards an Anthropology of Public Events*, New York: Cambridge University Press.

Katz, E. and Liebes, T. (2007) " 'No More Peace!': How Disaster, Terror and War Have Upstaged Media Events", *International Journal of Communication*, 1: 157–66.

Kornhauser, W. (1959) *The Politics of Mass Society*, New York: Free Press of Glencoe.

Levi-Strauss, C. (1963) "The Effectiveness of Symbols", in *Structural Anthropology*, translated by C. Jacobson and B. Grundfest Schoepf, New York: Basic Books, 186–205.

Liebes, T. (1998) "Television's Disaster Marathons: A Danger for Democratic Processes?", in T. Liebes and J. Curran (eds) *Media, Ritual and Identity*, London: Routledge, 71–84.

MacAloon, J. (1984) (ed.) *Rite, Drama, Festival, Spectacle*, Philadelphia: Institute for the Study of Human Issues.

Schudson, M. (1989) "How Culture Works: Perspective from Media Studies on the Efficacy of Symbols", *Theory and Society*, 18: 153–80.

— (2006) "L' Extraordinaire Retour du Journalisme Politique Ordinaire", in D. Dayan (ed.) *La Terreur Spectacle*, Paris-INA: De Boeck, 153–65.

Turner, V. (1985) "Liminality, Kabbala, and the Media", *Religion*, 15, 3: 205–17.

Weber, M. (1946) *From Max Weber: Essays in Sociology*, New York: Oxford University Press.

3

"NO MORE PEACE!"

How disaster, terror and war have upstaged media events[1]

Elihu Katz and Tamar Liebes

We sense a retreat from the genres of "media events" (Dayan and Katz 1992) – the ceremonial Contests, Conquests and Coronations that punctuated television's first 50 years – and a corresponding rise in the live broadcasting of disruptive events such as Disaster, Terror and War. We believe that cynicism, disenchantment and segmentation are undermining attention to ceremonial events, while the mobility and ubiquity of television technology, together with the downgrading of scheduled programming, provide ready access to disruption. If ceremonial events may be characterized as "co-productions" of broadcasters and establishments, then disruptive events may be characterized as "co-productions" of broadcasters and anti-establishment agencies, i.e. the perpetrators of disruption.

I

Media Events, as defined by Dayan and Katz (1992), are public ceremonies, deemed historic, and broadcast live on television. The genre, and its study, owes a lot to Anwar Sadat, President of Egypt. In 1977, Sadat announced that he would personally come to Jerusalem to offer peace in exchange for the territory which Israel had taken from Egypt in the war of 1967. Live television accompanied almost every moment of his three-day visit to Jerusalem, enthralling Israelis as well as Egyptians, attracting the reluctant attention of the other Arab countries, and the fascination of the rest of the world. His message – especially in his address to the Israel parliament (Liebes-Plesner 1984) – was "No More War."

Observing this near-hypnotic event, and its successful outcome, a first thought was to frame it as "media diplomacy," but clearly it was more than

Originally published in: *International Journal of Communication* 1 (2007): 157–66 that. Negotiation was certainly part of the picture, and implicit within it – indeed in Sadat's very arrival – was the recognition that Israel had so long awaited. Second thoughts led to the narrative underlying the event whereby a heroic leader crosses an enemy border unarmed in order to put an end to a long-standing conflict. This scenario applies equally well to the first visit of the Polish Pope to his homeland, then still under Communist rule, and, in certain respects to the Astronauts' first flight to the moon (Katz 1978). More than diplomacy, even more than ceremony, these events were "performative"; they actually enacted change! The key to such events, we thought, was in the charm of the televised hero, and his decision to risk the "breaking of a rule" in order to reach a goal; this is what the concept of charisma is about (Weber 1968).

Katz and Dayan (1986) decided to call broadcast events of this kind "Conquests" – great steps for mankind. Soon after, we added "Contests" – referring to sports events such as the World Cup and political events such as Presidential Debates – and "Coronations" – weddings, funerals, commemorations, and so on that mark the role-changes of the mighty. The common core of all three is (1) the live broadcast, (2) the interruption of everyday life and everyday broadcasting, (3) the pre-planned and scripted character of the event, (4) the huge audience – the whole world watching, (5) the normative expectation that viewing is obligatory, (6) the reverent, awe-filled character of the narration, (7) the function of the event as integrative of society, and typically, (8) conciliatory. To succeed, these events require the assent of their organizers, broadcasters and audiences – affirming that they are worthy of this kind of special attention – otherwise they are doomed to failure.

II

Critics complained that Dayan and Katz had omitted "major news events" – the kinds that shock the world (Scannell 1996). What is the point, they asked, of separating the Kennedy funeral from the Kennedy assassination, or, in other words, why focus on ceremony rather than on the disaster that provoked it? In reply, we pointed out that shocking news events are disruptive, not integrative, and – unlike ceremonial events – are not pre-planned. They are, of course, interruptions, but they are unexpected and mostly unwelcome. In short, they are a different genre.

But even if this distinction holds good, it is now clear that such major news events deserved inclusion. Doing so would have made it possible to juxtapose the two types of events – disruptive and integrative – and also might have raised a question about their changing proportions over time. For the fact is that media events of the ceremonial kind seem to be receding in importance, maybe even in frequency, while the live broadcasting of disruptive events such as Disaster, Terror and War are taking center stage. Hence our title, *No More Peace*.[2]

III

That media ceremonies are being upstaged, as we think, can be readily explained. First of all, there have been major changes in the technology and organization of broadcasting institutions. Channels have multiplied, and, because of fierce competition, they are less likely to band together, or to join hands with establishments – as once they did – in national celebrations. Television equipment, moreover, has become highly mobile – and ubiquitous. These institutional changes (1) have scattered the audience and undermined the shared experience of broadcasting; (2) have taken the novelty out of live broadcasting, and (3) have socialized us to "action" rather than ceremony, to a norm of interruption rather than schedule.

Increased cynicism offers a second set of reasons for the declining centrality of media events. The credibility of governments – co-sponsors of most media events – is at an all-time low, as is trust in the media (Cappella and Jamieson 1997). Altogether, people to believe in – Great Men – appear to be in short supply, says Scannell (1996). Establishment meddling in the media is widely suspected, and the media are thought to be bowing to these pressures.

Widespread realization that the miracles of media events are short-lived constitutes a third explanation for their apparent decline. The live broadcasting of "historic" ceremonies has lost its aura. Nixon's landslide triumph is soon followed by Watergate; drug scandals and hints of corruption have tainted the Olympics, not even to speak of the tragedy at Munich in 1972; the sentimentality induced by the Royal Wedding of Charles and Diana in 1981 is tainted by divorce and death; the stardom of John Kennedy, Anwar Sadat, and Yitzhak Rabin all end in assassinations.

The fate of Middle East summitry provides a cogent example of this process of disenchantment (Liebes and Katz 1997). The meeting of Sadat and Begin on Jimmy Carter's lawn was welcomed with breathless anticipation of a new era of peace in 1978. Lesser enthusiasm and less hopefulness accompanied the live broadcast of Clinton's attempt to bring Yasser Arafat and Yitzhak Rabin together on *his* lawn (1978); President Clinton fared even worse with Arafat and Ehud Barak at Camp David (2000); and the thrill had altogether dissipated when George Bush presided over the shotgun marriage of Ariel Sharon and Abu Mazen, the new Palestinian leader, in the tent at Aqaba (2003). A rare redeeming moment for the genre, and for Clinton, was the ceremonial signing of formal peace between King Hussein of Jordan and Yitzhak Rabin in 1994, muted by the fact that the parties only sought legitimation for their de facto marriage. On the whole, then, the live broadcasting of diplomatic summits seems to have turned sour, at least for now.

IV

Not all media events are benign. In fact, the very subgenre of "contest" – in sports, or politics or legal confrontations – engender tension; but it is the shared commitment to fairness and justice that unites the fans on each side. Of course, certain media events are intrinsically disruptive (see Lukes 1975; Rothenbuhler 1988; Carey 1998). Protests and strikes are agreed forms of sanctioned disruption. Watergate is an extreme example. The event is pre-planned, even scripted, and, in spite of the ostensible conflict there is, even here, an integrative aspect to the shared experience, as Lang and Lang (1983) and Alexander (2003) have argued. Moreover, ceremonial events may suddenly yield to an unplanned disruption. However much the producers try to avoid showing opposition, part of the thrill of live broadcasting is that something may go wrong. Thus, the Munich Olympics in 1972 were interrupted by the attack on the Israeli team (and the killing of 13 of its members), Lee Harvey Oswald was murdered in 1963 during the mourning over Kennedy, the *Challenger* exploded a moment after its ceremonial takeoff in 1986. Even scheduled media events – designed to celebrate or commemorate achievement – can go wrong.

The key difference between the two genres is in the element of pre-planning. As already noted, it is the difference between the shock and anxiety of learning that the President or the Prime Minister has been assassinated versus the carefully scripted grief during their funerals. Anticipation, and perhaps the comfort of orderliness, differentiate them.

V

The apparent decline of ceremonial events in both frequency and centrality does not, in itself, explain the reciprocal rise in the live broadcasting of traumatic events, and, more important, the extended, even obsessive coverage given to them by mainstream media. Liebes (1998) has dubbed these broadcasts "disaster marathons," alluding to the hours, sometimes days, spent recycling gory portraits from the scene, the heroics of rescue and relief workers, the mandatory interviews with experts and politicians speculating on what went wrong and why, and the implications that official neglect or worse may be involved.

Of course, these elements are legitimate aspects of journalistic inquiry, but whereas traumatic news events in the past were contained, mostly, in major "bulletins" and followed only later in the main news and in cooler analysis, the new coverage proceeds directly from the dramatic announcement that cancels regular broadcasting to the marathon mode that ensues. Of course, we know this formula from the Kennedy assassination (Greenberg and Parker 1965), but such extended interruptions were relatively rare at the time; by now, they seem to have usurped the place of ceremonial events. Thus, in addition to noting the ostensible displacement of scripted ceremonial events, it is worth noting also that these unscripted traumas have moved from "bulletin" mode to marathon mode.

Are major disasters really more frequent? It is difficult to say. Is paranoia more prevalent? That is probably the case. Are governments building on such events to legitimate their trigger-happy interventionism? Are the mainstream media trying to show off their newly mobile technologies in order to recapture their unfaithful audiences? Maybe.

VI

To get a better close-up view, let us have a look, however superficial, at the live broadcasting of Terror, Disaster and War – the three types of trauma that seemed to have resolutely moved to center stage and give no sign of abandoning it. A fourth type, which might be called Protest, and that may, however, also include Revolution, deserves attention as well, though we will not elaborate here.

Terror

Much has been written about the symbiotic relationship between terror events and the media. From the days of celebrity kidnappings, to airplane hijackings, to political assassinations to suicide bombings, it is well established that the perpetrators would have far less impact without media publicity, and that the media can hardly be expected to resist.[3] It is only recently, however, that such events have begun to be broadcast outside the regularly scheduled news.[4] From its beginnings, journalism saw such events as "major news," but they seemed somehow unfit – we are guessing – and unmanageable for full-scale treatment as live "specials." In most such cases, the event itself was over before even the most nimble television teams could arrive on the scene, and the equipment was far less mobile. Even the cameras at the ready at the Munich Olympics did not dwell long on this aberration of the ceremonial media event which it interrupted – at least partly because it was considered "incorrect" to do so. Only rarely is television there to witness such deeds in the doing. The explosion of the *Challenger* was such an example – again, like in Munich, because the cameras were already there – and 11 September is the extreme exception. Nevertheless, long before 11 September, the aftermath of terrorist events became a familiar, and frightening, part of television in Israel.

Liebes (1998) argues that marathon coverage of terror events puts pressure on governments to act more hastily, and more impulsively, than perhaps they might (or should) have done. Kellner (2004) argues, on the other hand, that such coverage is just the pretext that certain governments welcome; it allows them, he says, to speak in Manichean terms and to mobilize popular support for action against evil. The difference between the two is in Kellner's assumption about the pre-event eagerness of governments to act; but the effect of the marathon broadcast may be the same.

11 September directs us to the question of whether terror events are properly called "unplanned" when media schedules and availability are obviously implicated in the perpetrators' planning (Blondheim and Liebes 2002; Weimann 1996). The media also figure in the calculus of revolutionaries as seems to have been the case in 1989, at the overthrow of the Communist regimes in Czechoslovakia and Romania. For all their differences, both from each other and from terror events, the media were there *during* the event, not only in its aftermath (Dayan and Katz 1992). But to the extent that the element of surprise is central, it argues against their inclusion in the well-rehearsed integrative category of media events. Yet, it is not hard to envisage certain disruptive events where public and media are invited to attend, as is also the case with major protest events, which, because of their ceremonial aspect, approach the category of media events.[5]

Disaster

In the case of natural disasters or train wrecks (Boorstin 1964), the media cannot be said to have been manipulated by the perpetrators.[6] Yet, it seems to us that the marathon mode has been increasingly deployed here as well. Hurricane Katrina (in 2005) or the Tsunami of Southeast Asia (in 2004) may be the equivalents of 11 September in the realm of nature. Live broadcasting of these attacks and their aftermath mobilized world sympathy and support, but one wonders why the television systems of the world did not go outside their newscasts to portray other disasters of even greater magnitude. It is well known that the tragedies of starvation and disease in other parts of the world, and even other natural disasters, are all but ignored. Why the broadcasters suspected that their viewers would identify with the victims of the distant Tsunami is a good question, except perhaps for its allusion to biblical catastrophes such as the Flood, much as 9/11 inevitably recalls the pretentious builders of the tower at Babel. If one dares to say that the God of the tidal wave or the hurricane imposes surprise and disruption that parallels the work of the terrorist, it is no wonder that many a terrorist sees himself as an agent of God.[7]

Reality, however, suggests that terror may be experienced as more traumatic than natural disaster. The latter may be the work of an arbitrary God but is not due to a personalized, looming, demonic operator intent on the destruction of the nation, soul and body. Having said that, we must also report that we have evidence that the increasing frequency of massive terror attacks may not necessarily increase their effect (Liebes and Kampf 2007). The experience of the second Intifada in Israel suggests that repeated incidents of terror lead to a *decrease* in marathon-type coverage and are increasingly experienced as routine – even as in automobile accidents.

War

War is a third example of how the broadcasting of trauma has been upstaging ceremonial events. Of course, war is perhaps the most-studied case of tension between governments and the media. Putting surprise attacks like Pearl Harbor aside, it is likely that post-World War II military actions by Western powers have been publicly scheduled in advance, and that the problem of controlling the media has repeatedly arisen. These wars are more circumscribed than their predecessors, and fit the TV screen more readily, but hardly satisfactorily. Television has hardly been able to penetrate the smoke at the front, but the media attempt to frame what is happening is alleged to have had a major effect. In Vietnam, we know, it took days for filmed footage to be delivered to TV stations in the West, amid the implication that the huge American commitment would finally prevail, until the government began to believe – rightly or wrongly – that they were losing media support (Arlen 1982; Hallin 1994). Subsequent forays into the Falklands, Granada, Panama all placed restrictions on media access; in the Falklands, for example, a pool of journalists was invited abroad ship to wait, under surveillance, until the British Navy fired its first broadside at Argentina.

Even greater control characterized Gulf War I where journalists were kept away from the fighting, forced to report from General Schwarzkopf's regular briefings. Instead of presence at the front, television showed models of the new weapons that were being deployed (Katz 1992). Only the exceptions – Peter Arnett on the roof in Baghdad and Bob Simon who wandered off in the desert – called attention to the rule. The frustration of journalists during Gulf War I led to the brilliant idea of "embedding" in Gulf War II, where journalists were free to report what they could see from a front-line tank or helicopter, and, inside, to experience the morale of being a member of the crew. The extended, often live coverage went on for weeks amid much speculation about WMD, about the capitulation of Saddam's troops, the mystery of the whereabouts of Saddam himself, and very little evidence of loss – on either side. Wars of this kind are staged; certainly this was true of the live coverage of invasion, where the obvious interest of government is to keep journalists on its side by playing up the threat, and the evil of the enemy, and minimizing our own losses. Yet, disaster marathon it is, albeit of a different kind.

VII

To repeat, we assert that marathons of terror, natural disaster, and war have become established genres on mainstream television, each somewhat different than the others. We proposed explanations for the decline in salience of the live broadcasting of ceremonial events, and the rise of live coverage of traumatic events, even if these are mostly concluded before the media arrive, and mostly seen from afar. We speculated that the new media ecology, together with cynicism vis-à-vis establishments and media, have undermined the awe of ceremonial events and that the new mobile technology plus the paranoia of our times have propelled major news of disaster from the classic "bulletin" of tragedy to extended coverage of the trauma itself, or what remains of it.

In comparing ceremonial and traumatic events, we noted that the former are pre-planned and integrative, even when they end badly, whereas the latter are unwelcome outbursts of disruption and despair.[8]

In conclusion, we wish to emphasize another factor that distinguishes ceremonial from traumatic events, and that is the large difference between the extent to which establishments, and even the media, are able to maintain control. Thus, underlying the integrative versus disruptive character of each type of event, and the factor of pre-planning versus surprise, lurks the question of control, of who's in charge.

Media events, of the ceremonial kind, are essentially co-produced by broadcasters and organizers such as the International Olympics Committee, the League of Women Voters, and the Royal Family. They are establishment events, with wide public support, based on mutual agreement as to how the event will be staged. Disaster marathons, on the other hand, are obvious threats to establishments, in which the organizers – the perpetrators – are an invasive force, far out of the reach of establishment control. Thus, terror events, of course, are obvious co-productions of perpetrators and broadcasters; natural disasters are collusions between broadcasters and God; the script for war may well be in the hands of the enemy. The media, too, may lose control. Such events recall Molotch and Lester's (1974) paper on how establishment sources are in control of the news – except in the case of accident and scandal, where government loses control. While agreeing with Molotch and Lester that these are moments in which journalists achieve power vis-à-vis establishments, it is important to consider that the marathon treatment of terror events may deprive the journalist of the time and distance he needs to think, to investigate, and to edit. Ironically, even though he has attained the power to criticize establishment failings, he may find himself in the service of another master (Blondheim and Liebes 2002). In other words, if media events cause journalists to feel queasy about being exploited in the service of establishments, they should also be wary – in marathon mode – of unwittingly serving the anti-establishment.

39

Notes

1 Our debt to Daniel Dayan is evident throughout, and our work in this area, independently and together, continues in tandem (e.g. Dayan 2003; 2006; 2008). We wish to thank Zohar Kampf for his useful suggestions, and Jatin Atre and Deborah Lubken for ideas and research assistance. Earlier versions of this chapter were presented at the annual meeting of the Media, Communications and Cultural Studies Association, in Sussex, in December 2003; at the graduate seminar of the Department of Communication at Tel Aviv University, in March 2005; and at the Political Communication preconference, APSA, Washington, D.C., 31 August 2005. The present version was read as the Dr. Robert Rogoff Memorial Lecture of the Canadian Friends of the Hebrew University in Vancouver, in February 2006.

2 One wonders what Eric Hobsbawm (1985) might say about this shift in light of his functional (for the ruling elite) explanation of the proliferation of national ceremonies in Europe of 1870 to 1914. Our explanations here, like those of Dayan and Katz (1992), are more media oriented, but there may well be room for sociological speculation about the "need" for political spectacle in the second half of the twentieth century.

3 Hillel Nossek (1994) pioneered in the discussion of "fashions" or "genres" of terror. He also argues that terror events often integrate societies.

4 This shift is difficult to date, although nightly "action news" was surely its harbinger.

5 Broadcasting facilities are often the first targets of revolutions (and of military action). This was the case in 1989 Romania, but not in the more "democratic" Czechoslovakia. During the mass protest in Israel against the government's decision to "disengage" from Gaza, live radio coverage included the leader of the sometimes-violent protest as its on-the-air commentator. The mass protest at Tiananmen Square is another example (Calhoun 1994).

6 For Boorstin (1964), the ultimate news event is a train crash (before the PR personnel arrive on the scene).

7 Interestingly, in the case of the Flood, God gave Noah seven days' advance notice of his intention (Genesis 7: 4), deviating from "our" rule that disasters are always a surprise. Early-warning systems have a good model to emulate.

8 See Cottle (2006) for a somewhat similar typological effort.

References

Alexander, J.C. (2003) "Watergate as Democratic Ritual", in J.C. Alexander (ed.) *The Meanings of Social Life: A Cultural Sociology*, New York: Oxford University Press.

Arlen, M.J. (1982) *Living-room War*, New York: Penguin Books.

Blondheim, M. and Liebes, T. (2002) "Live Television's Disaster's Marathon of September 11 and its Subversive Potential", *Prometheus*, 20, 3: 271–6.

Boorstin, D.J. (1964) *The Image: A Guide to Pseudo Events in America*, New York: Harper & Row.

Calhoun, C. (1994) *Neither Gods Nor Emperors: Students and the Struggle for Democracy in China*, Berkeley: University of California Press.

Cappella, J.N. and Jamieson, K.H. (1997) *Spiral of Cynicism: The Press and the Public Good*, New York: Oxford University Press.

Carey, J. (1998) "Political Ritual on Television. Episodes in the History of Shame Degradation and Excommunication", in T. Liebes and J. Curran (eds) *Media, Ritual and Identity*, London: Routledge, 42–70.

Cottle, S. (2006) "Mediatized Rituals: Beyond Manufacturing Consent", *Media, Culture and Society*, 28, 3: 411–32.

Dayan, D. (2003) "Consenso e dissenso nos acontecimentos mediaticos: entrevista com Mario Mesquita", in D. Dayan, E. Katz and M. Mesquita (eds) *Televisa e Publicos*, Coimbra: Cuadernos Minerva.

—— (2006) "Terrorisme, Performance, Représentation: notes sur un genre discursif contemporain", in D. Dayan (ed.) *La Terreur Spectacle*, Paris-INA: De Boeck.

—— (2008) "Beyond Media Events: Disenchantment, Derailment, Disruption", in D. Dayan and M.E. Price (eds) *Owning the Olympics: Narratives of the New China*, Ann Arbor, MI: Michigan University Press, 391–401.

Dayan, D. and Katz, E. (1992) *Media Events: The Live Broadcasting of History*, Cambridge, MA: Harvard University Press.

Greenberg, B.H. and Parker, E.B. (eds) (1965) *The Kennedy Assassination and the American Public: Social Communication in Crisis*, Stanford, CA: Stanford University Press.

Hallin, D. (1994). *We Keep America on Top of the World: Television, Journalism and the Public Sphere*, London: Routledge.

Hallin, D. and Mancini, P. (1985) *Summits and the Construction of an International Public Sphere: The Reagan–Gorbachev Meetings as Televised Media Events*, Padova: Cedam.

Hobsbawm, E. (1985) "Mass Producing Traditions: Europe 1870–1914", in E. Hobsbawm and T. Ranger (eds) *The Invention of Tradition*, New York: Cambridge University Press.

Katz, E. (1978) "Sadat and Begin: Astronauts?", *Bulletin of the Annenberg School for Communication*, Los Angeles: University of Southern California.

—— (1980) "Media Events: The Sense of Occasion", *Studies in Visual Anthropology*, 6: 84–9.

—— (1992) "The End of Journalism", *Journal of Communication*, 42: 5–14.

Katz, E. and Dayan, D. (1986) "Contests, Conquests, and Coronations: On Media Events and their Heroes", in C.F. Graumann and S. Moscovici (eds) *Changing Conceptions of Leadership*, New York: Springer-Verlag, 135–44.

Kellner, D. (2004) "9/11, Spectacles of Terror, and Media Manipulation: A Critique of Jihadist and Bush Media Politics", *Critical Discourse Studies*, 1, 1: 41–64. Available HTTP: <http://www.gseis.ucla.edu/faculty/kellner/essays/911terrorspectaclemedia.pdf> (accessed 1 December 2008).

Lang, G. and Lang, K.L. (1983) *The Battle for Public Opinion: The President, the Press, and the Polls During Watergate*, New York: Columbia University Press.

Liebes, T. (1998) "Television's Disaster Marathons: A Danger for Democratic Processes?", in T. Liebes and J. Curran (eds) *Media, Ritual and Identity*, London: Routledge, 71–84.

Liebes, T. and Katz, E. (1997) "Staging Peace: Televised Ceremonies of Reconciliation", *The Communication Review*, 2, 2: 235–57.

Liebes, T. and Kampf, Z. (2007) "Routinizing Terror: Media Coverage and Public Practices: Israel 1996–2004", *The Harvard International Journal of Press/Politics*, 11–12, 108–16.

Liebes-Plesner, T. (1984) "Shades of Meaning in President Sadat's Knesset Speech", *Semiotica*, 48, 3–4: 229–65.

Livingstone, S. and Bennet, W.L. (2003) "Gatekeeping, Indexing and Live-Event News: Is Technology Altering the Construction of News?", *Political Communication*, 20, 4: 363–80.

Lukes, S. (1975) "Political Ritual and Social Integration", *Sociology*, 9: 289–308.

Molotch, H. and Lester, M. (1974) "News as Purposive Behavior: On the Strategic Use of Routine Events, Accidents and Scandals", *American Sociological Review*, 39, 1: 101–13.

Nossek, H. (1994) "The Holocaust and the Revival of Israel in the Press Coverage of Salient Terrorist Events in the Israeli Press", in T. Liebes (ed.) Special Issue of *Narrative and Life History*, 4: 1–2.

Rothenbuhler, E.W. (1988) "The Living Room Celebration of the Olympic Games", *Journal of Communication*, 38, 3: 61–81.

Scannell, P. (1996) *Radio, Television and Modern Life*, Cambridge: Blackwell.

Weber, M. (1968) *On Charisma & Institution Building: Selected Papers*, ed. S.N. Eisenstadt, Chicago, IL: University of Chicago Press.

Weimann, G. (1996) *The Influentials*, Albany, NY: Suny Press.

Part II

THE HISTORY AND FUTURE OF THE MEDIA EVENT

4

HISTORICAL PERSPECTIVES ON MEDIA EVENTS

A comparison of the Lisbon earthquake in 1755 and the Tsunami catastrophe in 2004

Jürgen Wilke

Introduction

The concept "media event" has only recently entered the scientific and even the common language. Dayan and Katz (1992: 1–53) gave to this term its "classical" character. They comprehended there under incidents with the following characteristics: (1) disruption of routine, (2) pre-planned, announced and advertised, (3) organized outside the media, (4) hegemonic TV live coverage, (5) presented with reverence and ceremony, (6) celebrating reconciliation, (7) electrifying, and (8) integrating large audiences. The two authors also described media events of this kind as "festive television" and "high holidays of mass communication." They distinguish three fundamental types (or scripts) of media events: contests (e. g. Olympic Games, TV debates in election campaigns), conquests (e.g. state visits to adversaries) and coronations (e.g. wedding ceremonies of royalty).

Obviously, Dayan and Katz thereby identified important aspects of today's media society. They were later criticized, however, for their narrow definition of the phenomenon of media events (Couldry 2003: 55–74). The limitation they placed on their concept had, for instance, the consequence that media events could not be said to have existed before the development of TV, and they also effectively ruled out the possibility that any type of event other than the three mentioned above could not be clarified as media events. With regard, however, to the media presentation of certain events, such limitations would seem to be unjustified.

Seen from the historical point of view, the concept of "media event" as defined by Dayan and Katz cannot be applied, since it cannot account for the fact that already, in earlier times, certain events attracted an enormous amount of public attention. The people who did not witness these events personally

45

learned about them primarily or exclusively through media coverage. They had no access to the "real" events, but only to the "mediated" events. It is therefore necessary to broaden the concept of "media events" to allow for a wider definition.

In what follows, I will improve two historical "media events" separated from each other by a considerable space of time: the Lisbon earthquake of 1755 and the Tsunami disaster of 2004. Both are natural catastrophes; the events are thus themselves similar. However, in the 250 years between them the world underwent dramatic changes. This is especially true in the case of mass media and journalistic coverage. In the eighteenth century, the printed press was still the only medium for dispersing current information. Since then, the media spectrum has broadened considerably with the introduction of radio, TV and, most recently, the internet. The extent to which today's media events differ from earlier ones can only be recognized by looking back at the past.

Both disasters were spontaneous, "natural" events, and the news value of each derived from their completely unexpected and surprising occurrences. Because of this surprise factor and due to their horrible consequences, they appeared sensational. In this respect they differ fundamentally from pre-planned, organized media events along the lines ensured by Dayan and Katz. What they have in common with the latter, however, is the extensive amount of attention paid to them. The following study examines the question of how these two media events came about, what contents and range they encompassed, and what consequences they had. The basis for this investigation is an analysis of the coverage of these events in Germany in 1755/56 and 2004/05. While, for the eighteenth century, only newspapers as media were used, other media must be included for an analysis of the current situation.

The events themselves

The two events will first be briefly described as such. The basic data may be found in Table 4.1.

On November 1, 1755, at about 9:30 a.m. local time, an earthquake shook the Portuguese capital of Lisbon (Kendrick 1956). The epicenter lay not far from the coast in the sea offshore the city. After a first quake, two more followed with the effect that a big sea wave was forced into the mouth of the river Tejo, flooding parts of the inner city. Many buildings collapsed, and fires broke out and devastated the city. The earthquake claimed many casualties, estimated between 20,000 and 60,000.

The size of the earthquake has been retroactively registered as an 8.5 on the Richter scale, though this figure cannot be verified, since the Richter scale as an instrument for measuring earthquakes was only introduced in 1935. The 1755 seismic shocks were not limited to Lisbon (or Portugal),

Table 4.1 The Lisbon earthquake 1755 and the Tsunami in Southeast Asia 2004

	Earthquake of Lisbon	*Tsunami*
1 Day of the event	November 1, 1755 (9:30 a.m. LT*)	December 26, 2004 (7:59 LT;* 1:59 a.m. CET*)
2 Force (Richter scale)	8.5	9.0
3 Number of victims	20,000–60,000	230,000

Note
* LT = Local Time, CET = Central European Time.

but were also witnessed in many other parts of Europe and even in North Africa.

The second event taken into account for comparison is the seaquake in the Indian Ocean on December 26, 2004. Because of contemporary technology, it could be dated and measured very precisely. It occurred at 7:59 a.m. local time (=1:59 a.m. CET). The Eurasian tectonic plate ground against the Indian-Australian plate at a depth of 10 kilometers, approximately 60 kilometers to the west of Sumatra. The pressure erupted with a jerk, and the earth shook on a length of 1,000 kilometers and a width of 100 kilometers. The ocean bed shot up by 10 meters. The earthquake had an intensity of 9.0 on the Richter scale and produced a gigantic seismic sea wave, a so-called "Tsunami". Despite the high speed (720 km/h) with which the Tsunami moved, it took a few hours to reach the coasts of the various countries on the Indian Ocean: Sri Lanka at 8:45 a.m. LT (=3:45a.m. CET), Thailand at 9:50 a.m. LT (=3:50 a.m. CET), India at 10:44 a.m. LT (=4:44 a.m. CET), the Maldives at 11:00 a.m. LT (=5:00 a.m. CET) and Africa at 6:00 a.m. LT (=9:00 a.m. CET). Where the Tsunami hit the coasts with its enormous strength, it left a scene of destruction in its wake, both in natural and man-made environments. Indonesia, with 168,000 casualties, and Sri Lanka, with 35,000 casualties, were the most severely affected. According to the United Nations, 230,000 people in total were killed – almost four times as many as in the Lisbon earthquake. Due to this number, the Tsunami was declared to be the biggest natural disaster in living memory.

Both natural disasters were predisposed to become media events, as earthquakes have a high news value. They quite literally shake the foundations of human existence, they are extremely life-threatening, and they cause (great) damage to persons and property. According to journalistic rules, the news value increases in proportion with these factors. Because such events are given coverage preference, especially if referring to certain parts of the world, the media have been reproached with perpetuating an "earthquake syndrome" (Rosenblum 1979).

The spread of news

In the 250 years separating these two events, the means of news transmission in particular have decisively changed. The result has been a difference in the speed with which these events became known to the world and were performed as media events. The dynamics of this transmission may be seen in Table 4.2.

The first instance in which people in 1755 learned about the Lisbon earthquake depended on how far away from the Portuguese capital they lived, and the communication channels that existed. The news reached the Spanish capital Madrid, also located on the Iberian Peninsula, within a few days. On November 8, 1755, it could be read in the newspaper *Gazeta de Madrid*. It took two weeks more to reach Paris and London. There, the news of the earthquake was published in the French *Gazette* and the English *Whitehall Evening Post* on November 22. In Germany (both in Hamburg and Berlin), the disaster only became known at the beginning of December 1755 – in other words, a whole month after the event.

Table 4.2 The dynamic of news reporting on both events: distribution of information

Earthquake of Lisbon Nov 1st, 1755	*Tsunami 1:59 a.m. (CET) Dec 26, 2004*
Newspapers • Madrid: November 8, 1755 • Paris: November 22, 1755 • London: November 22, 1755 • Hamburg: December 2, 1755 • Berlin: December 2, 1755	*News agencies* • AFP:[a] December 26, 2004, 2:59 a.m. • DPA:[b] December 26, 2004, 3:27 a.m. • AP:[c] December 26, 2004, 3:57 a.m. *Television* • CNN:[d] December 26, 2004, 4:00 a.m. • ARD:[e] December 26, 2004, 4:40 a.m. *Internet* • December 26, 2004, 4:30 p.m. *Newspapers* • Frankfurter Allgemeine Zeitung:[f] December 27, 2004 • Bild:[g] December 27, 2004 • Allgemeine Zeitung (Mainz):[h] December 27, 2004

Notes
a Agence France Presse (AFP).
b Deutsche Presse Agentur (DPA) (German Press Agency).
c Associated Press (AP).
d Cable News Network (CNN).
e ARD = First German TV Channel.
f German national daily newspaper.
g German tabloid newspaper.
h German local newspaper.

However, the news was not entirely unexpected for the people in Germany, since already, on November 8, 1755, the newspapers had reported signs of earth- and seaquakes close-by, and in the following weeks similar news trickled in from other parts of Europe. Thus people far away from the event were aware of the geological radiation of the earthquake long before they learned the origin and reason.

On the other hand, the seaquake in the Indian Ocean 250 years later became known with lightning speed and appeared all over the world within a few hours of its occurrence. The first news seems to have been sent by the French news agency, Agence France Presse (AFP), on December 26, 2004 at 2:59 a.m. (CET), one hour after the geological incident. Today, news agencies tend to stand at the origin of the news chain: Deutsche Presse-Agentur (DPA) and Associated Press (AP) followed half an hour from each other, after AFP. The American global TV station CNN brought the first news at 4:00 a.m. (CET), the first German TV station (ARD) at 4:40 a.m. On the internet, information is accounted for at 4:30 a.m. (CET), but the messages in this most recent "medium" are difficult to fix with any certainty. While the electronic media began coverage of the Tsunami within a few hours, although not all at the same time and not without delay, the newspapers were bound to the rhythm of daily publication. In addition, in the Christian part of the world, the newspapers were on a holiday schedule due to Christmas. Thus the first newspapers containing news about the Tsunami appeared in Germany on the morning of December 27, 2004.

Due to the acceleration of news technology, the clarification of the circumstances of events today is usually faster than in earlier times. However, for the Tsunami disaster this is true only with restrictions due to the wide-spreading nature of the sea wave. The number of casualties reported increased rapidly. The first news on German TV on December 26, 2004 at 4:40 a.m. still spoke of nine dead persons. At 5:00 a.m., the BBC reported 150 dead persons on Sri Lanka. According to AFP (12:40 a.m.), there were 4,000 dead or missing persons. On the same day, this number rose to 12,000. On the morning of December 27, the agencies spoke of 20,000 victims, one day later it was 40,000, and on December 29, the Red Cross already estimated the number at more than 100,000. On December 31, the number mounted to 150,000. One whole year passed before the UNO finally determined the number of victims. Surprisingly, 250 years before, the first news about the Lisbon earthquake in the German newspapers already spoke of 50,000 victims. Later announcements were also lower, but remained speculative, since at that time there were not yet any reliable statistics.

Our comparison shows that distance in space has lost its significance for the construction of media events. The electric and electronic technology of news transmission has shrunk the distances and has turned the earth into a "global village" in which knowledge no longer depends on proximity to the places where events occur. Today, big media events like the Tsunami circle the whole world within a very brief period of time.

Amount of coverage

Our next question is: How extensive was the coverage of these two events? It is the amount of coverage that makes media events. In order to answer this question, the coverage of both events was calculated. A direct comparison is only possible on the basis of newspapers. For this comparison, two German newspapers from the eighteenth century were analyzed, one from Hamburg (*Hamburgischer Unpartheyischer Correspondent* [HUC]), and one from Berlin (*Berlinische Nachrichten von Staats- und gelehrten Sachen* [BN]). The three current newspapers represent three different types: *Frankfurter Allgemeine Zeitung* (FAZ), a national newspaper, the *Mainzer Allgemeine Zeitung* (AZ), a local newspaper, and *Bild*, a tabloid. For the Lisbon earthquake, the coverage was calculated from December 2, 1755 to March 31, 1756, for the Tsunami from December 26, 2004 to January 22, 2005. The different condensation of coverage was decisive for the selection of time periods (three months vs. one). Table 4.3 shows the result of the calculation.

It is not surprising that modern newspapers covered the disaster to a far greater extent than did those of the eighteenth century. This is already a result of the format and the "capacity" of the respective medium. The eighteenth-century German newspapers normally appeared three or four times a week with four pages in small quarto. Thus, there was rather less space in 1755/56 than there is today, when newspapers are printed in large format and contain more pages.

Table 4.3 Amount of coverage

	Number of reports	Number of lines
Earthquake of Lisbon (December 2, 1755 – March 31, 1756)		
• Hamburgischer Unpartheyischer Correspondent (HUC)	36	1,981
• Berliner Nachrichten von Staats-und gelehrten Sachen (BN)	37	1,594
	Number of reports	Square centimeters
Tsunami (December 26, 2004 – January 22, 2005)		
• Frankfurter Allgemeine Zeitung (FAZ)	244	90,223
• Bild-Zeitung (BZ)	198	70,411
• Mainzer Allgemeine Zeitung (AZ)	178	46,727

However, the Lisbon earthquake was the event on which the two German newspapers reported the most for several weeks at the turn of the year 1755/56. No other event at that time was awarded such a high number of lines. This is particularly true if the reports on seismic shocks in other parts of Europe (and North Africa) are included. Therefore it is justified to talk about a "media event" at that time.

This is even more true for the 2004 Tsunami. In this case, the amount of coverage depended on the type of newspaper. The national newspaper *FAZ* contained the most reports, namely twice as many as the average local newspaper (*AZ*). The amount of coverage of the tabloid *Bild* was more similar to that of the national newspaper than to that of the local one.

Naturally, there are other media today which (may) exceed the scope of newspapers. Within four weeks, the *Tagesschau*, the newscast of the public TV station ARD, had 101 news reports with a total of 155 minutes about the Tsunami; and the commercial TV station RTL had 116 reports with a total of 244 minutes (Rehak 2006: 132). These numbers only refer to the main newscast in the evening. News at other times of the day as well as numerous special programs contributed additional reports. For this, the routine program flow was interrupted.

Means of coverage

Events do not become media events only because of the amount of coverage, but also because of the means of coverage. In this respect, there is also a big difference between the eighteenth century and today. The eighteenth-century newspapers, for example, did not yet have any headlines. News was printed stating merely the place of origin and the date. Thus, the first report about the Lisbon earthquake in the *Hamburgischer Unpartheyischer Correspondent* from 2 December 1755 appeared under the headline "Nachricht aus Madrid vom Erdbeben zu Lissabon, unterm 10 Nov." ("News from Madrid about the Lisbon earthquake under November 10.") The report was, how-ever, on the front page of the newspaper, though in general it was the date of entry of a piece of news rather than its significance which determined its placement.

Today, newspapers have a completely different layout. News reports have headlines, even catchlines, and they are also spatially distributed – as far as possible – in accordance with their significance. This at least applies for the first page. On eleven days (six thereof in sequence), beginning on December 27, 2004, the *Frankfurter Allgemeine Zeitung* devoted the lead story to the Tsunami. The Mainz local paper did this just as often (eight days in sequence). The tabloid paper used the event as a lead story on ten days in sequence. The TV news stations started their main news with this subject even more often: the ARD-*Tagesschau* (public service) did so on 15 days, *RTL Aktuell* (commercial TV) on 19 days (Rehak 2006: 57). Only afterwards did the subject lose its leading position, although it did not yet disappear. Top coverage of such duration is extremely unusual given the ever-changing nature of events.

The eighteenth-century newspapers offered exclusively verbal reports of the Lisbon earthquake. There were no pictures in the newspapers. This does not mean that there were no visualizations at all (see below), but the coverage of that period still had to make do without pictures as their production (woodcut, copperplates) was too costly and too inefficient. Today, the situation is totally different. It was not only the newspapers that presented many photos of the Tsunami disaster, but also the picture services of the news agencies, TV, and other visual media offerings (including the internet). Within four weeks, the German tabloid *Bild* showed 306 pictures, the highest number of all newspapers analyzed here, in fact three times as many as the other two newspapers. Within the same period of time, the *FAZ* published 116 pictures, the local Mainz newspaper 91 (Rehak 2006: 91).

Sources

From what sources did the information derive, through which the catastrophes became media events? With regard to this question, the two cases again differ immensely. In the eighteenth century, Portugal was a kingdom on the fringes of Europe, facing the Atlantic Ocean, but with Europe at its back. At that time, this situation had a different meaning than it has today. Portugal was an important trading nation, and its political and economic significance was such that two groups were primarily responsible for dispersing information: on the one hand, the ambassadors and residents in official functions in Lisbon; on the other hand, the representatives of foreign trading firms (including German firms). Since early modern times, these two groups often operated on the site as correspondents for printed papers. A further source of information was private correspondence. Information was brought to Spain, France and Germany via country roads by messengers, but letters were also transported by ships via sea routes.

With regard to this dynamic, news procurement has changed considerably since the eighteenth century, in both the technological and organizational domains. In the nineteenth century, telegraphy and telephone arose as means of transmission; at the end of the twentieth century, it was satellite technology. The primary role of the news agencies in spreading the Tsunami news has already been mentioned. They could do this even more effectively insofar as the region of the seaquake was – from a European perspective – far away from the centers of global interest. German mass media have only a few correspondents in this part of the world. All of them, however, were sent to the disaster area immediately. They were soon joined by so-called parachute reporters, i.e. reporters who, in cases of unexpected incidents, are flown in as fast as possible to give accounts from the "event front." Private persons who had witnessed the disaster constituted another source of information, especially regarding first images, since in some of the Asian countries affected by the earthquake, there are a number of tourist regions where many tourists (among them many from Germany) were traveling at the turn of the year 2004/05. So long as they themselves did not become victims of the catastrophe, they were able to take photos of the incoming Tsunami with their digital and mobile phone cameras before the professional photographers arrived.

Content and topics

The entire content of the coverage of these "media events" cannot be presented in detail. In 1755/56 "particularities" about the earthquake only became known little by little. Details about the damages and the fate of the survivors followed. It was not only the population that suffered, but also the royal family. As the prison had been destroyed, the liberated prisoners caused trouble in the city. Scavenging was reported, as well as its immediate punishment. Signs of the earthquake were also reported from other parts of Europe. Economic consequences and acts of sympathy were part of the coverage too. Furthermore, the readers were informed about relief operations.

In the coverage of the Tsunami in 2004/05, approximately one-third of the reports in German newspapers dealt with the concerned regions as such, especially with the situation of the locals (Rehak 2006: 77). More reports, however (i.e. approximately half), were devoted to German issues, namely the fate of Germans tourists. Furthermore, the beginning of fundraising campaigns and the political activities were covered. In approximately every fifth report, general issues (e.g. explanations for the Tsunami) were dealt with.

Ethnocentric reference

The fact that both natural disasters became media events is connected to their significance for Germany and German readers (or viewers). This, however, applies far more to the 2004 Tsunami than to the 1755 Lisbon earthquake. At that time, it was primarily German trading firms located in Lisbon that were affected by the earthquake (Anon. 1858). The extensive coverage was thus probably due more to the sensational nature of the event than to any direct consequences for the majority of the German population.

With regard to the 2004 Tsunami, it was significant for the media event that numerous German tourists were traveling in the earthquake region at the time because of the Christmas holidays. This fact gave the coverage an "ethnocentric reference," linked to what interested the readers mostly from their own country or town. It is noticeable that the German mass media reported primarily not about the regions with the highest number of victims, but about those with the highest number of German tourists (Rehak 2006: 75–81).

Visualization

It has already been mentioned that the media event of the Tsunami disaster derived much of its energy from its visualization, both in press and on TV. But already in 1755, the mediation of the Lisbon earthquake was not restricted solely to the printed press. Visual representations were also produced. Graphic illustrations, for instance, soon emerged and, in a certain sense, represented the forerunners of pictorial reports. In the beginning, however, they were not a result of the artist having immediately witnessed the event, but rather products of an imaginative reviewing of topographic settings (cf. Figure 4.1). Only later did authenticity become a goal.

There was also a second form of visualization owing to which one can assert that the Lisbon earthquake of the eighteenth century was also represented in a kind of pro-television, namely the so-called "looking box" which was set up at fairs as an optical toy. The "looking box" had a frontal opening equipped with a lens or glass through which the viewer could peer in (Sztaba 1996). Images were then inserted into this "looking box" to create a lively, three-dimensional impression of the motives displayed. The German engraver Martin Engelbrecht (1684–1756) mass produced such "scenery pictures" (also named as "perspective theater") (Füsslin et al. 1995). Engelbrecht also presented such a perspective theater of the Lisbon earthquake (cf. Figure 4.2).

Vorstellung und Beschreibung des ganz erschröcklichen Erdbebens, wodurch die Königl. Portugiesische Residenz-Stadt Lissabon samt dem gröſten Theil der Einwohnern zu grunde gegangen.

Figure 4.1 Woodcut of the Lisbon earthquake 1755 by Georg Caspar Pfauntz.

Figure 4.2 The Lisbon earthquake in Martin Engelbrecht's looking box
(around 1755).

Seven colored copperplates showed different episodes or "layers" of the event, and offered a dramatic, visually stirring series. Collapsing columns and constructive carriers frame the image, where the buildings, a steeple and vaults are about to cave in. A scattering of people seek refuge, make desperate gestures, or try to save each other's lives. Like the aforementioned graphic illustrations, the plates offer an imaginative vision rather than an authentic account. The "looking box" was a "medium" of popularization which sought to familiarize even those who could not read the news with the spectacle of the earthquake. Of course, the optical means were still modest compared to those offered by television today, but behind the means lay the wish to satisfy the visual needs which may have been even more important in times of wide illiteracy.

Journalistic recollection

Media events also stimulate journalistic recollection. In the coverage of the 2004 Tsunami, other, previous earthquakes were brought to mind. Sometimes real historic chronologies were printed, and there was an explicit connection to the Lisbon earthquake. Some German papers or journals even illustrated their reports on the Tsunami with copperplates of the 1755 earthquake (cf. Figure 4.1) – all this is a clear sign that this event has remained part of the collective memory of Europe.

Surprisingly, already 250 years ago, the *Hamburgischer Unpartheyischer Correspondent* was engaging in the same practice. The newspaper issue of February 11, 1756 offered the reader a list of similar earthquakes that had occurred since 1750. Ostensibly there had been more than 80, "obgleich die meisten nur in einer Erschütterung bestanden, die mehr Schrecken als Unheil angerichtet hat" ("although most of them merely consisted of a vibration which caused more fear than mischief"). The journalist then continues with the following thought:

> Most people are thus natured that they attach little value to a disaster happening far away, or even forget it quickly, if it does not concern them. Only the novelty of a matter grabs their attention for a few moments or days, and perhaps the disastrous earthquake of Lisbon will be as soon forgotten as the large number which we . . . want to bring back to the memory solely since 1750.
>
> (*HUC*, February 11, 1756)

In this case, however, the journalist's assumption turned out to be wrong.

Effects and consequences

Finally, there is the question about the effects of the media events. Obviously they elicit first of all agenda-setting effects. For Germany, this can be verified by data on the Tsunami disaster. A representative survey shortly after Christmas 2004 verified this (cf. Table 4.4).

Table 4.4 Agenda-setting effect of the Tsunami coverage in Germany 2004

Question: "About which topics did you converse with your family and friends during the Christmas holidays?"

Topics of our conversations	Population (in %)
The Tsunami in the Indian Ocean and the ensuing devastation	85
The costs of healthcare	48
Hartz IV, the earnings-related benefit (social topic)	45

Source: Institut Für Demoskopie Allensbach, Noelle (2005).

During (and after) the Christmas holidays 2004/05, five-sixths of the German population conversed with their families and friends about the Tsunami catastrophe. This is an extremely high percentage value. Other social issues which were significant for the German population at that time were discussed by only half the number of interviewees.

There are, of course, no comparable data for the Lisbon earthquake since such surveys were not yet common at that time. One must therefore rely on the reports of historical individuals. There are, however, numerous descriptions that refer back to the reception of the media event and offer an insight into the excitement of the people at that time. There is an especially noteworthy record in the autobiography *From My Life. Poetry and Truth* (originally published 1811/1814) by Johann Wolfgang von Goethe, the great German poet. The poet, who was born in 1749, described more than six decades after the disaster the shock which this incident had evoked in him (and in the world around him) when he was six years old. The passage will be cited here in full, as it obviously draws much of its details from the information which could be read about the event in the newspapers. Goethe describes very vividly the consequences triggered by its mediation in the newspapers. His words even suggest an agenda-setting effect:

> However the boy's tranquility of mind was deeply shaken for the first time by an extraordinary event. On the first of November, 1755, occurred the great earthquake of Lisbon, spreading enormous terror over a world grown accustomed to peace and quiet. A large, splendid city, both a port and a trading center, is hit without warning by the most fearful calamity. The earth quivers and rocks, the sea rages, ships collide, house collapse, churches and towers fall on top of them, the royal palace is partly swallowed up by the sea, and the severed earth seems to spit flames, for everywhere the ruins begin to smoke and burn. Sixty thousand human beings, who were calm and content just a moment before, perish together, and the happiest man among them is he who had no time to feel or consider his misfortune. The flames rage on, and with them rages a mob of criminals. Now coming out into the open, or perhaps set free by the disaster. The unfortunate survivors are exposed to robbery, murder, and every possible mistreatment; and so nature on every hand asserts her arbitrary will.
>
> Indications of this event preceded the tidings themselves over vast stretches of land. Weaker shocks were felt in many places, and an unusual cessation of flow was noticed in many springs, especially those with healing water. This only made the effect of the news greater when it finally came – first the general information and then shortly afterwards, the dreadful details. Hereupon God-fearing persons were moved to wise observations, philosophers offered consoling arguments, and clergyman preached fiery sermons. So much

happening at once drew the world's attention for a while to this one spot, and hearts already stirred by distant misfortunes were made still uneasier by worries about themselves and their families when reports, in even greater volume and detail, came in from every side about the wide-ranging effects of this explosion. Indeed, the demon of terror has perhaps at no other time spread its chill over the world as quickly and powerfully.

Having to hear all of this repeatedly, I was more than a little disconcerted by it in my boyish heart. God, the Creator and Preserver of heaven and earth, who had been presented to me as so very wise and merciful in the explanation of the first article of the Creed, had shown Himself by no means fatherly when he abandoned both the just and the unjust to the same destruction. My young mind tried in vain to resist these impressions, and it was not made any easier for me by the philosophers and scholars when they themselves could not agree on the way to view such a phenomenon.

(Goethe 1994: 34–5)

Beyond the twin tasks of agenda-setting and the transmission of knowledge, the coverage of the Lisbon earthquake of 1755 also "framed" the perception of the event. Although the eighteenth-century newspapers were constrained to reproduce the facts (and rumors) without additional commentary, the reports nonetheless reflected personal perspectives and opinions. Thus, for example, there were sometimes speculations about the geological causes of the earthquake. The *Berliner Nachrichten* (20 January 1756) reported that the English astronomer Edmond Halley linked the earthquake to the comet he had calculated and which he only expected in 1758 (when it was renamed after him). A few weeks later the same newspaper referred to a script by a professor of philosophy from Hamburg who also had an astronomic hypothesis (March 4, 1756).

Just as Goethe's cited confession indicates, the relevant "frame" for the perception of the Lisbon earthquake of 1755 was a religious-metaphysical one. How could this incident be linked to the Christian faith that prevailed across Europe? This aspect was not left out of the coverage. In several cases, newspaper articles ascribed the disaster to "heavenly providence" and considered it to be a kind of "Last Judgment." Correspondingly, hopes were expressed, as in a letter from Belem of March 9, 1756: "We hope from one day to the other that the heavenly providence watching over all will change our fate since November 1 [1755]" (*HUC*, April 4, 1756). Another reporter had already written before: "I had to reach the age of 72 to become a witness of the most frightening scourge the rage of the Highest can make palpable over the sins of mankind" (*BN*, December 19, 1755). This interpretation is suggested also by the analogy between the earthquake and the destruction of Jerusalem (*HUC*, December 10, 1755).

The metaphysical and moral "frame" shaped the treatment of the Lisbon earthquake above all in the wave of philosophic and literary publications in the years following the incident. They show that this incident, rather than any other similar event of modern history, drove cogitation (Günther 1994; Löffler 1999). Contributors included were, to name only the best known, Voltaire, Rousseau and Immanuel Kant (Breidert 1994). While for some, the earthquake shook the belief in a benign God and evoked the problem of theodicy, others saw this a justification for their doubts concerning the progress of enlightenment. The interest in a scientific explanation receded behind these ideological aspects.

Two hundred and fifty years later, the world and our view of the world have fundamentally changed. The coverage of the Tsunami was not only much more extensive and varied than the coverage of the Lisbon earthquake. It also framed the event in an entirely different manner. The geologic causes of the incident were mentioned more often than in 1755/56, despite the fact that journalistic personalization (i.e. the reporting of individual fates) tended to dominate. The media offered people (also with the help of charts) explanations as to how the seaquake had evolved and how it had spread. Metaphysical or moral questions barely featured in the coverage, at least in that of the German newspapers. All that was left of such questions was the inclusion of photos in the newspapers showing a man in the earthquake region in prayer posture or candles in a religious commemorative ceremony.

After the Tsunami, a religious or philosophic interpretation of the incident remained utterly absent as such interpretations were pervasive following the Lisbon earthquake. This requires the statement of the following paradoxical finding: although the Lisbon earthquake of 1755 claimed fewer victims and the media event was presented in smaller dimensions than in the case of its contemporary counterpart, it seems to have had a disproportionately deeper impact on the popular consciousness, or at least on that of the intellectuals, than the Tsunami of 2004. This reflects a general secularization of catastrophes in modern times (Imhof 2004). And today, media events are displaced much faster by other media events, and viewer's perceptions are presumably some-what dulled by the ongoing coverage of catastrophes. Such events develop in a dynamic of "hype" which – although not forgotten – were soon eclipsed. The consequences of the Tsunami were scientific and practical rather than intellectual and ethical. The seaquake gave geologists innumerable data points for their research and effectively led to the installation of an early-warning system, which in future will react more quickly in such cases and reduce the number of potential victims.

References

Anon. (1858) "Hamburg und das Erdbeben zu Lissabon am 1. November 1755", *Zeitschrift des Vereins für hamburgische Geschichte*, 4.

Breidert, W. (ed.) (1994) *Die Erschütterung der vollkommenen Welt. Die Wirkung des Erdbebens von Lissabon im Spiegel europäischer Zeitgenossen*, Darmstadt: Wissenschaftliche Buchgesellschaft.

Couldry, N. (2003) *Media Rituals: A Critical Approach*, London: Routledge.

Dayan, D. and Katz, E. (1992) *Media Events: The Live Broadcasting of History*, Cambridge, MA: Harvard University Press.

Füsslin, G. et al. (1995) *Der Guckkasten. Einblick – Durchblick – Ausblick*, Stuttgart: Füsslin Verlag.

Goethe, J.W. (1987/1994) *From My Life. Poetry and Truth. Parts One to Three*, Goethe's Collected Works, vol. 4, Princeton, NJ: Princeton University Press.

Günther. H. (1994) *Das Erdbeben von Lissabon erschüttert die Meinungen und setzt das Denken in Bewegung*, Berlin: Verlag Klaus Wagenbach.

Imhof, K. (2004) "Katastrophenkommunikation in der Moderne", in C. Pfister and S. Summermatter (eds) *Katastrophen und ihre Bewältigung. Perspektiven und Positionen*, Wien: Haupt, 145–63.

Kendrick, T.D. (1956) *The Lisbon Earthquake*, London: Methuen.

Liebes, T. and Curran, J. (eds) (1998) *Media, Ritual and Identity*, London: Routledge.

Löffler, U. (1999) *Lissabons Fall – Europas Schrecken. Die Deutung des Erdbebens von Lissabon im deutschsprachigen Protestantismus des 18. Jahrhunderts*, Berlin: de Gruyter.

Noelle, E. (2005) "Das Seebeben-Weihnachten", *Frankfurter Allgemeine Zeitung*, 21, 26 January: 5.

Rehak, S. (2006) "Katastrophenberichterstattung am Beispiel des Tsunami 2004", master thesis, Johannes Gutenberg University of Mainz.

Rosenblum, M. (1979) *Coups and Earthquakes. Reporting the World to America*, New York: Harper Row.

Sztaba, W. (1996) "Die Welt im Guckkasten. Fernsehen im 18. Jahrhundert", in H. Segeberg (ed.) *Die Mobilisierung des Sehens. Zur Vor- und Frühgeschichte des Films in Literatur und Kunst*, München: Wilhelm Fink Verlag, 97–112.

Wilke, J. (1996) " 'Daβ der Jammer und das Elend mit keiner Feder zu beschreiben sey.' Das Erdbeben von Lissabon 1755 als Schlüsselereignis in der Presseberichterstattung", *Relation*, 3, 1: 59–71.

5

FROM MEDIA EVENTS TO RITUAL TO COMMUNICATIVE FORM

Eric W. Rothenbuhler

In the years since publication of Dayan and Katz's (1992) *Media Events: The Live Broadcasting of History*, "media events" has become a well-established term of theory. The media event is understood to be an interruption of the normal routine for a live broadcast from a remote location of a pre-planned event organized independently of the media; the tone of the broadcast is more serious, ceremonial, or even reverential than normal, it attracts unusually large and attentive audiences, and it often has serious political and social consequences.

In the ten or so years before the book appeared, though, "media events" was not a concept or a well-defined genre of media content, but a project. The ideas were yet developing, the case studies still being gathered. The media events project involved faculty and graduate students as research collaborators, seminar participants, and discussion partners in Israel, the US, England, and elsewhere, while Katz and Dayan's shifting, developing ideas were presented in a series of articles (Dayan and Katz 1985a; 1985b, 1987, 1988; Dayan et al. 1984; Katz 1980; Katz and Dayan 1985, 1986; Katz et al. 1981). On the one hand, any interested reader could choose among the versions of the idea in those articles. On the other hand, Katz and Dayan were generous teachers who built their classes on a wide range of interdisciplinary reading materials and encouraged their students to read yet more widely and to forge their own conceptualizations. Their seminars were open-ended affairs in which visitors, teachers, and students, discussions in class and out, readings for this class and readings for others, assignments, plans, and new directions all blended together. For those of us lucky enough to participate in that heady activity, "Media Events" has always been an original concept, a conceptual opening, and an example of good thinking. This chapter is dedicated to that example with two goals. One is retrospective creative thinking to illuminate the influences of Dayan, Katz, and the media events project on the seemingly diverse areas of my own work in the 25 years since I was their student. The other is to imitate their example in the development of a new model for the analysis of an existing problem in media studies.

Media events

From the beginning, "media events" were objects of study and an approach to that study at the same time. The original collaboration of Katz and Dayan, a social scientist of the American tradition and a humanist of the French tradition, working together in Israel, was designed to provide a unique set of intellectual tools to address a unique phenomenon: the live media coverage of Sadat's first visit to Jerusalem. Katz convened a special group of academics for a seminar in which he and Dayan analyzed the broadcast of the Sadat visit as the group watched, listened, and participated. We can look back on that event as almost a type of media event itself. They interrupted the normal schedule of academic work and went live, they moved to a new location, planned ahead, invited special guests, and talked about it later. It was a historic event, a conquest story, and a reconciliation of the social sciences and the humanities; it attracted large audiences and altered the way we think about our field and its history.

When this work began to appear in articles and in Katz and Dayan's teaching, it represented a radical opening of what was known at the time as the field of mass communication processes and effects, exemplified by the then-canonically influential Schramm and Roberts (1971) reader. One reason was that if singular events were important, the concepts and methods with which we were working, designed for the statistical study of processes, simply would not work. From the statistical point of view the ordinary, everyday, often repeated, and average are most important; singular events are exceptions that may obscure understanding of the underlying processes. Yet here, in the media event, was evidence that the singular communicative event could produce permanent social change and that infrequently repeated communicative events were participating in the most basic social processes.

Thus, while mass communication researchers built their inquiries around theories, hypotheses, and measures, using whatever communicative materials were methodologically efficient, media events work began with the selection of communicative materials that were taken to be significant in and of themselves, and built the inquiry around them. This is a standard model of work in the humanities and in the opening pages of *Media Events*, Dayan and Katz presented their collaboration in that light, as bringing the humanist's expertise in the study of singular, meaningful objects to the social scientist's expertise in the study of social processes. In this it was part of a general rapprochement between the "two cultures" that was in the air at the time, and an enduring interest of Katz (e.g. 1959); but this was not without a sense of competitive mischief. Dayan reports that he "felt less like a representative of the humanities than like someone subverting a certain model of social science, by relying on Barthes, anthropology, les Annales, and philosophy of language." He also remembers the collaboration began with "a friendly challenge from Elihu to me: 'let's see what your semiotics can do, about real situations, while they are happening' " (Dayan 2008).

Another challenge for the early media events work was a suspicion of ceremony, media productions, and appearances, common to the humanities and the social sciences. Boorstin's (1964) critique in *The Image: A Guide to Pseudo-Events in America* reflected a dominant paradigm and ageless tradition. An excerpt from it was canonically entered in the Schramm and Roberts (1971) reader. Probably nothing has united the Right and the Left in academic politics so often as a presumption of guilt and cynicism regarding media appearances. Katz and his colleagues addressed this challenge directly (e.g. Katz et al. 1981), and they and their students went on to produce more complex and nuanced treatments of the necessary role of imagery, ceremony, and appearance in the communicative construction of social realities.

For both the study of singular events and the project of taking appearances seriously, the media events project turned to anthropological theory, and this may, in the long run, have been its largest legacy. Indeed, the study of media events turned out to be an important early source of what we more recently called media anthropology (Ginsburg et al. 2002; Rothenbuhler and Coman 2005).

Ritual and communication

The media events project did not just open the door to anthropology, it provided a purpose for reading and a conceptual organization of that territory. For our purposes the key idea was ritual – and especially Durkheim's theory of the roles of ritual in the establishment of social life (e.g. Dayan and Katz 1988; Rothenbuhler 1985, 1988, 1989). Such selective reading was a peculiar way to learn anthropology, but that was not our purpose. We were looking for ideas, methods, and models to help us understand particular problems in the study of communication. For us, Durkheim's (1912/1995) book *The Elementary Forms of the Religious Life* was a work of communication theory (Rothenbuhler 1993) and anthropological studies of ritual more generally provided important models for reconceptualizing communication theory (Carey 1988; Rothenbuhler 1998; 2006).

In ritual, individuals participate in symbolic action according to scripts encoded elsewhere and elsewhen, and with purposes, meanings, and implications already mostly set by convention (see esp. Rappaport 1979, 1999). Each individual will have his or her own thoughts about this while recognizing the socially encoded expectations and standardized outcomes. If you say "I do" in the ritually prescribed way, then you did: whether enthusiastically or doubtfully, it is done. There are different types of media events and different scripts they can follow, but it is their status as public ritual that attracts the massive attention they receive and creates the normative expectation of viewing. When they are successful, it is their capacity as ritual that produces the results of enthralling audiences, changing minds, and changing history.

Formal rites and ceremonies, such as weddings, funerals, church services, or bar mitzvahs, are constructed of verbal performances and layers of other symbolic forms. Such ordinary phenomena as standing up or sitting down, when performed in rituals, are ways of saying things that produce meanings, cognitions, and emotions. Even the non-performance of the disallowed is communicative, so that everything that is not required will be whispered or made small – or taken as signs of disrespect, ignorance, conflict, or something else ritually disallowed. So, from scripted verbal performance to body movement, posture, gesture, and clothing, through music, chanting, marching, food and drink, to decoration and architecture, rites and ceremonies are thickly communicative phenomena. Indeed, there is no rite or ceremony without communication and their communicative performances *are* the effective mechanisms of their consequences (Rothenbuhler 1998).

In the media event, the communication questions can be a bit more troublesome than in the usual examples of weddings, religious services, and funerals. The mass audience of a live television broadcast is essential to a media event. Is that audience, then, a participant in the ritual, akin to members of a congregation or witnesses at a wedding? MacAloon (1984) said no, there can be no ritual, festival, or community by television, only spectacle. Media events scholars, though, usually say yes (e.g. Rothenbuhler 1988). The argument is that the ritual nature of the communication, with the active participation of willing television audience members, constructs a symbolic world in which they are not ordinary viewers of ordinary television, but witnesses and participants.

The formality of communication in traditional rites and ceremonies and its recognized, usually intentional effectiveness, defines one end of a continuum: People use wedding ceremonies because they want to be married. On the other end of the continuum are the tiny bits of formality in otherwise very informal and often automatically performed communication, such as standardized greetings among friends, introductions, or the arrangement of seating at work or social gatherings. As Goffman (1959; 1967) showed these bits of symbolic formality are consequential; they create, maintain, or alter social identities and relations; they define situations and their obligations or licenses just as do the most formal and socially important of rites and ceremonies. Between these two extremes is a wide range of varying degrees of attention to form and propriety in communication and its consequences in meaning and morality. There is a widespread social tendency for a heightened sense of importance to be expressed in a heightened degree of attention to form and a corollary tendency to respond to certain communicative forms as signs of social importance. Competent communicators, from media producers to the hosts of dinner parties, from public relations consultants to groups of friends who gather to watch favorite TV shows, work with communicative form to produce desired social outcomes and to inhibit other ones. Essentially, they are engaged in ritualization (see Bell 1992; Coman 2005; Couldry 2003). The use of communication according to form for the production of a sense of occasion, or a good party, or the making of friends, may be different in degree, but it is not different in kind from the proper pronunciation at the proper time of the words "I do." So we can see that ritual or ritualization is present wherever formal performance is used to bring about desired social ends or to control undesired ones (Rothenbuhler 1998; 2006).

The concept of ritual, then, provided an explanation of the media event and also very useful and unique ideas for thinking about communication in general. Rituals provided examples of how communication could produce effects by processes very different than persuasion, imitation, or attitude change; ritual produces effects by the logic of speech acts, by symbolic implication, by entailment, acceptance, and other such modes the mass communication effects literature could not recognize. Rituals provided examples of how communication creates realities, and thus the way in which communication is part of the foundation of the social world.

Communicative form and self-organizing systems in the evolution of media worlds

Elsewhere I have argued for using ritual as a model of communication in general, as have others (Carey 1988; Rappaport 1999; Rothenbuhler 1998; 2006). Within this perspective, we would expect a range and diversity of media rituals, including ritual forms of media work, ritualized forms of media content, and ritualized activities of media audience members (e.g. Coman 2005; Cottle 2006; Couldry 2003; Rothenbuhler and Coman 2005). Here I want to pursue a narrower proposal: that the historical endurance of certain forms and formats in the media can be explained by analogy to the ways in which rituals are self-preserving and self-replicating. This may work where we can identify situations that parallel ritual in that: (a) the communication is according to form in some strict and at least partly self-conscious way; (b) that form allows a simple, scripted behavior to also symbolize valued ideas, produce desired social outcomes, or control undesired ones; and (c) the form is an essential element in a set of self-referencing and self-replicating activities. In that case, the form would endure against almost all odds.

A self-referencing, self-replicating system organized around ritualized communicative forms, would tend to reproduce the conditions of its own success. When audiences are cultivated to expect stories written in the form of "objectivity" (Tuchman 1972; 1978), for example, rookie reporters are taught to write that way, veteran reporters are sued for apparent violations, angry audience members charge bias and recruit advertisers to boycott, and newspapers defend themselves by pointing to adherence to the form, we see a self-referencing, self-steering, self-reproducing system. This is what Luhmann (1984/1995) and others call autopoiesis, a capacity of some systems to take self-organization to a new level of closure and autonomy vis-à-vis the environment. In essence, the autopoietic system constitutes its own world, like ritual communication does.

Assuming a finite set of communicative resources in any given society, when a form of communication is ritualized around the achievement of valued outcomes and an autopoietic system built around it, we should expect it (a) to succeed at the expense of other possibilities, and (b) produce a world in which its success is natural, expected, even desired. This model, then, promises a powerful new way to analyze the evolution of media worlds (Dimmick 1986; Dimmick and Rothenbuhler 1984; Rothenbuhler 1996; Stöber 2004).

This idea can be useful in analyzing a variety of cultural and media situations. I will start with a series of quick examples, then move into a more detailed analysis of the format in contemporary commercial radio.

For a first example, it is widely accepted among musicologists that the structure of blues songs and the style of blues performances have become less varied since commercial recording of the blues began in the 1920s. This has been a complicated historical process and the relevant literature is large (for just one example, see Rothenbuhler 2007). In the context of the present argument I would propose to explain it this way: the commercial interests of record producers, the recording motivations of musicians, the musical expectations of audiences, marketing strategies and images, and the circulating copies of successful records, all in the context of uncertainty about the other and the future, became a self-referencing loop organizing around an ever narrower song form. In other words, a self-referencing system in an environment, evolving toward reduced uncertainty, and producing a symbolic construct, the blues song form, as an operational reality.

Barnhurst and Nerone have shown how the newspaper, to take a very different example, operates in terms of a historically evolving visual form (Barnhurst 1994; Barnhurst and Nerone 2001). They argue that different forms of the newspaper have constituted their own different readers. I would predict it is something of an autopoietic system. Over time we should see how aspects of the newspaper business, printing technology, cultural constructs such as "democracy," "informed reader," or "Fourth Estate," and audience habits and expectations, organized around the communicative form so that the system reproduced the conditions of its own success. The current crisis of shrinking readership and profits in the newspaper industry, then, shows how autopoietic systems are also vulnerable to unanticipated change in their environments.

New media, on the other hand, require the invention of new communicative forms, and Scannell (1991; Scannell and Cardiff 1991) shows how early broadcasters had to develop an appropriate form for radio talks, a form of conversation that could work as communication in the studio and with the absent, dispersed audience members listening in their homes. There had not been a communication situation like this before and there was no established model for how to do it successfully. My hypothesis is that the model and the conditions of its success developed simultaneously as broadcasters and audiences trained each other, so to speak, and organized in a new form of relation around a new form of communication. The broadcasters learned to offer something that could work for listeners in domestic settings while the listeners learned to appreciate what the broadcasters could offer.

Ideas, ideals, and ideologies are also sustained by ritualistically performed communicative forms. Historical studies of the production of country music by Peterson (1997) and Jensen (1998) have demonstrated how authenticity developed as an idea, an appearance, a performance style, and presumably a set of audience expectations, over decades of the country music business. Again, we can interpret this in terms of communicative form in an evolving system: the appearance and performance are signifiers operating in a system that values tradition and authenticity and organizing itself so that particular styles of appearance and performance – communicative forms in my terms – can support their reality. There is an analogy between authenticity in country music and objectivity in journalism, as discussed above. Both are talked about as ideas, values, and goals. Both are widely recognized by their practitioners as fraught and by scholars as impossible – but that turns out to be irrelevant to everyday practice. Thus they reproduce themselves and the conditions of their success irrespective of any discussion of their unreality or impossibility. Why? How? Because they are communicative forms around which an autopoietic system organizes.

Luhmann (e.g. 1984/1995, 1995/2000) is the most widely recognized theorist of autopoietic systems in social analysis, and it is worth clarifying how my uses of the idea are independent of his larger system theory. Luhmann's (1996/2000) analysis of the mass media, for example, begins with "the assumption that the mass media are one of the function systems of modern society, which, like all the others, owes its increased effectiveness to the differentiation, operational closure and autopoietic autonomy of the system concerned" (Luhmann 1996/2000: 8). His interest is in how the mass media as a whole are internally systemic in such a way as to preserve their own operation and their integrated functional part in the social system as a whole. By contrast, I am proposing quasi-systemic outcomes to processes at a much lower level of analysis, performed by actors with goals in situations. The analytic vocabulary of systems theory is useful for describing some of the patterns that result, but I do not assume or propose a completely integrated system. Quite the contrary, I assume a messy world of mixed, uneven, and competing structures, processes, powers, resource flows, innovations, and accidental happenings.

There are other useful treatments of media forms and formats in the literature that deserve careful consideration. Altheide and Snow (1979) wrote about "media logic" analogous to what I call form, and some of their examples could be called ritualized forms. Their work has recently been picked up in the debate about mediatization, a concept for the ways in which previously independent social activities and objects take on the formats and logics prevalent in the media (e.g. Couldry 2008; Hjarvard 2008; Schulz 2004). Williams (1974) has also written about how existing cultural forms – such as drama, education, news, or sports – were adapted for television. Günter Thomas (2005) has analyzed how religious forms have migrated to television.

A concept of form and attention to its implications is not foreign to the media events literature either. Dayan and Katz's (1992) definition of the media event was explicitly formal, listing a series of necessary features for the syntax, semantics, and pragmatics of the media event. If we look back at that discussion with the idea of a self-referencing system in mind, we can see that when each element is present, the whole becomes a self-fulfilling and mutually-reinforcing logical circle. Similarly, Carey's (1998) analysis of denigration rituals and Liebes' (1998) of disaster marathons, each presented as complements to media events analysis, may also be read for evidence of self-policing, self-reinforcing communicative forms.

The system of radio formats

So forms and formats are ubiquitous in the media, in media events, other sorts of special coverage, and in everyday programming. Diverse examples hint that the idea of an autopoietic system organized around the ritualized performance of those forms could offer a useful explanation for how they endure and why, at key historical moments, they change so suddenly.[1] Let us consider a more detailed analysis, specifically of the formatting system of commercial radio stations in the United States.

In the US today radio stations program music, talk, and advertising within recognizable styles, whether new country or classic country, urban dance or smooth jazz, classical music or Latin. In the radio format, music, news, talk, and advertising are selected, produced, and blended for a consistent sound, so that the station sounds like itself and different from its competitors, 24 hours a day, seven days a week. Such reliable programming within recognizable styles attracts audiences with identifiable demographic tendencies, whose attention is sold to advertisers, whose spots are produced to fit the style. This system of commercial radio formatting was developed in the 1950s and 1960s, starting with Top-40 radio (MacFarland 1979; McCourt and Rothenbuhler 2004; Rothenbuhler and McCourt 2002).

Radio formats present themselves in public communication, not as business strategy, but as performances of taste, judgment, and style. The radio format portrays a world and an attitude toward it, and invites its listeners into that world. The Top-40 format of the 1950s was designed to attract everyone; it adopted an inclusive tone of fun and informality while playing diverse musical styles to attract teenagers and their parents, Anglo and African American, young, old, urban and rural. The presumption was that everyone wanted to hear the hits. In the ensuing years, as different styles of music and talk were sorted out and assigned to different stations, so were different audience members separated from each other. In cultivating their audiences, the radio industry also produced a nation-wide system of taken-for-granted knowledge. Today, no radio professionals, government regulators, or audience members, and precious few musicians or critics would expect a country station to play hip-hop or an urban African American to listen. Everyone knows better than that. But those are not natural facts; the system that produced them was invented within living memory.

What is the process by which this system could come into being, come into dominance, and then become so completely taken for granted? The answer may be the organization of an autopoietic system around the ritualistic performance of a communicative form.

The utility and the ritual of formatted radio

Forms of communication such as the radio format may spread through an industry because they are simply useful and have competitive advantage. They may also be associated with valued ideas – like objectivity in journalism and authenticity in country music – so that their repetition is also a ritualized performance that sustains the idea and the ritual itself. In that case we would expect the institution and its workers, the communicative form and its audience members, the ideas and their symbols, to organize autopoietically.

In the case of the radio format the mere fact of the form as such simplifies the job of radio station management in a series of ways. Formats radically reduce the number of decisions programmers must make, limiting the universe of musical choice to current songs of specified genres. Formatting allows a radio station to achieve a sound more consistent from moment to moment, by limiting the choices of the disk jockeys. The consistent sound of formatted radio is associated with ratings distributions that are less variable across parts of the day and within demographic groups. As there is less variability in the sample there is less difficulty in decision-making for programmers and managers who use ratings as indicators of success. The same advantages accrue to the sales staff, who can use the same pitch to all advertisers and have less need for special contracts to place certain advertisements at certain parts of the day (these points are taken from Rothenbuhler 1996.) Formatted versus unformatted radio would also be easier for audiences to recognize and choose, should they decide they like it, and easier for other radio stations to imitate if it is successful enough to be worth imitating.

Beyond the simple fact of form, as a specifically communicative form, the format solves one intractable problem and introduces a whole new territory of opportunities. The problem is that broadcasters work in a communicative situation of high uncertainty, at best, and often with fundamentally incoherent communicative goals. First, like all producers of cultural goods, the issues of demand, utility, value, and quality for their products and services are unclear and changeable. Second, their audience is unknowably large and diverse. Yet, third, like any other industrial enterprise, daily operation requires decisions, reliability, and a drive for efficiency. Non-commercial broadcasters can often reduce the ambiguity of their situation via a mission statement or some other commitment to a communicative, cultural, or social purpose.

Commercial, for-profit broadcasters, however, are in a situation that takes the basic problems of broadcast communication to another level (Rothenbuhler 1996). Because their purpose is essentially non-communicative (profit) but achieved with communication that works by misdirection (advertising), identifying the purpose does not solve any of the problems of communication (e.g. invention, style, audience adaptation). Further, their success in making profit is easily calculable by a metric incommensurable with the communicative means by which they make the profit. So profit can provide evidence of success, but it cannot provide information to reduce the uncertainty of communicating.

The format solves this problem via the a priori choice of a set of communicative rules. The purpose of the communication becomes the skilled performance of the format itself. The form of the communication becomes self-determining: autopoietic.

The radio format does more than that though because it is a public performance that participates in the everyday communicative worlds of its listeners. Unlike the program schedules of television and the earlier forms of network radio, which offered listeners discrete units of entertainment in return for their attention, formatted radio is more of a companion, an unusually reliable and undemanding communicative associate. This, then, represents a striking new opportunity for radio broadcasters, as the formatted flow of their communicative performance becomes a reliable communicative actor in the world of their audience. As the station has a voice, musical taste, news, and information, it takes on a communicatively performed character with which the listeners are encouraged to establish a relationship. Indeed when they were first discovering this new reality in the 1950s, there was an industry campaign to promote a new, more companionable radio format.

To the extent that a formatted radio station is successful in producing something catering for more than inertia or habit, but more akin to active listener loyalty, it is producing identity and relation in exactly the way Goffman (1959, 1967) analyzed those being produced in interpersonal rituals. The radio station is a communicative actor, offering a line in which are embedded proposed identities for self and other, performed rules of relationship, deference, demeanor, and so on. Listeners accept or reject the line and comport themselves accordingly for an ongoing interaction in which the identities, relationships, and so on are held to be true. This aspect of formatted radio as communicative form is, then, also ritualistic communication and from that point of view, such trite slogans as "your favorite radio station" or "we play more of your favorite music" are worth taking seriously. They could well be ritual invocations capable of creating the world they claim to represent.

Conclusions

The study of media events led to the study of ritual, which led to rethinking communication in general and a realization of the importance of communicative form. Form as such is useful, in communication as elsewhere. It reduces ambiguity and uncertainty. It is easy to recognize, to teach, to imitate, and so on. We should expect the practice governed by form to cultivate expectations in others more rapidly than one governed in some other way, such as by goals, or contracts, or situational response.

Second, form in communication produces patterned outcomes, predictable relationships, and so on. Patterned statements usually produce patterned responses and over time a communicative form can become a meta-signifier, whether shorthand or framing device. These aspects of form in communication are especially useful in the peculiar circumstances of commercial mass media, obligated to communicate for no clear communicative purpose with an unknowably large and diverse audience.

Third, above and beyond its basic usefulness, form in communication can work ritualistically to produce, alter, or maintain the reality of social constructs, such as authenticity, objectivity, femininity, masculinity, hipness, taste, and cultural categories.

To the extent that such communicatively constructed concepts are guides or evaluative standards for further communication, this illuminates one of the ways in which we live inside our communication. Our responses as communicators to the observable reality of communicatively constructed phenomena are aspects of the self-referencing patterns of communicative worlds. It is not a closed system but it is self-organizing through self-reference, so it does depend on circular logic.

Finally, because these systems are not alone and autonomous but competing in a messy world of mixed structures, processes, powers, trends, and happenings, we should be able to observe their competition, evolution, growth, and change in history. Even when we use the idea of system to organize our analysis, it is the study of history that shows us how it might have turned out differently, and so provides evidence of the ultimate contingency of whatever do become the structures in which we live.

Katz and Dayan created a conceptual opening in the study of mass communication processes and effects by drawing attention to singular events that punctuate ordinary everyday life and produce effects commensurate with the seriousness of their meanings rather than the frequency of their occurrence. I have tried to take what we learned from those studies and apply it back to situations of mediated communication that may appear trivial by the usual criteria of politics, religion, or art, but which are defining for the everyday cultural life of the masses of people who live within those media worlds.

In Dayan and Katz's terms, syntactically media events are interruptions, monopolistic, live, and remote; semantically they are historic, ceremonial, reverent, reconciliations; and pragmatically they enthrall large audiences, work with a norm of viewing, and celebrate. The radio format, by contrast, is syntactically uninterrupted flow, everyday, competitive, and in-studio; semantically it is unhistoric, has no memory, no future, unceremonial, irreverent, and reconciliation is irrelevant; pragmatically it entertains and amuses its audience and is indifferent to the rest.

If those two radically different forms can be analyzed using some of the same conceptual tools, especially the central idea of ritual, then two other important lessons follow. First, how important and how far-ranging was the conceptual example Katz and Dayan offered, from what was once called mass communication processes and effects to a new kind of humanistic media anthropology and styles of media studies we are still inventing; second, that media events may not be so radically unique after all. Media events, special as they are, are still part of the continuity of communicative worlds, and that is why lessons learned in their analysis can be so useful to the analysis of so many other situations of communication.

Acknowledgement

An earlier version of this chapter was presented as a Keynote address at Media Events: Globalization and Cultural Change, University of Bremen, Germany, 6–7 July 2007.

My thanks to Nick Couldry, Daniel Dayan, Andreas Hepp, Stig Hjarvard, Elihu Katz, Joost Van Loon, and several others who provided useful comments there and later. This work was supported by the Glasscock Center for Humanities Research, Texas A&M University, USA.

Note

1 This last issue is an important one that I have left mostly unaddressed here to simplify the discussion. Rituals and autopoietic systems can survive, produce their expected results, and reproduce themselves relatively independently of other changes in their environments. On the other hand, they do this through "operational closure" as systems theorists say, so that they only recognize and process information from their environment that already fits their self-reproducing model.

Such systems are, then, vulnerable to unanticipated changes that impinge on critical resources. Although Luhmann primarily theorizes system stability, I see this vulnerability as crucially important and use it to analyze how media forms come and go historically.

References

Altheide, D.L. and Snow, R.P. (1979) *Media Logic*, Beverly Hills: Sage.

Barnhurst, K.G. (1994) *Seeing the Newspaper*, New York: St. Martin's Press.

Barnhurst, K.G. and Nerone, J. (2001) *The Form of News: A History*, New York: Guilford Press.

Bell, C. (1992) *Ritual Theory, Ritual Practice*, New York: Oxford University Press.

Boorstin, D. (1964) *The Image: A Guide to Pseudo-Events in America*, New York: Atheneum.

Carey, J. (1988) *Communication as Culture: Essays on Media and Society*, Boston, MA: Unwin Hyman.

—— (1998) "Political Ritual on Television. Episodes in the History of Shame Degradation and Excommunication", in T. Liebes and J. Curran (eds) *Media, Ritual and Identity*, London: Routledge, 42–70.

Coman, M. (2005) "Cultural Anthropology and Mass Media: A Processual Approach", in E.W. Rothenbuhler and M. Coman (eds) *Media Anthropology*, Thousand Oaks, CA: Sage, 46–55.

Cottle, S. (2006) "Mediatized Rituals: Beyond Manufacturing Consent", *Media, Culture and Society*, 28, 3: 411–32.

Couldry, N. (2003) *Media Rituals: A Critical Approach*, London: Routledge.

—— (2008) "Mediatization or Mediation? Alternative Understandings of the Emergent Space of Digital Storytelling", *New Media and Society*, 10, 3: 373–91.

Dayan, D. (2008) Personal communication with author, 17 September.

Dayan, D. and Katz, E. (1985a) "Electronic Ceremonies: Television Performs a Royal Wedding", in M. Blonskey (ed.) *On Signs*, Baltimore: Johns Hopkins University Press, 16–32.

—— (1985b) "Television Ceremonial Events", *Society*, 22, 4: 60–6.

—— (1987) "Performing Media Events", in J. Curran, A. Wingate and P. Smith (eds) *Impacts and Influences: Essays on Media Power in the Twentieth Century*, London: Methuen, 174–97.

—— (1988) "Articulating Consensus: The Ritual and Rhetoric of Media Events", in J.C. Alexander (ed.) *Durkheimian Sociology: Cultural Studies*, Cambridge: Cambridge University Press, 161–86.

—— (1992) *Media Events: The Live Broadcasting of History*, Cambridge, MA: Harvard University Press.

Dayan, D., Katz, E. and Kerns, P. (1984) "Armchair Pilgrimages: The Trips of Pope John Paul II and their Television Public", *On Film*, 13: 25–34.

Dimmick, J. (1986) "Sociocultural Evolution in the Communication Industries", *Communication Research*, 13, 3: 473–508.

Dimmick, J. and Rothenbuhler, E.W. (1984) "The Theory of the Niche: Quantifying Competition among Media Industries", *Journal of Communication*, 34, 4: 103–19.

Durkheim, É. (1995) [1912] *The Elementary Forms of the Religious Life*, trans. K.E. Fields, New York: Free Press.

Ginsburg, F.D., Abu-Lughod, L. and Larkin, B. (eds) (2002) *Media Worlds: Anthropology on New Terrain*, Berkeley: University of California Press.

Goffman, E. (1959) *The Presentation of Self in Everyday Life*, New York: Anchor Books.

—— (1967) *Interaction Ritual: Essays on Face-to-face Behavior*, New York: Anchor Books.

Hjarvard, S. (2008) "The Mediatization of Society: A Theory of the Media as Agents of Social and Cultural Change", *Nordicom Review*, 29, 2: 105–34.

Jensen, J. (1998) *The Nashville Sound: Authenticity, Commercialization, and Country Music*, Nashville: Vanderbilt University Press.

Katz, E. (1959) "Mass Communication Research and the Study of Popular Culture. An Editorial Note on a Possible Future for this Journal", *Studies in Public Communication*, 2: 1–6.

—— (1980) "Media Events: The Sense of Occasion", *Studies in Visual Anthropology*, 6, 3: 84–9.

Katz, E. and Dayan, D. (1985) "Media Events: On the Experience of not Being There", *Religion*, 15: 305–14.

—— (1986) "Contests, Conquests, and Coronations: On Media Events and their Heroes", in C.F. Graumann and S. Moscovici (eds) *Changing Conceptions of Leadership*, New York: Springer-Verlag, 135–44.

Katz, E., Dayan, D. and Motyl, P. (1981) "In Defence of Media Events", in R.W. Haigh, G. Gerbner and R.B. Byrne (eds) *Communication in the Twenty-first Century*, New York: Wiley, 43–59.

Liebes, T. (1998) "Television's Disaster Marathons: A Danger for Democratic Processes?", in T. Liebes and J. Curran (eds) *Media, Ritual and Identity*, London: Routledge, 71–84.

Luhmann, N. (1995) [1984] *Social Systems*, trans. J. Bednarz, Jr., with D. Baecker, Stanford, CA: Stanford University Press.

—— (2000) [1995] *Art as a Social System*, trans. E.M. Knodt, Stanford, CA: Stanford University Press.

—— (2000) [1996] *The Reality of the Mass Media*, trans. K. Cross, Stanford, CA: Stanford University Press.

MacAloon, J. (1984) "Olympic Games and the Theory of Spectacle in Modern Societies", in J. MacAloon (ed.) *Rite, Drama, Festival, Spectacle: Rehearsals toward a Theory of Cultural Performance*, Philadelphia: Institute for the Study of Human Issues, 241–80.

MacFarland, D. (1979) *The Development of the Top 40 Radio Format*, North Stratford: Ayer.

McCourt, T. and Rothenbuhler, E.W. (2004) "Burnishing the Brand: Todd Storz and the Total Station Sound", *The Radio Journal*, 2, 1: 3–14.

Peterson, R.A. (1997) *Creating Country Music: Fabricating Authenticity*, Chicago, IL: University of Chicago Press.

Rappaport, R.A. (1979) *Ecology, Meaning, and Religion*, Berkeley: North Atlantic Books.

—— (1999) *Ritual and Religion in the Making of Humanity*, Cambridge: Cambridge University Press.

Rothenbuhler, E.W. (1985) *Media Events, Civil Religion, and Social Solidarity: The Living Room Celebration of the Olympic Games*, doctoral dissertation, University of Southern California.

—— (1988) "The Living Room Celebration of the Olympic Games", *Journal of Communication*, 38, 3: 61–81.

—— (1989) "Values and Symbols in Public Orientations to the Olympic Media Event", *Critical Studies in Mass Communication*, 6, 2: 138–57.

—— (1993) "Argument for a Durkheimian Theory of the Communicative", *Journal of Communication*, 43, 3: 158–63.

—— (1996) "Commercial Radio as Communication", *Journal of Communication*, 46, 1: 125–43.

—— (1998) *Ritual Communication: From Everyday Conversation to Mediated Ceremony*, Thousand Oaks, CA: Sage.

—— (2006) "Communication as Ritual", in G.J. Shepherd, J. John and T. Striphas (eds) *Communication as . . .: Stances on Theory*, Thousand Oaks, CA: Sage, 13–21.

—— (2007) "For-the-record Aesthetics and Robert Johnson's Blues Style as a Product of Recorded Culture", *Popular Music*, 26, 1: 65–81.

Rothenbuhler, E.W. and Coman, M. (eds) (2005) *Media Anthropology*, Thousand Oaks: Sage.

Rothenbuhler, E.W. and McCourt, T. (2002) "Radio Redefines Itself, 1947–1962", in M. Hilmes and J. Loviglio (eds) *Radio Reader: Essays in the Cultural History of Radio*, London: Routledge, 367–87.

Scannell, P. (1991) "Introduction: The Relevance of Talk", in P. Scannell (ed.) *Broadcast Talk*, London: Sage, 1–13.

Scannell, P. and Cardiff, D. (1991) *A Social History of British Broadcasting, vol. I*, Oxford: Blackwell.

Schramm, W. and Roberts, D. (eds) (1971) *The Processes and Effects of Mass Communication*, revised edn, Champaign-Urbana: University of Illinois Press.

Schulz, W. (2004) "Reconstructing Mediatization as an Analytical Concept", *European Journal of Communication*, 19, 1: 87–101.

Stöber, R. (2004) "What Media Evolution is: A Theoretical Approach to the History of New Media", *European Journal of Communication*, 19, 4: 483–505.

Thomas, G. (2005) "The Emergence of Religious Forms on Television", in E.W. Rothenbuhler and M. Coman (eds) *Media Anthropology*, Thousand Oaks, CA: Sage, 79–90.

Tuchman, G. (1972) "Objectivity as Strategic Ritual", *American Journal of Sociology*, 77, 4: 660–79.

—— (1978) *Making News: A Study in the Construction of Reality*, New York: Free Press.

Williams, R. (1974) *Television: Technology and Cultural Form*, New York: Schocken Books.

6

MEDIA SPECTACLE AND MEDIA EVENTS
Some critical reflections

Douglas Kellner

The mainstream corporate media today in the United States process events, news, and information in the form of media spectacle.[1] In an arena of intense competition with 24/7 cable TV networks, talk radio, Internet sites and blogs, and ever proliferating new media such as Facebook, MySpace, YouTube, and Twitter, competition for attention is ever more intense, leading the corporate media to go to sensationalistic tabloidized stories which they construct in the forms of media spectacle that attempt to attract maximum audiences for as much time as possible, until the next spectacle emerges.

By spectacle, I mean media constructs that are out of the ordinary and outside habitual daily routine which become special media spectacles. They involve an aesthetic dimension and are often dramatic, bound up with competition like the Olympics or Oscars. They are highly public social events, often taking a ritualistic form to celebrate society's highest values. Yet while media rituals function to legitimate a society's "sacred center" (Shils 1975) and dominant values and beliefs (Hepp and Couldry, Chapter 1, this volume), media spectacles are increasingly commercialized, vulgar, glitzy, and, I will argue, important arenas of political contestation.

Media spectacle refers to technologically mediated events, in which media forms such as broadcasting, print media, or the Internet process events in a spectacular form. Examples of political events that became media spectacles would include the Clinton sex and impeachment scandal in the late 1990s, the death of Princess Diana, the 9/11 terror attacks, and, currently, the meltdown of the U.S. and perhaps global financial system in the context of a U.S. presidential election. I will theorize in this study media spectacle as eclipsing and absorbing media events. I first indicate how my analysis is connected both to Guy Debord's notion of the society of the spectacle and theories of media events and spectacles, and then illustrate my theory with an analysis of the 2008 presidential campaign.

Guy Debord and the society of the spectacle

The concept of the "society of the spectacle" developed by French theorist Guy Debord and his comrades in the Situationist International has had a major impact on a variety of contemporary theories of society and culture. My notion of media spectacle builds on Debord's conception of the society of spectacle, but differs significantly. For Debord, "spectacle" constituted the overarching concept to describe the media and consumer society, including the packaging, promotion, and display of commodities, and the production and effects of all media. Using the term "media spectacle," I am largely focusing on various forms of technologically constructed media productions that are produced and disseminated through the so-called mass media, ranging from radio and television to the Internet and latest wireless gadgets.

As we proceed into a new millennium, the media are becoming more technologically dazzling and are playing an ever-escalating role in everyday life with proliferating media and cyberculture generating new sites such as Facebook, MySpace, and YouTube, as well as a propagation of complex computer games, which include role-playing and virtual immersion in alternative worlds. Thus, in addition to the spectacles that celebrate and reproduce the existing society described by Debord, and by Dayan and Katz and others as media events (see below), today there is a new domain of the interactive spectacle, which provides an illusion of interaction and creativity, but may well ensnare one ever deeper in the tentacles of the existing society and technology (see Best and Kellner 2001).

Thus, while Debord presents a rather generalized and abstract notion of spectacle, I engage specific examples of media spectacle and how they are produced, constructed, circulated, and function in the present era. In addition, I am reading the production, text and effects of various media spectacles from a standpoint within contemporary U.S. society in order to help illuminate and theorize its socio-political dynamics and culture, and more broadly, globalization and global culture. Debord, by contrast, was analyzing a specific stage of capitalist society: that of the media and consumer society organized around spectacle. Second, my approach to these specific spectacles is interpretive and interrogatory. In my studies of media spectacle, I deploy cultural studies as *diagnostic critique*, reading and interpreting various spectacles to see what they tell us about the present age, using media spectacles to illuminate contemporary social developments, trends, and struggles.[2] Third, I analyze the contradictions and reversals of the spectacle, whereas Debord has an overpowering and hegemonic notion of the society of the spectacle. Although he and his comrades in the Situationist International sketched out various models of opposition and struggle, and in fact inspired in part the rather spectacular May 1968 events in France, whereby students and workers rebelled and almost overthrew the existing government, Debord's notion of "the society of the spectacle" tends to be monolithic and all-embracing. By contrast, I see the spectacle as contested and have a notion of the reversal of the spectacle. In my conception, the spectacle is a *contested terrain* in which different forces use the spectacle to push their interests and agendas.

Media events and media spectacle

The notion of media spectacle also builds upon Dayan and Katz's notion of a "media event" (1992), which referred to how political systems exploited televised live, ceremonial, and pre-planned events, such as the funeral of President Kennedy, a royal wedding, or the Olympic Games to celebrate and reproduce the social system. Interestingly, Katz and Liebes (2007) have recently revised the original Dayan and Katz analysis to distinguish between "media events," "the ceremonial Contests, Conquests and Coronations that punctuated television's first 50 years," contrasted to disruptive events "such as Disaster, Terror and War" (Katz and Liebes 2007). My own view is that the Bush/Cheney administration has orchestrated media spectacle in its "war on terror" to strengthen their regime, but that the spectacle of the Iraq War got out of control and became a highly disruptive terrain of struggle (see Kellner 2005). In fact, war itself has arguably become an orchestrated media spectacle since the 1991 Gulf War (see Kellner 1992, 2005), with terrorism also using media spectacle for political ends (Kellner 2003b).

On my account, there are many levels and categories of spectacle (Kellner 2003a, 2008). Some media spectacles, such as Dayan and Katz's media events (1992), are recurrent phenomena of media culture that celebrate dominant values and institutions, as well as its modes of conflict resolution. They include media extravaganzas like the Oscars and Emmies, or sports events like the Super Bowl, World Cup, or Olympics, which celebrate basic values of competition and winning.

Politics too is increasingly mediated by media spectacle. Political conflicts, campaigns, and those attention-grabbing occurrences that we call "news" have all been subjected to the logic of spectacle and tabloidization in the era of media sensationalism, infotainment, political scandal and contestation, seemingly unending cultural war, the ongoing phenomenon of Terror War, and now the emergent era of the Obama spectacle.

Media spectacle thus includes those media events and rituals of consumption, entertainment, and competition like political campaigns that embody contemporary society's basic values and serve to enculturate individuals into its way of life. Yet the spectacle, as my allusion to the *political spectacle* attests, may also embody key societal conflicts, and so I see the spectacle as a contested terrain. Since the 1960s culture wars have been raging in the United States between Left and Right, liberals and conservatives, and a diversity of groups over U.S. politics, race, class, gender, sexuality, war, and other key issues. Both sides exploit the spectacle as during the Vietnam War when the war itself was contested by the spectacle of the anti-war movement, or the 1990s

Clinton sex and impeachment spectacle, whereby conservatives attempted to use the spectacle of sex scandal to destroy the Clinton presidency, while his defenders used the spectacle of the Right trying to take out an elected president to successfully defend him.

Spectacles of terror, like the 9/11 attacks on the Twin Towers and Pentagon, differ significantly from spectacles that celebrate or reproduce the existing society as in Guy Debord's "society of the spectacle," or the "media events" analyzed by Dayan and Katz (1992), which describe how political systems exploited televised live, ceremonial, and pre-planned events. Spectacles of terror are highly disruptive events carried out by oppositional groups or individuals who are conducting politics or war by other means. Like the media and consumer spectacles described by Debord, spectacles of terror reduce individuals to passive objects, manipulated by existing institutions and figures. However, the spectacles of terror produce fear which terrorists hope will demoralize the objects of their attack, but which are often manipulated by conservative groups, like the Bush-Cheney administration, to push through right-wing agendas, cut back on civil liberties, and militarize the society.

Spectacles of terror should also be distinguished from *spectacles of catastrophe* such as natural disasters like the Asian Tsunami or Hurricane Katrina that became major spectacles of the day in 2004 and 2005. Other recent U.S. spectacles of catastrophe include fires, dramatic failures of the system or infrastructure such as the Minnesota Bridge collapse and Utah mine tragedy, both becoming spectacles of the day in August 2007, and recurrent Hurricanes, such as Gustav in August 2008 which delayed the Republican party presidential convention by one day when it was predicted to be twice as powerful as Hurricane Katrina (although, fortunately, it was only half as powerful but totally dominated U.S. corporate media coverage for days).

Mega-spectacles constitute a situation whereby certain spectacles become defining events of their era. These include commodity spectacles such as the McDonald's or Nike spectacle, or Michael Jordan and the NBA basketball spectacle, which define an era of consumption (Kellner 2003a). Entertainment spectacle, such as Elvis Presley, rock and roll, and hip hop, came to help define a cultural epoch, The Age of Rock, that still rocks on. Mega-spectacles also include socio-political dramas that characterize a certain period, involving such things as the 1991 Gulf War, the O.J. Simpson trials, the Clinton sex and impeachment scandals, or the Terror War that was the defining point of the global nightmare of the Bush-Cheney era, now blessedly over.

Mega-spectacles are defined both quantitatively and qualitatively. The major media spectacles of the era dominate news, journalism, and Internet buzz, and are highlighted and framed as the key events of the age, as were, for instance, the Princess Diana wedding, death, and funeral, the extremely close 2000 election and 36-day Battle for the White House, or the 11 September terror attacks and their violent aftermath (Kellner 2003a). From 2003 to the present, the spectacle of Iraq, and the ongoing Terror War, have dominated our era and encapsulate basic conflicts and political dynamics, although these mega-spectacles can be overshadowed temporarily by the spectacle of the day, such as the interlude of the "Virginia Tech Massacre" (Kellner 2008), or the 2008 U.S. presidential party primaries and then election campaign, discussed below.

Media spectacles are thus becoming the form in which news, information, and the events of the era are processed by media corporations, the state and political groups, and institutions and individuals who have the power to construct political and social realities. In an earlier era of broadcasting, media events were the major form in which the media and the state constructed significant social rituals that reproduced the existing society. Media events tended to be temporally regular, discrete, temporary, and relatively pre-dictable. In the early era of television, as Lang and Lang have argued (1992 [1984]), media events became key markers and constituents of the political and social reality of the day, although as Boorstin warned (1961), they could also be constructed as pseudo-events.

Media spectacles, by contrast, are more defuse, variable, unpredictable, and contestable. Media spectacles emerged as a dominant form of defining and contesting existing social and political realities during the era of cable and satellite television and the metaphysical event of the Internet that changes everything. Whereas media events tended to be national, media spectacles are often global. In what McLuhan (1964) foresaw as a "global village," a networked and wired world can experience the same events simultaneously and in real time as during September 2008, when the entire world suffered through the Chinese milk poisoning and then the meltdown of U.S. financial institutions which threatened the global economy.

Media spectacles are orchestrated by the state in the case of wars, governing, or political elections, while media corporations on a daily basis constructed media spectacles out of "breaking news" and what are defined as the major events of the day. Media corporations want to hook consumers into big stories so that they will stay tuned, log on, or keep their eyes and attention on the big events of the day that are increasingly orchestrated as media spectacles. This was the case in the United States, and to some extent globally, with the 2008 U.S. presidential election whose outcome may well define a new historical era.

Cultural studies and political spectacle: the case of the 2008 U.S. presidential election

Since the establishment of the Centre for Contemporary Cultural Studies in Birmingham, England in the 1960s, as well as in subsequent versions of cultural studies throughout the world, there has been a long-standing tradition of taking on the big issues of the era (Kellner 1995). My version uses cultural studies and critical social theory to attempt to illuminate the contemporary moment.

Looking at the 2008 Democratic Party primaries we see exhibited once again the triumph of the spectacle. In this case, the spectacle of Obama and Hillary, the first serious African American candidate vs. the first serious woman candidate brought on a compelling spectacle of race and gender, as well as a campaign spectacle in incredibly hard-fought and unpredictable primaries. As a media spectacle, the Democratic Party primary could be read as a reality TV show. For the media and candidates alike the Democratic primary has been *Survivor*, or *The Apprentice* ("You're fired!"), with losing candidates knocked out week by week. With the two standing candidates Obama and Clinton, it has been *The Amazing Race*, as well as *American Gladiator* and *American Idol* rolled into one, with genuine suspense concerning the outcome.

From the first primary in Iowa where in January he won a startling victory, it has been the Obama spectacle, a spectacle of Hope, of Change, of Color, and of Youth. In addition to his campaign speeches on the stump everyday that have mobilized record crowds, after every primary election, Obama made a spirited speech, even after his loss in New Hampshire and other primaries. He gave a magnificent Super Tuesday victory speech that could have been the most watched event of the primary season and was probably the most circulated speech on the Internet that week, in which Obama pulled slightly ahead in a multi-state primary night. Obama then won 11 primaries in a row, and made another magnificent speech after the Wisconsin primary where he took over the airways for about an hour, providing a vision of the U.S. coming together, mobilizing people for change, carrying out a progressive agenda, getting out of Iraq, using the money spent there to rebuild the infrastructure, schools, health system, and so on. Even when he lost primaries, he gave inspiring and impassioned speeches.

There has also been an impressive Internet spectacle in support of Obama's presidency. Obama has raised an unprecedented amount of money on the Internet, he achieved over one million friends on Facebook, and he has mobilized youth and others through text-messaging and emails. The YouTube (UT) music video "Obama Girl," which has a young woman singing about why she supports Obama with images of his speeches interspersed, has gotten over five million hits and, along with Will,I,Am's Obama music video, is one of the most popular in history, while 12 Obama UT videos have received over one million hits a piece.[3]

In terms of stagecraft and spectacle, in Obama's daily stump speeches on the campaign trial, his post-victory and even defeat speeches in the Democratic primaries, and his grassroots Internet and cultural support have shown that Obama is a master of the spectacle. Hence Obama eventually secured the Democratic presidential nomination, setting himself to run against John McCain as the presumptive Republican Party candidate. Thus, during the summer months, we have had the Obama vs. McCain spectacle, intensified during the party conventions in late August and early September, and on full-blast for the final two months of campaigning. Since Obama is the master of the spectacle, McCain presumably had to give good spectacle himself, or produce anti-Obama spectacles. From the time Obama clinched the nomination, McCain largely attempted to create an anti-Obama spectacle through TV ads, planting anti-Obama stories in the press and circulating them through the Internet, and eventually savagely attacking Obama every day on the campaign trial.

Although Obama benefited significantly through his supporters' Internet and other cultural productions, he was temporarily put on the defensive in the summer with the YouTube released videos of the inflammatory speeches of the Reverend Jeremiah Wright, the Chicago pastor of his church. The deluge of Republican and then mainstream media circulating the Reverend Wright speeches and Wright's appearances on television and making inflammatory speeches led Obama to break with his pastor. However, Obama gave what many believed to be a brilliant speech on race in Philadelphia, another spectacle that became a major cultural event on both the Internet and mainstream media.

Underneath the spectacle on the broadcasting media, a Republican campaign circulated through the Internet claimed that Obama was really a Muslim, was, like the Reverend Wright anti-American, and even an Iranian agent.[4] In addition to these underhanded sneak attacks, parallel to the Swift Boat attacks against John Kerry in 2004, the McCain campaign released TV ads equating Obama with Paris Hilton and Britney Spears as an empty celebrity, leading Paris Hilton to create an ad attacking "the wrinkly old white dude" (i.e. John McCain) and arguing why she'd be a better president; her YouTube video received over one million hits in a single day.

While the McCain camp engaged in petty anti-Obama ads and attacks in summer 2008, Obama went on a Global Tour that itself became a major media spectacle as he traveled from Afghanistan and Iraq to Europe. Obama gave a rousing speech in Berlin that attracted hundreds and thousands of spectators and a global TV audience, and he was shown meeting with leaders in all of these countries as if he were the presumptive president.

As the campaigns neared their party conventions, traditionally a great TV spectacle, the presidential race seemed to be establishing once again the primacy of TV democracy where the election is battled out on television – although print media, Internet, and new media are also significant, as I have suggested. Following the great spectacle of the Democratic convention in late August with memorable speeches by Obama, Al Gore, Bill and Hillary Clinton, and a moving appearance by Senator Ted Kennedy, McCain desperately needed some spectacle and got it in spades when he announced and presented his Vice-President candidate, who generated the Sarah Palin spectacle, one of the more astounding media spectacles in U.S. political history: Palin, a short-term Governor of Alaska and former small town mayor who few knew anything about when McCain introduced her. It turns out, however, that Palin gives good spectacle: she's a gun owner and NRA activist, and footage all day showed her shooting guns. She was also a high school basketball star so there were good spectacles of her playing basketball (although Obama could probably beat her one on one). Palin's husband was a snowmobile champion so you got more good sports spectacle, and Sarah's a beauty contest winner, winning local competitions and coming runner-up as Miss Alaska, so there were a lot of images of her as pin-up girl that first day which introduced her to the American public. Governor Palin is a mother with five children, so you had great family pictures, including a newborn baby with Down's syndrome. After her initial speech with McCain introducing her, Palin's family and the McCains went shopping and she was shown as an enthusiastic shopper, marking her as a typical American.

Then, on Labor Day, 1 September, the public learned that Palin's 17-year-old daughter was pregnant and unmarried, so we had sex scandal spectacle all day and debates about whether a mother with all these problems should run for Vice-President and submit her family to media scrutiny. Many other scandals about Palin herself came out: she had fired state employees who would not do her bidding and had appointed unqualified high school friends and cronies to state jobs; she had supported corrupt politicians, had lied about her record, and had consistently taken positions to the right of Dick Cheney, so Sarah Palin suddenly became a spectacle of scandal, as well as adulation by the Christian and Republican Right.

The Republicans were forced to postpone their convention because of another spectacle, the Hurricane Gustav spectacle that was said to be twice as dangerous as Katrina, but turned out to be only half as bad. Once the Republicans got their convention started, it turned out that Sarah Palin gave an electrifying speech that mobilized the right-wing Republican base and a new star was born. For a couple of weeks after the Republican convention Sarah Palin was the spectacle of the day and the media buzzed around the clock about her past and her record, her qualifications or lack of them, and her effect on the election.

The Stupid Season in the campaign was over, however, when, on Monday 15 September 2008, the collapse of the Lehman Brothers investment company helped trigger what appeared to be one of the great U.S. and global financial crises in history. Suddenly, the election was caught up in the spectacle of the possible collapse of the U.S. and global economy, so economics took front and center stage. In two wild weeks of campaigning, McCain first insisted that the "fundamentals" of the U.S. economy were sound, and when everyone ridiculed him, he recognized the significance of the crisis and said that as president he would fire the head of the SEC (Security Exchange Commission), although this official does not serve directly under the president, and everyone from the *Wall Street Journal* to the television networks admonished McCain for trying to scapegoat someone who experts knew was not responsible for the crisis.

Obama seemed to gain the initiative during the economic crisis as he made measured and intelligent statements on the economy, and so the Republicans desperately began a strategy of the Big Lie, endlessly distorting his tax proposals, accusing him of crony relations with disgraced federal officials whom he hardly knew, and making ridiculous claims about Obama's responsibility for the economic mess. It was becoming apparent that the Republicans were pursuing the Karl Rove/George W. Bush strategy of simply lying about their opponents, trying to create an alternative reality. It was becoming clear that Sarah Palin's candidacy was based on Big Lies, as McCain introduced her as the woman who had stopped the Bridge to Nowhere in Alaska and was a champion of cutting "earmarks," that is, pork barrel legislation to benefit special interests in one's district. Palin repeated these claims day after day, but research revealed that she had supported the Bridge to Nowhere from the beginning, had hired a public relations firm to get earmarks for her district and her state, and had in fact received more earmarks per capita than almost any politician in the country.

With the September 22, 2008 economic meltdown, however, when it looked like the U.S. economy was in a freefall collapse and the Bush-Cheney administration proposed a multibillion dollar bailout package, John McCain embarked on one of the truly incredible political spectacles in U.S. history, trying to position himself as the savior of the economic system and then making an utter fool of himself as day after day he engaged in increasingly bizarre and erratic behavior. Immediately before the first presidential debate on September 26, McCain announced he was suspending his campaign, was going to Washington to resolve the financial crisis and would stay until it was resolved, threatening to miss the presidential debate. After a lot of negative publicity, he showed up for the debate, viciously attacking Barack Obama in probably the most thuggish debate performance in U.S. political history, with his website declaring him the winner before the debate even took place (subsequent polls showed that Obama got a bounce from the debate and the candidate's performances in response to the financial crisis).

Over the weekend, McCain came to Washington, claiming he was bringing together Congressmen to resolve the financial crisis, and attacked Obama for staying on the campaign trial. The morning of the Congressional vote on the debate, McCain and his surrogates claimed it was John McCain alone who had brought Democrats and Republicans together to resolve the financial crisis and continued vicious attacks on Obama. When, hours later, it was revealed that the bailout package pushed by the Bush-Cheney administration, and supported by McCain, Obama, and the Democratic and Republican Party house leaders, failed because two-thirds of the Republicans, who McCain was supposed to be leading, voted against it, McCain had more than a little egg on his face as the stock market plunged in the biggest one-day drop in history.

Trying in the face of his buffoonish spectacle to keep the initiative, McCain said that this was not the time to engage in partisan behavior, but to pull the country together, and blamed the failure of the bailout bill on Obama and the Democrats – surely a partisan claim! The Sarah Palin spectacle momentarily took the focus away from McCain's erratic efforts to take advantage of the booming economic crisis and the unpopular trillion-dollar-plus bailout, when the Vice-Presidential candidate debated the Democrats' Joe Biden. The lead-up to the debate featured daily sound-bites of Sarah Palin's interview with CBS's Katie Couric in which she was unable to mention one specific newspaper or journal that she read, could not think of a Supreme Court decision she opposed beyond Roe vs. Wade, and generally could not complete a coherent sentence, let alone provide a clear answer. During the debate she proved herself to be a good script performer as she acted out the predigested sound-bites to each question, winked and talked folksy if she wanted to distract the audience, and generally played cutesy rather than actually debate the questions with Biden, who provided coherent answers to questions and criticism of John McCain which Palin ignored.

Palin's conservative base loved her down-home hockey-mom performance and so Palin was unleashed as the attack dog on the campaign trail, as a desperate McCain, with polls indicating that votes were going Obama's way in key states, decided to attack Obama's personal character as a last-ditch way to try to win votes. After the *New York Times* published an article on Obama and former Weather Underground member Bill Ayers, Palin started referring daily to "Obama's pallin' around with terrorists," and John McCain began personally attacking Obama, raising the question "who is the real Barack Obama," with the audience screaming "terrorist!"

Throughout the second week of October, Palin and McCain continued to make the Ayers connection in their campaign rallies, media interviews, and TV ads, personally attacking Obama, and the frenzied Republican mob would scream "Kill him!," "Traitor!," "Bomb Obama!" When one confused woman in the Republican mob told McCain that she "didn't trust Obama" because of things she'd been hearing about him, stammering "he's an Arab!," it was clear that the Republicans lies and demagoguery had led their rabid right-wing base to believe that Obama was an Arab, a Muslim, a terrorist, and not an American. It was also clear that Palin and McCain had stirred up significant levels of mob fear, ignorance, and violence that were becoming extremely volatile and dangerous.

Investigative reporters indicated that Obama had only a casual relation with Ayers, whereas Palin and her husband were involved in an Alaskan secessionist party whose right-wing and anti-Semitic founder had a long history of outrageous anti-American ranting, racist ramblings, and ultra-right politics: Palin's husband had belonged to that party and just this year Sarah Palin addressed their party convention wishing them "good luck." Another investigative report linked Palin to a number of extreme right-wing groups and individuals who had promoted her career (McCain, too, it was revealed, had been associated with an unsavory lot). But Palin's week of infamy came to a proper conclusion when the Alaskan Supreme Court ruled on 10 October that a report into the "Troopergate" scandal could be released and the report itself pointed out that Palin had "abused her authority as governor" and violated Alaska's ethics regulations. Thrown off her moralistic high horse, Palin nonetheless continued to be McCain's attack dog and to raise controversy on the campaign trial.

It was clear that the Republicans were playing a politics of association to feed their media spectacles, just as the Bush-Cheney administration had associated Iraq with 9/11, Al Qaeda, and "weapons of mass destruction," connections that were obviously false, but the associations worked to sell the war to their base, gullible Democrats, and the media. Republicans had long sold their right-wing corporate class politics to voters by associating the Democrats with gay marriage, abortion, and secularism. Would the public and media wake up to the Republicans' politics of lying and manipulation or would they continue to get away with their decades of misrule and mendaciousness?

The major theme of the final debate pushed by McCain that remained a touchstone of his campaign was how Obama's answer to Joe the Plumber proved that he was going to raise taxes on small businesses. In an Obama campaign event the previous weekend, the man who McCain referred to as Joe the Plumber told Obama that he had been a plumber for 15 years and was trying to buy the business he worked for – and, since it cost over $250,000, he would be forced to pay higher taxes since Obama's tax reform proposal would increase taxes on those making over $250,000 and lower those making less. It turned out that Joe wasn't the dude's first name, whose real name was Samuel J. Wurzelbacher; that he was not a licensed plumber; that his income the previous year was around $40,000; and that he owed over $1,000 in back unpaid taxes.[5] These paltry facts did not stop McCain and Palin, who continued to raise Joe the Plumber in every campaign stop and were making it the major theme of their campaign to generate opposition between Obama the tax-and-spend liberal who would raise your taxes and McCain and Palin who took the side of Joe the Plumber, Ted the Carpenter, and a daily array of allegedly working-class people who opposed Obama.

As the two campaigns entered their last week of campaigning before the November 4 election, Obama made speeches with his "closing arguments" hoping to "seal the deal." During September, Obama raised an unprecedented $150 million, much of it from small Internet and personal donations, and was also getting soaring poll numbers, showing him pulling ahead nationally and in the significant battleground states. As he entered the last week of the campaign, Obama presented the spectacle of a young, energetic, articulate candidate who had run what many considered an almost flawless campaign and attempted during the election's final days to project images of hope, change, and bringing the country together to address its growing problems and divisions – exactly the message with which Obama started off his campaign.

The McCain-Palin camp seemed to close with the same basic argument with which most Republican candidates end their campaign: the Democrats want to raise taxes and spread around the wealth, an accusation increasingly hyped by the right-wing base and McCain and Palin themselves that Obama was really a "socialist." McCain continued to raise questions about Obama's experience and the risk that the country would undergo with an untried president, while Obama retorted that the real risk was continuing with more of the last eight years of catastrophic economic policies and a failed foreign policy.

Meanwhile, Obama tried to seal the deal with a multimillion-dollar info-mercial played on major networks during prime-time just before the World Series game on October 29. In a Hollywoodesque production, the Obama spectacle came together with "American stories" about hard times and struggles and how Obama would deal with these problems and help people. The Obama TV spectacle also contained a rare acknowledgment of the seriousness of problems with the economy and what Obama would do to deal with the crisis; a reprise of his story, highlighting his biracial heritage and close relations to his white mother and grandparents; testimonies from a variety of individuals concerning Obama's experience in community, state politics, and the national level; and highlights from some of Obama's greatest moments of his speeches.

This event was followed by a live appearance with former president Bill Clinton in a midnight campaign rally in Florida, his first campaign event with the former president and husband of his primary campaign rival Hillary Clinton. Bill enthusiastically endorsed Obama, indicating that Obama was regularly calling him for advice concerning the economic crisis and praising Obama's reaching out for experts on the issue, and that the Clintons and Obama had made up, at least for the present. Obama returned the compliments with praise for Clinton's presidency and a comparison between good times under Clinton and the Democrats contrasted with the messes of the past years under the Republican Bush-Cheney regime, which Clinton and Obama both claimed John McCain would basically continue.

Barack Obama continued to draw large and adoring crowds throughout his fall campaign, but consistently tried to present an image of himself as cool, calm, competent, and presidential on the campaign trail and during media interviews and the presidential debates. Unlike the McCain-Palin campaign, he avoided dramatic daily shifts and attention-grabbing stunts to try to present an image of a mature and intelligent leader who is able to rationally deal with crises and respond to attacks in a measured and cool manner, giving him the current moniker "No drama, Obama."

The election night spectacle

Election night is always a major political spectacle when the country, and parts of the world, watch the election results come in with maps flashing new red and blue colors on the states, with the exciting swoosh of Breaking News!, followed by results and trends of the election in the inevitable countdown for a candidate achieving the magic number of votes to gain the presidency.

All day long the television networks gave us the exciting spectacle of record turnouts all over the country, with images of people patiently waiting in line to vote, the candidates making their last electoral stops and pitches and then voting, followed by the period of waiting for the polls to close so that the networks could release votes.

The November 4, 2008 election started slowly, with Obama getting the predictable Democratic Party states in the Northeast and McCain getting predictable Republican Southern states. Excitement mounted when Obama was awarded the plum of Pennsylvania, which McCain and Palin had campaigned hard for, and when an hour or so later Obama was given Ohio it was clear that he was on the way to victory. At 11:00 p.m., the networks opened the hour with the banner heading "Barack Obama Elected 44th President of the United States," or just "Obama Elected President." His sweep of the west coast states of California, Oregon, and Washington, plus the bonus of Hawaii and the hard-fought southern state of Virginia sealed it for Obama who was on his way to a big win.

Meanwhile, in Grant Park in Chicago – the scene of the spectacle "The Whole World is Watching" during the Democratic convention in 1968, when the police tear-gassed anti-war spectators, and the site a year later of the Weather Underground abortive "Days of Rage" spectacle – this time a peaceful assembly of a couple of hundred thousand spectators, mostly young and of many colors, had assembled to celebrate Obama's historical victory. In the crowd, close-ups appeared of celebrities like Jessie Jackson, tears streaming down his face, a jubilant Spike Lee, a solemn and smiling Oprah Winfrey, and other celebrities who joined the mostly young crowd to hear Barack Obama's victory speech. The park hushed into silence as John McCain gave his concession speech and the audience nodded and applauded respectfully, suggesting that the country could come together.

When Obama, his wife Michelle, and their two beautiful daughters took the stage the place went wild, and the eyes of the world were watching the spectacle of Barack Obama becoming President of the United States. Television networks showed the spectacle of people celebrating throughout the United States, from Times Square to Atlanta, Georgia, and even throughout the world. There were special celebrations in countries like Kenya and Indonesia where Obama had lived, and his former residencies in these countries were becoming national shrines that would be tourist destinations. Obama was indeed a *global spectacle* and his stunning victory would make him a world superstar of global politics.

Deconstructing the spectacle

In this chapter, I have focused on the dimension of presidential campaign as media spectacle and have described the spectacles of the 2008 presidential election, surely one of the most exciting and fascinating political spectacles in U.S. history. While I have argued that presidential campaigns in the U.S. and elsewhere are primarily orchestrated as media spectacles, I do not want to suggest that this is the most important aspect of determining who wins an election, or the master key to victory. Obviously, money plays a major part in presidential elections and often whoever raises the most money wins. In a media age, money allows candidates to produce their own spectacles in the form of TV ads and they need millions to raise money to orchestrate campaign events and produce an organization. Obama had raised an unprecedented amount of money, including record donations from small contributions and a record amount of money raised through the Internet.

People also vote because of political affiliations and ideology, their economic interests, and sometimes even because of issues and substance, no matter what the spectacle of the day has to offer. Yet while I write this shortly after the election and serious scholars have not yet fully explained Obama's victory, I would suggest that certain resonant images and media spectacles contributed to Obama's victory. People obviously wanted change and hope, and Obama offered a spectacle of both, since he was the first candidate of color and also represented generational change. The Obama campaign pushed daily the spectacle of the connections of John McCain with the Bush administration, in TV ads, daily rallies, the debates, and other forums with TV news playing endlessly pictures of Bush and McCain embracing and graphics showing that McCain had voted with the most unpopular and failed president of recent history 90 percent of the time.

The global collapse of the financial markets and crisis of the U.S. and global economy produced one of the major media spectacles of the campaign, and the McCain spectacle of erratic pronouncements and daily stunts to exploit the crisis appeared to have turned voters off, while Obama remained cool and rational during this spectacle and time of danger, showing he was more presidential and better able to deal with crises. During this difficult period in U.S. and global history, voters reacted against the politics of distraction with the Republican spectacles of daily attacks on Obama backfiring, and the negative spectacle of Republican crowds screaming "terrorist," "traitor," "kill him!" and the like produced an extremely negative spectacle of a Republican mob stirred up by McCain and Palin, and seeming to inspire rational voters to line up, for hours if necessary, to vote for Obama and a new politics. Thus campaign spectacles can backfire, and, while the Sarah Palin spectacle did not alone destroy the Republican campaign, it certainly did not help recruit voters, although it made Palin a darling of the Republican extreme Right and a media superstar.

89

No doubt other factors too will become part of the story of how Barack Obama emerged from relative obscurity to beat Hillary Clinton in a hard-fought Democratic Party primary, and then whipped John McCain in one of the wildest and most spectaclesque elections in U.S. history, one that is transformative and will be pondered for years to come.

Finally, to be a literate reader of U.S. presidential campaigns, one needs to see how the opposing parties construct narratives, media spectacle, and spin to try to produce a positive image of their candidate to sell to the American public. In presidential campaigns, there are daily photo opportunities and media events, themes and points of the day that candidates want to highlight, and narratives about the candidates that will win support from the public. Obama's narrative from the beginning was bound up with the Obama spectacle, a new kind of politician representing change and bringing together people of different colors and ethnicities, ages, parts of the nation, and political views. He has effectively used media spectacle and Internet spectacle to promote his candidacy and generally been consistent in his major themes and story-lines, although the Republicans tried to subvert his story with allegations of close connections with radicals such as the Reverend Jeremiah Wright and Bill Ayers.

An informed and intelligent public thus needs to learn to deconstruct the spectacle to see what are the real issues behind the election, what interests and ideology do the candidates represent, and what sorts of spin, narrative, and media spectacles they are using to sell their candidates. This chapter limited itself to describing the media spectacle dimension of the campaign. I do not want to deny that presidential campaigns also depend on traditional organizing, campaign literature, debate, and getting out the vote, the so-called "ground game." But I would argue that media spectacle is becoming an increasingly salient feature of presidential and other elections in the United States and many other countries today.

Notes

1 This work draws on my studies of media spectacle in Kellner 2001; 2003a and b, 2005; 2008.
2 On diagnostic critique, see Kellner (1995: 116–17).
3 See the videos at http://www.youtube.com/watch?v=wKsoXHYICqU and David Carno, "MyBo Brigade Awaits Orders", *Los Angeles Times*, 19 November 2008: E1.
4 See "An Attack That Came out of the Ether", *Washington Post*, 28 June 2008.
5 For a dossier of articles on Joe the Plumber, see http://topics.nytimes.com/top/reference/timestopics/people/w/joe_wurzelbacher/index.html?inline=nyt-per.

References

Best, S. and Kellner, D. (2001) *The Postmodern Adventure. Science Technology, and Cultural Studies at the Third Millennium*, New York and London: Guilford Press and Routledge.

Boorstin, D. (1961) *The Image: A Guide to Pseudo-events in America*, New York: Harper & Row.

Dayan, D. and Katz, E. (1992) *Media Events: The Live Broadcasting of History*, Cambridge, MA: Harvard University Press.

Debord, G. (1967) *Society of the Spectacle*, Detroit: Black and Red.

Katz, E. and Liebes, T. (2007) " 'No More Peace!': How Disaster, Terror and War Have Upstaged Media Events", *International Journal of Communication*, 1: 157–66.

Kellner, D. (1992) *The Persian Gulf TV War*, Boulder, CO: Westview Press.

—— (1995) *Media Culture. Cultural Studies, Identity and Politics between the Modern and the Postmodern*, London: Routledge.

—— (2001) *Grand Theft 2000*, Lanham: Rowman & Littlefield.

—— (2003a) *Media Spectacle*, London and New York: Routledge.

—— (2003b) *From September 11 to Terror War: The Dangers of the Bush Legacy*, Lanham: Rowman & Littlefield.

—— (2005) *Media Spectacle and the Crisis of Democracy*, Boulder: Paradigm.

—— (2008) *Guys and Guns Amok: Domestic Terrorism and School Shootings from the Oklahoma City Bombings to the Virginia Tech Massacre*, Boulder: Paradigm.

Lang, G. and Lang, K.L. (1992 [1984]) *Politics and Television*, Edison: Transaction Publishers.

McLuhan, M. (1964) *Understanding Media: The Extensions of Man*, New York: McGraw-Hill.

Shils, E. (1975) *Center and Periphery*, Chicago, IL: Chicago University Press.

Part III

MEDIA EVENTS IN THE FRAME OF CONTEMPORARY SOCIAL AND CULTURAL MEDIA THEORY

7

CREATING A NATIONAL
HOLIDAY

Media events, symbolic capital and
symbolic power

Friedrich Krotz

Introduction

Since Dayan and Katz's ground-breaking book (1994), we at least know two things: First, that there is a media genre which is called "media events" – it had not been totally ignored before, as the work of Lang and Lang (1953) or the pseudo-event concept of Daniel Boorstin (1987) show, but it lacked a name, a theoretical context and it was not given enough attention by communication and cultural research. Second, Dayan and Katz offered many tools to describe and analyze media events and created a content-based typology. In contrast to a lot of concepts of communication and media studies, their work was theoretically based as it referred to the work of Max Weber, Emile Durkheim and other "classics" of social research and social theory. Perhaps this is a reason for the fact that the discussion of media events today is conceptually broad and theoretically challenging, and that there are many overlaps with other theoretical approaches, mainly from cultural studies and ritual theory.

More supplements and complements to the concept of media events have been created since then; for example, the concept of popular media events and the labeling of Dayan and Katz's approach as a ritual media event theory by Andreas Hepp and his colleague (cf. Hepp and Vogelgesang 2000; Hepp 2001) or Nick Couldry's ritual theory perspective of media events (2003). Nevertheless, the concept of media events still remains in large part a basic concept of functional sociology. This means more precisely that Dayan and Katz's approach only holds for specific media events and aims to establish how media events take place and how they are celebrated: "We think of media events as holidays that spotlight some central value or some aspect of collective memory" (1994: 9). Evidently, event theory is being developed from a perspective which is very close to an analysis of ceremonial holidays organized by government or a church. This is especially true of the work of Katz on the national holidays of Israel, which are all simultaneously Jewish religious holidays (cf. Handelman 1990). In some sense, this type of media event is rather close to myths in the sense of Roland Barthes (cf. Liebes and Curran (1998) with further hints). They also emphasize the role of media events in social integration, and thus create a rather affirmative theory. The work of Michael Real on the academy awards (1989) and his presentation of this award as a machine to promote movies, and Murray Edelman's even more general concept of symbolic politics (1976), show that Dayan and Katz's concepts need further elements if we are to understand media events as an instrument for doing politics or for improving viewer ratings, earning money or for controlling values and interpretations of the people.

Thus, the starting point of this chapter is the assumption that media events play an important role in the mediatized societies of today, helping people to orient themselves and to understand what is important and what not. This then means that the scene-setting of a national media event with reference to politics should be seen as part of a nation's political game and as having political and economic goals. Thus, we should *enhance the functionalist approach of Dayan and Katz by adding a perspective on power that may be created, legitimated or maintained by the staging of media events*. Therefore we intend to propose a view of ritual media events that connects Dayan and Katz's theory with some ideas of Pierre Bourdieu, especially his concepts of symbolic and economic capital and of symbolic violence.

The reason for that of course is not just a theoretically guided interest, but the result of empirical work on media events. To make this clear, we refer to two case studies about the founding in 1990 of Germany's new national holiday, October 3. We will ask what this holiday means and who was interested in such a meaning as the basic orientation of German unification. From that we approach some further questions which can be answered with reference to the work of Bourdieu.

The empirical material of this chapter thus stems from two research projects, both of which have been done by a group of researchers from western and eastern Germany. The first was done in 1990 in order to analyze the relations between the media and the German unification process. The relevant TV programs of October 2 and 3 were recorded and most of the newspapers from across Germany were collected and analyzed. In addition 2,400 diaries were distributed to households in Hamburg, Berlin-East, Berlin-West and some cities of eastern Germany, mostly in Potsdam and Leipzig. We got back 145 of them – about two-thirds from western Germany, the others from eastern Germany. The results of this study are published in a book and an article (Krotz and Wiedemann 1991; Krotz et al. 1991). At that time the researchers had no knowledge of the Dayan and Katz concept of media events. In a theoretical sense, the project referred to cultural studies (Williams 1981;

Carey 1989; Gramsci 1991) and to Edelman's (1976; cf. also Sarcinelli 1987; Dörner 1996) understanding of symbolic politics. We lacked the perspective to understand that day as a media event; instead, the power perspective was foregrounded compared with the work of Dayan and Katz.

In 1997, a second study, financed by some German media regulation institutions, attempted to analyze how eastern Germany was depicted on German national television. This examination took place owing to the ongoing economic, political and cultural difficulties and irritations between the two former parts of Germany which resulted from their different cultural backgrounds and because there was a suspicion that national German TV was Western dominated (as was indeed the case). In this context we also studied what happened to the 1990 media event in the years up to 1997. The detailed results of this study may be read in Früh et al. (1999). There is some additional interpretative work in Weichert's paper (1999) on specific programs which dealt with the national holiday or the German unification on October 3, 1997.

The emergence of the new German national holiday

As is well known, the Second World War in Europe ended in 1945 with the occupation of Germany by the Soviet Union, the USA, the UK and France. Four years later, the former Soviet sector was reconstituted as the German Democratic Republic (GDR), as a part of the Soviet empire. This happened as an answer to developments in the western part of Germany, where the former American, French and British sectors at first had formed a common economic unit and then were transformed into the Federal Republic of Germany (FRG). The idea to install a unified Germany as a neutral state between the two Cold War opponents was never accepted by the western German government. As is well known, the FRG was a great economic success in the decades which followed and then developed into an important member of NATO and the EU, while the GDR always had huge economic problems although it was an important political and economic part of the Eastern Bloc during the so called "Cold War."

Both German countries had their own political symbols, their own anthem, their own flag and their own national holiday. In the GDR this holiday was October 7, the day on which the country was founded. In the FRG the national holiday, by being placed on June 17, was politically directed against eastern Germany. This holiday was a reference to 1953, the year when the workers and other people of the GDR revolted against the so-called socialist system and were put down by the Soviet military (cf. Wolfrum 1999). Indeed, some literature has set out to deal with why exactly this day became the western German national day, and not, for example, July 20, the date in 1944 of the bourgeois revolt against Hitler, which in the years after the Second

97

World War marked an important point of reference of German Democracy and the political system (Holler 1994).

It is common knowledge that the Soviet system began to collapse after Michael Gorbachov took the first step with his popularization of "Perestroika." Subsequently, in all countries of the Eastern Bloc people began to agitate to change their restrictive governments in order to gain more freedom and economic success. In May 1989, Hungary opened its frontiers to Austria enabling anyone who wanted to leave to travel westward. By November 1989, 200,000 inhabitants of the GDR had availed themselves of this opportunity and moved to western Germany. At the same time, more and more manifestations and other acts of collective civil disobedience in eastern Germany followed under the motto "We are *the* people." The political system of the GDR could not withstand that, and suddenly and unexpectedly gave up. On November 9, 1989 the Berlin Wall and the whole frontier to the FRG were opened and the last communist GDR government resigned, leaving the government to be overtaken by non-communists. Nevertheless the agitation went on, but now under a different slogan: "We are *one* people." Thus, there was a lot of pressure on German governments to found a common nation with a common economy and a common political system. This, at least, met the interests of the West German government, which was supported by conservative and liberal parties. Besides these movements, a lot of political bargaining took place that involved the two Germanys, the former Soviet Union, the USA and their allies from the Second World War. As a consequence, on July 1, 1990 the western Deutschmark also became the currency in eastern Germany, and the western government selected October 3 to become German (Re-) Unification day and a national holiday. It was the day when the five eastern German states (Länder) formally became members of the federation FRG. Thus the former GDR ceased to exist.

Celebrating a national holiday

That October 3, a Wednesday, was the first day of German (Re-) Unification, and since then it has served as the new national holiday of the new common nation, which is still called the Federal Republic of Germany. From the perspective of communication research, national holidays should be analyzed as media events or at least as something similar in concept. Of course, national holidays are usually public events, as in most countries most people do not work on such days, children stay at home and public institutions organize celebrations for that day (e.g. meetings or army parades).

Indeed, October 3,1990 was a huge media event for Germany. More precisely, it was a ritual media event as described by Dayan and Katz, as may be seen if we look at their characterization:

Syntactically the holiday was preplanned and staged by the government and the media. For example, some weeks before, the people were informed that this would be a national holiday on which schools would be closed and no one would have to work, in other words like any Sunday. There were two main events on that day: a huge public festival in Berlin on the night from October 2–3, including fireworks at midnight, as this was the moment when the official unification took place, and a celebration including music and government speeches declaring what had happened and explaining how to think about it. On the evening of October 2 and throughout the day of October 3 (and even the whole week) more or less all TV channels interrupted their usual program schedule and broadcast a lot of programs with reference to the German unification.

Semantically events are media events if the media celebrate the event and handle it with "reverence and ceremony," according to Dayan and Katz (1994: 7). All newspapers referred to German unification, as may be seen from the collage in Figure 7.1. The title of the tabloid *Hamburger Morgenpost* on October 2 was even "Black, red and gold on all channels," which contains a slight media criticism about too much national joy. Every TV channel was full of programs about the event. In particular, the public service channels even transmitted entertainment programs related to the event (e.g. movies about the German–German separation or talk shows about the two Germanys). The most important public service channel, ARD, transmitted a lot of symbolical political acts from all over the country.

Figure 7.1 Headlines of German newspapers, October 2, 1990.

Finally, *pragmatically* an event in Dayan and Katz's view becomes a media event if the people really consider it to be a remarkable event – for example, if they prepare for it and celebrate it together with good friends or their families, perhaps serving special food and drinks. As the collected diaries showed, a lot of people did indeed celebrate actively on that day. Interviews quoted on TV also showed that a respectable portion of the population involved themselves in the day. It is also worth mentioning that a lot of local and regional live events were held in the different German states, regions and cities on both October 2 and 3.

Thus October 3, 1990 was a media event in the sense of Dayan and Katz. It is, nevertheless, rather more complicated to find out what really was the character of the upcoming national day. We will briefly mention some points concerning the unification process that found, or did not find, an expression in the media event of that day.

First, we have the question as to why exactly October 3 became the national holiday. On the one hand, the day was designated by the western German government with an eye on the upcoming election of a new parliament. On the other hand, there was a public discussion about which day should be the future national day of the united Germany. Other proposals were November 9 (the day on which the Berlin Wall was opened in 1989), May 8 (the day on which the Deutsches Reich surrendered in 1945 and Germany was freed from the Nazi regime), the already mentioned July 20 and other dates, including a day to commemorate the failed 1848 Revolution. Here we want to emphasize that the German government did not select a day of freedom and political participation, but rather a day of national unity, and thus turned German unification remembrance into a bureaucratic event which could not be experienced by the ordinary people.

Second, the mode of the unification process and hence the celebration made it evident that German unification was less a unification of equals than a more or less friendly takeover of eastern Germany by the western part. Not only the national symbols such as the name, the anthem or the flag remained the same as in the FRG before 1990, but also the political structure, the government and the constitution didn't change. Moreover, the central participants of official celebrations on October 3 were the members of the government and the President of the FRG; representatives from the eastern Germany were rare.

Third, the TV shows and the media generally portrayed "normal" people involved in the events as being happy or at least content. The mood as seen on TV was characterized by loud cheers and fundamental happiness, while our diaries showed more mixed emotions. A possible interpretation of this difference would be that it meant that the media, especially the TV channels, were simulating what people should feel in order to give the government what it wanted.

Fourth, other elements of the unification process were left out of the celebrations: the economic takeover of the eastern German by the western economy; the disappearance of eastern German lifestyles, while western German people continued to live as before. Further, there was no critical reflection of the 45 years of separation or of the revolutionary activities of the eastern people. In particular, the important dialectic between freedom and democracy on the one hand, and national unity on the other, did not become a topic of public discussion or of a celebration of the event.

All of this shows that in order to understand the media event "German unification," it is necessary to do more than merely describe what happened. *Public and national holidays, in particular, are symbols whose meaning is the product of the activities of the public, the political and social actors and the media.* Such days are of importance for the population, the culture and the nation which is represented by such symbols: the narrative "We are a common Nation and this Nation is based on common ground and on common goals" is intended to give the people a common basis for their further life. Thus, public holidays are interwoven with ideological definitions of reality; they depend on power relations and on economic success. The narratives that belong to a media event do not exist "naturally," and thus must be analyzed with regard to hegemonic relations and in the context of political, cultural and communicative conditions.

Thus, we would propose a slightly altered definition of a media event, one that emphasizes the role of its intended meaning: *A media event is an event with a specific narrative which gives the event its sense and meaning. To become a media event, an event must be arranged and presented by (all or a great part of) the media of a society at great expense and in a specific way such that the usual schedules of radio and TV channels and the usual concepts of how to make a newspaper are not maintained. Further, for a narrative to be seen as constituting a media event it is necessary that TV channels and newspapers present it with the intention of emphasizing specific values – to give people a collective orientation as to what is good and bad and how they should get involved. Finally, it is necessary that the public as the audience participate in this event, and that the whole nation or at least a good part of a specific subculture must be impressed by that event – only people's active involvement can make an event into a media event.*

This approach does not emphasize what happens but emphasizes the narratives, values and orientations which are articulated by a media event, as it is interested in the contexts of the event. Thus, in analyzing a media event, one should take into account what interests are behind this media event.

Bourdieu's concept of capitals and its application to media events

With this intention in mind we refer to Bourdieu's concept of capitals (Bourdieu 2005). Traditionally, "capital" is – following Marx and others – used for economic capital. But one can also be successful in capitalism if one has the right friends, if one is well educated or if one is respected by others.

Thus, Bourdieu generalized the concept of capital to include cultural, social and symbolic capital by stating that all such forms of capital have something in common.

Cultural capital includes collected experiences, the ownership of cultural goods, institutional titles, and these capitals may be incorporated, objectively present or institutional. Social capital consists of knowing the right persons to deal with specific issues – if you need a job or some information, such nets may be a helpful resource to solve that problem. Symbolic capital includes any honor, credibility and legitimation to do or to speak in specific situations. These three types of capital are generalizations of the economic capital in the following sense: They:

- have a value defined by society and culture,
- are important for power and life chances of any actor,
- can be accumulated,
- can be exchanged for other capitals.

Thus, Bourdieu's generalization may be used to describe how society functions through the resources of its actors. For example, they may be used to analyze digital inequality, as a change in media may change the value of capitals, and thus mediatization (Krotz 2001, 2007) may be a source to enhance inequalities that can be described by those capitals. This is much more helpful than the usual digital divide approach, which refers to technical developments and not to social ones (cf. Krotz 2006). Thus, Bourdieu's concepts may serve as an instrument for analyzing cultural and societal phenomena, as they offer a language and allow phenomena to be compared in different fields. In doing so, they relate social and other phenomena to the central category of power and hegemony in society and culture.

What then is the result if we connect media events with Bourdieu's idea of economic, social, cultural and symbolic capitals? In the case of the above case study, we may say that the organizing institution of the national holiday, the government of western Germany, did not merely celebrate a political act. Instead, we should understand its activity as an investment of symbolic and financial capital in order to reach specific goals. The government invested its legitimacy and its credibility, supported by its power, to define a holiday. Schools and all official institutions, shops and places of work were told by law to close on October 3 as on any other holiday. In addition, the government and its bureaucracy organized a ceremony and festivals all over the country, and declared the holiday to be the German state national holiday, thus articulating the common ground of future politics. This was an investment of capital, and at first it was open what would happen with this investment, whether the media and the public would accept it and whether the legitimacy and credibility of the west German government would increase as a result of this investment.

In the case of the German unification, the media followed the government and turned the day into a media event in the sense of Dayan and Katz. They also invested symbolic and financial capital to do so. With this investment, both actors, the government and the media, together offered the people an interpretation of what had happened in the past months and years, by arranging a celebration, by celebrating the day in the media and by defining October 3 as the future state national holiday of the unified Germany. Nevertheless, the selected national day celebrated only the bureaucratic completion of German unification. This day thus neither referred to freedom and democracy nor to the end of some consequences stemming from the Nazis, but instead to national unity. Symbolic emphasis was thus given to the common nation and state as the relevant factor for living together, and that the government and its bureaucracy and its values appeared to be at the heart of future development.

In this narrative, the media took on their own role. They told the people what they should feel on this day and how history was to be interpreted. The event thus became a reinforcement of law and order, anti-communistic and national thinking, as it fitted with the conservatively dominated government. The majority of the German people seemingly accepted this interpretation and at the coming elections the government was re-elected. Thus, the investment of the government was successful, as the invested symbolic capital generated voters and credibility.

To sum up, we should conclude that ritual media events like national holidays are an investment of symbolic and economic capital by the organizing institutions, which articulate its values, and by the media, which support the institutions, and at the same time as an investment by sponsors or similarly participating actors – enterprises or stars. *If the investment of the government and the media is successful, in so far as the people support the media event, then the government as the organizing institution gets back symbolic capital (e.g. credibility, image, reinforcement of values) while the media gain symbolic and financial capital.*

Symbolic violence and habitus

This leads us to two further basic concepts of Bourdieu: symbolic violence and the habitus of the people. These concepts of Bourdieu may be helpful in understanding how the German government operated and achieved its aims.

"Symbolic Violence," according to Bourdieu, "is the imposition of systems of symbolism and meaning (i.e. culture) upon groups or classes in such a way that they are experienced as legitimate" (Jenkins 1992: 104). Symbolic violence, to put it simply, works by addressing people in their habitus as the shared body of dispositions, classificatory categories and generative schemes, in which social practices, individual experiences, views and expectations of culture and society are included (Jenkins 1992).

Bourdieu developed this concept in his studies about education in France: when we grow up we not only learn knowledge – we learn to inscribe the rules of society into our bodies, our thinking, our emotions and intentions. We even consist as social beings of these rules, which we learn by interacting with parents, with school and which are reinforced by the media – maybe in a changing form – throughout our lives. Habitus thus includes the consequences of symbolic violence; it depends also on class and gender. Symbolic violence (similar to Gramsci's concept of hegemony (Gramsci 1991; cf. Krotz 1992) and its consequences for the habitus of people are thus not only intertwined with school and education, but also with media and communication (which is ignored by Bourdieu).

Empirically, the pressure put on Germans by the October 3 celebrations to join in was similar: in the diaries of western and eastern dissidents, we found descriptions of fear, shame or guilt if they failed to conform to the norm and did not celebrate (e.g. if they were not happy that Germany was once again united). On the other hand, the announced sense of what the future in the new and unified German nation would bring was different for eastern and western Germans, as the strategy of unification addressed different elements of the habitus of eastern and western people: the habitus of eastern Germans in general contained the lifelong experience that consumption was not possible. This contrasted dramatically to what they would observe when watching western German television. Unification thus addressed their hopes for an end to the lack of consumer articles and that their demands for satisfaction might be met. This had already been happening with the introduction of the Deutsche Mark into the east in July 1990, and now it was being symbolically repeated in many TV programs. On the other hand, the habitus of western Germans contained the traditional wish for national unification which had been part of symbolic politics for decades and which reinforced their feeling of being on the right side of history and the Cold War. In western Germany unification day thus demanded personal joy and an expectation that nothing would change in general, but everything would become better. Thus both subcultures were addressed in different ways, but this was successful.

The declining career of a former media event

The decline of the state national holiday may be seen if we look at the further career of October 3. In short, this day in 1990 was a media event, but it was not a media event in 1997. Seven years later, the number of information-oriented programs on October 2 and 3 dealing in any sense with German unification had declined remarkably (see Table 7.1).

In general, we may say that in every year since 1990, there have been at least two official events with which the government celebrated the unification officially. On the one hand, a solemn celebration featuring the President and the Chancellor takes place each year in another one of the sixteen German

Table 7.1 Numbers of programs referring to German Unification by channel

Year	ARD Publ	ZDF Publ	SAT.1 Priv	RTL Priv	PRO7 Priv	N 3 Rpubl	MDR Rpubl	All
1990	13	17	3	6	–	10	–	49
1991	6	9	1	2	–	9	–	27
1992	7	7	–	–	–	8	2	24
1993	5	8	–	1	–	5	1	20
1994	5	7	–	–	–	10	5	27
1995	6	7	2	1	–	6	5	27
1996	11	7	–	–	–	4	5	27
1997	8	9	–	–	–	8	5	35
1998	2	9	–	1	–	5	2	22
Ges.	63	80	6	11	0	65	25	250

states. Usually, there is music and speeches by the head of government of the organizing state, the Chancellor of the Federal Republic and one specific invited guest, usually an elder statesman. In 1997, this was the former US president Bush. This official celebration is usually broadcast by public service TV. Afterwards, there is a people's parade in Berlin, which in 1997 took place with hardly any spectators watching it on the streets. The same is true of the respective TV transmission of the celebration: less than one million people (of 81 million) watched the broadcast, a market share of only 12.5 percent in western Germany and of 7.7 percent in eastern Germany. The audience consisted mostly of people over 60. In 1990 far more people watched the respective programs. The same is true for all other programs that were concerned with the German unification.

Further, in contrast to 1990 the private German channels did not refer to the German national holiday in 1997 at all. They mostly offered the same programs they usually offer on a Sunday or any other holiday: attractive movies and shows, but with no reference to the national holiday. One could in general say that private TV ignored the German unification anniversary. Even the politically important and sensitive problem of the relations between eastern and western Germans that was discussed in public in 1997 was not mentioned in the regular news and information programs on private TV. Of course, the unification holiday and the connected narrative were shown in the news, but not as a topic of great interest. For example, some political magazines on private channels only mentioned the day, but were more concerned with other questions. In the field of entertainment, the situation is even worse. Only public service TV presented some entertainment programs related to German unification, but there was no real new material.

The conclusion is that in 1997 October 3 was no longer a media event. Germans mostly see the holiday as an occasion to have a day off work, private

TV channels see it as an occasion to attract a larger audience, as they would do on any holiday, while the public service channels use the national day to show viewers and politicians that the TV license and the fees they receive are justified and that they are doing something for the integration of eastern and western Germany. But it seems that they had not been interested in investing money, creativity or energy into it.

From a broader perspective, the symbolic story of the national holiday of October 3 and the way the media dealt with it illustrates exactly the problems to be found in Germany within the inner social and cultural unification. German unification occurred through the admission of some new states to western Germany, and people couldn't experience anything on that day other than that it was not a working day. Whereas western Germany didn't change, eastern Germany and its culture and history disappeared.

In the categories of Bourdieu, the investment of the government was successful for the elections coming after unification, but it did not carry the unification process. The promises that were made to the people have not been kept: west Germans have found out that unification is expensive, and east Germans found out that their culture has disappeared and that their economy has been taken over by much more experienced western capitalists. Nevertheless, it is taught in schools and reported in the media that German unification was unavoidable and the only right solution. That the concrete forms of this unification were by no means unavoidable and that they have probably produced a lot of the problems Germany is suffering today cannot be discussed rationally, as it is part of what cannot be thought.

In addition, and with reference to our understanding of a ritual media event, we can learn that a phenomenon should not just be analyzed simply as a phenomenon, but in its relation to the essential ways in which society, politics, media and people function. This may be done using Bourdieu's helpful approach, which concentrates on the core mechanisms of society and culture.

The media event may thus be seen as an investment by the organizers trying to ratify and consolidate their values. In the case of October 3, it was an investment by the conservative government: the symbolic interpretation of the past and the future reproduction of the event as the basis of the German nation, which children learn in school and which is celebrated each year anew, should thus be seen as the result of symbolic violence and as a celebration of unity and order and not of freedom and democracy. This is one result of applying Bourdieu's concepts to media event theory, which thus gets a critical dimension, as it refers to the core mechanisms of a capitalistic society.

Such an overtly critical perspective is especially important, as in mediatized societies of the future (Krotz 2007) the role and the influence of media and thus of media events seem to become more and more important. In general, television at least in Europe and the United States increasingly becomes an institution, interested in influencing the behavior and lifestyle of the people, for example, by showing so-called reality TV and by educating people in motivating them to become superstars or top models and thus to offer them values of a specific type. Media events may be an important part of such strategies.

References

Boorstin, D.J. (1987) *Das Image: der amerikanische Traum*, Reinbek: Rowohlt.
Bourdieu, P. (2005) *Die verborgenen Mechanismen der Macht*, Hamburg: VSA.
Carey, J. (1989) *Communication as Culture. Essays on Media and Society*, Boston, MA: Unwin Hyman.
—— (1998) "Political Ritual on Television. Episodes in the History of Shame Degradation and Excommunication", in T. Liebes and J. Curran (eds) *Media, Ritual and Identity*, London: Routledge, 42–70.
Couldry, N. (2003) *Media Rituals: A Critical Approach*, London: Routledge.
Dayan, D. and Katz, E. (1994) *Media Events: The Live Broadcasting of History* (2nd edn), Cambridge, MA: Harvard University Press.
Dörner, A. (1996) *Politischer Mythos und symbolische Politik*, Reinbek: Rowohlt.
Edelman, M.J. (1976) *Politik als Ritual*, Frankfurt am Main: Campus.
Früh, W., Hasebrink, U., Krotz, F., Kuhlmann, C. and Stiehler, H. (1999) *Ostdeutschland im Fernsehen*, München: Kopäd.
Gramsci, A. (1991) *Marxismus und Kultur. Ideologie, Alltag, Literatur* (3rd edn), ed. S. Kebir, Hamburg: VSA.
Handelman, D. (1990) *Models and Mirrors: Towards an Anthropology of Public Events*, New York: Cambridge University Press.
Hasebrink, U., Krause, D., Krotz, F. and Nebel, B. (1991) "Der 3. Oktober 1990 ein Medienereignis im Erleben der Deutschen in Ost und West", *Rundfunk und Fernsehen* 39, 2: 207–31.
Hepp, A. (2001) "Medienwandel als kulturelle Differenzierung von Artikulationen: Zur Mediatisierung des emotionalen Erlebens am Beispiel des Medien-Events 'Titanic' ", in E.W.B. Hess-Lüttich (ed.) *Medien, Texte und Maschinen: angewandte Mediensemiotik*, Wiesbaden: Gabler, 67–90.
Hepp, A. and Vogelgesang, W. (2000) "Kino als Media Event. Dargestellt am Beispiel des Films 'Titanic' ", in W. Gebhardt, R. Hitzler and M. Pfadenhauer (eds) *Events. Soziologie des Außergewöhnlichen*, Opladen: Leske + Budrich, 239–61.
Holler, R. (1994) *20. Juli 1944: Vermächtnis oder Alibi?*, München: K. G. Saur.
Jenkins, R. (1992) *Pierre Bourdieu*, London: Routledge.
Krotz, F. (1992) "Kommunikation als Teilhabe. Der 'Cultural Studies Approach' ", *Rundfunk und Fernsehen*, 40, 3: 412–31.
—— (2001) *Die Mediatisierung kommunikativen Handelns. Wie sich Alltag und soziale Beziehungen, Kultur und Gesellschaft durch die Medien wandeln*, Opladen: Westdeutscher Verlag.
—— (2006) "Rethinking the Digital Divide-approach: From a Technically Based Understanding to a Concept Referring to Bourdieu's Social Capital", in N. Carpentier et al. (eds) *Researching Media, Democracy and Participation*, Tartu: Tartu University Press, 177–89. Available HTTP: <http://www.researching communication.eu/reco_book1.pdf> (accessed 10 December 2008).

—— (2007) *Mediatisierung: Fallstudien zum Wandel von Kommunikation*, Wiesbaden: VS.

Krotz, F. and Wiedemann, D. (eds) (1991) *Der 3. Oktober 1990 in den Medien und im Erleben der Menschen*, Hamburg: Hans-Bredow-Institut.

Krotz, F., Hasebrink, U., Krause, D. and Nebel, B. (1991) "Der 3 Oktober 1990: Ein Medienereignis im Erleben der Deutschen in Ost und West", *Rundfunk und Fernsehen*, 39, 2: 201–31.

Lang, G. and Lang, K.L. (1953) "The Unique Perspective of Television and its Effect", *American Sociological Review*, 18, 1: 103–12.

Liebes, T. and Curran, J. (eds) (1998) *Media, Ritual and Identity*, London: Routledge.

Real, M. (1989) *Super Media. A Cultural Studies Approach*, London: Sage.

Sarcinelli, U. (1987) *Symbolische Politik*, Opladen: Westdeutscher Verlag.

Weichert, S.A. (1999) *Der Tag der Deutschen Einheit im Fernsehen*, Master thesis, University of Hamburg.

Williams, R. (1981) *The Sociology of Culture*, London: Fontana.

Wolfrum, E. (1999) "Politik mit der Erinnerung – Die Folgewirkungen des 17. Juni 1953", in J. Wilke (ed.) *Massenmedien und Zeitgeschichte*, Konstanz: UVK Medien, 467–75.

8

MODALITIES OF MEDIATION

Joost van Loon

This chapter attempts to provide a refocusing of some of the insights on media events offered in the ground-breaking work of Dayan and Katz (1992). Drawing on Heidegger and Latour, it explores mediation as an attunement of our existential being to our being in the world. This attunement consists of three modalities: affect, understanding and reason. By considering these three modalities, we are able to analyze the process of mediation as both translation and enrolment. Media events then emerge when mediation is revealed; when translations are incomplete; when enrolment "adds to but does not add up" (Bhabha 1990: 312). That is to say, media events become apparent only because their "immediacy" is exposed as "an illusion of transparency" (Vattimo 1992). Hence, media events are not 'bad' *because* they invite staged perfomances (instead of 'authentic' politics). Instead, the relevant question is whether media events *enable* experiences of authenticity.

I want to argue here that the value of media events lies in their capacity to "add to" without "adding up"; that is, in their capacity to disclose an existential moment of "being-in-mediation." What they then disclose is not simply the event as such, but the event-in-mediation. Rather than becoming "transparent," mediators are to be disclosed as transformers of experiences by engendering "affect." The litmus test of such an event would be whether anything was "given," or was everything dissolved in simulation? This "gift" is the inauguration of the enigma: "What is happening?"

The event

That the distinction between event and media event does not really hold is fairly straightforward. The distinction relies on the Platonic separation of the "real" and the "representational" (the Idea). This separation finds its culmination in the Cartesian dualism of *res extensa* and *res cogitans*. According to Deleuze (1994), the separation entails a basic fear of the shadow, or simulacrum. The media event is a simulacrum. It is therefore from the outset problematic to create a simple contrast between a mediated or staged event and a so-called non-mediated "authentic" event as that which takes place "outside" the realm of signification.

This was already noted by Dayan and Katz (1992) in their seminal work on media events which appeared over 15 years ago as a critique of Boorstin's notion of pseudo-event and George Moss' lament over the loss of "real" politics. Dayan and Katz were not making some facile allusion to postmodernity as if once upon a time the separation (real event versus media event) was feasible but now it is no longer. Instead, they made the mere logical assertion that for an event to exist at all, it has to have entered into signification. Moreover, they insisted that the mediation of events was not intrinsically a bad thing, but part and parcel of how politics are done in complex modern democratic societies. That is, media events are not by themselves bad but there are good and bad media events. For them, good media events are those that contribute to enhancing solidarity through the "enfranchising" of a "sense of occasion" (Dayan and Katz 1992: 8), while simultaneously enabling a sense of "pluralism" (Dayan and Katz 1992: 9).

It is in the light of this "political" note (which is in essence a moral note, as it is about the "good" and "evil" of media) that this chapter seeks to make a modest intervention. This intervention will take the form of a (false) paradox; namely that in order to engender authentic experiences, mediation requires more, not fewer, mediators. This paradox is false because one can only really speak of this being a paradox when one accepts, as a priori, that there is an inverse correlation between quantity of mediators and authenticity. The paradox is borne out of mainly Marxist lamentations over the way in which ideological state apparatuses (Althusser 1971) have managed to sugar-coat popular common sense with ideological gloss. The masses are no longer politically able to enact their innate class instinct because they have been "mono-dimensionalized," to quote Marcuse (1964). Media are complicit as they have provided a replacement for religion in providing opiate to the people (and primarily through the production of "false needs"). Boorstin's pseudo-event, the staged and *therefore* inauthentic experience, testifies to this aestheticization of everyday life (Featherstone 1993). In this sense, Boorstin echoes a more negative resonance of Benjamin's (1971) allusions to the aestheticization of politics, and provides a more accessible version of Guy Debord's (1994) famous thesis on the *Society of the Spectacle* which became the hallmark of post-1968 radical socialist critique of the consumer society.

Indeed, when considering "media events," our attention is most naturally drawn to the spectacle (see Kellner, Chapter 6, this volume). In this view, the spectacle is a distraction, an escape from the grim reality of everyday life, which is a reality of exploitation and subjugation; a reality in which "the system" of medio-cracy (i.e. "modernity") prevails in the reproduction of "Das Mann" (the herd-man). Yet, at the same time, since we tend to see events as distinctive interruptions of the otherwise continuous, ordinary goings-on of everyday life, we separate being from event, and reserve the latter for those special onto-existential moments of revelation when our being is shown up in terms of what Heidegger (1927/1986) called *Dasein* (Badiou 2006). That is to say, as much as the spectacular nature of events would prevent us from becoming political, they are also our only hope of entering into an existential moment at all.

Time

It is because the paradox is false that we are in a stalemate. In order to turn away from this, I propose that we turn towards a form of phenomenology I would call "materialist." It draws primarily on the work of Martin Heidegger. Rather than seeing being and event as opposites, Heidegger's work shows us that *Dasein* is disclosed as event (Derrida 1982; Haugeland 1992) and it is through this disclosure that it is possible for us to encounter being at all. It is the splitting of this existential moment from the ordinary everydayness that marks being as event.

What enables us to recognize the event is time. The event is what is marked, what stands out, in time. Standing out in time becomes a time out, as if time itself ceases – even for the briefest of moments – to be. The paradox of existential being is that we only come to an existential moment if it is allowed to deceive us as a "time out" (Van Loon 1996). Normality is regained only if this moment is narratively recuperated into the biographical continuity of writing-being. The existential moment, the moment where the narrator moves outside the *timescape* of the narrative, is the inauguration of mediated being. It is on this intersection, this *paradoxa* (and this time it is no false paradox), that we can make a start with reconsidering media events.

Ontologically speaking, the event is a rupture of time, a moment of release from the "numbness imposed upon our senses" (McLuhan 1964) that enables us to "live" in an orderly yet unremarkable way. Dayan and Katz (1992: 5) insist on "live-ness" as the defining feature of the media event. However, they thereby show themselves to have a rather naïve understanding, philosophically, of the nature of time, and practically, of the nature of media production. As Hemmingway (2007) has shown, "live-ness" is an accomplishment of a series of networked enactments that can hardly be called "live"; they evolve a complex technological configuration of distinctive temporalities that by their very nature extend the presence of the "live" and stretch what we might refer to as "simultaneity."

Philosophically, the idea of media events being simultaneous with the events themselves entails a regression to "metaphysics of presence" (Derrida 1982; Van Loon 1996). That is to say, it fails to problematize the relationship between language and being, and assumes an "empty" (Euclidian) notion of time as merely an abstract interval. Not surprisingly perhaps, this view of time in relation to live-ness also reinforces a notion of media as "channels of transmission" which has been strongly criticized by, among others, James Carey (1992) for their instrumentalism and idealism (Van Loon 2007).

The notion of "live-ness" that is implied in Dayan and Katz's under-standing of media events thus also implies the non-event, the ordinary, that which is unremarkable and this easily overlooked, ignored, forgotten, as the backdrop. In narrative analysis (e.g. Todorov 1990) it would be called the "initial equilibrium" (which is disturbed by the event – the turbulent rupture). This implication of "ordinariness," however, is exactly that which Heidegger (influenced by Nietzsche) associated with inauthenticity, as *"durchschnittliche Alltäglichkeit"* (common everydayness). In *Being and Time*, Heidegger (1927/1986) asserts that this common-ness is considered the ground for the forgetting of being and thus as the enemy of authentic being. It is this existentialist moment in Heidegger's early philosophy that provides the basis of a more radical-critical materialist phenomenology. Noting that this can also have more dangerous implications, for example, in terms of celebrating a certain violent radicality – such as the pseudo-vitalist endorse-ment of strength one finds in national socialism – a different mode of thinking about time as "dense materiality" (and hence not as continuity or simul-taneity) will enable us to see how media events, strictly speaking, have no "outside."

What is specific about media events is that this paradox, this rupture of the "out-of-time-ness" of the existential moment of being-as-event becomes "objectified"; it becomes inscribed with significance, and this significance is derived from what mediation is: a form of translation and of enrolment. Mediation translates as a coming-in-between (Van Loon 2007). Mediation enrols because it binds "third-ness": communication is a gathering of sense (hence common sense); and this gathering is an enrolment of actants. As Latour (2005) wrote: "mediation entails transformation." Following Latour, we could also see that without enrolment, mediators would be mere "inter-mediaries." Intermediaries are empty vessels, they merely "pass on" and do not inaugurate events; they have nothing to offer and nothing to give. Intermediaries merely perform simulations in the sense of annihilating what is given. Whereas intermediaries inform and empty out meaning, mediators transform and inaugurate "affect." Only mediators are able to open up media events as having moral implications. This is quite similar to what Dayan and Katz (1992: 147–87) refer to as "shamanizing media events."

It is with this in mind that I propose we consider what we mean by media event as that which reveals being-as-mediated. That is, being-as-event becomes a media event when what is shown as the existential moment is no longer disconnected from the forms of translation enrolment by which is enframed.

Technological mediation

In *Being and Time*, Heidegger (1927/1986) showed how existential being, or *Dasein*, is its disclosedness (Haugeland 1992). Whereas this may sound at once

112

overly cryptic and blatantly obvious, it is a useful antidote against the naïve realist presumption that being is just "there." Regardless of whether one agrees with Latour's (1993) anti-Heidegger polemic that no one but Heidegger himself has actually forgotten being, an identical problem remains to be explored for both thinkers: how is order possible in everyday life? Whereas for Heidegger this was a negative question which led him to assert that the entire Western metaphysical tradition has been geared up to maintain the forgetting of being, for Latour (2005) it is an affirmative question that "social" order solely exists by virtue of non-social forces (see also Couldry 2003). What both thus share is the starting point of not taking the taken-for-granted for granted.

This not-taking-for-granted is the rupture that inaugurates theory. And this is why for media theory, considering what is a media event is an issue of fundamental ontology. The media event is what discloses mediation. The event as "rupture" may be seen as a distinctive existential moment in which *Dasein* finds itself "disclosed" in its being-in-the-world. And this being in the world is what we have commonly accepted as "the social" (Latour 2005).

What facilitates such a disclosure? In Latour's inimitable provocation: what are the non-social forces that make a media event possible as a *social* event? By what means does *Dasein* become endowed with a sense of its disclosedness that is experienced, in some sense of commonality, as a social event?

A clue to this may be found in Heidegger's (1977) essay on the question concerning technology, where he starts with the assertion that the essence of technology is revealing. In the modern age, the age of technology, this is so evident that it becomes almost banal. What does it mean, however, to say that the essence of technology is revealing? When deploying the hammer, the technology of hammering reveals the nature of the matter of hammering as an act of applying force on an object in order to impact on a surface. If the hammering concerns driving a nail into a wall, it also reveals something about the matter of the nail (its purposefully designed flat head to enlarge the surface for hitting; its pointed tail to wedge itself into a wall or piece of wood) and the wall (its *resistance* to penetration is the essence of the wall as a protective device). In so doing, hammering could, for example, "reveal" the usefulness of a wall to hang something on as well as its generic function to produce space.

Heidegger relates this revealing to a reflection on "causality." That is, he forces us to think of that which technology reveals as reflecting back on how a particular technology has come into being, and not simply in terms of its material development, but also of its *functions*. The function of technology is its purposefulness. Purposefulness is an essential part of technology and this enables us to understand why we cannot think of technology and intentionality as mutually exclusive. That is, technology is designed and developed for a particular purpose, even though the outcome may be completely different

113

from the original intention. It would be nonsensical to exclude human intelligence from technology as what technology reveals also discloses intentionality. This is not to suggest that the revealing is completely contained by this intentionality, far from it. Instead, it is merely to remind us that technology is not some completely external and autonomous force that comes from nowhere and acts completely of its own accord.

In our ordinary everyday being, we inhabit technology (Van Loon 2002). Inhabiting technology means two things: (1) we habitualize technology as a means to relate to the world, and (2) we deploy technology to modify our habitat. The first enables us to "take technology for granted" in our ordinary everydayness which in turn makes it possible for us "to get on with things" (and technology becomes what McLuhan (1964) problematically (Fuller 2005) calls "an extension of human faculties"). The second enables us to overcome obstacles or problems that reveal themselves when we "cannot get on with things." In modern life, comfort and convenience (immediacy) are essential values within modes of habitation and they form a significant part of the motivation for technological innovations (Shove 2003). Those moments of discomfort and inconvenience are significant interruptions in the taking-for-granted of our technological inhabitation. They are moments of rupture, of incompleteness, of lack and of discord.

Of course, there are obvious examples that spring to mind here: 9/11 being only one of them; the recent (near) collapse of the global finance sector would be another. These are, strictly speaking, not singular *media* events in the ideal-typical sense of Dayan and Katz, but they are clearly media *events*. That 9/11 entailed a lot of media-related planning and staging is obvious; that it was "spectacular" in the most negative sense of the term as implicated by Debord is also hard to refute. Whereas the credit crunch may be less of a single event, it does consist of a series of related events: record-breaking dips in the value of shares, banks and mortgage lenders filing for bankruptcy, emergency speeches, votes in parliaments, resignations, all play their part. But what is clear in all of these events is that media perform less of an informative and more of a transformative function. Media generate terror, they externalize our neural systems, they drain confidence, they perform "the crash." In so doing, they have opened up existential moments in which we can engage with the question of being mediated. These are not "ideational" operations but material ones. We are "affected" beyond what we perceive and believe.

On ordering

For Heidegger, technology reveals by structuring our relationship to the world. Resonating Ong (1982), we could translate this by stating that technology engenders particular perspectives. Especially in today's world, perception is never pure but technologically mediated, or as Heidegger would say, it is *"enframed"* (*ge-stellt*). Enframing is a particular way of "bringing forth" (*dar-stellen*) into presence. In other words, for Heidegger, technology is not a tool, or a piece of equipment *as such*, but a way of presencing, or *en-presenting*. This en-presenting is first of all a form of "showing" or "making visible." Whereas most media analyses talk about media in terms of representation, the term *en-presenting* suggests that as technology, media do not simply "pass on" but instead are more creative; they produce or engender "presence." Representation suggests that something returns as the same, en-presenting highlights, however, the close association between revealing and creating as "a bringing into being" (Fry 1993: 31).

This more productive reading of technology enables us to talk about the technological condition of being as "calling into presence" or "ordering." In other words, what we experience as "pure reality" is in fact not only already mediated, but reconstructed by the same process of mediation that called it forth. This presents an alternative to the linear model of mediation as that which comes in between reality and its perception. For example, in "live news" it is assumed that something "real happened" (in the sense of "it really happened") and that a crew is sent to "cover it" by means of audio-visual recording, photography or simply verbal testimonies. The real "live" event is then mediated to the millions of viewers, listeners or readers. However, as Hemmingway (2007) has brilliantly shown in her ethnographic work on regional news production, the "live event" is not what it seems; it is not an *immediate* presencing, but instead a highly mediated and complex techno-logical accomplishment of *actualizing* a particular reality that is visualized and narrated according to a set of pre-established heuristics of what it takes to "get the job done" (which are often at some distance supported by "guidelines and rules" but can by no means be reduced to these).

Instead of the linear model (intention–production–message–consumption–interpretation), which provides the basis of the transmission view of commu-nication (Carey 1992; Fiske 1990), Heidegger's phenomenology suggests a different type of technological ordering. Media technology orders the world by calling it into being. Mediation is the creation of 'media events.' There are no media events outside of mediation. Moreover, the "reception" of the media event is also part of its mediation. Without a reception there is no mediation and thus no media event. This is why Baudrillard (1995) could so confidently say that "the Gulf War did not take place"; it did not happen "by itself"; its "taking place" was the consequence of its mediation, which he argued is a form of simulation (virtual war).

Mediation 'calls into presence' in the form of ordering as both (1) putting into its proper place and (2) bringing forth or challenging (*Herausfordern*). Hence when we associate mediation with representation we should always bear in mind that this is not simply "reflecting" or "associating" between symbolic forms and "real" objects or events, but *en-presenting*, the actualization of being-as-event.

The narcissus narcosis

The event as a rupture in the ordinary, mundane flow of everyday life is the actualization of mediation-as-such. That is, it is the moment when mediation is unconcealed. Ordinary life is unnoticeable because the operations of mediation remain hidden. We are completely habitualized to the orderings that they provide. Our existential being *(Dasein)* is dormant because our being-in-the-world does not pose an existentially significant hermeneutic crisis.

In the ordinary everydayness of being in the world, we fall victim to the forgetting of being. We are in a state of relative comfort and convenience and one of the hallmarks of this is that we perceive the world as "immediate" (non-mediated) and "transparent" (self-evident). Our bodies become accustomed to our technologically mediated environment by incorporating the ergonomics of diverse technical systems. Driving a car is an example of this, but so is typing, or playing the piano, or even working in the kitchen with a multiplicity of appliances.

In such a world, when nothing seems concealed because everything is immediate and transparent, we live in a state of *Narcissus Narcosis* as McLuhan (1964) so aptly phrased it. The story of Narcissus, who is cursed by the gods for badly treating his fiancée, is often referred to as a case of someone falling in love with himself. However, the curse Narcissus suffers from is the misrecognition of himself for someone else. He fails to see his own reflection as himself; he has been excommunicated from the mirror-stage, to speak with Lacan (1977), and has lost his subjectivity. No longer able to relate to himself as himself, and to recognize himself as subject; he thus becomes trapped in a spiral of self-externalization and alienation. He becomes trapped within a negative dialectic, doomed to dwell in the "fake universe" of his own image. This is perhaps not entirely unlike the experience of people addicted to playing computer games and how they relate to their avatars (as "needing them").

The point of this chapter is to argue that this state of miscognition is induced by the modalities of mediated being themselves. Our "failure" to recognize ourselves in an existential manner is not a matter of a lack of cognitive disorientation (e.g. as in ideology), but of technological concealment inherent in the process of mediation itself. That is to say, when mediation does its work, when it translates and enrolls, we are inhibited from encountering its disclosure; this is when we live in the non-event.

In *Symbolic Exchange and Death*, Baudrillard (1993) contrasts symbolic exchange (as an expression of "communication" as an actual interaction based on some form of gift-exchange, and "simulation" as forms of mediation that solely consist of relationships between signifiers that are mistaken as signs (myths, as Barthes called them). For Baudrillard, this entails a historical-social shift in which simulation is taking the place of symbolic exchange, as a result of which reality loses its significance and becomes hyperreality. Despite

Baudrillard's oft-reviled blasé-posturing (which is in fact a form of irony), he is concerned about this virulent expansion of insignificance (death) and there is an unmistaken lament for the loss of sociality (Merrin 2005). However, mediation is not necessarily leading into insignificance. It is not in itself destined to only engage simulation. In Baudrillardian terms (but against his lamentations), there are forms of mediation that can engage in forms of symbolic exchange as well. In order to argue this, we need to explore the modalities of mediation.

Modalities of mediation

How does mediation come about or what is the essence of mediation? If we accept that the essence of technology is revealing and that mediation is a technological practice, then we need to ask: What is revealed by mediation? The answer to this is actually quite straightforward. Mediation reveals the attuning of our existential being to our environment, and thus that *mediation is the attuning of* Dasein *to our being in the world.* This revealing, however, is not a simple disclosure, but also one that entails forms of concealment. Regardless of what is being communicated, media technology en-presents the nature of communication as mediated; that is, as something that extends from ourselves by *coming-in-between*; by offering a means to facilitate an exchange of signs and symbols.

Heidegger uses the term *Entbergen* (unconcealment) to highlight that every form of "showing" already presupposes a "hiding" or concealment. Technology reveals what is being concealed. That is, if one looks properly at a medium, one does not simply see an empty vessel carrying a message, but also how the medium is intertwined with the message. As Ong (1982) has show with reference to literacy; the arrival of writing and later print changed the nature of human interactions and thereby the nature of communication.

At first sight, this seems to go completely against the more commonly accepted view that the essence of media is concealment. Indeed, the entire essence of structuralist semiotics, for example, is predicated upon the assumption that the real structures – from which meaning is derived – remain hidden (like the unconscious). Indeed, even when we look at the technological nature of mediation it is easy to see that in everyday use this is often simply taken for granted and thus concealed. It is for this reason that it often looks as if media technology conceals itself behind content. Indeed, in everyday media use, instead of mediation we encounter representation because as media technology conceals the mediated nature of communication, it brings into presence something else, something "with which" the communication in question is concerned. This goes even as far as communication itself – which is most generally referred to as an "immediate" exchange of signs and symbols, for which technology is merely an amplifier or vehicle rather than a prerequisite.

However, we need to remember that media never emerge from nowhere and never land in a vacuum. Media evolve, and in their evolution they cannot but show forth the mediated nature of their content (Levinson 1997). This is because media technologies are more than mere instruments of communication. Technologies also structure how we think because they are themselves engines of thought; they *form* at our perceptions and sensibilities and in*form* the content of how and what we perceive. This is the core of what William Connolly (2002) referred to as '*neuropolitics.*' It is for this reason that we cannot understand media events if we take media to be mere vehicles. Hence, we must also analyze media events as technological accomplishments and are forced to explore the production of specific media events empirically. For example, television is a neuropolitical engine *pur-sang*; it is a mood-machine exactly because it affects us, in the first instance, in a non-cognitive sense (unlike print, for example). A clear historical example is Hitler. He would have been a rather different phenomenon without radio and without Leni Riefenstahl's *Triumph of the Will*. Radio enabled Hitler to address the German people as if they were all "illiterate." As it asks so much of our own imaginative capacities, radio involves us as a tribal drum; providing a call to embrace primordial belonging. This is also why radio has been so effective in popularizing Rock 'n Roll, which, after all, stems from the tribal drums of Africa which were mediated and transformed through the experience of slavery and racial segregation into agitators of "youth"; a resurrection of bodies against Puritanism and rationalist civilization (Browning 1998).

It is this understanding of technology which relates to Heidegger's concept of "disclosure" or "laying open." In *Being and Time*, Heidegger (1927/1986) discusses three modalities of disclosure: understanding, feeling and discourse. The modalities of disclosure are neither pure form nor pure content, but different intensities of existential involvement, or what Heidegger refers to as *Dasein*.

Heidegger (1927/1986) explores the fundamental question of how to provide a phenomenological understanding of being that does not presuppose a forgetting of the basic presupposition that whatever is reflecting on Being is itself a being. It is this basic premise of reflexive, non-linear thought (Curtis 1977) that we must always include with thought the conditions of the practices of the thinking that make thought possible to begin with. Or to put it in simpler terms: How can we understand the conditions of our own understanding of the conditions of our existence?

Heidegger referred to the entity that is trying to come to terms with existence as *Dasein*. The German word *da* refers to "here," *Sein* means being. Literally *Dasein* means being-here. For Heidegger (1986: 114) *Dasein* is existential because it is always tied to the "I," irrespective of the manner of being I engage with in everyday life. The relationship between the existential properties of being as *Dasein* and their manifestations as being in the world are indeed mediated. That is to say, our reflective encounter with our own being in the world, which stems from the fact that we are existential beings to begin with, is not *in itself* self-evident (*selbstverständlich*). Its self-evident-ness is accomplished through an encounter (Heidegger uses the term *Befindlichkeit*, which is translated as so-found-ness) between *Dasein* and a reflection on its "being in the world." The manner in which we come to terms with this so-found-ness of ourselves-in-the-world is what we might call "mediation" (although it must be stressed that Heidegger did not do so himself).

Mediation is thus the interplay between concealment and unconcealment of the relationship between our existential being (*Dasein*) and our ordinary everyday being (being-in-the-world). Mediation is a "coming-to-terms-with" exactly because it enables meaningful relationships between ourselves and the world; it immerses us into the work of "making sense." The "coming to terms with" is like a trade-off. Whereas we gain sociability by attuning our *Dasein* to the world, we lose existential clarity as we have to abandon the purity of insight (authenticity) into the conditions of our so-found-ness.

More implicitly than explicitly drawing back on Aristotle's work on rhetoric, Heidegger identifies three main modalities of so-found-ness. The first is *pathos* or affect (feeling), which is an intuitive encounter that is mediated by our embodied sense-experiences (Stein 1917/1989). Heidegger further develops this thematic, which was also central to, for example, the work of Max Scheler (who criticized Husserl for his exclusive emphasis on conscious-ness), through the concepts of anxiety (*Furcht*) and fear (*Angst*). We can identify these as affective *attunements* towards being-in-the-world. Leaving aside the critical issue of why Heidegger chose to associate pathos with fear (i.e. it is in Angst that we are concerned for being itself), it suffices to conclude here that the first dimension of mediation, pathos, facilitates a generic attunement to our being in the world.

The second domain is that of understanding (*Verstehen*), or what in Aristotelian rhetorical analysis is called ethos. By invoking the term "ethos," I want to stress that the German concept of *Verstehen* is not limited to cognitive processes, but to a more diffused set of sense-making practices by which the world becomes significant (e.g. insight, intuition). By attributing significance to its being in the world, *Dasein* becomes "disclosed"; that is, what may have been mere feelings generated through affective attunement (or mood) now become significant. It is through this modality of signification that *Dasein*'s being in the world begets a sense of purpose, a sense of "why" and a sense of possibility (between what is not yet and what is no longer) in terms of becoming (Heidegger 1986: 143).

The third modality of mediation is *Logos* or reason (*Rede*). Reason (discourse) fulfils signification as the attribution of meaning. Heidegger stresses that discourse does not follow from affective so-found-ness and understanding, but is co-constitutive with them of the way in which *Dasein* encounters its being in the world. It is with discourse that this encounter becomes intelligible and

119

meaningful and thus valued. Heidegger's concept of discourse is not limited to forms of expression (speech) but also gives equal weight to forms of reception (hearing). This further underlines the compatibility of his theory of *Dasein's* disclosure to its being in the world and a phenomenology of mediation that is perhaps more evident in his later writings (Heidegger 1977, 1987; Fry 1993).

Critical media analysis

It is this unconcealment that brings the critical dimension to every analysis of mediation and thus possibilities for answering the otherwise debilitating "so what?" question that usually plagues phenomenological approaches. When we encounter our being in the world in the mundane, ordinary settings of everyday life, we are invited to experience them as an innocuous, timeless flow of "things passing." We may even learn to overcome mild irritations and incorporate them as routine encounters with inconvenience and discomfort without this becoming problematic.

For example, when exposed to daily news, we have to gloss over the personal tragedies associated with victims of war, famine or disasters. Indeed, as Neil Postman claims (1987), the news may be seen as a perfect training ground to become desensitized to our own existential being by the very format of "newsmaking" ("and now for something completely different. . . ."). The news invites us to "forget" about the existential properties of being, it invites us to separate ourselves from the world as "audience"; we are taught to take a completely spectatorial approach to our being in the world.

Debord (1969/1994) described this in great detail in his *The Society of the Spectacle*. Whereas in common vernacular speech we associate the spectacle with special events, it is in fact the "murdering" of events. The spectacle is an engine of commodification, of alienation, objectification, distancing; it is the ultimate producer of *narcissus narcosis*. Why? Because the spectacle turns the event into something else, it turns it into the opposite of a media event, which is in effect a non-event. The spectacle no longer enables translation and enrolment, but instead establishes self-referentiality. In the spectacle, simulation no longer has an "outside" with which anything is being exchanged; there are no gifts, there is no "sociality." Because there are no non-social social forces that disrupt, create lack and enable the creation of objects than can *ob-ject*.

Hence, media events may be spectacular but they remain outside the spectacle. Real media events are existential "moments of truth and revelation that snap us out of the *Narcissus Narcosis*" (McLuhan 1964). They do this because the "attunement of our existential being to our being in the world" is disclosed to us: something does not feel right, we cannot affirm our sense and sensibility with understanding, reason is incomplete. At this point, what is disclosed is "a lack" of translation, which is really an excess of translation: the transformative capacity of mediators becomes visible, as without media there is no event.

At this same moment, the enrolment performed by mediation adds to but does not add up (Bhabha 1990: 312). It is the dissonance of the too-many that marks the media event: too many voices, too many points of view, too many cameras, too much information. Therefore, instead of the spectacle, and following McLuhan more closely, we should be looking for *hybrid media*. It is in the unplanned, unexpected intersections of media that immediacy and transparency become unconcealed:

> The hybrid of the meeting of two media is a moment of truth and revelation from which new form is born. For the parallel between two media holds us on the frontiers between forms that snap us out of the Narcissus-narcosis. The moment of the meeting of media is a moment of freedom and release from the ordinary trance and numbness imposed by them on our senses.
>
> (McLuhan 1964: 63)

Hence, contrasting media events and the spectacle, we are enabled to follow Dayan and Katz in their sidestepping of the critique of "staged events" of "pseudo-events" (such as that of Boorstin 1964). The involvement of media in the "staging" of a happening does not in itself turn the event into an inauthentic experience. It is an empirical matter which completely depends on the particular constellation of mediators, human and non-human, that are invoked to "make sense" and "order" experiences. That is, the morality of media events is tied to the heterogeneity of its coming into being. If the media hybrids allow us to snap out of the narcissus narcosis, it is because they have succeeded in creating significance as ob-jects. This happens when the modalities of mediation take us out of the comfort zone and inaugurate being-as-event. Where we need to depart from Dayan and Katz's original work is in the understanding of time and mediation. Rather than continuing a metaphysics of presence of parallel universes of real events and media events, we need to engage with mediators, human and non-human actors, that inaugurate "events."

Conclusion

To bring this back to the issue of unconcealment, we need to ask ourselves: What is the role of media analysis? What does it point towards? What does it turn away from? In turning towards a more existential-phenomenological critique of mediation, it turns away from modes of critique that portray media as political vehicles, engines of representation. More specifically, the three aspects of attuning enable us to overcome the prevailing conception of mediation as primarily concerning "ideas". This in turn may enable us to overcome the reduction of critical media analysis to mere forms of "ideology critique" (where being critical is simply identifying the difference between the prevailing assumptions of media texts and one's own opinions).

The test of whether this approach has any value will only come with attempts to explain particular events. Spectacular "mass" media events will not engender a profound existential turning (awakening) of large populations because they lack significant connections; they do not reveal mediation as excess translation and enrolment. Recent changes in the nature of mediatization towards more personalized and individualized modalities of attuning us to our being in the world are also not likely to inspire radical changes. However, the latter may very well entail more personalized "conversions" of snapping us out of our narcissus narcosis. One of the profound aspects of, for example, 9/11 has been the intertwining of nationwide media events with personal mediated testimonies, thereby enabling a remediation of this media event, leading us away from a spectatorial self-distancing towards a more personalized, affective, sensible sense-making.

Acknowledgment

I would like to thank the organizers of the Media Events conference in Bremen for giving me the opportunity to present this paper, the editors of this volume for their constructive criticism, and Emma Hemmingway, Michael Schillmeier, Andreas Hepp and Tobias Werron for the discussions that have inspired me to subsequently rewrite this paper as a chapter.

References

Althusser, L. (1971) *Lenin and Philosophy and Other Essays*, New York: NLB.

Badiou, A. (2006) *Being and Event*, London: Continuum.

Baudrillard, J. (1993) *Symbolic Exchange and Death*, London: Sage.

—— (1995) *The Gulf War Did Not Take Place*, Bloomington: Indiana University Press.

Benjamin, W. (1971) *Illuminations. Essays and Reflections*, New York: Shocken.

Bhabha, H. (1990) "DissemiNation: Time, Narrative, and the Margins of the Modern Nation", in H. Bhabha (ed.) *Nation and Narration*, London: Routledge, 291–322.

Boorstin, D. (1964) *The Image: A Guide to Pseudo Events in America*, New York: Harper & Row.

Browning, B. (1998) *Infectious Rhythm: Metaphors of Contagion and the Spread of African Culture*, London: Routledge.

Carey, J. (1992) *Communication as Culture. Essays on Media and Society*, London: Routledge.

Connolly, W. (2002) *Neuropolitics. Thinking, Culture, Speed*, Minneapolis: University of Minnesota Press.

Couldry, N. (2003) *Media Rituals: A Critical Approach*, London: Routledge.

Curtis, J.W. (1977) *Culture as Polyphony*, London: Routledge.

Dayan, D. and Katz, E. (1992) *Media Events: The Live Broadcasting of History*, Cambridge, MA: Harvard University Press.

Debord, G. (1969/1994) *The Society of the Spectacle*, New York: Zone Books.

Deleuze, G. (1994) *Difference and Repetition*, London: Athlone.

Derrida, J. (1982) *Margins of Philosophy*, Hemel Hempstead: Harvester Wheatsheaf.

—— (1989) *Of Spirit*, Chicago, IL: University of Chicago Press.

Featherstone, M. (1993) *Consumer Culture and Postmodernism*, London: Sage.

Fiske, J. (1990) *Introduction to Communication Studies* (2nd edn), London: Routledge.

Fry, T. (1993) "Switchings", in T. Fry (ed.) *R U A TV? Heidegger and the Televisual*, Sydney: Power Publications, 24–44.

Fuller, M. (2005) *Media Ecologies. Materialist Energies in Art and Technoculture*, Cambridge, MA: MIT Press.

Haugeland, J. (1992) "Dasein's Disclosedness", in H. Dreyfus and H. Hall (eds) *Heidegger: A Critical Reader*, Cambridge: Blackwell, 27–44.

Heidegger, M. (1927/1986) *Sein und Zeit* (16th edn), Tübingen: Max Niemeyer Verlag.

—— (1977) *The Question Concerning Technology and Other Essays*, New York: Harper & Row.

—— (1987) *Over Bouwen, Wonen en Denken*, Nijmegen: Sun

Hemmingway, E. (2007) *Into the Newsroom: Exploring the Digital Production of Regional Television News*, London: Routledge.

Lacan, J. (1977) *Écrits. A Selection*, London: Routledge

Latour, B. (1993) *We Have Never Been Modern*, Hemel Hempstead: Harvester Wheatsheaf.

—— (2005) *Re-assembling the Social. An introduction to Actor-network-theory*, Oxford: Oxford University Press.

Levinson, P. (1997) *The Soft Edge. A Natural History and Future of the Information Revolution*, London: Routledge.

Marcuse, H. (1964) *One Dimensional Man. Studies in the Ideology of Advanced Industrial Society*, Boston, MA: Beacon Press.

McLuhan, M. (1964) *Understanding Media. The Extensions of Man* (2nd edn), Harmondsworth: Penguin.

Merrin, W. (2005) *Baudrillard and the Media*, Cambridge: Polity Press.

Ong, W.J. (1982) *Orality and Literacy. The Technologizing of the World*, London: Routledge.

Postman, N. (1987) *Amusing Ourselves to Death. Public Discourse in the Age of Show Business*, London: Methuen.

Shove, E. (2003) "Converging Conventions of Comfort, Cleanliness and Convenience", *Journal of Consumer Policy*, 26, 4: 395–418.

Stein, E. (1917/1989) *On the Problem of Empathy*, Washington: ICS Publications.

Todorov, T. (1990) *Genres in Discourse*, Cambridge: Cambridge University Press.

Van Loon, J. (1996) "A Cultural Exploration of Time: Some Implications of Temporality and Mediation", *Time and Society*, 5, 1: 61–84.

—— (2002) *Risk and Technological Culture. Towards a Sociology of Virulence*, London: Routledge.

—— (2007) *Media Technology: Critical Perspectives*, Maidenhead: McGraw-Hill Open University Press.

Vattimo, G. (1992) *The Transparent Society*, Cambridge: Polity Press.

9

MEDIA EVENTS, EUROVISION AND SOCIETAL CENTERS

Göran Bolin

Introduction

Since its publication, Daniel Dayan and Elihu Katz's (1992/1994) *Media Events* has become increasingly influential in media theory. At the time, it opened up new ways of thinking about the role of the media in society, as it combined traditional mass communications theory with a qualitative and humanities-inspired approach. It was also an important alternative to the then-mushrooming qualitative audience research, in which David Morley's (1986) *Family Television* study was an important landmark that initiated approaches emphasizing the ordinariness and everydayness of media use. Contrary to this, media events theory emphasized the uniqueness of specific, highly extraordinary, media interruptions of the quotidian that helped integrate society.

Although media events theory has become increasingly popular, it has also met with criticism, not least in the light of changes in the media landscapes, the dramatic increase in broadcasting channels, audience fragmentation, and other features characteristic of contemporary media, such as the phenomenon of non-integrative or disruptive media events (e.g. Carey 1998; Katz and Liebes 2007). The most elaborate critique comes from Nick Couldry (e.g. 2003), who argues that Dayan and Katz's work aligns itself with arguments from within the media industry, and is used as a way for the industry to highlight its own societal importance.

In the following I depart from that discussion, and by pointing to a few of the major features in the theory (although far from all) try to advance it by discussing its ontological and epistemological bases, as a way of both overcoming the critique and possibly also updating and developing it to better fit the contemporary media environment.

First, I summarize the main arguments in the debate between Dayan and Katz and Couldry. I then relate both theories to an empiric example – the Eurovision Song Contest – to contribute with reflections on the theoretical standpoints in the debate (how the ESC works as a media event and what societal values it might produce). In the second part of the chapter I return to the Dayan and Katz–Couldry debate, discussing its ontological and epistemological premises, and suggest a way to overcome the opposing standpoints between the functionalistic strands of the media events theory and Couldry's stance.

Media events as function and myth

Dayan and Katz (1992/1994) define media events as a genre unique to television. It interrupts the everyday routines of television programming with live broadcasts across all channels. Typically, say Dayan and Katz, "these events are *organized outside of the media*, [and] the media only provide the channel for their transmission" (1992/1994: 5, emphasis in original). They are thus not orchestrated from within the media, but by "public bodies with whom the media cooperate, such as governments, parliaments (congressional committees, for example), political parties (national conventions), international bodies (the Olympic committee)" (1992/1994: 6). The events are "pre-planned" (which excludes major news events) and "presented with *reverence* and *ceremony*" (1992/1994: 7, emphases in original). And they have a ritual quality of being "ceremonial enactments of the bases of authority" (1992/1994: 43).

In his re-evaluation of Dayan and Katz's thesis about the ritual aspects of media events, Nick Couldry (e.g. 2000, 2003, 2006a) suggests that they overestimate the workings of the media in holding society together. Media events, Dayan and Katz argue, are ceremonial and celebrate order. They stand in for the moral, ethical and sacred in society (they are "civil religion"; Dayan and Katz 1992/1994: 16), and their message is one of reconciliation, in which "reintegration of society is proposed" (1992/1994: 12). Contrary to this theory, in which media events are seen as an expression of, or a connection to, a wider social order, Couldry proposes the thesis of "the myth of the mediated center" (Couldry 2003). By this he naturally does not reject the idea that there are several basic organizational, or administrative, centers in society. Obviously there are, at least if by society we (as Couldry clearly does) refer to the nation-state: when the Bank of Sweden adjusts interest rates all Swedish banks need to follow, which is a typical example of how economic centralization works in society. Instead, Couldry argues that although societies indeed have organizational centers such as parliaments, they do not have *a social or moral center* for which the media stand in, or to which they have exclusive access. In fact, he argues, the media would have us believe that they are the channels through which we access the symbolic center of society, while what they are actually engaged in is constructing this center for us. And this is, according to Couldry, where the real power of the media lies. By media power, he means "the particular concentration of symbolic power in media institutions" (Couldry 2005: 63). So, what he proposes is that the mediated center is created or constructed by the media themselves in close collaboration with mainstream media theory, "where it fulfils a direct institutional purpose: self-justification" (Couldry 2006b: 179). So, the myth, or ideology, that the media present us with is that there is indeed a center, and that the media are our main connection to it.

Now, if we consider a phenomenon such as the European Song Contest, which was the event that first led me to consider the theory of media events, we can try to think how this event can help us understand both Dayan and Katz's and Couldry's ways of understanding the media's role as involved in "mega-events," as Maurice Roche (2000) would term them. I will discuss the implications for the theory of media events, and then in relation to the myth of the mediated center. First, however, I give a short introduction to the ESC for readers who are not entirely familiar with the phenomenon.

Notes on the Eurovision Song Contest

The Eurovision Song Contest was launched in 1956 on the initiative of the European Broadcasting Union (EBU). The EBU was founded in 1950, with the aim of producing pan-European broadcasts. The first event broadcast was the coronation of Queen Elizabeth in Britain in 1953, also one of Dayan and Katz's examples. At that time the EBU had 23 members, which had increased to 70 members in 52 states by 2004. In Sweden, for example, both public service broadcasters Sveriges Television (SVT) and Sveriges Radio, as well as commercial TV4 that have some public service obligations, are members. Geographically, the EBU has expanded to countries outside Europe; for example, North Africa (Algeria, Tunisia, Egypt, Morocco), Israel, Jordan and Lebanon, as well as Japan and Canada. With the exception of Israel, these broadcasters have not entered the ESC.

When the ESC started in 1956, seven Western European countries competed for the title of having produced and performed the best song. The next year another three countries joined the contest, and since then the number of countries has continuously increased. In 1993, the International Radio and Television Organization (OIRT), an equivalent organization of broadcasters from Central and Eastern Europe, merged with the EBU. Consequently, in 1993 Yugoslavia was replaced by three of its former constituent states, and nine post-Soviet countries also entered the competition.

Naturally, a number of changes have occurred over the years. Since 2004, due to the expansion of the number of competing countries, the show stretches over two days. Furthermore, the artists need no longer sing in their national language, meaning that most contributions are sung in English; the studio orchestra has disappeared to the benefit of pre-recorded music; and so on. However, the main formula has not changed: we see the performances, then a short interlude with national artists performing, and then the voting procedure with each contributing nation accounting for their tele-votes.

If the organizational format has changed slightly, there has been a more significant shift in the cultural-political context of the contest. Not only has a shift occurred in the evaluation of Eastern Europe's potential to win; two kinds of reception attitudes towards the event have also evolved. The Western, more ironic stance, with its camp ideology, connections to gay culture, and so on, may be seen as opposed to the more sincere and strategic attitude on the part of the participating countries from Eastern Europe. The ironic stance among certain West European audiences is revealed in some of the national commentators' comments, here exemplified by BBC's Terry Wogan:

> Hope you enjoyed it as much as I have. . . . Congratulations to everybody involved here – a very polished show, a very entertaining show, in some ways, as always (laughter) . . . a very foolish show. But that's the charm. That's what the Eurovision Song Contest is all about. Not really a song contest, as such, a piece of . . . extraordinary entertainment. Just some fun. Grandiose fun. Nothing like it in the world. Hope you in Australia enjoyed it. And all over Europe. And all over the world!!!
>
> (Wogan; quoted in Ericson 2002)

Not everyone shares the ironic stance Wogan and others entertain. After Latvia's victory, and the success of other Eastern European countries in Tallinn in 2002, some were quite upset and argued that there should be separate competitions for Eastern and Western Europe. These statements revealed contempt for Eastern European culture, and an irritation over the fact that the audiences of (Western) Europe were not aware of the presumed cultural backwardness of Eastern Europe. In Sweden, when it was clear that the winning nation once again belonged to the eastern part of Europe, there were calls for "reviving the iron curtain," and others argued for a split of the competition: one for Eastern Europe and one for Western Europe (cf. Štětka, 2009).

Over the past decade there have been a few attempts at "hijacking" the event (cf. Dayan and Katz 1992/1994: 72), mainly for political purposes. The final in Kiev in May 2005, shortly after the political turmoil surrounding the national elections in Ukraine, ended with the new President, Viktor Yushchenko, entering the stage and presenting the winner with a "special prize" from the host country: "a special pictorial to the song that unites the whole Europe" (cf. Bolin 2006a).

This is not the first obvious example of how politicians and governments have tried to "hijack" the ESC for political purposes. Already when Estonia won in 2001, the Estonian government took advantage of the fact that the nation would for at least a short while have the attention of the rest of Europe. British public relations bureau Interbrand, which had previously worked on the Blair administration's campaign "Cool Britannia" was hired, and a strategy for promoting Estonia abroad was developed, including typefaces, maps and pictures of "typical" Estonian nature and people (cf. Bolin 2006b). A statistical analysis had even been performed before Estonia won in Copenhagen in 2001, in which voting patterns over the past decade were analyzed to develop a strategy for winning (Tart 2000).

Media events in new media landscapes

Although the ESC has already been labeled a media event by Dayan and Katz (1992: 6, 136), some of its features depart from the theory. First, the ESC is clearly organized from within the media (by the EBU). However, we might ask to what extent it is possible – today – to theorize *any event* as "organized outside the media." On the one hand, very few media events are as clearly orchestrated from within the media as the ESC; on the other hand, very few events are orchestrated by *other* powerful institutions of society *without them having the media in mind*. The ESC is perhaps orchestrated more obviously from within the media than are other events, but most other events are certainly also produced with the media in mind – even terror or war events such as the Gulf War (cf. Katz and Liebes 2007).

You could even argue that the phenomenon *could not* exist outside the media. It would indeed be pointless to have an international competition of supposedly great national interest if no citizens could partake of it. In fact, all international contests presuppose media to report back to their respective national audiences.

Following from this, *all* international events are orchestrated with the media in mind, at least if by "media" we mean TV, press, radio, the Internet, and so on. This makes the Olympic Games entirely similar to the ESC – a case in point being that the Olympic Games of modern times did not exist before mass press towards the end of the 1800s.

Second, if we accept that media events can be produced from within the media, how would we think about their interruptive qualities? The ESC has appeared annually for over half a century. In what way, then, is it at all possible to consider the ESC an interruption of the everyday routines of television broadcasting? It should be noted here that Dayan and Katz point to how television is produced, rather than how it is perceived. Media events theory has recently been taken up by fan studies, also in connection with the ESC (e.g. Jackson 2007), and here focus is entirely on whether the fans perceive the event as an interruption of *their* daily routines. However, it is fair to say (and Daniel Dayan seems to align himself with this thought in recent discussions of the theory[1]) that there is an intentional component that is very important for the theory. Dayan discusses media events as *willed*; that is, set up by someone for a specific purpose, similar to a visual speech act that enunciates a message to someone, with a specific intention. Naturally, audience response should be taken into consideration, as Katz has recently emphasized (Katz and

Liebes 2007: 158). However, to dismiss the intentional components would be to miss out on the will to communicate that media events express. Admittedly, Dayan and Katz pay very little attention to the social subjects in the audience and their ways of receiving this intended communicative act. Nonetheless, a media event needs to include both the willed staging of the event and its successful reception (or rejection). If no one paid attention to it, it would certainly be a failed event. The audience hailed thus needs to acknowledge that it has been addressed.

I will return to this question, but want to signal already that I believe that the ESC is produced as a special event, especially if we consider the tabloid press, the Internet, and the other media surrounding television, which build up the expectations before the event each year. I will also argue that some ESC finals can be considered as breaking more with everyday routines than others. The example I highlight is the 2002 final in Tallinn (the first to be broadcast from Eastern Europe), which I argue is the most important turning point in the history of the ESC, and I would also argue that we can use the theory of media events to understand why.

Third – and this moves into my main theoretical argument – if we can agree that the ESC is a kind of media event (that media events can be orchestrated from within the media, and that although the phenomenon is characterized by its predictability and repetitive features, the ESC is orches-trated as an interruption of everyday routines), and that it actually touches on (or, if we side with Couldry, produces) some fundamental "bases of authority," we then need to discuss what the bases of authority *are* in this specific case. What are the deeper, fundamental beliefs that the ESC broadcast touches on/produces? How are the bases of authority articulated by the event? In addition, what if the bases of authority orchestrated become challenged by the event itself?

Before I enter this discussion, I want to highlight one of the features in Couldry's theory that I find especially important if we are to understand the workings of the ESC – either as an integrative or a myth-producing event.

Self-referentiality as the myth of the mediated center

Important in the construction of 'the myth of the mediated center' is, according to Couldry, the constant self-referentiality and self-justification the media engage in. When it comes to the broadcast of the ESC itself, in typical self-referential style it points to the complex nature of the production by providing production details: how many cameras are involved, the number of computers used, lighting equipment, staff, wires, and so on, all indicating the high professional standard of the production (and hence the ability of the broadcasting institution). In the technical handbook distributed to accredited journalists at the event in Tallinn, we learn that there are 27 people involved in the lighting arrangements and that 3,000 meters of cable have been used.

For the camera work there are 18 cameras, for the transmission three satellites are being mastered from Tallinn, and the tele-voting has been organized through a special transmission center in Tallinn (cf. Forsman 2002: 73ff.). Many of these production facts were reproduced in both the Estonian and the Swedish press, and in the international press generally.

In 2005 the organizers in Ukraine were equally keen on informing about the work and preparations before the final in Kiev, and were proud of having constructed the lighting even more sophisticatedly than previously:

> Light was used to increase the depth of the stage. The visual effects were based on 300 moving lights and 500 conventional light sources.
>
> A team of 30 people spent more than 40 days programming and adjusting the lighting desk to give each participant their own unique stage and light design that harmonised with the mood of the music.
>
> (www.eurovision.tv/english/1786.htm, accessed 24 July 2005)

This is one way in which the media point to their own capacity, and hence importance (with so much effort, so much technical and economic investment, it cannot possibly be insignificant). Most vocational groups in society naturally hold what they do as important: doctors and nurses, street sweepers, teachers. It is hard to imagine anyone with sufficient work satisfaction thinking of what they do as totally meaningless or insignificant. This is naturally also true of those who work within the media. As I have discussed in more detail elsewhere (Bolin 1996), it would be unbearable for a journalist to imagine that nothing he or she wrote or said in the media mattered at all. Journalists, however, contrary to other groups, have the power to announce this importance of their own profession. This importance is enforced by the prominence some politicians give them, and so the fact becomes established. Looking at the ESC, we can see that the political presence of national heads of state, and other markers of importance, lends prominence to the events (if the President were at the ESC, it would surely be important, would it not?).

The bases of authority/the myth produced

If we now return to the problematics laid out initially, against the debate between Dayan and Katz and Couldry we can ask ourselves what specific values the ESC does, or does not, connect us with (depending on where our sympathies lie in the debate). What is expressed in the grand speech act that is the ESC? Let us for the moment set aside the ontological question concerning whether or not these values exist (or whether they are merely suggested by the media in their efforts to self-justify their activities). I will return to this question, but for now let us suppose that there are values – real or constructed – to which a connection is made.

I should also say that by value I mean something deeply connected to beliefs. Value as a concept, says Douglas Magendanz (2003: 443), is indefinable. But a basic meaning of value is "the worth of a thing" – an "agreed or assumed standard, criterion or measure." Value is then a social product, something negotiated and agreed upon, or indeed contested and struggled over, as in Bourdieuan field theory.

I suggest that there are (at least) two basic values at play in relation to the ESC and especially the Tallinn event: on the one hand, the idea of the nation-state and, on the other, the value of Europeanness. I would furthermore argue that the more basic of these values is the one connected to the nation-state – not specific nation-states, but *the idea of the nation-state as a basis for cultural identity*. One critical remark that can be made regarding the degree to which the ESC connects us to specific, and foundational, basic values (the ability of the ESC to "enact the bases of authority") is, naturally, the lessons we have all learned from reception theory and media ethnography (the approaches to which media events theory was an alternative). Based on the massive audience research over the past few decades, few would dispute the fact that audiences interpret media phenomena variously. This is naturally also evident for the ESC. The meaning produced by the gay community is supposedly another than that produced by a straight family audience, for example. And the meanings produced by audiences from Southern Europe will differ from those of Northern Europe, not least in the meanings given to the musical content, which is obvious if one studies the voting patterns of the tele-voting national audiences (cf. Yair 1995; Tart 2000). It is also revealed in the commentaries from different nations, as mentioned above. However, although there may be different opinions on which song is best or which performance was classy, tasteless, etc., one thing is uncontested: the fact that there are nations, that they can indeed compete, and that songs stand in for the respective nations. In this, few opposing voices are heard.

If this idea of the nation seems uncontested, the same does not apply to the idea of a common and shared European cultural entity. As is obvious from the comments after each event since 2002, there are outspoken voices arguing for a separation of Europe into two halves – East and West. One could argue that the idea of Europeanness is centered on Western Europe (probably not a controversial remark). In this respect, the 2002 ESC in Tallinn actually functioned as an interruption of that everyday concept. This interruption was hardly integrative in its function, at least not at the level of Europeanness. It rather challenged the authority of the Western European cultural supremacy, and in this provoked reactions in the form of discourses on Eastern backwardness and so on. So, it turns out that the same event can be analyzed as both integrative and conflictual simultaneously.

But why do I argue that the turning point is Tallinn 2002, and not Copenhagen the year before? Was it not in 2001 that Estonia was the first Eastern European nation to win? I would say that the victory in Copenhagen was perceived as a one-off, which made it possible for the Western European audiences to approve of it, as a gentle gesture towards a small and quite unknown nation, recently freed from oppression by its former Soviet rulers. Obviously it was expected that Western Europe would retain its cultural supremacy, and that the West would still function as a role model for the newly freed nations. The *interruptive event*, the real provocation, was produced through *winning again*, as the Latvian artists did in Tallinn. This was the real challenge to the bases of authority, the fundamental beliefs held by Western European audiences.

Now, after having described and briefly discussed how the ESC fits into the theory of media events, and how it illustrates some of the features in the critique of the myth of the mediated center, I return to the wider theoretical relationship between these opposing perspectives. I then end the chapter by suggesting the implications this has for how we can understand the ESC and its workings in society.

Ontological and epistemological dilemmas

So, how can we understand the different standpoints taken by Dayan and Katz and Couldry? The explicit critique by Couldry of the functionalistic strands in the theory of media events and other "neo-Durkheimian" theory (Couldry 2005) could, in my understanding, be said to boil down to, first, ontological questions of the nature of reality and, second, to epistemological questions concerning our abilities to gain access to, or indeed explain, that reality. My suggestion is to explain this as an opposition between functionalist thinking and critical theory. I end the chapter with first trying to clarify how I interpret these two relationships to reality, and the two ways of approaching that reality, represented in the debate between Couldry and Dayan and Katz. Second, I argue that, these differences notwithstanding, there is also a difference in how the role of the media in society is considered by the two positions, and that this might be the root to the different standpoints.

The critique of functionalist reason and the role of a critical theory

The main argument Couldry poses in his critique of the theory of media events is its functionalist position, and its affirmative evaluation of these events as integrative. In functionalist reasoning, the main research question posed concerns the internal workings of the societal machinery: How do the different parts of the societal organism function in relation to each other? What are the tasks each individual part has to play for the societal whole? Critical theory poses the opposite question: Why does society not fragment into pieces? Admittedly, there are functionalist explanations that can also be attached to the critical theory explanations, although the fundamental difference concerns the evaluation of the integrative forces, and to Couldry the main critique concerns the positive, uncritical stance in Dayan and Katz's theory.

This eternal question of the "problem of order," as Dennis Wrong (1995) has termed it, makes the conceptualization of the myth of the mediated center take on Kantian qualities: Reality is out there, outside the human subject, and it is not ordered. It is we who make order through our senses or faculties. However, we need to be suspicious of our own apprehensions (*apprehensio*) of reality, because they can delude us. Our faculties are not entirely reliable: things are not what they immediately seem to be. In Couldry's version it is the media that shape this apparent order for us, and would have us believe that the world is ordered, that societies have centers of basic moral authority, whereas the truth is that they actually do not (or at least that this is an assumption that should be tested empirically: Couldry 2006a: 16). The media are thus a prolongation of our faculties.

This part of the Kantian critique appears later in critical theory in Marx, and later the Frankfurt School, where it is developed to analyze the workings of capitalist society in the nineteenth and twentieth centuries, producing theories of "false consciousness," "pseudo-individualization" and other explanations for why society does not fall apart or why the revolution was postponed (e.g. Horkheimer and Adorno 1947/1981). The critique is further analyzed, elaborated and discussed by Jürgen Habermas (1981/1989 and 1981/1991) in his massive work *The Theory of Communicative Action*. In fact, Habermas tries to bridge the opposition between functionalism and an "action-theoretical approach" based on hermeneutics, phenomenology, linguistics and symbolic interactionism through rethinking the relationships between functionalist thinkers like Durkheim, Parsons and others, with Gadamer, Wittgenstein, Schutz, etc., and attempts to incorporate all into his theory of communicative action. The tool for doing so is the lifeworld-systems model, with the administrative and economic systems making up the functionalist part while the lifeworld stands for the phenomenological, action-oriented world of our immediate social relations and the individual's own hermeneutical perceptions that guide his or her actions:

> [T]he conceptualization of societies cannot be so smoothly linked with that of organic systems, for unlike structural patterns in biology, the structural patterns of action systems are not accessible to [purely external] observation; they have to be gotten at hermeneutically, that is, from the internal perspective of participants.
>
> (Habermas 1981/1989: 151, second square brackets in original)

Although Habermas does not dismiss functionalist explanations altogether, he considers them insufficient for explaining even how systems reproduce, because systems – besides having their own systems logic – are also dependent on and reproduced through individual action. It is then not so much society *as* system, but society as containing *both* systems and individual action that should be incorporated into social analysis. This is then a theory that tries to explain societal development in terms of systemic integrative forces as well as the ambivalent replies to these from individual action based on life-world experiences – some of which will resist integration, and some of which will not.

In his analysis, Habermas strives to move beyond an ontological position based on solely a material reality, through a three-part analytical division in an objective, social and subjective world (that is, the world "about which true statements are possible"; the world of "regulated interpersonal relations"; and the world of subjective experiences to which the individual "has privileged access": Habermas 1981/1989: 120). We can then use these three worlds as levels of understanding (they are not mutually exclusive in that sense), and it seems to me that Dayan and Katz and Couldry do not discuss the phenomenon of media events at the same level of understanding. In my interpretation, the difference is that Couldry speaks about the objective world (Do societies have centers or not?), whereas Dayan and Katz execute their analysis within the framework of the social world level (How are societies integrated through communicative relations between a willed media event and an audience response?).

As a postscript to the work on communicative action, Habermas updates the critical program of the Frankfurt School for the "tasks of a critical theory of society" (Habermas 1981/1989: 374ff.). Here, and with special reference to the media, Habermas argues that we need to acknowledge ambivalences, complexities and inner contradictions within media organizations as well as in reception. These ambivalences point to the fact that the workings of the media do not have uniform influences (something already noticed by functionalist uses and gratifications research long ago: Habermas 1981/1989: 390ff.). As far as I can see, the empirical fallacy of both Couldry and Dayan and Katz is to speak in terms of uniform influences. Even when Dayan and Katz (1992: 226) speak of interpretive audiences, they speak of *the* audience having "veto power," whereas it would certainly be more accurate in light of the example of the ECS above, and the divergent opinions on the event, to speak of several interpretive stances among viewers, or perhaps contradictory positions among different viewers.

What Dayan and Katz propose in their theory, but do not fully consider, is not that these events actually bind society together, but that their message is one of *proposed reintegration*. This proposal can, naturally, be rejected by various audiences in line with their respective interpretation of the phenomenon (see the Czech example in Štětka, 2009). But neither acceptance nor rejection will be uniform, as has been proven by reception research. This brings us to the question of the status of the media in the construction of media events.

Different ways of constructing values: the role of the media

If we conclude that reception is not uniform, we should also ask whether it is indeed possible to speak about "the media" with the same ease as both Dayan and Katz and Couldry do. Can we think of "the media" as one, unified locus of authority (given that we grant at least some media authoritative power)? I have already hinted at the fact that both Couldry and Dayan and Katz take for granted that we all understand what they are aiming at with their respective "media" concepts. But would it then not be an empirical question whether certain media have authoritative power, whereas other media have very little of that quality? And would we not have to differentiate between different media technologies (and content)? Few would be likely to defend the gossip weeklies as bases of authority (that is, guardians of the bases of authority in society). Even if we restricted ourselves to the mass media (and I agree with Couldry (2006b: 182f.) that we should not), we would most certainly find contradictory messages even there.

Another question of importance concerns the status of the media (any media), and their role in the construction of reality. If the media claim that there are such things as centers in society, and can also convince audiences/ readers/citizens that they have privileged access to that center (and this is obviously an important part of journalistic rhetoric), these apprehensions will have real social effects. "If men define situations as real," the Thomas theorem goes, "they are real in their consequences" (Merton 1949/1957: 421ff.). And as long as the media construct themselves as powerful with or without the help of media researchers, will they not, if their audiences take them seriously, be treated as powerful? And will they not, then, be seen as connecting us to that center? And if they construct that center and we believe it is real, is it then not real? And would the media not have the function of being integrative? To argue against this, one would need to analyze the media's effects as producing "false consciousness," and I suspect that this is not the intention behind Couldry's arguments, although he says that "the problem with such functionalism . . . is that it closes down massively our options for explaining *what is actually going on*" (Couldry 2006b: 182, emphasis in original).

There is another possible reading of Couldry's quote however. If by "actually" we do not refer to some objective reality but rather to "what is actually constructed," this certainly makes the analysis more sophisticated.

So, does it at all matter whether or not the media actually have access to a mediated center? Indeed, does it matter whether the center is a construct, and is it then less real (as a basis for acting in society)? And, indeed, to what extent is it at all possible to judge the real from the mediated? How can we, from the example of the ESC event in Tallinn described above, separate what Couldry calls "the media" from any surrounding "reality"? How can one distinguish "the power of the media to construct reality" from the political, economic

135

powers that cooperate in the production? This is indeed an important point at which we need to update the theory of media events, as very few events today happen without the media in mind, and – more broadly – because the media are so embedded in society that they can be separated from it only analytically.

If the media's true power, as Couldry argues, is their ability to construct reality for us, are they then not in fact one of the "bases of authority" in society? Admittedly, there are several other "bases of authority" connected to other power fields of society (e.g. economic, political, cultural), but does this make any one of them less authoritative in this respect? Quite rightly, we need to "decenter" media studies, as Couldry argues, but we also certainly need to remind ourselves (and perhaps even more so scholars within other areas of study) not to forget about the role of the various media technologies and content that surrounds us.

Conclusion

As I have tried to argue above, we can use the media events theory of Dayan and Katz, and with slight modifications and updates have that theory explain a phenomenon such as the Eurovision Song Contest – indeed one of the more long-lived events within television. However, we can also, despite the apparent disagreement between Couldry and Dayan and Katz, use the features from the theory on the myth of the mediated center to understand aspects of the phenomenon. As I also have tried to show, this is not so much because the theories are incompatible, but rather that they perform their analysis from different perspectives and perhaps also on different analytical levels.

It has been my argument throughout this chapter that whether we agree with Couldry or Dayan and Katz in this debate will not depend so much on whether we subscribe to certain ontological positions, or on the way we understand the workings of the media in society. Some have attempted to move beyond these ontological positions, for example, Habermas in his work on communicative action. I have tried to suggest some paths along which one can travel further – in the company of mediated events such as the ESC or otherwise.

Note

1 For example, in the talk "Public Events" at the workshop Media Events/Public Events, Södertörn University, 26 May 2004, and the opening address "Revisiting Media Events, or Struggling over Expressive Events: Ownership, Appropriation, Validation, Identity" at the conference Media Events, Globalization and Cultural Change, Bremen, 5–7 July 2007.

References

Bolin, G. (1996) "Det journalistiska våldet. Rapportering och tro i nyhetsmedierna", *KRUT*, 80: 74–80.

—— (2006a) "Visions of Europe. Cultural Technologies of Nation States", *International Journal of Cultural Studies*, 9, 2: 189–206.

—— (2006b) "Electronic Geographies. Media Landscapes as Technological and Symbolic Environments", in J. Falkheimer and A. Jansson (eds) *Geographies of Communication. The Spatial Turn in Media Studies*, Göteborg: Nordicom, 67–86.

Carey, J. (1998) "Political Ritual on Television. Episodes in the History of Shame, Degradation and Excommunication", in T. Liebes and J. Curran (eds) *Media, Ritual and Identity*, London: Routledge, 42–70.

Couldry, N. (2000) *The Place of Media Power. Pilgrims and Witnesses of the Media Age*, London: Routledge.

—— (2003) *Media Rituals: A Critical Approach*, London: Routledge.

—— (2005) "Media Rituals. Beyond Functionalism", in E.W. Rothenbuhler and M. Coman (eds) *Media Anthropology*, Thousand Oaks, CA: Sage, 59–69.

—— (2006a) *Listening Beyond the Echoes. Media, Ethics, and Agency in an Uncertain World*, Boulder: Paradigm.

—— (2006b) "Transvaluing Media Studies, or, Beyond the Myth of the Mediated Centre", in J. Curran and D. Morley (eds) *Media and Cultural Theory*, London: Routledge.

Dayan, D. and Katz, E. (1992/1994) *Media Events. The Live Broadcasting of History*, Cambridge, MA: Harvard University Press.

Ericson, S. (2002) "Rösten från andra sidan. En kommentar till kommentaren", in S. Ericson (ed.) *Hello! Europe! Tallinn Calling! Eurovision Song Contest som mediehändelse*, Huddinge: Mediestudier vid Södertörns högskola, 43–68.

Forsman, M. (2002) "Direktsändning som teknologi och kulturell form", in S. Ericson (ed.) *Hello! Europe! Tallinn Calling! Eurovision Song Contest som mediehändelse*, Huddinge: Mediestudier vid Södertörns högskola, 69–80.

Habermas, J. (1981/1991) *The Theory of Communicative Action, Vol. I, Reason and the Rationalization of Society*, Cambridge: Polity Press.

—— (1981/1989) *The Theory of Communicative Action, Vol. II, The Critique of Functionalist Reason*, Cambridge: Polity Press.

Horkheimer, M. and Adorno, T. (1947/1981) *Upplysningens dialektik. Filosofiska fragment*, Göteborg: Röda Bokförlaget.

Jackson, P. (2007)"The Significance of the Song: The Eurovision Song Contest as a Media Event", paper presented at the conference Media Events: Globalization and Cultural Change at the University of Bremen, 5–7 July.

Katz, E. and Liebes, T. (2007) " 'No More Peace!': How Disaster, Terror and War Have Upstaged Media Events", *International Journal of Communication*, 1: 157–66.

Magendanz, D. (2003) "Conflict and Complexity in Value Theory", *Journal of Value Inquiry*, 37, 4: 443–53.

Merton, R.K. (1949/1957) *Social Theory and Social Structure* (revised and enlarged edn), Glencloe/London: The Free Press/Collier-Macmillan.

Morley, D. (1986) *Family Television. Cultural Power and Domestic Leisure*, London: Routledge.

Roche, M. (2000) *Mega-events and Modernity: Olympics and Expos in the Growth of Global Culture*, London: Routledge.

Štětka, V. (2009) "Media Events and European Visions: Czech Republic in the 2007 Eurovision Song Contest", *Communications* 34, 1: 21–33.

Tart, I. (2000) "Estonia on the Eurovision Landscape", *Estonian Human Development Report 2000*, Tallinn: Tallinn Pedagogical University.

Wrong, D.W. (1995) *Problem of Order. What Unites and Divides Society*, Cambridge, MA: Harvard University Press.

Yair, G. (1995) "'Unite Unite Europe.' The Political and Cultural Structures of Europe as Reflected in the European Song Contest", *Social Networks*, 17, 4: 147–61.

Part IV

MEDIA EVENTS AND EVERYDAY IDENTITIES

10

PERMANENT TURBULENCE AND REPARATORY WORK

A dramaturgical approach to late modern television

Peter Csigo

Introduction: from ritual to dramaturgy

The Event, as an observable phenomenon and a concept, has for long carried a potential to refine and improve mainstream, modernist visions of media power.[1] Turning to "extra-ordinary" events has promised to gain insight into a "sacred time" of turbulence, when the crystallized power circuits typical to modern media are suspended. The energies released by events have been found to dissolve the burdens that had been erected – in the practice of doing and studying popular media equally – by the "binary-producing machine" of modernism (Grossberg 1996:94). Unquestionably, the opposition of "producers" and "consumers," of "subordinate" and "resistant" registers of use, of top-down "power" and bottom-up "agency" seems rigid and artificial in times of emotional turbulence, when audiences and performers "fuse" (Alexander 2006a) and jointly engage in "concerts of performances" (Dayan and Katz 1992). Such an understanding of events as rituals, liminoid dramas or ceremonies (see also Alexander et al. 2006; Cottle 2006; Jacobs 1996) has an incomparable potential to grasp power flows from a different perspective: as "mutual accommodations" (Dayan and Katz 1992: 227) between performers and audiences.[2]

At the same time, the very idea of sacred time as standing out of the ordinary social machinery suits very well the time management typical to the "high modern" media system. Broadcast TV programming was tailored to the presumed life rhythm of the "average" viewer. The strict temporal regulation of "ordinary" watching experience has been commonly presumed to bring far-reaching consequences to viewers' meaning making. Broadcast television's "economies of time and consciousness" (Uricchio 2004: 180) have been conceived to be intermingled and inextricable: the temporal structure of broadcast programming has been seen as mirrored in feelings of familiarity, trust, cohesion, stability and meaningfulness at the level of audience experience (Silverstone 1994). "Ritual" approaches to mediated dramas and events have engaged less in challenging than in enriching the above concept – this friendly conceptual relationship mirrors the fact that "extra-ordinary" events themselves tended to suspend and complement, instead of bursting apart, the ordinary flow of programs in the era of broadcasting. Media events and dramas, embodying a "sacred time" of turbulence, did have their proper function in the broadcast production of stable and meaningful reality.

The days when the predictable regularity of TV programming maintained a familiar mediatic environment and a sense of coherence have gone. What recent, late modern cultural circuits seem to produce instead is media "torrent" (Gitlin 2002), media "clutter," and media "plenty" (Ellis 2000) – an environment over-saturated by spectacular performances that distort the familiar rhythm of ordinary programming. Today's "media clutter" constitutes a realm filled by spectacular "event-claims" which routinely draw all kinds of occurrences out of the sphere of "normality," and promote them as extraordinary, never-seen events. Should we conclude that, along these transformations, broadcast TV has ceased to be a medium of intimacy, of "ordinary stability"? Certainly, there are good reasons to argue that in our era when excess is becoming ordinary and part of "ritualized formats of representation," audiences may find themselves left with an impression of "television as an increasingly disruptive intruder upon the stability of everyday life" (Coleman 2007: 49). Increasingly, today's media events, dramas and rituals – stripped from their anchorage into a "sacred time" – seem to fall into routine and banality, given their mutual invalidating effects and their exposure to audiences' reflexive suspicions.

The fact that in the recent era of media plenty events have become the milestones of ordinary TV programming has been reflected in various scholarly accounts on "event television" (Hesmondhalgh 2002: 243) and "event-status programming" (Caldwell 1995: 160). In the above context, ordinary media time is less "suspended" by sacred media events and dramas than burst apart and blown up by profane ones. Today's truncated events, non-cathartic dramas, and priestless rituals cannot create a sense of sacred media time that would cooperate with ordinary discourses in weaving a dense web of meanings and communal feelings. The collapse of the broadcast temporal régime that gave meaning to media events has incited some protagonists of the ritual approach to grasp late modern "media torrent" as a menace – as Elihu Katz's (1996) pathetic exclamation, "Deliver Us from Segmentation" clearly illustrates. Indeed, stripped from their anchorage into "sacred time," late modern rituals may fail to counterweigh, and may even sharpen, profane forces of disruption – those of tribalism, partisan polarization, segmentation and alienation.

The above association between media multiplication, loss of meaning, and social disintegration is not unique at all. Today's media torrent has been widely blamed for establishing an unsurmountable distance between the individual and the broader social community. This distance has been theorized in three basic ways: either as the self-centered distance of the lifestyle tribe,[3] or as the over-moralized distance established by political or cultural polarization.[4] The most discussed one of all has certainly been the "alienated distance" of the bondless passer-by. Many media theorists have warned that the breakdown of the seamless repetitivity of TV use will annihilate the viewer's sequential temporal experience that allows meaningful narratives to unfold. As a consequence, it has been argued, the "tell me more" viewer would give place to the "browser" (Ellis 2000: 173), and depth would surrender to the "sensuality of the surface" (Fiske 1987). A similarly negative view of media torrent lurks behind Jameson's famous postmodern association between "the fragmentation of time into a series of perpetual presents" (Jameson 1988) and the parallel falling apart of the modern Self into a schisophrenic set of unbounded attachments to random points of the timeless, affective space of media spectacle. Importantly, all the above narratives of disruption share the underlying idea that the social disintegration process as diagnosed is somehow entwined and mutually determined with the all-absorbing and inevadable forces of media "spectacle" (Kellner 2003).

In a word, all the signs are that television has ceased to be the trusted anchor it once was,[5] and became the carrier of an unstoppable torrent of profane events. The above critical voices have denounced new television as a medium of disruption, "socializ(ing) us . . . to a norm of interruption rather than schedule" (Katz and Liebes 2007: 158). Although such a reversal of old integration theories into new disintegration narratives has gained widespread popularity, this approach severely oversimplifies the transformation of television, and overlooks the deep inner tensions with which the "eventization" of late modern TV is imbued. There are good reasons to argue that the disruptive force of profane events has not entirely supplanted forces of integration, which keep providing media users with symbolic resources. True enough, these symbolic resources of integration are less to be located in high, orchestrated, integrative media rituals, which, apparently, have had their day. In lack of sacred rituals rising out of the disruptive media torrent, it may be more fruitful to inquire into the unanticipated ways in which the opposed forces of disruption and integration may coalesce in various contexts. Due to this coalescence, media users' sense of a trusted, worthy, and just ordinary world does survive, although in a "paradoxical continuity" (see Dayan 2006: 182–3) with the torrent of profane rituals that try to cannibalize it.

This chapter seeks to explain why the potential of (re)integration is inherent in the above disruptive mechanisms. Our point of departure is the obvious fact that competing media events, harsh and expressive as they are, necessarily make their own persuasive intent visible for the receiver, similar to advertisements (see Muniz and O'Guinn 2001). As a consequence, today's media torrent accentuates the distinction between the front-of-stage reality of mediated performances and the behind-the-scenes, unmediated reality of performers themselves who always act on stage with a purpose. The rise of this distinction signals an ambiguous doubling of "media reality" in the late modern media environment, a centrifugal movement that diametrically runs against the supposed fusion of reality with spectacle, diagnosed by postmodern theories. As opposed to critical postmodernists who envisage the "loss of the real" (see van Oldenborgh 2007: 68) in the self-referential universe of media spectacle, my aim is to point here to an ever-sharpening distinction between the apparent/spectacular and the hidden/"deep" reality of media.[6] The separation of the two above-mentioned media realities feeds a popular wish to see behind the untrusted realm of media spectacle, to step beyond the clutter of profane events. This revelatory wish is becoming a common drive behind (factual) media consumption, which makes people work to re-establish coherence and engage in what will be called in this chapter "symbolic practices of repair."

The term "repair" refers here to symbolic micro-practices of reconstituting coherence that is felt to be broken, tactics of re-establishing the sentiment that one's society is, after all, liveable and just. The symbolic practices of repair in which people engage might also be called acts of "integration against all odds," given the fact that they are not produced by integrative rituals, but emerge as side products of the disintegrating, alienating processes of late modern television. Acts of repair are to be seen as coping strategies by which people struggle to find meaning in a media environment they deeply distrust: thus, "repair" is half symptom of and half cure to the alienating clutter of late modern media.

While broadcast media has rightly been blamed for constructing a frustratingly coherent "normality," the late modern media environment faces us with a new challenge: that of repairing "normality" in spite of the sense that everything is continuously broken, and all actors are acting upon us (and not with or for us). The above sense of brokenness will be grasped with the help of Ervin Goffman's dramaturgical theory. Following the late Goffman's arguments, I will argue that people's sense of disintegration and distrust should not be misperceived as a paralytical, anomic lack of agency, since it also feeds a relentless, bitter, determined quest for insight into the unvisible, backstage "reality" behind the realm of deceptive media performances. The hidden, backstage intentions, convictions, coalitions, competences, and so on of media actors (politicians, parties, experts, journalists) have become objects of permanent speculation, basic measures by which people judge actors' well framed front-of-stage performances. According to Goffman, in a distrusted symbolic environment, behind-the-scenes insights ("frame breaks") are regularly used as prime windows to actors' "real" identity. Although such frame breaks feed a "negative experience," this has not to be corrosive at all: in Goffman's view, it may also serve as the prime fuel of people's emotional involvement. The above involvement, I argue, may activate people's "reparatory" labor, the work of maintaining a sense of a just and liveable society against the torrent of potentially deceptive performances.

Repairing a broken media world, repairing permanent disruption, looking through the veils of spectacle in the hope of a more universal truth – these instances of the reparatory work that will be addressed here are not the privilege of the most literate. Reparatory work – and the underlying idea that by stepping beyond spectacle we may repair the disruption it caused – is a "conduct of existence based on distrust" (Luhmann 1979, quoted in Burns 1992: 373), a common "way of life" of people doomed to face a torrent of excessively harsh performances with hopelessly discrepant validity claims.

Why Goffman?: permanent disruption and reparatory work in dramaturgical sociology

I have proposed above to switch focus from the old question whether rituals can bring people together to whether people can bring together what has "fallen apart," and how they use "profane" media performances as symbolic resources in this reparatory work. In other words, I have proposed to conceive *forces of fragmentation and those of repair as interdependent* at the level of personal media experience. In order to understand the "paradoxical continuity" of disruption and repair at the level of personal experience, I will turn to Goffman, a main theorist of the paradoxes of modern experience. Goffman's dramaturgical sociology has so far proved to be the most sensitive social theory of the troubled dialectics of coherence and disruption, immersion and distanciation, authenticity and alienation in modern societies.[7]

What makes Goffman's sociology especially relevant to late modern media is the fact that it challenges classical modernist social theory in a similar way that late modern television has challenged the integration model of "high modern" broadcast TV. Goffman has challenged the view that society would socialize us into a coherent symbolic world (as broadcast TV did once, for good or bad, according to the mainstream view). By contrast, in Goffman's view, our ordinary life is marked by the highly uncomfortable necessity of maintaining integrity while facing a multitude of discrepant role expectations and situations that are ready to tear us apart. Goffman's heroes are all wanderers, antecedents of late modern zappers and browsers: wandering across various discrepant situations, being addressed by discrepant voices, playing discrepant roles. Modern social life in Goffman's view is moved by the fertile tension between strong symbolic integratory forces that prescribe with a Durkheimian strictness the adequate mode of conduct in each social "situation," and disruptive forces which emerge due to the simple fact that individuals are constrained to wander among the above, mutually invalidating situations. The above experience of wandering across mutually discrepant normative situations appears as everyday "normality" in Goffman's analysis.

Accordingly, people have to invest ceaseless effort into rebuilding coherence and maintaining personal integrity in the fragmenting settings of modern society (Messinger et al. 1961; Burns 1992).

Goffman's tense vision of modern experience apparently applies to the late modern media landscape where forces of emotional/normative involvement are strong, but always partial and exclusionary, and people continuously jump "from situation to situation"; that is, they wander among harsh and discrepant media performances.[8] In such an environment, the Goffmanesque media wanderer would not have an internalized key to "normality"; neither would s/he "fall apart" – by contrast, s/he would invest effort into accommodating his or her discrepant affective attachments, without being able to fully reconcile them. The above work of "accommodation" may be explored with the help of the late Goffman himself who aimed to include mediated communication into his place-bound interactionist perspective.[9] As I will argue, the late Goffman develops a sociology of "repair," where people are conceived of as "repairers," doomed to a constant task of rebuilding, restoring, retrieving their ever-shattering identities in their inescapable flight from performance to performance.

The late Goffman's dramaturgy is a sociology of "repair," with social actors permanently preoccupied with the question: "Is this really Me?" If this question appeared as troubling in *The Presentation of Self*, it has reached unprecedented depths of existential uncertainty in the late Goffman's work – which makes this study particularly consonant with the sense of "permanent disruption" cultivated by today's media torrent. The dramaturgical spiral of disruption and repair assumes a considerably different shape in *Frame Analysis* than in *The Presentation of Self*. The early vision of the individual as wandering between predefined Durkheimian roles gives place to a new understanding of individual wanderers who ramble, either as spectators or as participants, between staged performances that are stripped from a deap-seated consensus regarding their meanings. While the early Goffman's ramblers have been asking whether they can "believe in the role (they) play" (1959), the late Goffman's wanderers have to face an even more troubling question: can we believe in anything at all (reality frames, authority claims, boundaries)? The answer is yes, no doubt, for Goffman, who develops new visions of integration and repair to his new understanding of social "situations" as fundamentally contested events-performances.

Goffman's late work foreshadows the radical erosion of trust characterizing the late modern media era. In *Frame Analysis* (1974) and his later works,[10] he examines the micro-strategies of involvement that may be followed in a context of overall distrust in any public or private speaker who claims the authority to frame a "situation." The late Goffman explores the possibilities of experiencing coherence and belongingness in an era when "whatever it is that generates sureness" may be rightly suspected to be "employed by those who want to mislead us" (Goffman 1974: 251, quoted in Burns 1992: 273).

Today's advertising (Muniz and O'Guinn 2001: 415) and political communication (widely blamed to be "all spin, no substance" Scammell 2003: 133) make people ask questions similar to Goffman's. In a cultural context so deeply and apparently polluted by machineries of deception, as Goffman has argued, what heightens the most audiences' emotions are not frames but frame breaks : those accidental moments when the "real" intentions of performers come to light and the veils of deception can be peered through. However, the above "gotcha" attitude, and people's related fascination with "mistakes," "debates," and "ambiguities" around media framing would be misread if identified with "falling apart" (tribalism, polarization, anomy). For, what bewildered people enact in such moments is not some masochist celebration of disintegration. People do not deepen the "breach" on such occasions, but perform its potential *repairability*. "[A]s Goffman insists . . . his concern is not to show how the world around us is filled with lies and falsity, and must therefore be constantly regarded with doubts and suspicion, but 'to learn about the way we take it that our world hangs together' " (Goffman 1974: 440, quoted in Burns 1992: 281).

Repair or breakdown?

Goffman's above works allow us to rethink late modern television and the torrent of profane events (many of which are, as we shall see, "orchestrated frame breaks") from a dramaturgical angle. Accordingly, people's fascination with scandals and revelations of various sorts, and their never-ending interest in the actual success or breakdown of events-performances, should not be simply decried as symptoms of "falling apart." Critical scholarly narratives about disruption have typically derided viewers' fascination with the above "frame breaks" either as a futile affect that supplants substance or as a violent pleasure in the breakdown of the political enemy demonized by tribal politics. By contrast, a Goffmann-inspired approach would grasp people's interest in performances' success and breakdown as a coping strategy, a work of meaning-making and repair in the overall context of hypermediation.

Following Goffman's lead, we can diagnose an ambiguous doubling of the real in late modern culture: the "in-frame" reality of a staged performance is increasingly perceived as separate from the "out-of-frame" reality where the real intentions, characters, and interests of performers are thought to reside behind the deceptive machineries of mediated communication. The fact that the connection between the two media realms cannot be self-evidently established is a source of constant frustration that feeds media users' permanent attention to "frame breaks": that is, instances when the two realities can be meaningfully attached. Frame breaks, these "negative events," appear to be self-evident interfaces which connect the mediated with the unmediated, and compare the on-stage reality claims of performers with the measure of their out-of-stage identity that has been coincidentially revealed. The above matching of the framed with the unframed has become a common coping strategy in today's media environment, where people develop a monitorial attitude to media spectacle: constantly browsing it for signs that lead beyond it, "anchoring," as Goffman says, the reality of staged performance to the background reality that lies outside the stage, grasping the meaning of a performance not only at its heights but also at its breakdown. In the spirit of Goffman, the above monitorial practices may be thought of as elements of a distinctive "conduct of existence based on distrust" (Luhmann 1979) in late modernity.

However, it is obvious that frame breaks have become the key stakes of communicators' struggles, who seek to destroy their opponents' "out-of-frame" authenticity. Given the obvious fact that frame breaks themselves are prime targets of framing, deliberately scripted and staged by malicious performers, is not people's fascination with frame breaks just another sign of their submission to disruptive forces (polarization, tribalism, or mere voyeurism)? Is the above "doubling of the real" itself an illusion, as van Oldenborgh argues in line with Zizek and Baudrillard (van Oldenborgh 2007: 68)? Would the "flickers of authenticity" that light up when a performance breaks down (Roscoe 2001) be set up by forces of disruption? Indeed, the mere fact that "frame breaks" are themselves framed and orchestrated by potentially disruptive forces may cast doubt on our claim that they may allow people to "repair" the permanent disruption which they perceive.

Indeed, at first sight, it is hard to attribute such a reparatory potential to frame breaks. Let us take the example of infotainment shows that are performing politicians' "frame breaks" every day, by ridiculing their unintended misformulations, outcropping ignorance, or lies. Certainly, the well-orchestrated daily revelations by partisan hosts like Bill Maher or Bill O'Reilly may arouse viewers' concerns for the whole of the political community, but these worries risk being subjacent to partisan identification. The logic of such "orchestrated" frame breaks usually combines universalistic concerns with the degradation of subaltern groups, the Others of partisan ideology, be they "rednecks" or "illegal aliens." This is not to say that orchestrated frame break performances would not be able to mobilize "reparatory" energies at all – they may do so, but these energies risk being subordinated to the ideological project of the performer. The partisan exploitation of frame breaks' communal potential is quite common in our media environment.

However, introducing a counter-concept, that of at least "relatively" unorchestrated and genuine frame breaks as opposed to orchestrated ones, would be an unacceptable solution to the above problem. Such a move would represent a return to the modernist trope of normative binarizing – the mainstream scholarly practice that researchers of media events have mostly sought to transcend.[11] What will be proposed instead is dropping the idea that genuine frame breaks can exist at all, and examining instead the burdens of the control that performers who orchestrate frame breaks can exert over these "negative events." These burdens do exist and they may serve as a starting point for our understanding of why people's necessary reliance on mediated resources in their "journeys into the unmediated" does not necessarily compromise their emotional reactions. Frame breaks open up a wider horizon than that of their revealers' partisan ideology – they allow people to look "behind" spectacle, far beyond their fatal immersion into the make-believe world feared by many critics.

The role of frame breaks in the profane ritual of laughing at Bush

When inquiring into the burdens of performers' control over the frame breaks they orchestrate, it may be worth making a recourse to the late Barthes' work on photography (1981). Indeed, there is an astonishing consonance between Goffman's idea of frame break and Barthes' widely popular notion of "punctum." At the level of reception, both concepts refer to the intensification of subjective experience and meaning-making at incidental moments that suspend the distant, distrustful, monitorial practice of "browsing" over a torrent of performances or images (in my understanding, this work of browsing is called "studium" by Barthes). The photographical "punctum" in Barthes' work is a piece of unusual detail that picks the viewer, a voice that can bring the viewer to new dimensions because it is believed to be different from the voice of the photographer, a piece of reality that somehow does not fit the photographical reality codes the viewer is used to and expects. For Barthes, punctum itself is a potential: a potential presence of the unframed, a potential lapse of the performer's control, a potential that opens up a place for contemplation and the elaboration of the viewer's subjective experience. This labor is made possible by the subject's conviction that the detail that moves him or her represents at least a piece of "unframed" reality and that s/he is not entirely set up by malicious communicators.[12] The above imaginary distance from the discourse of the performer will be half-illusiory and half-real; no guarantee of its final status can ever be established. Still, it *is* a sense of potential distance, it *is* a sense of freedom: which allows the receiver to pick up that dissonant "unframed" detail and run with it far from the performer.

My point in line with Barthes is that orchestrated frame break performances, by claiming that they give direct access to off-stage reality, necessarily downgrade the importance of who exactly the "orchestrator" is, and how his or her ideological project may exploit the momentum the frame break may create. In other words, the orchestration of a frame break is itself a vulnerable performance that may establish a distance between "revealer" and audience. In the following, I would like to illustrate this vulnerability with a short and hypothetical example. In popular media, staged performances that reveal frame breaks often lean on humor and laughter. Humorous revealings of frame breaks may open up a wide associative space, beyond the control of the performer, even if this latter is widely objected by opponents for enacting excessive and disruptive propaganda. My example is an instance of the movie *Fahrenheit 9/11*, where Michael Moore ridicules the semantic overlap between Hollywood cowboy movies and the press conferences announcing the war in Afghanistan: the first quotes originate from film actors, the last from government officials.

> We will smoke them out of their holes.
> We're gonna smoke them out.
>
> We'll smoke him out of his cave.
> Let's rush them and smoke them out.[12]

Moore's performance is an orchestrated frame break, challenging the government's media framing of the war on terror. In the light of Moore's creative and unusual association of political rhetorics with fictional discourse, the same slogan that may have seemed to be powerful and mobilizing in the ordinary settings of political communication now appears as an illuminating, eloquent mistake of framing. The above presentation of Bush hawks as a group of cowboys out of touch with reality has been created by aesthetic techniques powerfully condensing an already existing and elaborated political opinion, widely dispersed through hundreds of newspaper columns.

However, Moore's claim that he has revealed a hidden truth behind the framed one derails to some extent his own performance as well. For, as opposed to the more serious, ideologically closed and bitter parts of Moore's performance, his rhetoric of laughter introduces a sense of ease and lightness, a sense that normality will be restored, fallacious hawkish ideology removed from the system, once the cowboys leave the scene. Moore's performance of frame break has a potential to cultivate the civil conviction that the permanently experienced crisis is repairable, is a matter of a particular group of wrongdoers and not of structural determinations, and that there is hope that normality will be restored. In the past few years, Bush has been laughed at enough to be stripped of his institutional background and seen as an awkward coincidence in American history. However, this is an idea Moore would certainly not identify with, an idea which, by the way, has spread wide enough to undermine the Democrats' message that today there is a crisis of "American-ness" which could not be solved simply by electing a "normal" Republican president in 2008. Although many of us may sympathize with this last message, I propose to read its relative failure positively: as a sign of the fact that orchestrated frame breaks are not necessarily subjugated to the performer-revealer's ideological project. In those (numerous) cases when Bush's framing mistakes were laughed at, it is exactly the relative freedom of the frame break from the "revealer" that enabled an important idea to spread through the community: that discarding the Bush administration is not a partisan conviction but a consensual basis for moving forward, and that this administration's performance is a common (negative) measure against which the identity of the whole community may be compared.

My example was used to show that even harshly partisan "frame breaks" may have reparatory potential and may incite non-exclusive concerns for the political community as a whole. The above concerns and hopes may allow rudimentary articulations of universalistic principles of responsibility, compassion, and solidarity to emerge – which is a basic condition of "reparatory" labor. As Goffman himself argued in relation to interpersonal "performance disruptions," "when such an incident occurs, the members of an audience sometimes learn an important lesson, more important to them than the aggressive pleasure they can obtain by discovering someone's dark, entrusted, inside, or strategic secret. The members of the audience may discover a fundamental democracy that is usually well hidden" (Goffman 1959: 235, quoted in Burns 1992: 139). Although Goffman refers here to the community of speaker and listener in a face-to-face situation, his idea may be broadened to mediated frame breaks, as potentially allowing for inclusive understandings of a dispersed social community. The rhetoric of frame breaks allows one to experience a community the members of which are doomed to be "jointly lost" in an environment of permanent disruption. The above integrative potential of frame breaks, these profane events, may mobilize more universal insights than those actually made available in the realm of the "framed." This universal orientation may allow the reparatory work connected to "ordinary" frame breaks to serve as a resource for, to use Alexander's appealing terminology, acts and movements of "civil repair" (2006b).

Conclusion

This chapter has addressed how people react to the fact that their media space is permanently torn apart by profane events (like the film *Fahrenheit 9/11* itself), divergent "intensities," tribal and partisan voices. Most of today's profane events claim to break down the opponents' frames, and to reveal some "unmediated" truths about them – which meets the expectations of audiences, who themselves are permanently monitoring media for instances of such "breakdown." As I have argued, the fact that frame breaks are perceived as connection points between the mediated and the unmediated provides audiences with relative independence from the performer who reveals the frame break. This ephemerality of orchestrated frame breaks may allow their audiences to perform, although without acknowledging themselves as a community-in-performance, universalistic standards of commonality and civil society, independent of the revealer's partisan ideology. Truncated, profane events of late modernity may not be entirely stripped of the communal orientation that was typical of media ceremonies of an earlier era.

By allowing the universalizing codes of solidarity and responsibility to emerge, events of late modernity, profane and vulnerable, may contravene forces of fragmentation, tribalization, and polarization – even if they cannot create the "sacred time" in which media rituals have conventionally been thought to be anchored.

Notes

1 For a similar argument on ritual and media power, see Cottle 2006.
2 This "ritual" perspective has been expressed in various conceptualizations of perceived media veracity as an "achievement" in turbulent times. Accordingly, "media events require not only the consent of the viewer, they require his or her active involvement" (Dayan and Katz 1992: 120), "ritual only comes alive experientially, emotionally, subjunctively, when actively read" (Cottle 2006: 429), ritual "is not something the meaning of which is above or beyond or behind the backs of its participants" (Rothenbuhler 1998: 125).
3 Lifestyle tribes typically absorb individuals who lose their interest in society as a whole (Maffesoli 1996; Turow 1997).
4 Mechanisms of cultural/political polarization allow concerns about society as a whole to arise, but urge people to condemn their ideological opponent as lethal to society (see Evans 2003).
5 Well-established scholarly evidence about record heights of distrust in political establishment has been complemented in the past few years with new data documenting a similar erosion of loyalty to television. Recent polls have shown that 46 percent of American respondents claim not to trust TV news (outweighing the number of trusters (36 percent)). A similar proportion of UK audiences (48 percent) have recently claimed to distrust television. The number of people distrusting TV as such does not lag far behind the number of those (60 percent) who disapprove of reality shows, the least trusted of all TV genres. Would people then see TV itself as they see reality shows, that means, "generally misleading as a result of severe and dishonest editing?" See: http://broadcastengineering.com/newsrooms/half_americans_not_trust_news_0314/, http://news.bbc.co.uk/2/hi/entertainment/6960987.stm.
6 Later we will return to the problem that, obviously, people's efforts to see through the looking glass and access the "unmediated" side of media could hardly be treated as a sign of autonomy (in some cases, indeed, such attempts do no more than further affirm the symbolic power of media; see Couldry 2000: 88–9). People inevitably rely on mediated sources in their attempts to see behind mediated make-believe. One of the aims of this chapter is to show why this inevitable reliance should not be misinterpreted as a final proof of people's immersion into spectacle, and why the sharp distinction people maintain between the mediated/visible and the unmediated/hidden media realms allows them relative freedom in their attempts to judge peformances on the visible stage of media.
7 It is the same "dialectics" that has been exploited in Goffman's recent reapplications in media studies. Although far yet from a renaissance, the last few years have certainly brought a revival of Goffman's performance theory in the research of popular media and politics (Abercrombie and Langhurst 1996; Corner and Pels 2003; Waskul 2005; Alexander 2006a). Most recent usages of Goffman have returned to his vision of the interactive context of performance as one where

authenticity, substance, and self-integrity necessarily amalgamate with, and indeed emerge through, artifice, manners, self-surrender, and even self-denial (denial of self-performances in previous contexts). The above authors have exploited this fertile ambiguity in their efforts to grasp today's media as more complex than the socially disruptive spectacle envisioned by critics.

8 The furthest-reaching application of Goffman to broadcast television, Meyrowitz's *No Sense of Place* (1985), has declared that broadcast TV eliminates such self-contained "situations" that once were able to absorb the individual. Meyrowitz was speaking in the name of a broadcast media environment that was able to integrate people into its all-encompassing universe. In the post-broadcast media era, however, the broadcast media space and its collective visibility seem to surrender to a plethora of new local "situations," this time not physical but virtual and mediated ones: harsh media performances with strong "gravitational force."

9 Importantly, the late Goffman's interest in the "framing" of situations (of "staged performances") has downplayed the once-fundamental difference between face-to-face and mediated communication. Accordingly, he expands the scope of his empirical analysis to the field of "depicted social situations presented commercially in movies, TV and print" (Goffman 1974: 379, quoted in Burns 1992: 283). The late Goffman places all forms of communication under the general categories of staged performance and framing.

10 Goffman's arguments will be reconstructed mostly on the basis of Tom Burns' monography (1992).

11 As presented in the introductory arguments of this chapter.

12 Such a malicious communicator would be, for Barthes, a photographer who would use an explicit, didactic rhetoric of astonishment, an all-encompassing spectacular appeal, overwriting all signs that would lead outside the rhetorical "frame." By contrast, honest photographers would create a balance between their framed, rhetorical message and the "unframed," surrounding spheres of reality which is not under the artist's direct control. Apparently, the idea lurking here is, again, that of a "paradoxical continuity" between the framed and the unframed, between involvement and distanciation.

13 *Fahrenheit 9/11*, 00:44:59–00:45:06.

References

Abercrombie, N. and Longhurst, B. (1996) *Audiences: A Sociological Theory of Performance and Imagination*, London: Sage.

Alexander, J. (2006a) "Cultural Pragmatics: Social Performance between Ritual and Strategy", in J. Alexander, B. Giesen and J.L. Mast (eds) *Social Performance. Symbolic Action, Cultural Pragmatics and Ritual*, Cambridge: Cambridge University Press, 1–28.

—— (2006b) *The Civil Sphere*, Oxford: Oxford University Press.

Alexander, J., Giesen, B. and Mast, J.L. (eds) (2006) *Social Performance. Symbolic Action, Cultural Pragmatics and Ritual*, Cambridge: Cambridge University Press.

Barthes, R. (1981) *Camera Lucida: Reflections on Photography*, New York: Hill and Wang.

Burns, T. (1992) *Erving Goffman*, London: Routledge.

Caldwell, J.T. (1995) *Televisuality: Style, Crisis, and Authority in American Television*, New Brunswick: Rutgers University Press.

Coleman, S. (2007) "Mediated Politics and Everyday Life", *International Journal of Communication*, 1: 49–60.

Corner, J. and Pels, D. (eds) (2003) *Media and the Restyling of Politics*, London: Sage.

Cottle, S. (2006) "Mediatized Rituals: Beyond Manufacturing Consent", *Media, Culture and Society*, 28, 3: 411–32.

Couldry, N. (2000) *The Place of Media Power. Pilgrims and Witnesses of the Media Age*, London: Routledge.

Couldry, N., Livingstone, S. and Markham, T. (2007) *Media Consumption and Public Engagement: Beyond the Presumption of Attention*, Basingstoke: Palgrave Macmillan.

Dayan, D. (2006) "Quand montrer c'est faire", in D. Dayan (ed.) *La Terreur Spectacle*, Paris-INA: De Boeck, 165–85.

Dayan, D. and Katz, E. (1992) *Media Events: The Live Broadcasting of History*, Cambridge, MA: Harvard University Press.

Ellis, J. (2000) *Seeing Things*, London: I B Tauris & Co.

Evans, J.H. (2003) "Have Americans' Attitudes Become More Polarized? – An Update", *Social Science Quarterly*, 84, 1: 71–90.

Fiske, J. (1987) *Television Culture*, London: Routledge.

Gitlin, T. (2002) *Media Unlimited: How the Torrent of Images and Sounds Overwhelms Our Lives*, New York: Henry Holt & Co.

Goffman, E. (1974) *Frame Analysis: An Essay on the Organization of Experience*, New York: Harper & Row.

—— (1990) [1959] *The Presentation of Self in Everyday Life*, London: Penguin.

Grossberg, L. (1996) "Identity and Cultural Studies", in S. Hall and P. du Gay (eds) *Questions of Cultural Identity*, London: Sage, 89–108.

Hesmondhalgh, D. (2002) *The Cultural Industries*, London: Sage.

Holt, D.B. (2002) "Why Do Brands Cause Trouble? A Dialectical Theory of Consumer Culture and Branding", *Journal of Consumer Research*, 29: 70–90.

Jacobs, R.N. (1996) "Producing the News, Producing the Crisis: Narrativity, Television and News Work", *Media, Culture and Society*, 18, 3: 373–97.

Jameson, F. (1988) "Postmodernism and Consumer Society", in E.A. Kaplan (ed.) *Postmodernism and its Discontents: Theories, Practices*, New York: Verso, 13–29.

Katz, E. (1996) "And Deliver Us from Segmentation", *The Annals of the American Academy of Political and Social Science*, 546, 1: 22–33.

Katz, E. and Liebes, T. (2007) " 'No More Peace!': How Disaster, Terror and War Have Upstaged Media Events", *International Journal of Communication*, 1: 157–66.

Kellner, D. (2003) *Media Spectacle*, London: Routledge.

Liebes, T. (1998) "Television's Disaster Marathons: A Danger for Democratic Processes?", in T. Liebes and J. Curran (eds) *Media, Ritual and Identity*, London: Routledge, 71–84.

Luhmann, N. (1979) *Trust and Power*, Chichester: Wiley.

Maffesoli, M. (1996) *The Time of the Tribes: The Decline of Individualism in Mass Societies*, London: Sage.

Messinger, S.L., Sampson, H. and Towne, R.D. (1961) "Life as Theater: Some Notes on the Dramaturgic Approach to Social Reality", *Sociometry*, 98–109.

Meyrowitz, J. (1985) *No Sense of Place*, New York: Oxford University Press.

Muniz, A.M. and O'Guinn, T.C. (2001) "Brand Community", *Journal of Consumer Research*, 27, 4: 412–32.

Roscoe, J. (2001) "Big Brother Australia: Performing the 'Real' 24/7", *International Journal of Cultural Studies*, 4, 1: 473–88.

Rothenbuhler, E.W. (1998) *Ritual Communication: From Everyday Conversation to Mediated Ceremony*, Thousand Oaks, CA: Sage.

Scammell, M. (2003) "Citizen Consumers: Towards a New Marketing of Politics?", in J. Corner and D. Pels (eds) *Media and the Restyling of Politics*, London: Sage, 117–36.

Schulze, G. (1998) "The Experience Society. Excerpts", in A. Wessely (ed.) *A kultúra szociológiája,* Budapest: Osiris, 186–204.

Silverstone, R. (1994) *Television and Everyday Life*, London: Sage

Turow, J. (1997) *Breaking Up America: Advertisers and the New Media World*, Chicago, IL: University of Chicago Press.

Uricchio, W. (2004) "Television's Next Generation: Technology/Interface Culture/Flow", in L. Spigel and J. Olsson (eds) *Television After TV: Essays on a Medium in Transition*, Durham: Duke University Press, 232–61.

van Oldenborgh, L. (2007) "Performing the Real", in D. Sutton, S. Brind and R. McKenzie (eds) *The State of the Real*, London: Tauris, 62–72.

Waskul, D.D. (2005) "Ekstasis and the Internet: Liminality and Computer-mediated Communication", *New Media and Society*, 7, 11: 47–63.

11

MEDIA EVENTS AND GENDERED IDENTITIES IN SOUTH ASIA

Miss World going "Deshi"

Norbert Wildermuth

Introduction

In November 1996 the South Indian metropolis Bangalore hosted the annual Miss World pageant show. The live event and its televisualization, produced for the first time in India, became a "key moment" in the ongoing transformation of India's media landscape. Not only does the glamorous beauty contest qualify as the single most controversial television programme in India since the arrival of transnational television in 1991, but the televised event also became discursively embedded in the broader ideological and political struggles over competing definitions of the Indian nation state and Indian culture unfolding over the past decade. As I will try to show, the 1996 pageant has spelled out these discursive struggles – which were shaping both the final "textual" construction of the show and the public controversy that accompanied the televised event – in a nutshell. However, I will argue that the new audio-visual services, in general, and particular media events like the Bangalore Miss World pageant, were not only the object of public debate and textually framed by the discourses employed in them, but have also constituted an increasingly important and prominent, mass mediated "platform" for Indian society to actively reflect upon its contemporary modernization. In this sense, the new structures and forms of television emerging from 1991 onward, in addition to symbolizing and imagining India's globalized modernization, have created a crucial communicative space for the discursive construction and exploration of the very notion, meanings and problematic of this socio-historic change.

To study a particular media controversy is to study phenomena of societal transformation associated with and negotiated within a changing public sphere. Thus, my reading of the 1996 Miss World pageant will seek to explore the symbolic constructive capacity exercised by India's transformed contemporary media institutions in general and by the Indian transnational producers of the Bangalore pageant in particular. To that purpose, I will examine the latter's symbolic power to engage the gendered identity constructions and conceptualizations of "modern India" that were vehemently contested over the televised event. This will bring me to my main thesis, that the show's textual realization was successful in offering the audience the vision of an unproblematic and productive relation between the local and the global as a preferential frame of interpretation of the event. In theoretical terms I seek therewith to contribute to a case study-based, empirical qualification of our understanding of media institutions' power to shape the modernizing societies under the transition of which they are a part through the symbolic practices of mediated representation they exercise; contested representative practices which point beyond the mere reproduction of the dominant discourses and ideologies. Let me start this endeavour by outlining in which sense the pageant and its televisualization has been indicative of the emergence of a profoundly altered, audio-visual popular culture in India.

Transnational satellite television has made spectacular inroads on the Indian subcontinent, starting with the transmission of the BBC World Service and CNN International during the first Gulf War. Facilitated by the parallel unfolding far-reaching economic reforms and a swift market liberalization, some dozen television channels, private- and state-owned, from India and abroad, were by the mid-1990s competing for the attention of a growing Indian cable and satellite (c&s) audience. While the state broadcaster Doordarshan's exclusive monopoly was gradually eroded, the "liberalization of the skies" provided Indian c&s homes with access to an unprecedented amount of both domestic and international programming. By the mid-1990s, especially in urban, middle-class India, satellite television had taken over as the dominant form of cultural consumption and (mediated) leisure activity. While the private broadcasters' programming was predominant among the lucrative c&s homes, the state broadcaster was more or less left behind with the less affluent and socio-politically empowered terrestrial TV homes.

Doordarshan's decision to bring The Miss World pageant to India and to transmit the show both via c&s and terrestrially nationwide may thus be understood to have been part of a broader attempt (under Doordarshan's then director general, Rathikant Basu) to turn around this "negative" development and to win back the middle- and upper-class audience segments. However, what followed obviously took Doordarshan, the event organizers and producers by surprise.

Welcome to India's *Garden City*

In August 1996 the South Indian metropolis Bangalore decided to host the annual Miss World pageant; an event which was propagated by its Indian organizers as "the right opportunity to showcase Indian culture and talent to the world". Claims to put India and its IT industries centre Bangalore on the global map were expected to appeal to India's burgeoning, confident and assertive new middle classes that "have now come to meet the West in the global arena of commerce, enterprise and consumption on equal terms [and] . . . are animated by the vision of setting India on a newly liberated path of progress and economic prominence on the world stage" (Chakravarty and Gooptu 2000: 91). While the event held the promise of global cultural recognition and of a highbrow live entertainment event for the Indian urban elites to participate in, Godrej, a leading Indian fashion and cosmetics house with a substantial turnover in India and abroad, was appointed as main sponsor to the show.

As for Godrej's motivation to become the main sponsor it is important to know that the centre of gravity (that is, the audience and sponsorship focus) of the global beauty pageant industry has shifted, slowly but steadily, from the Western hemisphere towards the East and South, encompassing an increasing number of Asian countries in recent years. Thus, while the Miss World pageant is ever more ignored by the mainstream media in the USA, Canada, Australia and most of Western Europe, it has found major new audiences in the developing economies of Eastern Europe and Asia. Subsequently, the international beauty queens no longer come from the Western countries and Latin America alone. Over the past decade several Indian beauty queens were formally acknowledged to represent a new international, idealized look and paradigmatic female character. In consequence, India has become both the site of a major audience segment and an important participating nation in global pageants in the course of a few years[1] and is thus not surprisingly a potential site of venue in the eyes of the British Miss World organization.

But who else was in support of the Bangalore pageant? Apart from the South African TV producer "Combined Artists Productions" and the executive producer Johannesburg "Gillian Gamsy International", the Indian event organizer ABCL deserves our attention the most. For ABCL, bringing the Miss World finals to India constituted a valuable chance to promote the newly established company, set up by former Bollywood superstar Amitabh Bachchan, and to prove its competence in making happen a globally broadcast live event of comparable scale.

As for the pageant's supposed national audience, Doordarshan's 200 million-plus viewership, the fact that national and regional beauty pageants have been around in India for three decades, were widely broadcast by the private TV channels and well received by a growing c&s audience was taken as sufficient evidence for certain success of the show.

To the Indian public at large the Miss World pageant was presented as an outstanding chance to raise funding for charity and welfare programmes. Notwithstanding these noble intentions the announcement that Bangalore would host the global media event caused considerable turmoil. In the weeks prior to the contest, Bangalore was the site of four minor bomb blasts accompanied by boycott calls and peaceful demonstrations. While opinion polls in major newspapers showed overwhelming support for the beauty contest, a number of feminist activists threatened to set themselves on fire during the final show.[2] Arguably these actions scared off additional sponsors, impacted on ABCL's reputation and landed the company in a financial mess.[3]

Who were these protesters and how can we explain the fact that they, while failing to mobilize a broad base of direct support for their protests, were successful in raising a nationwide debate which put those organizers and Indians who publicly sympathized with the fact of the event taking place (on grounds of principle and not necessarily due to a personal preference for the genre of pageants) "morally" on the defence?

A qualified answer demands more than a face-value consideration of the opponents' main arguments. As in the case of the counter-arguments, we have to scrutinize the protesters' critique for the latent meanings and interests it less obviously contains. While a description of the opponents' line of reasoning may provide us with an initial point of understanding of the issues at stake, we must proceed to examine how exactly both sides have product-ively mobilized broader discursive positions with regard to Indian society's contemporary transformation, including the role that media institutions and audio-visual representations play in this process, in their rhetoric positions. Only then will we be able to perceive the larger picture that tells us in which sense the particular case under examination may be related to the dynamics of India's contemporary "globalization-localization" with all its contested inherent contradictions, inconsistencies and disjunctures.

Media images of the New Indian Woman

In the Indian public the "uncontrolled" proliferation and spectacular success of the private audio-visual service providers was, from 1991 onward, widely perceived to constitute the most spectacular, visible and controversial aspect of a cluster of interdependent processes of structural change subsumed under the labels of India's consumer revolution, economic liberalization and cultural globalization. Not surprisingly, their "socio-cultural" impact became a highly problematized and politicized question within the Indian public. However, as for the concrete significance and meanings of India's c&s revolution, the articulations which came to dominate the Indian public were deeply split.[4] On the one hand, there was a certain enthusiasm about India having joined the electronic flow of a globalized media culture, not only on the level of consumption, but increasingly also in terms of broadcasting production. On the other hand, there was an equally powerful line of interpretation under circulation – rooted conceptually in the contested but still very powerful notions of how best to safeguard the country's cultural, economic and political sovereignty – according to which India's "globalized" modernization (and in particular its electronic media's transnationalization) constitutes a destabilizing external pressure on Indian society and culture. Arguably, many Indians were "split" between both positions, giving evidence to the often stated ambiguity of the new Indian middle classes with regard to the moral and sexual dimensions of Indian society's and culture's contemporary transformation.

Indisputably, with the spread of pan-Asian Star TV, CNN, MTV, Zee TV and so on, a far-reaching reconfiguration of the female image could be observed. Until then, the "traditional" (Sati/Savitri) role model had been the predominant representation of Indian womanhood in the male viewer-oriented Indian film and family-oriented TV fiction production. Yet from 1991 onward, the hegemonic articulation of this "ideal" in Indian popular culture was thoroughly challenged with the imagery of the *New Indian Woman* emerging in the new print media, in advertising, at public events and on the small screen. As the number of satellite channels and the volume of their output increased, a plethora of new female faces (and bodies) appeared which soon became synonymous with post-liberalization, "modern" India: the sexy and self-assured MTV Video Jockey, the Bombay socialite, the "Non-resident Indian" talk-show presenter, the cosmopolite fashion designer, Miss World and Miss India.

Archana Puran Singh, the lively presenter of *Kya Scene Hai*, sported body-hugging suits and mini-skirts on El TV (the Zee network's second channel), a sari-clad compare asked men about the state of their libido, while a slew of private television chat shows were blowing the lid on previously taboo subjects such as adultery, breast augmentation, homosexuality, incest and complaints about lack of sexual satisfaction. Jain TV, a private Hindi general entertainment satellite channel, went so far as to relay a weekly erotic movie on Saturday nights (Shah 1997: 134).

As indicated by the vehemence of reactions, the meanings imputed to these new topics and female ("body") images, though far from being unified and completely determined with regard to individual and public reception, were not open to any possible reading. The reconfigured images of Indian womanhood and female agency became a highly controversial issue, the representation of the New Indian Women on c&s television probably the "most contested site in the Indian cultural landscape" (Malhotra 1999: 84). To their growing horror, India's "conservative" middle-class majority,[5] enwrapped in an almost Victorian code of morality, saw itself confronted with the products of a popular culture which portrayed the possibility of an independent, female agency – including autonomous control over her sexuality – as socially acceptable and even desirable.

To add to these concerns, this "shameless" female behaviour and disregard for gendered roles, determined by the "logics" of a male-dominated kinship structure, was not only displayed by the female stars of a larger-than-life Indian cinema or a super-rich Westernized, urban elite. The audience, increasingly, came to witness the deviance of otherwise rather ordinary women from the urban middle- and upper-middle classes and/or the characters representing them in entertainment programmes and serial fiction. Yet the closer these images came to the life worlds of the bulk of Indian middle-class families, and the more they became drawn into the public, the more they unleashed a whole set of deep-rooted and unresolved social anxieties and uncertainties around the larger cultural transition and ongoing renegotiation of gender relations. As early as 1993, the secular women's action group *Jagriti Mahila Samiti* filed a petition in the Delhi High Court against the excessive display of sex and violence on television. Foremost, however, were the Hindu nationalists who were ready to lead the verbal and legal attacks on the "vulgar" and "obscene" electronic media.

A spiral of moral panics with media

Shohini Gosh, a media scholar and member of the feminist film collective Media Storm, has traced what she calls a spiral of regular recurring "moral panics" from 1992 onward. The first major controversy about "obscenity" in the media focused on the song-and-dance sequences in *Choli Ke Peechey Kya Hai?* (What's Behind the Blouse?) from the Hindi film *Khalnayak* (The Villain, 1993). The ritual and moral outrage around the "*choli*" song was re-enacted and escalated around subsequent movies, songs, advertisements and television programmes, culminating in November 1996 when the Miss World Beauty Pageant was held in Bangalore amid violent protests and threats.[6]

According to Gosh, "the images and representations that have simultaneously provoked outrage from both the Hindu right and secular feminists", though extremely diverse in their cultural form, share "sexually coded representations primarily articulated around women's bodies" (Gosh 1999: 236). If the Hindu Right was mobilizing the "moral" and cultural" agenda, neither the Congress Party, nor the United Front government, in power from June 1996 onward, has refrained from highly publicized, legislative attempts to curb "the growing obscenity and vulgarity" in the media. Pressured by non-government groups and the Hindu Right which claimed to represent a "concerned" majority, and following a furore in Parliament, the Congress government introduced, for example, a voluntary "Programming and Advertising Code" in 1995. The Code condemned objectionable content, but while it urged advertisers not to offend morality, decency and religious sentiment, it did not require them, legally, to do so, providing the protagonists of "greater accountability in satellite programming" with a powerful political agenda.

By this time, Indian and transnational satellite broadcasters clearly felt the heat; above all, Rupert Murdoch's Star TV network, publicly branded as the archetypal cultural alienator. In the mid-1990s, India's Film Censor Board initiated a number of legal proceedings against Star TV for showing "indecency" in its movies. The Censor Board objected to the network's overdosed, explicit sex scenes on more than 175 programmes shown by Star Movies, Star Plus and the Hindi-language channel, Zee TV (Sinha 1998: 36). The private satellite broadcasters, far from being immune to the public accusations and demands made against them, acted highly responsively from 1995 onward, trying to accommodate at least some of their critics with the implementation of a redefined and readjusted channel identity and programming strategy. In this repositioning endeavour localization strategies came to play a central role. While Star TV started to "Indianize" programming on Star Plus, replacing Anglo-American with Hindi prime-time serials, Zee TV made efforts to reinvent itself as *the* Indian satellite network. Ironically, even Doordarshan, the (former) state broadcaster, who was commonly blamed for not being sufficiently internationalized in terms of its production standards and programme formats, was accused of being accomplice to an "essentially non-Indian" entertainment event, the Bangalore Miss World pageant.

The protesters' "moral" coalition

To come back to the particularities of the controversy unfolding around the 1996 pageant: organizations ranging from the women's wings of the Communist Party of India to the Hindu Right BJP protested against the pageant on the grounds that it represented a "cultural threat" to the Indian nation. In an unusual coalition of interests, various groups ranging right across the party political and social activist spectrum found common ground.[7] On one side, there were feminist activists and non-government women's organizations denouncing a major incident of "female exploitation". On the other, there were communist, Hinduist and Islamic (political party-affiliated) movements, describing the pageant as an imminent "threat to Indian civilization". So, for example, Uma Bharati, representing the Hindu nationalist BJP, claimed that the protesters were not against being "modern" but against being "Western". As she elaborated: "We want women to become doctors, engineers, IAS (Indian Administrative Service) and IPS (Indian Police Service) officers and ministers, but we don't want them to smoke, drink and adopt a Western style of living."[8]

The secular women's movement's engagement with female representation emerged from demands for women's right to equality and a concern with violence against women, arguments basically different from the Hindu nationalists' indictment of obscenity as detrimental to "traditional Indian values". However, the merging of lines between communal forces and autonomous women's organizations did not stop at the level of symbols and slogans, but found expression in some of the more concrete demands raised by the secular women's movement. "Obscenity" was such an issue. Thus the feminists' campaign received support from all sorts of people and social forces, ranging from Victorian moralists to the Hindu fundamentalist *Sangh Parivar*. Thus, the Hindu/Muslim Right and the secular women's groups have, despite their basic ideological divergence, not only targeted the same representations but also demanded similar censorious measures (Gosh 1999).

Projected to exemplify the (above-outlined) cultural threat of India's "satellite revolution", the 1996 Miss World contest provided this aggregation of social and political interest groups with a chance to approach the Indian public with their particular ideological positions, which framed protests effectively as gendered nationalist discourses. While the BJP depicted the Bangalore pageant as an assault on Indian national culture and womanhood, organizations from the ideological Left argued that the contest would encourage the entry of foreign capital into the country and reinforce Indian women's patriarchal-capitalist exploitation. That is, the Miss World controversy provided an occasion to problematize and to debate not just some specific questions of media regulation (e.g. the "need" for censorship and/or a programming code policy), but the sociocultural "impact" of c&s television and India in general, presumed to be a central dimension of India's current process of globalized modernization.

In consequence, the Miss World event was interpreted and discursively linked to a series of highly politicized debates about the essence and future of India and Indian culture, about gender issues, India's position in a globalized world, the return of Indian society to a Hindu cultural core and so on. As in the case of other controversial media images of the *New Indian Woman*, the representation of an *Ideal Indian Womanhood* became the symbolic battlefield in which competing visions of national identity and the "Indian way to modernity" came to confront each other throughout the 1990s.

Where did all this leave those who still sought to bring the 1996 Miss World pageant to Bangalore? And what was the actual outcome of this unified agitation? Were the pre-pageant protests just the foreplay to a final escalation over the public meanings and legitimate forms of Indian television in the satellite age? And to which extent were the Indian masses mobilized for or against the Miss World show? Did they buy into the urgency of the protesters' "moral" agitation, or was the majority willing to agree with the organizers' affirmative interpretation of the event?

No swimsuits, no liquor, no provocation

Admittedly, the federation of opponents can claim some partial success. Due to "unfavourable publicity" the Miss World pageant's beachwear round was moved by the organizers to the Seychelles.[9] Eighty-eight beauties displaying their lush bodies on a tropical beach, wearing nothing but tight swimsuits, were deemed – under the given circumstances – too much of a provocation to be staged and filmed in India. Other sub-events, like the Miss Photogenic contest and the Miss Personality contest, lead-ups to the main show, remained in India, but were moved outside Bangalore for security reasons.[10]

Also on the legal front the protesters challenged the show. In an appeal to the Karnataka High Court, the Mahila Jagran Manch demanded a blanket ban on the event "in the interest of Indian culture and heritage and to save the country from AIDS". The Karnataka High Court, while holding that no direction could be issued to ban the pageant, asked the police and the registrar of the High Court to monitor the show to ensure the observance of certain conditions imposed on the event, including prosecution charges against contestants in case of "indecent exposure of the body of the participants". In addition, the Karnataka High Court in its verdict stipulated that the holding of the event should be subject to the strict observance of the laws of the land and that liquor in any form should not be served.

Yet the Indian Supreme Court overruled most of these restrictions on the eve of the main contest after it had taken on record an affidavit from the Indian organizers, the Amitabh Bachchan Corporation Limited which stated that "liquor will be served only as a welcome toast at the beginning of the pageant and as a toast at the end of the contest. This service will be in selected enclosures and will be served only to the invitees, organizers and dignitaries seated in the enclosures."

On Saturday, 23 November 1996, the main contest was conducted in Bangalore's cricket stadium without further incident, even though strong forces within the opposition BJP, in a last decisive bid to frustrate the event, had given a call for a 24-hour Bangalore *bandh* (general strike). Obviously, the opponents to the event had crudely misjudged the public support they could mobilize. Audience shares for the show on the Indian market were reportedly high, as was the pageant's global reach. The majority of the Indian TV viewers were seemingly not impressed by the protesters' boycott calls, or simply too curious not to judge and to enjoy the spectacle themselves. The de facto local popularity of the 1996 Miss World contest may thus not only indicate male and female viewers' fascination with a glamorous media event. It may also indicate the audiences' demonstrative rejection of any attempt to re-establish a paternalist regime of media consumption, telling them what they were supposed to see and what not to see.

"Indianizing" a globalized media event

Methodologically, a qualitative reception study done at the time could tell us about some of the de facto readings and interpretations by Indian viewers watching the final contest. To the best of my knowledge, no such qualitative audience study has been done, nor have the results of some survey-based, quantitative enquiries into the subject been published. What we have, in terms of an indicator, are the reactions of the ordinary Indian viewer selected and purported by a far from impartial Indian press. However, given the principal ambiguity of many Indians with respect to a fast-transforming popular culture and media landscape, an ambiguity that has been pointed out by numerous authors, it seems safe to assume that a substantial part of the Indian audience had not yet decided whose line of interpretation to follow by the time the pageant went on air. That is, they could still either be won over by the event, or be pushed to embrace the opponents' rejection.

Obviously this unsettled situation, following weeks of speculation about how the final show would actually "solve" some of the most contested issues (e.g. the "semi-nudity" of the contestants), placed an extraordinarily "creative" pressure on those responsible for the pageant's final realization as a telecast event. Thus, how have the producers/organizers managed to overcome the diffuse but consistent accusations of the show as vulgar, voyeuristic, male chauvinistic, non-Indian and so on by a well-orchestrated set of narrative and representational practices? How have they textually constructed and audio-visually imagined the show with the intention to deflect the protesters' accusations and how successful have they been in (re-)establishing the legitimacy and credibility of their own (promotional) interpretation of the productive and "unproblematic" character of the event with the Indian viewer?

Let me sum up the results of a detailed, "textual" analysis-based answer to this question, which I have provided and discussed (including its method-ological and analytical challenges) in earlier publications (Wildermuth 2003; 2005). Its relevance for my present argument aims less at demonstrating how the narrative construction and enactment of particular social relations and the representation of particular social identities, realized in the 1996 Miss World final contest, have undergone a strategy of "Indianization". Rather it serves as a necessary basis to characterize the Bangalore pageant as the "mediated imagination"[11] of a hybridized conjuncture, in which the contested politics of India's economic liberalization were negotiated through the delineation of a new, productive relationship between the national and the global.

While the Indian and foreign media professionals in charge of the show were not to transgress the contemporary generic conventions of the Miss World pageant, they certainly had some room for manoeuvre with regard to the selection of the hosts and prescription of their performance. Furthermore, they could decide on the setting, the performing artists and the promotional ("land and people") videos shown between stage acts. In this way, they could attempt to create a popular and broadly acceptable impression for the Indian viewers, accomplished in accordance with the generic expectations of the global viewers, advertisers, broadcasters and the Miss World organization.

The outcome of this need for the accommodation of both global and local viewer expectations was a contest show characterized by an excess of dramatic, ornamental and atmospheric codes which sought to signify classical Indian culture and traditions. On the level of visual presentation the Miss World pageant's "localization" materialized in a theme-park-like exotic Indian setting, including the on-stage parading of two "holy" temple elephants, as used in religious processions. Furthermore, it materialized in an elaborate stage design inspired by the ancient and world-famous temples of nearby Hampi; a decorative reference to the historical greatness of Indian culture which was explicitly pointed out by the pageant's two hosts, American Richard Steinmetz and Indo-Canadian Ruby Bhatia.

In my reading, the 1996 pageant tried desperately to maximize its cultural credibility and "moral" reputation with its (specific) implied Indian audience. This endeavour was pursued by linking the representational practices of the genre discursively to "respectable" symbolic forms and expressions of Indian classical culture, India's rural, pre-modern traditions and the iconography of Brahminical Hinduism. The folkloric touch and localized ambience present in the Bangalore pageant were made the explicit point of a discursive emphasis and the focus of an imagined nostalgia, a "nostalgia for things that never were" (Appadurai 1996: 77) wrapped around the notion of "instant pleasure" (Ang 1996: 31).

Visual and conversational references to the heritage of Indian high culture – enabling the discursive reconstruction of Indian "tradition" within the field of modern, popular culture – thus became the underlying theme established throughout the show. Basically, the Bangalore pageant's projected image of present-day India reproduced a tourist brochure vision which excluded images of social hardship, political turmoil, corruption, communal riots and all the other "embarrassing" dimensions of the country's continued social reality. Instead, all the admiring attention was focused on India's ancient glory and its modern-day technological and cultural achievements. Thus, the pageant addressed the audience with a flattering image of India that corresponded – apart from its controversial, gendered representations – to a high degree with India's cultural nationalists' imagination of a politically and economically potent nation state, able to assert itself as a sovereign player, while protecting and projecting a hegemonic national culture. That is, the final Miss World show, as realized in concrete, allowed for some cognitive and emotional reconciliation, winning back potentially some of those viewers who had bought into the sceptical, anti-Indian interpretation of the event.

Negotiating the parameters of hybrid modernization

Importantly, the pageant's viewer reconciliation strategy was consequently enacted by Richard and Ruby in the form of a simple role play, in which Richard was acting as the open-minded Western observer and visitor, who looks with a certain ignorance and naivety but great sympathy at India and its "timeless" yet "modern" culture. Ruby, on the other hand, played the role of the inside-outside interpreter: the India-returned non-resident Indian who is able and willing to translate the essential truths and values of Indian/Hindu culture to Richard and through him to an ignorant but in principle not prejudiced global audience.

A prerequisite for Ruby's and through her for India's cultural recognition, projected by this enactment, was her cosmopolitan life and education. Hence, her fluent English, "modern" attitudes, knowledge of the world and other forms of cultural capital which combined with the attributes of Indian feminity were shown to earn her the respect of a Western and male-dominated audience. Thus her hybrid cultural identity enabled, metaphorically, India's cultural recognition on a global stage.

As the worldwide history of anti-pageant protests shows, it can be an arduous job to convince a critical audience/public that this kind of contest is more than a cheap exploitation of the participants' physical attractiveness. In general, respective attempts may fail or succeed with the ability of the hosts (and their scriptwriters) to handle the delicate balance between visual exhibition – the public parading of some dozen bare-legged girls – and respectful esteem, expressed in their conversational comments. Likewise, the Indian viewer had to be encouraged to recognize both the ambitious, sexually unmarked virgin daughter and the sexually attractive but virtuous bride, future wife and mother, in the modesty and desire invoking imagery of the beauty queen.

Through the hosts' enacted conversational comments the bodies of the contestants, potential objects of the male gaze and desire, became redefined as the receptacle of an order and a morality, imagined to be firmly embedded in the contestants' cultural identity. Essential Indianness in this chain of association was imagined in the female form, with the (Indian) beauty queen an avatar of *the* culture of her imagined nation. The feminine construct of Indian culture was thus projected as assertive against the cultural ignorance of those (viewers) who don't see more than the sexualized bodies which meet the eye. The Miss World pageant is perfectly Indian, the implicit message went; you may just not have known this (until you were told).

As Robertson (1995: 29) rightly points out, the reaffirmed national-local which is acknowledged in its continued significance is (subject to some qualifications) not so much asserted *against* globalizing trends; rather it seeks recognition and acknowledgement by the dominant, meaning Western Other, *within* a globalized "structure of common difference" (Wilk 1995). Cultural assertion, in the form of the feminine as "emblematic of a non-alienated, non-fragmented identity" (Felski 1995: 37), and India's political-economic-military assertion in the form of a modern, masculine Hindu culture capable of protecting *Bharat Mata* (Mother India) – if necessary by exercising the "nuclear option" – appear thus as two sides of the same desire to secure India a place among the leading cultures and nations in the world. Yet while the first is a seductive, promotional and courting form of competition, the latter nurtures an aggressive, confrontational and imposing approach. In the

Miss World pageant's discursive structure the imagined, identified with and asserted Indian community was hence not *patrios*, with its territory and its women's honour to be defended by the sword, but rather of a motherland delineated by a clear emphasis on the female aspects of its culture's ability to assert itself and its essential cultural core in a globalized world.

Concluding remarks

Globalization as unfolding in the context of India's post-Nehruvian economic liberalization has given rise to forms of symbolic reterritorialization which centre around middle-class women's imagined ideal roles. Contemporary Indian television actively negotiates and articulates these reimagined female roles. As the example of the Bangalore pageant shows, the delineation and symbolic assertion of the Indian nation is discursively constructed along particular gendered social codes. The *New Indian Woman*, as predominantly imagined by the majority of c&s channels, glossy print magazines and other new media, suggests an "optimistic" vision of "the global" as fully compatible with being (in essence) perfectly Indian.

The images offered by the new national-transnational media actively produce, project and communicate a particular dominant vision of the Indian nation based on an idealized depiction of the urban middle classes and new patterns of commodity consumption. This does not imply a view of the Indian television landscape as a monolith, speaking in one voice with no space for alternative visions. I maintain, however, that the logic of the market and the politics of consumerism do tend to privilege particular visions and undermine others in contemporary India. In the process of advancing a consumerist ethos, television reconfigures and reorients existing ideas in particular, highly decisive ways, and at the same time it privileges some ideas while submerging others, as has become most visible around the unfolding of the 1996 Miss World pageant.

Constitutive of the dominant utopia of India's global modernity is a desire to appropriate and take part in certain forms of Western otherness: the ability to travel and study abroad, to marry a non-resident Indian, to consume foreign goods and to appropriate other aspects of a Western lifestyle (Inden 1999: 56). Meanwhile, the new assertive middle classes' desire to exhibit their adoption of a new cultural standard, associated with the privileged consumption of the non-Indian, goes hand in hand with their longing for the preservation of an internationally strong and independent nation state and with a resurgent nostalgia for local and national traditions (Hogan 1999). The representational practice of the new electronic media may thus be understood to be oriented (in tendency) towards the mediated imagination of an unproblematic and pleasurable "Indian" way to take part in the practices of a globalized modernity, a vision that seeks to accommodate the new middle classes' ambiguous structure of aspirations within a singular narrative of consumption.

As I have sought to demonstrate, the 1996 Miss World pageant's "optimistic" view on India's ongoing glocalization was visualized in a juxtaposition of modernity and tradition that succeeded in reconciling parts of the sceptical and undecided Indian public, by allowing for a reading of the event in congruence with a non-chauvinistic, non-essentialized rearticulation of the self-assertive, national sentiments of India's new middle classes. This chapter has therewith hopefully provided some deeper understanding of how a particular media representation and event has become a critical site in which the politics of economic liberalization and modernization characterizing India's ongoing social transformation were successfully mediated through the delineation of a new, productive relationship between the national and the global.

Notes

1 With Aishwarya Rai (1994), Diana Hayden (1997), Yukta Mookhey (1999) and Priyanka Chopra (2000) winning the Miss World pageant, and Miss Universe titles for Sushmita Sen (1994) and Lara Dutta (2000), India's predominance in the 1990s was remarkable.

2 How serious these threats had to be taken became clear on 15 November 1996, eight days prior to the final contest, when Suresh Kumar, a 24-year-old male activist of the Marxist Democratic Youth Federation of India, committed self-immolation in a desperate attempt to mobilize additional public support against the show.

3 *The Hindu* (27 August 1996) reported that ABCL secured the rights for marketing, television and sponsorship for the next three years, and that it was going to invest IRS80 million (more than US$4 million). ABCL is reported to have lost US$1 million over the event, while numerous suppliers remained unpaid for years (*Screen India*, 7 July 2001).

4 Historically, the national (English-language) press, expressing the views and interests of the educated, non-vernacular elite within a deeply "split" Indian public (Sheth 1995), has played a central role in the articulation and negotiation of intra-elite conflicts and ideological contestations regarding the systemic relations between the postcolonial state and civil society. In the early 1990s, this "free" press was trying to come to terms with the challenges and prospects of a fast and profoundly changing public sphere and media environment, providing a major platform for general debates on Indian media policies and debates regarding Indianness and its bodily depiction (Butcher 1999: 191).

5 "Conservative" refers here less to a set of political ideas and priorities than to a "sociocultural" conservatism in terms of a fundamental rejection of reconfigurations in the cultural and social fabric of society and resistance to a change that is discursively constructed as in conflict with "tradition".

6 See Gosh (1999), Shah (1997) and Wildermuth (2001, 2005).

7 For a detailed account see Gosh (1999) and Wildermuth (2003, 2005).

8 *The Indian Express*, 31 October 1996.

9 "Unfavourable publicity" was the expression used by the Indian organizers of

the Miss World Contest pageant to circumscribe the surprising opposition leading up to the final event.

10 They were finally conducted under "gaol-like security". Police and private security forces had arranged, allegedly, for double-frisking and metal detectors, as well as sniffer dogs doing the rounds (*The Hindu*, 17 November 1996).

11 I have borrowed this concept, with modifications, from the work of Arjun Appadurai (1996).

References

Ang, I. (1996) *Living Room Wars: Rethinking Media Audiences for a Postmodern World*, London: Routledge.

Appadurai, A. (1996) *Modernity at Large*, Delhi: Oxford University Press.

Butcher, M. (1999) "Parallel Texts: The Body and Television in India", in C. Brosius and M. Butcher (eds) *Image Journeys: Audio-visual Media and Cultural Change in India*, New Delhi: Sage.

Chakravarty, R. and Gooptu, N. (2000) "Imagination: The Media, Nation and Politics in Contemporary India", in E. Hallam and B.V. Street (eds) *Cultural Encounters: Representing "Otherness"*, London: Routledge.

Felski, R. (1995) *The Gender of Modernity*, Cambridge, MA: Harvard University Press.

Gosh, S. (1999) "Feminists Engage With Censorship", in C. Brosius and M. Butcher (eds) *Image Journeys: Audio-visual Media and Cultural Change in India*, New Delhi: Sage.

Hogan, J. (1999) "The Construction of Gendered National Identities in the Television Advertisements of Japan and Australia", *Media, Culture and Society*, 21, 6: 743–58.

Inden, R. (1999) "Transnational Class, Erotic Arcadia and Commercial Utopia in Hindi Films", in C. Brosius and M. Butcher (eds) *Image Journeys: Audio-visual Media and Cultural Change in India*, New Delhi: Sage.

Malhotra, S. (1999) "The Privatization of Television in India: Implications of New Technologies for Gender, Nation and Culture", doctoral dissertation, University of New Mexico.

Robertson, R. (1995) "Glocalization: Time-space and Homogeneity-heterogeneity", in M. Featherstone, S. Lash and R. Robertson (eds) *Global Modernities*, London: Sage.

Shah, A. (1997) *Hype, Hypocrisy and Television in Urban India*, New Delhi: Vikas.

Sheth, D.L. (1995) "The Great Language Debate: Politics of Metropolitan versus Vernacular India", in U. Baxi and B. Parekh (eds) *Crisis and Change in Contemporary India*, New Delhi: Sage.

Sinha, N. (1998) "Doordarshan, Public Service Broadcasting and the Impact of Globalization: A Short History", in M.E. Price and S.G. Verhulst (eds) *Broadcasting Reform in India*, Delhi: Oxford University Press.

Wildermuth, N. (2001) "Negotiating a Glocalised Modernity: Images of the 'New' Indian Woman on Satellite Television", in T. Tufte and G. Stald (eds) *Global Encounters – Media and Cultural Transformation*, Luton: University of Luton Press.

—— (2003) "Miss World Going 'Deshi' ", in S. Hjarvard (ed.) *Media in Globalized Society,* Copenhagen: Museum Tusculanum.

—— (2005) "A Cultural Economy of Satellite Television in India", Ph.D. dissertation, University of Copenhagen.

Wilk, R. (1995) "Learning to be Local in Belize: Global System of Common Difference", in D. Müller (ed.) *Worlds Apart*, London: Routledge.

12

MEDIA EVENT CULTURE AND LIFESTYLE MANAGEMENT

Observations on the influence of media events on everyday culture

Udo Göttlich

> We should look not for the components of a product but for the
> conditions of a practice.
>
> (R. Williams, *Culture*, 1981)

Introduction

The influence of so-called "media events" on our present media culture reveals a strong relation with new marketing strategies over the past two decades. Television, often seen as evasion from daily routines, turns out to use more and more aspects of daily life for programming as well as for the development of new television formats. The question of what consequences this has for television and programming itself as well as for our understanding of everyday life is still open. What can be shown and analyzed at this point are the different phases through which the new marketing strategies gain their power on programming by producing media events. The thesis is that as an integral whole, the strategies discussed have a determining influence on the creation of *media events* as *produced realities*. This means that such *events* play a special role in *the dramatization of everyday life*. From this point of view I will discuss how changes in everyday life within media culture are related to media events.

Over the past decade we have investigated the special cultural features connected with the production of programs like the German soap operas, *Big Brother* or casting shows that may be grouped under the heading of *factual entertainment formats* (cf. Brunsdon et al. 2001).[1] A substantial part of the functions of these programs cannot be viewed separately from the strategic interests of media providers, who use these formats to fulfill the requirements of marketing. The marketing and merchandising strategies which are becoming more and more important in view of the competition between public and private channels include a great many new forms of targeting different audience groups and advertising tactics, and it is no accident that in German television daily soaps became the spearhead of experimentation in the early 1990s before the factual entertainment formats like *Big Brother* or casting shows like *Deutschland sucht den Superstar* (*"DSDS"*) or *Germany's Next Topmodel* took over this role. Comparable examples may be discussed for British television when we consider the term "factual entertainment" that is used to point to a special development in the early years of the new century, when shows like *The Naked Chef* or *Idols* came out. The examples discussed here concentrate on the developments in German television.

In the first part of the chapter I focus on different strategies which can be identified behind the creation of an *additional popular framework of events* – one that loosens up the boundaries between formats – and in different *aspects of lifestyle staging*. The chapter discusses the different phases in German television, starting with the German daily soaps using strategies of "Kult-Marketing," then the role of *Big Brother* in strengthening such event strategies in programming, and currently *DSDS* as the latest phase in building not only a fan-culture but also an event-culture. It is here where we must pose questions about how an event-culture and everyday life affect one another. One question concerns the way in which new forms of media consumption depend on the new TV formats. A second question concerns the way in which the new forms of media consumption lead to different forms of lifestyle management and are related to media events.

In the second part of the chapter I ask about the role and function of media events as *produced realities* in our media culture from a sociological point of view. Going back to Anthony Giddens' (1991) notion of "life politics" and Raymond Williams' (1989) investigation of "drama in a dramatized society" I will show that different media events are not only the products of marketing-related strategies but also expressions of changed cultural relations. From this point of view I will ask if the term "event" is appropriate to understand current changes in media culture.

Societal change – media change: new challenges for television production

"You have 15 seconds to impress me!"

With this phrase the actual situation confronting television can be easily grasped. The "Kampf um Aufmerksamkeit" (struggle for attentiveness) (Franck 1998) is the main reason for ongoing developments within pro-gramming that changed television over the past 20 years in Germany and in other European countries as well. There are different forms of reaction to these changes and we all know some of them quite well. Over the past decade different marketing strategies and event strategies may be seen as the most successful ways to cope with audience fragmentation. One aim was to produce program highlights not only to attract the audience but also to get hold of the younger target groups (between the ages of 14 and 29) that are relevant for advertisement revenues. But does the formula "Kampf um Aufmerksamkeit" explain why events have become successful or why we now confront the role of events within television as well as within media culture? This seems to be too easy a way to resolve the point but within television things are indeed sometimes that easy.

Media change and societal change are complementary processes and the structure of each may be subdivided into stages of development where the changes are influenced by technological, economic, political, legal, social and cultural conditions (cf. Bruns et al. 1996). The changes in television which may be observed on the level of programming since the 1990s are accompanied by a series of processes which are not only the result of the development of a public and commercial broadcasting system, but are accompanied in the social and cultural domain by the development known as *individualization* (cf. Beck 1997).

To put it in a nutshell: *individualization* as one aspect of cultural change forms the counterpart to marketing strategies on the other side; both form the prerequisite for the success of "produced media realities," i.e., media events. In this understanding, television may be determined as the "object and carrier of social change." The following processes may be identified as a group of factors which led to a change in the production of television entertainment (and other genres) in German as well as in European television and that have their influence on our understanding of the role of "events" in media culture:

1 *On the media and program levels* we find as a result of the competition between public and commercial broadcasters for market shares and audience ratings a convergence. The former differences between the two types of broadcasting do not lead to a persistence of their program and marketing forms. On the contrary, as the program strategies of public and commercial broadcasters show, we find a convergence in addressing audiences by nearly the same strategies and formats.

2 *On the sociocultural level* one reason for this development may be found in the disintegration of traditional ties, values and orientations in the course of individualization that lead to sameness in media use. As a reaction to these changes, television in the 1990s, with the target group of a young audience in mind, already aimed – by using different marketing strategies to create "events" – at:

- building a regular audience, and together with this
- organizing the audience flow
- cultivating a channel image by broadcasting certain product families, i.e., formats and genres, as anchors for the different levels of audience, and

174

- testing new advertising strategies and concepts, which went far beyond the soaps and led to the creation of additional popular events as "produced realities."

What is of interest about the daily soaps that were on German screens in the 1990s is not only that they were all German in-house productions. More interesting is that these soaps started to build different music events, so that the audience was attracted by different products – from music CDs to fan-magazines as well as T-shirts, towels and bed linen – that were linked with the soap. This was the first step toward creating a reality that not only loosened up the borders of the traditional soap opera format but also thereby followed new ways to connect itself with the everyday life of the young audience. The music stars were already known by video clips on VIVA.[2] Their appearance on soaps changed the look of the soaps – something that we normally think of as programs for housewives now drew on images from adolescent rather than middle-aged culture.

One may therefore conclude that the media change which can be observed at present is not only a consequence of the restructuring of industry and the working world, of markets, technologies and resources, but also of media organizations searching for ever new formats that affect the social context of the media user. This program offensive has not ended; instead, it has shifted to the introduction of ever new formats that have a connection with the soap opera form when we consider how they dramatize the everyday.

Accordingly, we must take a closer look at the different phases of television change over the past 20 years to see how marketing began to structure the formats as well as the program flow and how events have become the most striking outcome of this development, a development that has led to produced realities as one form assumed by events within television. This form goes back to the evolution of the so-called reality television programs that play a special role in building media events (cf. Bondebjerg 1996, 2002; Göttlich 2004).

Daily soaps and "Kult-Marketing"

As the German daily soaps are directed at a target group different from those of the American or British soaps, in the German context one can speak more precisely of youth and lifestyle marketing rather than generally of marketing or program marketing. Where the young audience is concerned, marketing since the 1990s was faced with a new challenge. This was met by those responsible with a combination of aspects of "Kult-Marketing," "culture marketing" and "Erlebnis-Marketing" (cf. Göttlich and Nieland 2002).

The concept of "Kult-Marketing" (cult marketing) was first described by Bolz and Bosshart in the early 1990s as the reaction of the advertising and marketing industries and the producers of consumer goods to market contingencies. By *reverting to rituals* and *trends* an attempt is made to create and to reinforce "cults" in order to offer structuring and fascinating opportunities to consume (Bolz and Bosshart 1995: 74ff.). The development of events seems to be one strategy that could be easily applied to marketing different products. "Kult-Marketing" itself covers a variety of strategies that reach from image transfer of different brands to "event-marketing" as a special form of communication with consumers.

Bolz and Bosshart use the term "cult" because it points at the structuring function in social and cultural orientation which was previously determined by variables of social structure such as age, class, status and profession. The connection with advertising, marketing and merchandising strategies (and nowadays with factual entertainment formats) is that television with all its different genres conveys symbolic worlds and that the lifestyle aspects associated with "cults" in popular culture probably have an ordering nature for the viewer that replaces the older, status- and class-related forms. At the very least, television, with its genres promoting fashions, styles, trends and symbols, opens a window on to youth and everyday culture. Nowadays, the so-called factual entertainment formats make use of this mechanism and begin to play their own role in the process of "eventization."

"Culture marketing" as one strategy within Kult-Marketing has greater relevance for most companies due to its clearer connotations. The main thrust of culture marketing is to relate socially significant cultural events to the aims of companies. The "image transfer of the cultural event to the company and its sectors, brands and products" increases its degree of recognition, share of the market and competitive advantages (Graf 1995: 22). Image transfer refers here to a strategy that uses the name or image of an existing brand to market new products under this heading.

The third form of marketing is "Erlebnis-Marketing," which, in reaction to social change, is "the creation of sensuous consumer experiences which are embedded in the emotions of the consumers and influence their values, lifestyles and attitudes" (Weinberg 1992). The main categories are the product-specific "Erlebnis value" and the "Erlebnis transfer" associated with it. *"Lifestyle symbols"* are used to direct *"Erlebnistransfer"* at the consumer and this form can be integrated into events as well. The decisive factor for this form of marketing is the individualization of consumption, requiring strategies to emphasize individuality through "Erlebnis values" such as youthfulness to achieve differentiation from competitive products. The event then is an opportunity to bind together the different groups or different interests.

According to our observations, different *factual entertainment formats* use combinations of these three marketing forms. The result is the development of a new strategy, mainly directed at younger audiences, of creating, introducing and using an additional framework of popular events that may be understood as "produced realities" leading to different forms of lifestyle management (cf. Göttlich and Nieland 2002).

From this point of view, "events" of this new kind are nothing else than "produced realities," playing their role in the dramatization of everyday life. The aim of the different strategies is to link the channel image and the program as closely as possible with various products and product-related events. This finds expression in: on-air and off-air promotion, targeting of different audience groups, publication of fan magazines, creation of fan clubs and the development and marketing of numerous merchandising products and special events. For this context we have used "Kult-Marketing" as an umbrella term, as here the aim is to market popular products and turn the purchasing of them into a "cult." The exhibition of lifestyle settings makes an input through the complex development of marketing scenes.

When events are understood as produced realities we have to deal with a differentiation of events as the result of media change. Events may be seen – as by Dayan and Katz – as real-life situations like weddings or funerals or sport- and music-related events or political speeches or demonstrations that are broadcast to mass audiences all over the world. But events do not always need such "real" situations as the starting point from which the ritual function in structuring everyday life emerges. As the result of media change, such "situations" can be produced by the media industries themselves and these situations can become as real – and ritualistic – as the events Dayan and Katz have in mind. One may think of virtualization, but it is more than that. It is the creation of reality by events that are used by the cultural industries to bind audiences with brands that are the outcome of different strategies which industries produce to gain market shares for their channels. In this process the border between real life and entertainment loosens up. As one result, this development changes events in the traditional sense of Dayan and Katz too, because these events also start to use entertainment and marketing strategies to gain a greater market share and audience ratings.

Creation of an additional framework of popular events

The consequences may largely be shown through a closer look at developments in music television. Most frequently event marketing in the aforementioned sense resorts to the symbols and lifestyles of popular music, although even for professionals an enormous variety of styles and scene codes exists so that events facilitate in this field a structuring and ritualistic function. And there seem to be no exceptions, because the so-called underground or independent music scene is being instrumentalized itself more and more rapidly by the marketing and entertainment industry in staging different events. This process is being accompanied and driven by innumerable music magazines for various music trends, youth and lifestyle magazines, the constant diversification of radio stations, numerous music programs on television and television music channels such as MTV and VIVA/VIVA2, as well as by the Internet. MTV in particular is considered to have sparked off the so-called clip culture which is regarded as a formative influence in the media socialization of young viewers. This clip culture was also immediately used in advertising and in daily soaps. In connection with this, pop stars were given the opportunity of guest appearances in daily soaps; later on, with the new formats like *Idols* and *Popstars* – and in Germany *DSDS* – people participate in castings and dream of their pop careers.

The effects of the forms of presentation mentioned here are as obvious as they are deliberate. Reality and fiction intermix in a new way. This development suggests not only that the success of certain music groups increases the success of the series, soaps or films, but also that the trend groups and the new formats acquire a structuring function when they become fixed points of reference for everyday life and leisure activities. The interlinking between music scenes and film/television leads to the use and creation of an additional popular framework of events. These offer further potential for adherence in the form of lifestyle management. At the turn of the century, these strategies were aggressively used by *Big Brother* and further developed by *DSDS* on the German screen. But the strategies derive from the 1990s and have experience in soap opera production and marketing as their background (cf. Göttlich 2004).

The reason for speaking of "Kult-Marketing" and not just marketing is above all the fact that through the different formats discussed above an additional popular framework of events is created, making it possible to stage performances and events, and to market music above and beyond the actual screening of programs and thereby to form ties with a particular target group through a wide range of products, brands and lifestyle symbols.

In addition, the interrelation between formats and the music scene serves another important aim. Most of the formats *are standardized in structure* and the only way the programs of one channel can be clearly distinguished in the long run from the programs of another channel in this sector is if the more or less identical ways of dramatization can be packaged differently. Program design, served by the music groups, offers an opportunity for differentiation via packaging. At the same time the music groups guarantee further ways of promoting the formats, ways that are independent of regular broadcast episodes and that exist within the framework of additional popular-culture events.

Four phases of implementing marketing strategies

To sum up, it can be asserted that the makers of such formats pursue the following aims which considerably affect the production of new genres and formats:

- picking up (music) trends
- presenting (music) products
- rationalizing the development of characters
- creating high recognition and identification values for individual characters.

Over the past decade we can make out four phases that affect as well as delimit present developments (cf. Göttlich and Nieland 2002). The first and longest phase started in the early 1990s and lasted until 2000. It itself can be subdivided into four parts. Against the backdrop of the debate on quality in television programming between public-service and private channels, the production of soap operas became an approach to sustaining quality and to promoting the strength of particular formats and programs.

To do this, special events were created to present soap stars to younger audiences on new stages such as talk shows and in music television as well as in radio talks. This process was amplified when music channels themselves cast soap actors as hosts. The same is true of game shows where former soap actors now serve as hosts. A third aspect is manifest with soap opera guest appearances by prominent actors as well as by VJs and DJs; the latter is a special sign of how in touch the production is with youth culture. At a fourth stage the soaps themselves function as a platform to assist the music careers of some of their actors. Soap actors and entire productions participate in this process, as with the "Love Parade."[3] It is with this step that the media marketing and the branding of a production became one of the key instruments in eventization (cf. Karstens and Schütte 1999; Siegert 2001).

The second phase represents the expansion of "Kult-Marketing" strategies. It is no accident that the format *Big Brother* served as its bearer (around 2000). Even after most of the former *Big Brother* housemates had ended their music careers, some of them persisted in television as hosts of game shows. But it is here that we should not understand the terms "career" and "stars" in terms of their usual denotations. The development shows how we are presented with part-time "stars," cult objects for cults induced by marketing efforts against the backdrop of the struggle for attention.

The third phase is represented by the development of formats that surround the show *Big Brother* to broaden audience share. So we have Saturday evening shows as well as daily shows on RTL and its little sister channel RTL II. It is in this phase that channels start to develop casting shows. The format *Teen Stars* on RTL II is one example, where a young singer is the host for a casting show of this sort, in which kids act as singers or dancers.

The fourth phase, with shows like *DSDS*, has its forerunner in American television. The show *Becoming* on MTV was the first program that started as a music casting show in search of young talent. Here "Kult-Marketing" cumulated in near-industrialization of the search for talent, with ever new casting shows. Financial risk for the producers is not particularly great, because with different strategies like branding of shows, developing a channel image, securing the audience stream or selling merchandise they make earnings in one way or another.

The most effective feature of the show in terms of gaining audience and marketing share is that it is suitable for a Saturday evening. The show is the sought-after platform from which the "struggle for attentiveness" can be directed, with different marketing strategies on different stages and phases, while the show develops over weeks and comes to an end with a grand finale.

Marketing the soap aesthetic as a lifestyle option

Picking up, presenting and reinforcing trends of youth culture is, however, not found only with regard to pop music on the German screen. The formats are also trend amplifiers for fashion and style from clothing to furnishings, accessories, hairstyles and so on. This results in direct references to everyday life that are, right from the start, not related to any particular class or lifestyle and that offer the possibility of combinations, thus complying with the *bricolage* attitude of the young cultural scene. The effect of media events is not limited to messages via these processes. Media events also play the role of an *amplifier* of cultural change by introducing forms of lifestyle management.

An explanation for the role of lifestyle presentation, or the presentation of lifestyle semantics within such events is provided by Anthony Giddens in his numerous investigations of high modernity. According to Giddens, the detraditionalizations which may be observed result in the need of each and every individual for "life politics" (1991: 214). Processes of identity-forming are no longer based on orientation toward traditions external to the individual but more and more on self-reflexive decisions. Institutions and traditions offering security are being replaced by *life politics* (*Selbstkultur*). This development undermines the classic patterns of behavior and of stratification, and draws from the reservoir of popular culture symbols.

Thus new aspirations and identities are developed. The increasing orientation toward lifestyle has the effect that "culture and symbolic worlds are used more strongly as a resource" (Michailow 1994: 119). This explains the role of the media in cultural orientation and in the preference for lifestyle patterns and lifestyle semantics over traditional norms. An increase in differentiation results through media events and through event-related formats. After all, it is not by accident that "a supply industry develops which not only produces these articles and goods indicating lifestyle and provides services to support the lifestyle, but also delivers a whole *structure of contexts for use and connecting patterns* which causes the lifestyle to boom" (Michailow 1994: 121). The lifestyle semantics in factual entertainment formats can be understood, taking a sociological view of their consequences, as a response to increased demand for promotion of a public image and to subsequent changes in public images.

Raymond Williams' concept of *drama in a dramatized society* (1989) also allows an understanding of the ongoing process of eventization when he draws on *conventions in performance that can lead to the "dramatisation of consciousness itself"* (Williams 1989: 9) and so can become a *"basic need"* (Williams 1989: 5). Williams continues as follows:

> The specific conventions of this particular dramatisation . . . are not abstract. They are profoundly worked and reworked in our actual living relationships. They are our way of seeing and knowing, which every day we put into practice, and while the conventions hold, while the relationships hold, most practice confirms them.
>
> (Williams 1989: 10)

Media events related to fictional genres on television can form a background for orientation by demonstrating lifestyle patterns. Thus lifestyles not also form new bonds but answer to new needs that particularly derive from media events. If a particular lifestyle is associated with additional distinction, social acceptance and a feeling of satisfaction, the demand for this lifestyle pattern increases and media events can function as one carrier. This standpoint permits one to observe how the so-called factual entertainment formats not only offer an almost perfect background for the presentation of new brands, fashions, trends and music *but also lead to an increase in dramatization of the everyday.* This means that the older perspective on media events as rituals is transformed into an understanding of media events as produced realities. These produced realities are more than sources from which the everyday takes examples of fashion and lifestyle. They are also stagings of the everyday in which people perform rituals and where forms of lifestyle management are exhibited. Evidently the levels of daily life and of "Erlebnis" (experience) are entering into a new relationship with these formats. The formats thus amplify a commodification of everyday culture but on the other hand they foster processes of *"doing culture"* (Hörning and Reuter 2004).

To ask such questions means to analyze marketing in its relation to the performances and stagings from which new ways of "doing culture" can derive. In analyzing such questions, it is also necessary to relate questions of social constructivism at the macro-level to questions of cultural practices at the micro-level. In looking at the recent development and proliferation of media events we can obtain an understanding of what drama in a dramatized society is actually about.

Notes

1 The research was conducted together with Jörg-Uwe Nieland at the Rhine-Ruhr-Institute for Social Research at the University Duisburg-Essen in the years 1996 to 2002. Our project took part within the dedicated research section on theatricality,

funded by the German Research Council. Many thanks to Alex S. Knisely for his help in translating the text.
2 VIVA is a German music TV channel that applies a counter-strategy with MTV in broadcasting German music groups and music productions.
3 The "Love Parade" is a techno event that started in Berlin in the early 1990s and took place there every year on one summer day. Nowadays the "Love Parade" takes place in the cities of the Ruhr Area; participating cities have been Essen and Dortmund.

References

Beck, U. (1997) "Die uneindeutige Sozialstruktur. Was heißt Armut, was Reichtum in der 'Selbst-Kultur' ", in U. Beck and P. Sopp (eds) *Individualisierung und Integration,* Opladen: Westdeutscher Verlag, 183–97.

Boltz, D.-M. (1994) *Konstruktion von Erlebniswelten. Kommunikations- und Marketingstrategien bei Camel und Greenpeace,* Berlin: Vistas.

Bolz, N. and Bosshart, D. (1995) *Kult-Marketing. Die neuen Götter des Marktes,* Düsseldorf: Econ.

Bondebjerg, I. (1996) "Public Discourse/Private Fascination: Hybridisation in 'True-Life-Story' Genres", *Media, Culture and Society,* 18, 1: 27–45.

—— (2002) "The Mediation of Every Day Life. Genre, Discourse and Spectacle in Reality TV", in A. Jerslev (ed.) *Realism and "Reality" in Film and Media. Northern Lights Film and Media Studies Yearbook 2002,* Copenhagen: Museum Tusculanum Press, 159–92.

Bruns, T., Marcinkowski, F., Nieland, J.-U., Ruhrmann, G. and Schierl, T. (1996) "Das analytische Modell", in H. Schatz (ed.) *Fernsehen als Objekt und Moment des sozialen Wandels,* Opladen: Westdeutscher Verlag, 19–74.

Brunsdon, C., Johnson, C., Moseley, R. and Wheatley, H. (2001) "Factual Entertainment on British Television. The Midlands TV Research Group's '8–9 Project' ", *European Journal of Cultural Studies,* 4, 1: 29–62.

Deese, U., Hillenbach, P.E., Kaiser, D. and Michatsch, C. (eds) (1995) *Jugendmarketing. Das wahre Leben in den Szenen der Neunziger,* Düsseldorf: Metropolitan Verlag.

Franck, G. (1998) *Ökonomie der Aufmerksamkeit,* München: Hanser.

Gerken, G. and Merks, M.J. (eds) (1996) *Szenen statt Zielgruppen. Vom Produkt zum Kult. Die Praxis der Interfusion,* Frankfurt am Main: Deutscher Fachverlag.

Giddens, A. (1991) *Modernity and Self-identity,* Cambridge: Polity Press.

Göttlich, U. (2004) "Produzierte Wirklichkeiten. Zur Entwicklung der Fernsehproduktion am Beispiel von Factual Entertainment Angeboten", in M. Friedrichsen and U. Göttlich (eds) *Diversifikation in der Unterhaltungsproduktion,* Köln: Herbert v. Halem, 124–41.

—— (2005) "Öffentlichkeitswandel, Individualisierung und Alltagsdramatisierung. Aspekte der Theatralität von Fernsehkommunikation im Mediatisierungsprozeß", in E. Fischer-Lichte et al. (eds) *Diskurse des Theatralen,* Tübingen: Francke, 291–309.

—— (2006) "Reproduktion des Alltags? Factual Entertainment als Bühne kultureller Performanz: Zur Durchdringung von kultureller Performanz und sozialer Praxis", in U. Rao (ed.) *Kulturelle Verwandlungen. Die Gestaltung sozialer Welten in der Performanz,* Frankfurt am Main: Lang, 217–31.

Göttlich, U. and Nieland, J.-U. (1997) "Politischer Diskurs als Unterhaltung? Präsentationslogiken von Daily Soaps als Wegweiser", in H. Schatz, O. Jarren and B. Knaup (eds) *Machtkonzentration in der Multimediagesellschaft? Beiträge zu einer Neubestimmung des Verhältnisses von politischer und medialer Macht*, Opladen: Westdeutscher Verlag, 188–200.

—— (1998a) Daily Soap Operas: "Zur Theatralität des Alltäglichen", in H. Willems and M. Jurga (eds) *Die Inszenierungsgesellschaft*, Opladen: Westdeutscher Verlag, 417–34.

—— (1998b) "Daily Soaps als Umfeld von Marken, Moden und Trends. Von Seifenopern zu Lifestyle-Inszenierungen", in M. Jäckel (ed.) *Die umworbene Gesellschaft*, Opladen: Westdeutscher Verlag, 179–208.

—— (2002) "Kult-Inszenierungen und Vermarktungsstrategien im Kontext von Endlosserien und Musiksendungen: Grenzen und Perspektiven", in H. Willems (ed.) Die *Gesellschaft der Werbung. Kontexte und Texte. Produktionen und Rezeptionen. Entwicklungen und Perspektiven,* Wiesbaden: Westdeutscher Verlag, 549–64.

Graf, C. (1995) *Kulturmarketing. Open Air und Populaire Musik*, Wiesbaden: DUV.

Hörning, K.H. and Reuter, J. (eds) (2004) *Doing Culture. Neue Positionen zum Verhältnis von Kultur und sozialer Praxis*, Bielefeld: Transcript.

Jäckel, M. (1996) *Wahlfreiheit in der Fernsehnutzung. Eine soziologische Analyse zur Individualisierung der Massenkommunikation*, Opladen: Westdeutscher Verlag.

Karstens, E. and Schütte, J. (1999) *Firma Fernsehen. Wie TV-Sender arbeiten. Alles über Politik, Recht, Organisation, Markt, Werbung, Programm und Produktion*, Reinbek: Rowohlt.

Michailow, M. (1994) "Lebensstilsemantik. Soziale Ungleichheit und Formationsbildung in der Kulturgesellschaft", in I. Mörth and G. Fröhlich (eds) *Das symbolische Kapital der Lebensstile*, Frankfurt am Main: Campus, 107–29.

Schatz, H. (ed.) (1996) *Fernsehen als Objekt und Moment des sozialen Wandels. Faktoren und Folgen der aktuellen Veränderungen des Fernsehens*, Opladen: Westdeutscher Verlag.

Siegert, G. (2001) *Medien, Marken, Management. Relevanz, Spezifika und Implikationen einer medienökonomischen Profilierungsstrategie*, München: Fischer.

Weinberg, P. (1992) *Erlebnismarketing*, München: Vahlen.

Williams, R. (1981) *Culture*, Glasgow: Fontana.

—— (1989) "Drama in a Dramatised Society", in A. O'Connor (ed.) *Raymond Williams on Television. Selected Writings*, New York: Blackwell, 3–13. Translated into German as: Williams, R. (1998) "Drama in der dramatisierten Gesellschaft", in U. Göttlich, J.-U. Nieland and H. Schatz (eds) *Kommunikation im Wandel. Zur Theatralität der Medien,* Köln: Herbert v. Halem, 238–60.

Part V

MEDIA EVENTS AND GLOBAL POLITICS

13

IN PURSUIT OF A GLOBAL IMAGE

Media events as political communication

Nancy K. Rivenburgh

Introduction

Advances in information technology have dramatically altered the conduct of international relations. Images and information now move effortlessly through interconnected media networks. Television saturation of the globe is near complete. Internet use is rapidly increasing. This global communications infrastructure allows political actors to speak past national governments directly to world publics. In turn, world public opinion has become a more significant factor in foreign policy planning, putting a premium on a nation's ability to proactively manage its image on a world stage.

In light of this, efforts at political communication by governments have evolved well beyond international radio broadcasting and cultural exchanges aimed at target audiences. Contemporary government public diplomacy, or image management efforts, increasingly resembles corporate public relations or global branding campaigns. Governments employ media-sophisticated strategies aimed at influencing world public opinion in order to influence foreign governments, tourism, and corporate investment (Signitzer and Coombs 1992). Government websites and email distribution lists are flourishing. Most governments hire public relations firms to help manage, and monitor, their ongoing international media presence (Manheim 1994). And, increasingly, nations and cities attempt the more "spectacular" image strategy of hosting global media events (GMEs), such as the Olympic Games, UN Summits, World Cup Soccer, Miss World Beauty Pageants, and other high-profile events in order to attract favourable, and saturated, media and public attention. As Kunczik (2003: 120) puts it, government "statecraft [has] become stagecraft".

There are many reasons why cities and nations compete vigorously to host GMEs. These include political (promote an ideology, establish diplomatic ties, foster domestic unity), economic (enhance foreign investment, tourism or trade, promote an image of "modernity", improve local infrastructure), cultural (enhance intercultural understanding, promote an identity, challenge stereotypes) and altruistic (promote peace or a global cause). Whatever mix of reasons motivate a prospective host, common to all bids is a belief that the hosting of a GME will *enhance or change* an international image by positively associating the host city or country with: particular values (e.g. peace, cooperation, human rights); development or modernization; a role (e.g. mediator, peacemaker, leader); or a topic (e.g. environment, human rights).

Yet the hosting of a mega-event is, in fact, a high-stakes gamble. While the "world is watching" a host can succeed or fail in an equally spectacular way, and governments can become politically and economically vulnerable if the event fails. In fact, from a risk/reward perspective the choice to host a GME as a global image strategy is a curious one. GMEs are extremely expensive endeavours in terms of providing adequate infrastructure, technology, security, and promotion, as well as ensuring the well-being of tens of thousands of participants, spectators, volunteers, officials, media, and local citizens during the event. The threat of terrorism is ever present. GMEs always attract a range of interest groups seeking to promote and protest their causes. Planning conflicts among local, regional, national, and international organizations invariably arise. GME hosts cannot control the actions of participants or spectators. Perhaps most unnerving is that a host cannot control the group it depends on the most for image success: the 8,000 to 15,000 international media personnel that arrive to cover a typical UN Summit or Olympic Games.

Certainly GME hosts can influence the media by monitoring security clearances and providing event information, but the media ultimately construct the event, and the host image, for global audiences. Media outlets edit the international signal (visuals and natural sound provided by the host broadcaster); they add visuals; they overlay commentary; they interpret and evaluate what they see according to their own agenda – which may or may not coincide with the host image agenda. As stated by Dayan and Katz (1995: 177) and Katz et al. (1984: 135), the media are "active negotiators" of the event and "must decide . . . whether to accept the definition of the event provided by the organizers".

What makes the difference in terms of how a host city or nation is portrayed in international media? How might one predict the potential effectiveness of hosting a GME as a political communication strategy? More practically, how might host cities and nations better achieve a more positive global image by hosting a GME? To answer these questions this chapter reviews research conducted on global media events over a 20-year period for insights into the key factors that determine whether a GME host will meet its global image goals in the face of a largely independent, international media. What emerges from this meta-analysis is the identification of five critical variables consistently found to make a difference in the visibility, valence and quality of the host image in international media. It is hoped that the identification of these variables provides some theoretical insights into the study not only of GMEs as strategic political communication, but more broadly into the media's role in international relations.

Background

The results of this study are foreshadowed by key research findings in two related areas of international political communication scholarship: (1) strategic image management, and (2) influences on global news content. These are briefly reviewed below.

Strategic image management

Image politics or "soft power" – the ability to project a prestigious or powerful image – has become as vital to a nation's well-being and foreign policy arsenal as economic or military strength (Ebo 1997; Kunczik 2003; Nye 2004). From a strategic perspective, research in international political communication has identified several considerations relevant to nations who would seek to influence their "soft power" by hosting a GME.

Optimal path for image enhancement

Manheim (1994: 131–5) investigated the effectiveness of governments that hire public relations firms to promote a favourable image in international media. His results reveal that, strategically, governments need to follow an optimal "path" in order to achieve a more favourable and visible news presence on a world stage. In his model, countries are categorized on axes of high to low visibility and negative to positive image valence in international news. Assuming that all countries desire a high-visibility, positive world image, Manheim argues that a country with primarily negative valence in international news cannot successfully move directly to a high-visibility, positive valence image. Instead, that government must first lower visibility if necessary, then use both time and positive actions to shift global perceptions from negative to positive before attempting to increase its positive visibility on a world stage.

Manheim's model is relevant because GMEs are a high-visibility image-enhancement strategy. Deutsch and Merritt (1965: 135–6) distinguish between "cumulative" and "spectacular" events where spectacular events are of high profile and impact, but short duration and cumulative events are "myriad lesser events" spread over many years. So, in the case of a high news visibility negatively perceived country, hosting a high-profile GME may not be the best image management decision (e.g. Atlanta USA Olympics). Nations with low visibility and negative or positive valence must still follow the same "path". However, here the hosting of a GME may prove helpful to a city or nation's image (e.g. Olympics Games in Lillehammer, Sydney; UN meetings in Trinidad).

The rhetoric must reflect reality

Jervis (1970: 18) argues that a nation's projected image must correspond with its national behaviour in order to be effective in international politics. He refers to the role of "signals", defined as statements or actions sent forth in an effort to influence others' image of the sender. For example, the signal might be hosting a UN summit on human rights in order to be seen as a global leader in this area. However, receivers of the signal – other governments, foreign publics, and international media – will remain sceptical of this "leadership" image until there is adequate supporting evidence. Along these lines, Kunczik (2003) refers to "structural" image management aimed at correcting false images and "manipulative" image management that attempts to create positive images that don't reflect reality. In either case, strategies where the signals or rhetoric don't reflect reality – or where the public relations effort is too overt – tend to backfire under the scrutiny of global media.

The "Menace of Unreality": images out of control

Finally, Tehranian (1984: 59) describes how, in the potent mix of rapid technology, intra-media sourcing patterns and a "world that is watching", events can quickly "snowball" out of control for a nation or government. Drawing on Daniel J. Boorstin, Tehranian refers to this phenomenon as the "menace of unreality" where media-constructed imagery becomes so vivid or skewed as to create a new political reality that governments must deal with. The case of the Mohammed cartoon competition in Denmark – with global media scrutiny triggering a series of international riots – would be an example of this snowball phenomenon.

The media agenda

The scholarship in political communication readily refers to the "functional dependency" or symbiotic relationship between governments and the mass media as an inherently uneasy relationship (i.e. where media are not govern-ment owned) (Kunczik 2003: 119). Similarly, in the context of GMEs, media thrive on an event planned with them in mind, yet bring to it an agenda that frequently diverges from that of the host.

The concentric rings of influence

Shoemaker and Reese (1996) offer an excellent model of the layers of influence that compose the media agenda. Conceptualized as a series of concentric circles, they identify – in order of degree – the following types of influence on news content: *Individual* journalists who bring personal knowledge, experience, beliefs and ambitions to their work. *Media routines* that value efficiency, consistency, and balance and support professional norms and practices such as the "beat" system, formula stories, factory news production, reliance on stereotypes, and conflict (two-sides) reporting. *Organizational* influences such as the need for profits in a commercial media environment, resulting in content decisions based on minimizing cost while maximizing audience appeal. *Extramedia* influences which refer to both the inputs (e.g. public relations materials) and pressures from external actors such as the government, corporations and the public. *Ideological* influences which refer to mainstream media's largely unconscious way of seeing, interpreting and supporting the status quo in society based on a "common-sense" perspective of political and economic ideology.

Shoemaker and Reese's model explains much about media coverage of GMEs. What is missing, according to Clausen (2003), is the influence of media as a national and cultural actor. Based on her analysis of Japanese and Danish coverage of the UN conference on women, Clausen argues that the processes of "domestication" are a key attribute at all levels of global news production. She cites an abundance of research confirming that, despite the use of common news formats, national media outlets routinely adapt content to enhance the appeal to, understanding and identity of their national audiences (cf. Gurevitch et al. 1991; Rivenburgh 2000).

Media routines surrounding special events

Dayan and Katz (1995) have written at length about the "specialness" of media events in terms of how they are covered, particularly by broadcast media. They characterize media events as "interruptions" and "rarities" despite being "preplanned" with media in mind. At the same time, they identify narratives qualities – such as the language and tone of heroics, awe, consensus and respect – that are common across successful GMEs. In other words, they suggest that there are routines of coverage surrounding these "unique" events. Similarly, Hallin and Mancini (1992: 126), in their analysis of the Reagan/Gorbachev superpower summit as a GME, emphasize that routine reporting "buildup" to a GME plays a key role in "shaping the conversation" that emerges surrounding the event.

In summary, key research in the areas of strategic image management strongly suggests that not all countries will benefit from engaging in a "spectacular" image strategy such as hosting a GME. If a city or nation endeavours to host a GME its rhetoric must align with reality in the face of a naturally sceptical global media. Further, it is well established that hosts simply cannot control the media construction of the GME. Finally, research on influences on news confirms that despite a relationship that is "functionally dependent", the system of media production – ranging from cost considerations to professional routines to domestication practices – will tend to promote a media agenda that is distinct from the GME host city or country agenda.

Method

In order to identify what makes a difference in terms of GME host image portrayal in international media, the author conducted a meta-analysis of results of her own original research on 11 GMEs over the past 20 years, starting with the 1988 Seoul Olympics, as well as research findings on an additional 14 GMEs conducted by others.

Event sample

More specifically, this study analyses research conducted by the author from four Olympic Games: 1988 Seoul (Larson and Rivenburgh 1991; Rivenburgh 1992); 1992 Barcelona (Moragas et al. 1995); 1996 Atlanta (Rivenburgh 2008); and 2000 Sydney (Rivenburgh et al. 2003); six UN summits: 1992 Rio de Janeiro on the environment, 1993 Vienna on human rights, 1994 Cairo on population and development, 1995 Copenhagen on social development, 1995 Beijing conference on women, and 1996 Rome world food summit (Giffard and Rivenburgh 2000); and the 1999 WTO meeting in Seattle (Rivenburgh 2007). These data were supplemented by both original and secondary source work done by others on G8 and IMF meetings (Giuffo 2001), the 1996 Miss World Pageant (Parameswaran 2001), Olympic Games (Chalip 1989; Klausen 1996; Ladrón de Guevara et al. 1995; Larson and Park 1993; Manheim 1990; Papa 1996; Sun 2002; Tomlinson 1996); UN and superpower summitry (Clausen 2003; Fortner 1994; Hallin and Mancini 1992; Ogan 1987; Rusciano et al. 1997; Silcock 1996; Zaharopoulos et al. 1995); and audience image surveys of the Seoul, Barcelona and Sydney Olympic Games conducted in various countries (Chalip 1989; Moragas et al. 1995; Rivenburgh et al. 2003; Sakamoto et al. 1999; Sun 2002).

Study approach

For each GME analysed, the author asked and answered the following questions: (1) What were the GME host's primary image goals? 2) In what way were they reflected, or not, in international media coverage? and (3) What key conditions characterized the GME internally (e.g. media operations), immediately surrounding the event (e.g. event-based protests), and externally (the global news context)?

A host's primary image goals were determined through review of organizing committee documents, interviews, news stories and marketing materials, as well as secondary source references to these data. The international media image for each host was determined from results of systematic content analyses conducted on each GME. Conditions surrounding the GME (internal, immediate and external) were determined through author participant observation, news accounts, and other primary and secondary accounts of each event.

Three caveats are worth noting. First, the focus here is on host *image* success. A GME can be successful in terms of world record sports results or a multilateral treaty signed, but not in terms of host image goals. For example, the Atlanta 1996 Olympics were a sport and financial success (Yarbrough 2000), yet a host image disaster (Rivenburgh 2008). The Sydney 2000 Olympics, while successful by most measures, did not fully meet organizers' image goals of depicting Australia as a cosmopolitan, multicultural and "green" society. In fact, international media coverage increased foreign audience awareness of Australia's history of racial discrimination toward aboriginal peoples (Rivenburgh et al. 2003). Second, each GME is an extremely complex event and case study situated in its own culturally, historically and politically unique moment. For that reason, this study does not compare GMEs, but considers them as a collectivity of a type of event. The analysis looks for relationships and media-related phenomena common across all the events. Finally, although the author's GME research focused on host imagery, the full body of GME research reviewed here posed a variety of research questions, employed a range of methodologies, and looked at diverse media outlets and data sources from over 60 different countries, so not all of the meta "survey" questions could be adequately answered about each of the 25 GMEs reviewed. Even so, clear patterns across events did emerge.

Results

The results of two decades of research into GMEs reveal five key variables that make a difference in how the GME host is presented in international media.

Variable 1: Host organization and treatment of media

Paradoxically, it is the GME aspects that seem most trivial but which are, in fact, most critical to media presentation of the host image. Quite simply, anything that affects the media's ability to do its job during the event is attributed to the quality, and even personality, of the host. These "trivialities" include the language, time and format of materials for media and operational logistics that affect media performance.

Materials for the media

GME hosts produce an abundance of materials for media (books, brochures, web information, video features, documentation and guides, advertising). One challenge to international media is that organizers, for cost considerations, typically limit production of these materials to a few languages. For example, Olympic Games materials are produced in French, English and the host language. In the case of Opening Ceremonies – a moment critical to host image portrayal – the media guide is typically released only a few hours ahead of the ceremony to maintain an element of surprise. This practice discourages some media from using the guide; there is not enough time to translate it. As a result, despite years of careful image planning, remarkably little cultural detail makes it into the broadcast or newspaper media (cf. Moragas et al. 1995). In addition, some GME hosts are more adept at formatting media materials to encourage media use. Media guides created by the Seoul Olympic organizing committee were written in a flowery, rhetorical style generally ignored by Western media. As a result, nuanced cultural and historical performances about Korea became simply "a traditional dance" in broadcast commentary (Rivenburgh 1992). By contrast, the Barcelona organizers combined attractive, media-ready materials with an arsenal of "beauty cameras" set around the city, generating sensational visuals readily incorporated into international broadcasts (Moragas et al. 1995).

Logistics that affect media performance

Basic event operations such as computer systems, transportation, media facilities and accommodation significantly influence media portrayals of the GME host. Most notably, journalists are extremely critical of the host when they cannot get their job done. At the 1996 Atlanta Olympics, the computer system wasn't fully operational until day *six* of the Games (Rivenburgh 2008). This situation was intolerable for media on deadline. Further, the information that did appear was not credible. The computer displayed incorrect start lists, 95-year-old archery competitors, and a fencer credited with a 400-metre world record (Yarbrough 2000). The resulting media portrayal of Atlanta as host was disastrous. During the 1999 WTO meetings protesters, and police trying to control them, literally blocked journalists from getting across the street to the meeting venue. Stuck in hotel rooms, what did they do? Journalists filed stories about chaos on the streets and the incompetence of the host city Seattle (Rivenburgh 2007).

Similarly, journalists routinely complain about bus drivers who take them to the wrong Olympic sports venue, traffic jams that snarl a city during a UN summit, bad food, air pollution and the weather as reflective of the host "culture". After weeks of rain, journalists at the women's conference in Beijing characterized the "muddy, half-finished site" as "typical" Chinese construction (Giffard and Rivenburgh 2000). In other words, the immediate, lived experience of journalists can become the host personality in international media.

Drawing on Shoemaker and Reese (1996), it is easy to explain these tendencies in terms of the professional expectations and competitive pressures placed on media. Katz et al. (1984: 135) also refer to the challenge to media of telling a story "whose end is unknown". This causes journalists to search for information from which to judge whether the GME in progress is "succeeding" or "failing". They find clues in the daily logistics of the event.

Variable 2: Media as national and cultural actor

Despite claims that GME coverage is distinct from news (Dayan and Katz 1995), coverage of event hosts adhere to many patterns familiar to international news coverage. International media are influenced by: (1) their nation's relationship to the host nation; (2) processes of domestication and national bias; and (3) intercultural challenges.

Cultural, political and geographic orientation to host nation

Media tend to present more positive images of GME hosts "more like them". For example, Western news agencies (Associated Press, Reuters) were significantly more negative toward Cairo, Beijing and Rio de Janeiro as UN summit hosts than toward the three European hosts (Copenhagen, Vienna and Rome). By contrast Inter Press Service, a "Southern hemisphere" news agency, did not show the same bias (Giffard and Rivenburgh 2000). Media also focus on home nation relationships with the host. For example, NBC (US) video features during the Seoul Olympics emphasized US–Korean military and economic relations, and South Korea's move to a US-style democracy (Rivenburgh 1992). Olympic images of Australia differed in Malaysian media – which highlighted political and immigration tensions – and US media – which focused on Australia as a US tourist destination (Rivenburgh et al. 2003).

Domestication and national bias

It is well established that patterns of ethnocentrism, combined with the need to appeal to audiences, result in the domestication of international news coverage (Clausen 2003; Gurevitch et al. 1991). These same patterns affect the image of a GME host. First, international media prefer to focus on the "home team". For example, Clausen (2003) in her comparative study of Japan and Danish coverage of the 1999 Beijing summit found that each national medium focused on their own diplomats, not the host. Rivenburgh (1992) found that NBC feature stories during the Seoul Olympics focused primarily on US athletes, or on the US as mentor, partner and actor in South Korean affairs. Second, international media portrayals of GME nations tend to be comparative in ways that make the home country look positive. For example, Giffard and Rivenburgh (2000) found that Western media criticisms of logistics and accommodation in Cairo, Rio de Janeiro and Beijing during UN summits were based on Western standards for efficiency, comfort and customer service. US media coverage of the Seoul Olympics portrayed South Korea as striving to "be like us" in terms of democratic government and consumer culture (Rivenburgh 1992). Conversely, Atlanta was portrayed by international media during the 1996 Olympics as "not like us" and an example of all that is wrong with capitalist consumer culture. Rivenburgh (2008) writes:

> [Atlanta] was characterized as a trade fair, flea market, product exhibition center, shopping mall, temple of consumerism, streets full of junk, state fair, tacky, cheap, a superstore, supermarket, oriental bazaar, with pushy vendors and naked hucksterism. Such an atmosphere of profiteering was said to be an "attack on the Olympic spirit" and the "rape" of the Games.
>
> (Rivenburgh 2008: 25)

Silcock's (1996) analysis of international broadcasts of the 1991 Maastricht summit also found patterns of national and ideological bias.

Intercultural challenges

GME hosts often seek to educate foreign publics about the local culture. In fact, much time and negotiation is spent designing the host "look" and image for a mega-event such as the Olympic Games. However, a review of coverage of host cultural performances, such as Olympic ceremonies, reveals a significant amount of misinterpretation, simplification ("it's very traditional"), or vague ("it's very beautiful") descriptions by international media. Similarly, there is little explanation as to the "logic" of daily life in the host culture. Instead of learning why a cultural activity is important, audiences more typically hear or read that Koreans (Seoul Games) "speak to the dead" during the Chusok holiday, Norwegians (Lillehammer Games) believe in underworld spirits and fairies, the French (Albertville Games) are "avant-garde", and the Australians . . . well, according to Sun (2002) the Chinese media had absolutely no idea what the lawnmowers in the Sydney Opening Ceremony signified.

Variable 3: Media resources and financial constraints

A typical GME involves hundreds of international media organizations. While all have the same assignment to cover the event, their financial means to do so vary dramatically. This variance plays a significant role in the amount, and quality, of attention given by a media outlet to the host city or nation. For example, better funded national media (e.g. British, German, Japanese, US) devote more journalists to do host-related stories in advance of and during the event, visiting historical and cultural sites, talking to locals, and crafting features on the local culture. Financial constraints also affect access to event venues. For example, Olympic Games pricing structures for accredited media are typically pay-as-you-go (i.e. a broadcaster pays extra for commentary stations at venues or for extra cameras). Underfunded, understaffed media are less able to – literally – leave the media centres and experience the host city. Rivenburgh (2002) also notes the trend toward remote production of Olympic Games, where media are handling more of the event production at home. This cost-saving strategy means that fewer media personnel visit and "experience" the host culture, affecting the kind of image they may present.

Variable 4: Media routines for GME reporting

This research review revealed that media coverage of GMEs combines typical patterns of international news coverage with its own set of reporting conventions.

Formula reporting for a unique event

All GME hosts can expect a similar collection of pre-event news stories on security (terrorism threats); site preparation (e.g. construction delays, host efforts to "clean up" lower income areas); funding issues (e.g. lagging hotel bookings and tickets sold, cost overruns); and political conflicts (e.g. organizational in-fighting, protest groups). According to Hallin and Mancini (1992), this type of pre-event buildup sets a tone and framework for how the host will be portrayed and evaluated during the event. In the author's hometown newspaper, *The Seattle Times*, the pre-event coverage to the Beijing 2008 Olympics included all of the above, plus stories on algae overtaking the Olympic sailing venue, fears of locust swarms migrating from Mongolia to Beijing, detained journalists, and reported anti-terrorism missiles hidden near Olympic venues.

During the GME, four more reporting patterns emerge. First, and not surprising, significant media attention shifts away from the host to event proceedings (Giffard and Rivenburgh 2000; Ogan 1987; Zaharopoulos et al. 1995). Second, host culture visibility tends to mimic that nation's visibility (high or low) in international news more generally. For example, a Chinese, US or French city gets relatively more media attention during the event than an Austrian, Danish or Caribbean city. Third, the coverage of the GME host is predominantly event-based (versus enduring qualities of culture and place) and focused on logistics (traffic, facilities, politics, weather) (Giffard and Rivenburgh 2000; Moragas et al. 1995; Rivenburgh 2008; Rivenburgh et al. 2003; Rusciano et al. 1997). Fourth, story selection about the host is driven by typical news values of drama, conflict, oddity and good visuals – although not necessarily characterized by negativity. For example, during the 1996 Miss World Pageant in southern India, media were drawn to the conflicts between organizers and critics of the event (Parameswaran 2001).

Reliance on stereotypes

Media are well known for perpetuating stereotypes of other nations. High on the goal list of most GME hosts is to challenge national stereotypes. Seoul organizers hoped to dispel Korea's M*A*S*H image (Larson and Park 1993). Barcelona organizers sought to be seen as Catalan instead of Spanish (Moragas 1992). Atlanta organizers wanted to be about Southern hospitality instead of Hollywood (Yarbrough 2000). Sydney organizers wanted Australia to look more cosmopolitan than outback. This study merely confirmed the difficulty of confronting stereotypes. Despite some extraordinary image campaign efforts, the GME hosts analysed fell victim, repeatedly, to formulaic stereotypes. The BBC broadcast of the Barcelona Games opened with an image of a rose and flamenco dancer. In fact, most broadcasters made no reference to Catalonia (Moragas et al. 1995). South African, US, Malaysian and Hong Kong audiences saw an abundance of kangaroos and koala bears during the Sydney Games (Rivenburgh et al. 2003). Islamic fundamentalism was the primary cultural theme during the Cairo summit (Giffard and Rivenburgh 2000). Both Papa (1996) in her study of the Albertville 1992 Winter Games and Silcock (1996) in his analysis of the Maastricht summit found that host image portrayals reflected existing foreign perceptions. As Manheim (1994) would predict, stereotyping of GME hosts was strongest in the case of high news visibility countries. For example, Atlanta was readily associated with the "top ten" list of US stereotypes, including violence, racial tensions, consumerism, Hollywood, and obesity (Rivenburgh 2008). Beijing as summit host was subject to persistent communist stereotypes of government control and political censorship (Clausen 2003; Rusciano et al. 1997).

Media scepticism

As noted above, efforts at image change are met with scepticism. If the rhetoric does not match the reality the image campaign will not only fail, but will be "exposed" by media. This happened to Atlanta seeking to be an "international city" when its computers failed to work. At the 1992 environmental summit in Brazil and 1995 summit on women in China, the hosts suffered from media criticisms of "host image hypocrisy". Instead of being portrayed as leaders in these global issue areas as the hosts hoped, journalists pointed out that Brazil destroys its rain forests and China engages in human rights violations (Giffard and Rivenburgh 2000; Rusciano et al. 1997). As Giffard and Rivenburgh (2000: 19) stated, "the tendency on the part of the . . . news agencies was to highlight precisely those negative images that the . . . hosts hoped to ameliorate".

Variable 5: Intervening news events

Of least control to host organizations are the unplanned news events which occur within, surrounding and external to the GME. These happenings not only attract the attention of media already at the event site, but can also bring to the city a flood of non-accredited media personnel that hosts must cope with.

News external to the event

All GME hosts must compete with other news – whether natural disasters, war, domestic events such as elections, and more. For example, in the lead-up to the 1996 Atlanta Games, the host was eager for stories about Atlanta as the "Cinderella" of the US South. Instead, TWA Flight 800 crashed over the waters of New York ten days before the Opening Ceremony, riveting international media attention on the prospect of a terror attack at the Games (Yarbrough 2000). Reports of mass starvation in Rwanda and Zaire coincided with Rome's World Food summit, and civil war raged in Bosnia at the time of the Vienna human rights conference, drawing media attention away from the host (Giffard and Rivenburgh 2000).

News internal to the event

Unexpected news that occurs within the context of the event can also distract media attention from the host – or contribute to negative associations with the host. This "menace of unreality" (Tehranian 1984: 59) are situations such as the Centennial Park bombing one week into the Atlanta Games, the Kerrigan–Harding debacle during the Lillehammer Winter Games, the Salt Lake City ice-skating judging scandal, Olympic drug scandals, and summit stalemates where media coverage can snowball and derail the most meticulous of host image plans.

News surrounding the event

GMEs have become magnets for a variety of local, national and globally organized protest groups – an issue of increasing importance and expense (Giuffo 2001). Daniel Dayan calls this phenomenon "stealing attention". The five days of protests surrounding the 1999 WTO meetings in Seattle were disastrous for the host image of Seattle as headlines such as "A Sensational Failure" (Italy); "Fiasco in Seattle" (Croatia); and "The Flop of the Century" (Belgium) dominated press accounts. Parameswaran (2001: 74) called the media coverage of vigorous public and special interest protests surrounding the 1996 Miss World Beauty Pageant in Bangalore a "spectacular form of public embarrassment that only underscored anti-nationalistic, negative stereotypes of India as chaotic, unstable, and unfit for modernity".

Conclusion

Based on this review of 25 GMEs over a 20-year period, there is little question that hosting a GME is a high-risk/high-reward image strategy and one where hosts can at best expect "generalized" image results largely consonant with existing foreign perceptions. However, GMEs are higher risk for some than for others. Drawing on the results of this study, and confirming prior research in international political communication, one can reliably predict the greatest hosting challenge will be for: (1) nations that have an existing international news presence of high visibility and negative valence (often with strong stereotypes); (2) nations whose image goals are not grounded in reality; and (3) nations who are not organizationally prepared for smooth event operations and to cater to the daily needs of media personnel.

Conversely, hosting a GME may be a desirable image strategy for lower news visibility nations who seek high-impact global attention, but not dramatic image change. In this case it is best to match the event to some positive (or at least non-conflicting) aspect of the existing host image (e.g. Athens and Sydney with Olympic sport). Such hosts will also benefit significantly from careful preparation of favourable yet balanced media-friendly materials in a variety of languages and media formats. They should offer free on-site translation and cultural interpretation, and consider pricing structures that allow less well-funded media to cover more aspects of the event and host setting.

In other words, while risks remain, the most successful GME hosts will focus on the variables above over which they have the most influence and be well prepared to respond to those that they don't – such as surprise news events or no-surprise, pre-event reporting topics. More broadly, any city or nation considering the "spectacular" image strategy of hosting a GME must seriously weigh a number of issues, ranging from the increased attractiveness of GMEs as sites of protest to the extraordinary security costs, before deciding whether such an endeavour is worth it.

References

Chalip, L. (1989) "The Politics of Olympic Theatre: New Zealand and Korean Cross-National Relations", paper presented at the Seoul Olympiad Anniversary Conference in Seoul, South Korea, September.

Clausen, L. (2003) *Global News Production*, Copenhagen: Copenhagen Business School Press.

Dayan, D. and Katz, E. (1995) "Political Ceremony and Instant History", in A. Smith (ed.) *Television. An International History*, Oxford: Oxford University Press, 169–88.

Deutsch, K.W. and Merritt, R.L. (1965) "Effects of Events on National and International Images", in H.C. Kelman (ed.) *International Behavior: A Social-psychological Analysis*, New York: Holt, Rhinehart & Winston, 130–87.

Ebo, B. (1997) "Media Diplomacy and Foreign Policy: Toward a Theoretical Framework", in A. Malek (ed.) *News Media and Foreign Relations: A Multifaceted Perspective*, Norwood, NJ: Ablex, 43–57.

Fortner, R.S. (1994) *Public Diplomacy and International Politics: The Symbolic Constructs of Summits and International Radio News*, Westport, CT: Praeger.

Giffard, C.A. and Rivenburgh, N.K. (2000) "News Agencies, National Images and Global Media Events", *Journalism and Mass Communication Quarterly*, 77, 1: 8–21.

Giuffo, J. (2001) "Smoke Gets in Our Eyes: The Globalization Protests and the Befuddled Press", *Columbia Journalism Review*, 5, September/October: 14–17.

Gurevitch, M., Levy, M. and Roeh, I. (1991) "The Global Newsroom: Convergences and Diversities in the Globalization of Television News", in P. Dahlgren and C. Sparks (eds) *Communication and Citizenship*, London: Routledge, 195–216.

Hallin, D. and Mancini, P. (1992) "The Summit as Media Event: The Reagan/Gorbachev Meetings on US, Italian, and Soviet Television", in J. Blumler, J.M. McLeod and K.E. Rosengren (eds) *Comparatively Speaking: Communication and Culture Across Space and Time*, London: Sage, 121–39.

Jervis, R. (1970) *The Logic of Images in International Relations*, Princeton, NJ: Princeton University Press.

Katz, E., Dayan, D. and Motyl, P. (1984) "Television Diplomacy: Sadat in Jerusalem", in G. Gerbner and M. Siefert (eds) *World Communications: A Handbook*, New York: Longman, 127–36.

Klausen, A.M. (1996) "The Lillehammer '94 Winter Games", in M. de Moragas, J. MacAloon and M. Llines (eds) *Olympic Ceremonies: Historical Continuity and Cultural Exchange*, Lausanne: International Olympic Committee, 269–74.

Kunczik, M. (2003) "States, International Organizations, and the News Media", in P.J. Maarek and G. Wolfsfeld (eds) *Political Communication in a New Era*, New York: Routledge, 117–38.

Ladrón de Guevara, M., Cóllier, X. and Romaní, D. (1995) "The Image of Barcelona '92 in the International Press", in M. de Moragas and M. Botella (eds) *Keys to Success*, Barcelona: Universitat Autònoma de Barcelona, 107–23.

Larson, J.F. and Park, H.S. (1993) *Global Television and the Politics of the Seoul Olympics*, Boulder, CO: Westview Press.

Larson, J.F. and Rivenburgh, N.K. (1991) "A Comparative Analysis of Australian, U.S. and British Telecasts of the Seoul Olympic Opening Ceremony", *Journal of Broadcasting and Electronic Media*, 35, 1: 75–94.

Manheim, J.B. (1990) "Rites of Passage: the 1988 Seoul Olympics as Public Diplomacy", *Western Political Quarterly*, 43, 2: 279–95.

Manheim, J.B. (1994) *Strategic Public Diplomacy and American Foreign Policy: The Evolution of Influence*, New York: Oxford University Press.

Moragas, M. de, (1992) *Los Juegos de la Communicación. Las multiples dimensiones commuicativas de los juegos Olimpicos*, Madrid: Fundesco.

Moragas, M. de, Rivenburgh, N.K. and Larson, J.F. (1995) *Television in the Olympics*, London: John Libbey.

Nye, J.S., Jr. (2004) *Soft Power: The Means to Success in World Politics*, New York: Public Affairs.

Ogan, C. (1987) "Coverage of the Development News in Developed and Developing Countries", *Journalism Quarterly*, 64, 1: 80–7.

Papa, F. (1996) " 'The Albertville Olympic Games' Ceremonies: An Imago Mundi", in M. de Moragas, J. MacAloon and M. Llines (eds) *Olympic Ceremonies: Historical Continuity and Cultural Exchange*, Lausanne: International Olympic Committee, 213–25.

Parameswaran, R. (2001) "Global Media Events in India: Contests over Beauty, Gender, and Nation", *Journalism and Communication Monographs*, 3, 2: 53–105.

Rivenburgh, N.K. (1992) "National Image Richness in US-televised Coverage of South Korea during the Seoul Olympics", *Asian Journal of Communication*, 2, 2: 1–39.

—— (2000) "Social Identity Theory and News Portrayals of Citizens involved in International Affairs", *Media Psychology*, 2, 4: 303–29.

—— (2002) "The Olympic Games: Twenty-first Century Challenges as a Global Media Event", *Culture, Sport, Society*, 5, 3: 31–50.

—— (2007) "Global Media Events as Public Diplomacy", paper presented at the Conference on Media Events, Globalization, and Culture Change at the University of Bremen, Germany, 5–7 July.

—— (2008) "For the Cinderella of the New South, the Shoe Just Didn't Fit: The 'Most Exceptional' Games of 1996", *International Journal of Sport Communication*, 1, December: 465–86.

Rivenburgh, N.K., Louw, P.E., Loo, E. and Mersham, G. (2003) *The Sydney Olympic Games and Foreign Attitudes towards Australia*, Gold Coast: CRCST Publishing.

Rusciano, F.L., Fiske-Rusciano, R. and Wang, M. (1997) "The Impact of 'World Opinion' on National Identity", *Press/Politics*, 2, 3: 71–92.

Sakamoto, A., Murata, K. and Takaki, E. (1999) "The Barcelona Olympics and the Perception of Foreign Nations: A Panel Study of Japanese University Students", *Journal of Sport Behavior*, 22, 2: 260–80.

Shoemaker, P.J. and Reese, S.D. (1996) *Mediating the Message*, New York: Longman.

Signitzer, B.H. and Coombs, T. (1992) "Public Relations and Public Diplomacy: Conceptual Convergences", *Public Relations Review*, 18, 2: 137–47.

Silcock, B.W. (1996) "Television News Coverage of the Maastricht Summit", in D. Paletz (ed.) *Political Communication in Action*, Cresskill, NJ: Hampton, 119–39.

Sun, W. (2002) *Leaving China: Media, Migration, and Transnational Imagination*, Lanham, MD: Rowman & Littlefield.

Tehranian, M. (1984) "Events, Pseudo-events, Media Events: Image Politics and the Future of International Diplomacy", in A. Arno and W. Dissanayake (eds) *News Media in National and International Conflict*, Boulder, CO: Westview Press, 43–61.

Tomlinson, A. (1996) "Olympic Spectacle: Opening Ceremonies and Some Paradoxes of Globalization", *Media, Culture and Society*, 18, 4: 583–602.

Yarbrough, C.R. (2000) *And They Call Them Games: An Inside View of the 1996 Olympics*, Macon, GA: Mercer University Press.

Zaharopoulos, T., Punitha, C., Reinert, V., Chuang, L., Foos, B., Sandness, T. and Yeh, S. (1995) "International Press Coverage of the 1992 Rio Earth Summit", *International Communication Bulletin*, 30, 1–2: 10–12, 23.

14

9/11 AND THE TRANSFORMATION OF GLOBALIZED MEDIA EVENTS

Agnieszka Stepinska

Introduction

Although journalists have been covering acts of terror for a few decades, on September 11, 2001 they seemed to be surprised by the "combination of detailed planning and coordination in well orchestrated high concept terror spectacle" (Kellner 2004). Even the journalists and audiences in such countries as Great Britain and Spain that have been experiencing and reporting terrorism for a long period recognized that the attacks were different, both in scale and intent, from the terrorist atrocities of the IRA or ETA (La Porte Alfaro and Sadaba 2007; McNair 2007).

The attacks revealed a comprehensive picture of contemporary relations between political actors (including terrorists) and journalists. They clearly showed that terrorist organizations are able to respond not only to the previously established criteria of newsworthiness for both domestic and foreign news, but also to some new trends in the modern media, namely mobility and immediacy. The event exemplified the consequences of the proliferation of new communication technology around the world, including a new perception of time, space, and proximity. In particular, the 9/11 attacks provided us with arguments that the distinction between foreign and domestic news flow is no longer easily distinguishable. Furthermore, depending on the context and the audience, the same event may be considered to be a domestic or foreign news story, as well as a national or international media event.

This chapter argues that although the 9/11 event shared almost all the features that determine whether or not the event is reported, the uniqueness of that event lies in those that were actually *not* fully shared, namely the *unequivocal character* of the event and *frequency*. I suggest that the analysis of these two criteria of attacks' newsworthiness will lead us to one of the fundamental questions raised by the media event concept, which concerns the role of the media organizations in providing meaning and integrating the audience (society). In the following section I will present the theoretical background and some empirical findings regarding: (1) the relationship between terrorists and journalists, and (2) terrorist acts as media events. Moreover, I suggest combining the categories of news stories and media events in order to deepen our understanding of a nature of preplanned, disruptive media events.

Theoretical background

Relationship between terrorism and the media

The view that the newsrooms' routines have provided a set of useful hints for terrorist organizations has been repeated, discussed, supported or denied since the 1970s, soon after the international mass media terrorism occurred in the late 1960s. Primarily, as Alex P. Schmid and Janny de Graaf wrote, it was the outgrowth of minority strategies to get into the news: "since the Western mass media grants access to news-making to events that are abnormal, unusual, dangerous, new, disruptive and violent, groups without habitual access to news-making use these characteristics of the news value system to obtain access" (Schmid and de Graaf 1982: 217).

In the 1960s and 1970s terrorist organizations most frequently used direct pressure and force against journalists in order to attract their attention. Gabriel Weimann and Conrad Winn (1994) enumerated examples of such coercive actions: using guns to force journalists and editors to diffuse manifestos, messages and speeches; kidnapping or attacking executives of the papers, corporate officials and journalists; and kidnapping family members of press moguls (e.g. the case of Patricia Hearst). At the same time, the hijacking of airplanes and threatening governments by making the hostages' right to life conditional on media cooperation were frequently used by terrorist organizations (see Weimann and Winn (1994: 112–17) for some examples).

Since the end of the 1970s the relationship between terrorism and the media has become increasingly extensive. The desire for maximum publicity has created a tendency to select a target and engage in types of symbolic actions that translate well visually in coverage and broadcast (see Nacos (1994, 2002) for some examples) with respect to the media's schedules and routines. As Abraham H. Miller (1982) observed, terrorism has become "a triple composition of mortal performance, high politics and abject crime. It suits the aim of mass media so perfectly that they just cannot deny themselves reporting such events completely."

Weimann and Winn (1994) showed, however, that not every single act of terror is covered by journalists. While analyzing results of numerous studies they recognized that a location (Western countries), a nationality of targets (Americans and representatives of other Western nations), and the significance of the perpetrators were the factors predicting coverage of terrorist attacks.

In addition, in a world characterized by media saturation and with news stories already devoted to coverage of so many issues relating to violence, death, and tragedy, guaranteeing coverage of terrorism stories requires visually compelling, dramatic, and therefore devastating violence on a larger scale. Consequently, we may observe the escalation of violence and upgrading "sophistication" of the scripts of terror acts (Miller 1982; Schmid and de Graaf 1982; Nacos 1994).

Considering the terrorists' strategies in terms of relationship with journalists, one may distinguish between two main types of acts of terror. The first one is a *negotiation-like type*, when terrorists seek direct contact with journalists to introduce themselves and present their objectives or demands. Since the act is usually designed to catch the media's attention for at least a few hours or days, its script is developing: when the intensity of a situation appears to be abating, terrorists can re-establish a sense of crisis by introducing deadlines for compliance with their wishes and by making threats in the event of non-compliance (e.g. kidnapping, hijacking, and taking hostages).

The second type is a *show-like* act of terror, when terrorists seek publicity, but their identity is not disclosed and their objectives are not immediately presented, since terrorists do not show any interest in having contact with journalists (see Blondheim and Liebes (2003) for a similar distinction). The strategy exemplified by bombing incidents and assassinations includes a short duration and a complete script of an event. Since journalists in many countries around the world have been covering terrorism for at least a few decades, they possess the routine organizational procedures and frames for responding to most of the negotiation-type acts of terror. In cases of terrorist acts of a show-like type, by contrast, the potential power lies in breaking those previously used routines (Noll 2003).

Terror acts as media events

It has already been noted that some acts of terror seem to match most of a key characteristics of a media event introduced by Daniel Dayan and Elihu Katz (1992) in their book *Media Events: The Live Broadcasting of History*. In particular, they may share the following features: a live broadcast, a highly dramatic narrative, an event rich in symbolic values, heroic actions and individuals, and important personalities at the center of drama.

Only some of the terrors, however, have been regarded as historic moments transforming daily life into something special through obligatory watching of their coverage by the media (see Weimann and Winn (1994); Paletz and Schmid (1992) for some examples). Even fewer have received extensive, *live, global* media coverage and the undivided attention of audiences from all around the world (Weimann and Winn 1994). Although they share most of the characteristics of the media events defined by Dayan and Katz (1992), terror acts do not fit neatly into any of the three main types of ritual media events. What they usually lack is a contract between three partners: media, audience, and the event organizers, as well as a consensual role of the center (media), providing interpretation and definition of the event.

In other words, although acts of terror might be considered as preplanned events structured not by the media organizations themselves but externally (as is required for the media event), their media coverage is not the result of negotiation, but rather of a coercion or advanced media management strategy employed by the perpetrators. Thus, the contract is only semi-voluntary and mutual services are forced rather than agreed upon (Bouvier 2007). In addition, the event organizers are usually anti-establishment, whereas Dayan and Katz (1992) noted that the organizers should be "well within the establishment."

The classic concept of ritual media events has been criticized for being insufficient for focusing on all media events since 1980s. Therefore, some attempts have been made to establish distinctive categories that account for terrorist attacks and other types of shocking and traumatic events, namely: coercion (Weimann and Winn 1994), disaster marathons (Blondheim and Liebes 2003), crisis and catastrophe (Doane 2005), and terror, disaster and war (Katz and Liebes 2007). Table 14.1 outlines the differences among classic genres of ritual media events and some more recently introduced categories of disruptive media events.

Most of the latter share the following features: victims in substantial number or victims having celebrity status, the dramatic failure of visible and supposedly foolproof technologies, or the collapse of a well-established and salient institutional practice, and the element of surprise that underscores its diametrically opposed relationship with the establishment. Furthermore, a disruptive media event is the most effective when television arrives in time to cover the ongoing event "while it still lacks symbolic or even narrative closure, rather than landing in its bloody aftermath, when the structure is already established and involves easily identifiable villains and heroes" (Blondheim and Liebes 2003: 186). Finally, in the case of any disruptive media event it is not the media that plays the role of narrator and interpreter of the ceremony. Journalists and editors have no control over the beginning and the ending of a "spectacle."

News stories and media events

A ritual media event has been presented as in sharp contrast to a news story, since a routine news story has a narrative structure that pre-exists any given circumstances, while an event violates the narrative control and management of the news media, at least for a moment, as well as interrupting routine time (Dayan and Katz 1992: 1–9; Wark 2005). Facts, when they emerge, can be fitted into a story, while weird global media events are unique: each of them is singular and none conforms to any predetermined narrative.

Table 14.1 Categories and characteristics of media events

Characteristics	Ritual media events			Disruptive media events		
	Contests	Conquests	Coronations	Coercions	Disasters	Wars
Periodicity	Fixed, cyclical	Not fixed, predictable	Not fixed, Current	Not fixed, Surprise	Not fixed, Surprise	Fixed
Drama	Who will win?	Will he or she win?	Will ritual succeed?	At what price?	How it could happen?	Will the goals be achieved?
Rules	Agreed rules	No rules	Ritual rules	Against rules	No rules	Agreed war rules
Conflict	Person vs. person	Person vs. Nature or society	Culture, Society vs. Nature	Person or group vs. person, group, society & culture	Nature/technology vs. humankind Man vs. humankind	Nation vs. nation; army vs. army
Conflict resolution	Fixed, symbolic resolution	Invites identification	Reflexive recall basic Values of society	Condemnation and identification	Restoration	Capitulation/pledge
Message	Rules are supreme; victory & defeat are reversible	Giant leap for humankind	Continuity is assured	Violence leads to nowhere	We will survive	It was a necessity
Time orientation	Present	Future	Past	Present	Present/future	Present/future
Role of performers	Demonstrate character	Demonstrate charisma	Ritual performance	Demonstrate power	Demonstrate power/will to survive	Demonstrate power
Analogue to TV genres	Quiz	Western	Soap opera	Crime series/reality shows	Catastrophic movie	TV Series

Source: Based on Dayan and Katz (1992), Weimann and Winn (1994), Katz and Liebes (2007).

Moreover, most of the news is routinely broadcast to the domestic or international audience, while media events "happen within a space and time saturated in media and global media events traverse borders and call a world into being" (Wark 2005: 119). In other words, most of news stories are presented according to the media schedules and deadlines, and only some of them, once they become "breaking news" and are presented despite the media organizations' routines, may be eventually considered as media events.

Finally, analyses of the impact of international news coverage on audiences show the usual lack of affect and compassion fatigue. As Roger Silverstone (1994) and Kevin Robins (1994) put it, news media seem to be usually "distancing and denying" or "defusing painful reality." Media events, by contrast, have to be watched in one or several nations, or even on a global scale, in such a way that the experience integrates societies and evokes a renewal of loyalty (Dayan and Katz 1992: 1–9).

In cases of disruptive media events, however, the organizers need to design the event in a way that will satisfy expectations held by a highly competitive and news-hungry media to achieve their attention. In order to capture that feature, I will combine media's definitions of newsworthiness, namely (1) Herbert J. Gans' (2004) media considerations for important and interesting domestic news stories, (2) Johan Galtung and Mari Holmboe Ruge's (1965) media criteria of newsworthiness of a foreign event, (3) Pamela J. Shoemaker and Akiba Cohen's (2006) criteria of deviance and social significance, with (4) Gaye Tuchman's (1978) distinction between hard and soft news stories, and (5) Daniel Dayan and Elihu Katz's (1992) concept of media events.

First, to be recognized by both broadcasters and audience as a historic moment with a highly dramatic narrative (Dayan and Katz 1992: 1–9) an event must be exceptional, extraordinary (Bouvier 2007) and of a high significance for the past and future (Gans 2004). Thus, it might be negative, scary, or destructive. As Shoemaker and Cohen (2006) showed, people want to know about things that are deviant and/or socially significant in order to protect themselves and their societies and because of their interest in things that are unusual, break laws or norms, or threaten to change their societies.

Second, to achieve extensive media coverage and undivided attention, an event should be perceived as relevant and meaningful to the majority of a society (or societies). Thus, it should refer to elite nations, elite individuals, high-ranked officials in governmental and other hierarchies, or to a large number of people. Considering those characteristics we may conclude that a hard news story is at the core of many media events.

Finally, Dayan and Katz's criterion of heroic actions and individuals corresponds closely to Galtung and Ruge's criterion of personalization. It may be also be considered as the core of Gans' distinctive category of an interesting story and Tuchman's category of a soft news story.

From a domestic news story to a global media event?

Despite their political, economic, and security significance, the 9/11 attacks seemed to be a disruptive media event of a show-like type with a spectacular script, a short duration, and no message attached to the terror act.

A unique character of the script was formed by a combination of previously used elements and new ones. The construction of the attacks included: hijacking four airplanes to attack a few very carefully selected, symbolic targets, the pace of the attacks (two airplanes crashing into two towers one after the other within 15 minutes), a number of victims and the drama of their families, strong emotions (shock and lack of sense of security), the material effects disrupting the airline industry and business centered in downtown New York, and the global economy through the closure of the U.S. stock markets. Undoubtedly, all those features met the media's expectations toward domestic, both important (hard) and interesting (soft) news stories.

The event also fulfilled most of the criteria of newsworthiness for a foreign story presented in a previous section, including: unexpectedness ("the most extravagant strike on U.S. targets in its history and the first foreign attack on the continental U.S. since the war of 1812" as Kellner (2004) described it), a scarcity, a relevance and meaningfulness (an act of terror as an experience of numerous countries around the world), a continuity (the developing narrative of the act and its longitudinal social, political, and military consequences), a personification, and a reference to elite nations and elite individuals (Stepinska 2005).

However, two classic criteria of newsworthiness, namely the *unequivocal character* of the event and its *frequency*, were not fulfilled, or required a redefinition. Paradoxically, these two seem to be highly significant in understanding not only the global extensive media coverage of the 9/11 attacks, but also the changes of globalized media events in general. The theory of catastrophe captures this paradox. Based on the theorem in typology that is used to provide the formal language for the description of sudden discontinuities within a gradually changing system, the theory is most often used for a study of sudden, unexpected effects in a gradually changing situation (Doane 2005). Since television itself is most frequently theorized as a system of discontinuities emphasizing heterogeneity, the concept seems to be extremely useful in studying the media in times of crisis.

Technological capabilities that facilitate live transmission from various sites in parallel, combined with the economic pressure of ever-increasing competition, seem to result in bypassing the process of traditional editorial practices. Instead of preceding a careful selection and cross-checking of sources, journalist are encouraged (or forced) to "act on instinct" (Mogensen et al. 2002). This, as Blondheim and Liebes (2003) see it, pushes for the relaxation of standards in favor of the juiciest sound bites, the goriest images, and the most unlikely rumors. Hence, the classic definition of news by

209

De Fleur (1966) describing it as an "imperfect result of hurried decisions made under pressure" seems to be even more adequate today than it was at the time of its origin.

New timing of the media production and a global sense of proximity

Apparently, the perpetrators of the 9/11 attacks responded to a new timing of the newsrooms. Instead of planning the activity around the deadlines, they decided to select the moment of time in order to maximize the damage (airplanes and buildings crowded with people) and to reach audiences in all parts of the globe (it was 2:46 p.m. in most European countries, about 9:46 or 10:46 p.m. in most Asian countries, and 10:46 p.m. in Australia).

The timing combined with a careful selection of the city (one of the most media-saturated cities in the world) and targets (symbolic buildings crowded with people) resulted in the media dropping regular content and shifting to all-news programming on the event. The interruption of the television flow was pervasive to the extent that certain broadcasters stayed on the story for more than 24 hours straight. For example, in Germany, radio stations broadcast the first news about the attack four minutes after the Associated Press announcement (Haes 2003), and in Poland the RMF FM radio station broke the news at 2.47 p.m. and broadcast its own first live reports from New York City 15 minutes later (Pukniel 2001; see Pludowski (2007) for results of studies on more countries). The ABC was reporting news about the attack for 91 hours, the CBS for 93 hours, the British Sky News for 24 hours, while 4,000 reporters of the CNN were devoted exclusively to collect and spread news about the attack for 48 hours after the attack (Pukniel 2001).

As the results of the studies on a news diffusion showed, in the eastern time zone one-third of American citizens had heard about the first plane crashing into a WTC tower by 9:00 a.m. (the crash occurred at 8:46 a.m. eastern daylight time) and 90 percent knew by 10:30 a.m. (Carey 2003). Less than half an hour was needed for people living in Europe to learn about this event. Interestingly, time zones hardly affected the way in which people learned about the attacks: television and interpersonal communication were crucial sources of information for people in the U.S. and abroad.

For example, on the East Coast of the U.S., most people learned about the crash from another person, but 22 percent learned about it from television (Carey 2003). Also in Germany, although it was afternoon and many people were still at work, most of the people learned about the attacks from TV and radio (Haes 2003).

The extensive global media coverage resulted in a "worldwide synchronization of attention" (Debatin 2002), while the exposure of emotional suffering exacerbated existential anxiety through empathy with the tragedy of other human beings. In contrast to a general assumption that, since for the few past decades images of terrorism and destruction have been commonly displayed in the news of printed and electronic media, such images seem unlikely to shock the viewer, the media coverage of the event resulted in reactions of distress and emotional breakdown (Greenberg 2002).

In addition, the material damage underscored by a physical collapse of the symbols of U.S. economic power and psychological effects of the message that revealed the vulnerability of the superpower and terrorists' dedication to their objectives caused, as Ingrid Volkmer (2002) wrote, "the traumatic desta-bilization of the sense of security previously felt by Western nations." Furthermore, the attacks showed that terrorism is no longer tied to crisis regions or to some particular national "spaces" and that "isolated events may be transforming into terrorism on a global scale" (Volkmer 2002: 235). As a result, on the day of the attacks and in the aftermath even countries usually perceived as being highly critical, such as France and Germany, or Syria and Iran, responded with a deep sympathy toward America. The sense of unity, togetherness, and belonging was expressed succinctly by French *Le Monde* in the statement "We are all Americans," and repeated by some other media (Portes 2007).

The way the event was covered resulted in, as A. Sreberny put it, an *over-identification*:

> So many international writers and commentators were somehow merged with Americans in a cultural geography of attachment. This was partly an effect of America as the global, universal, an indication of the internalization of a steady drip-feed of hegemonic values and partly of the geographical and cultural proximity or a mass mediated sense of proximity, "our familiar and much loved NY of the movies, television, tourism".
>
> (Sreberny 2002: 223)

Since the whole world saw the same pictures at the same, real time, the attacks became a common mass-mediated experience for many. Thus, 9/11 has been frequently compared to the explosion of the *Challenger*, or the assassination of President J. F. Kennedy. This time, however, one may ask a distinctive question "What did you do when the attacks happened?" not only of American citizens, but also of people all around the world.

Although the unanimity appeared to be fragile (the reactions and attitudes toward the U.S. response to the attacks showed a large discrepancy among countries), it may be argued that the 9/11 events became a significant element of a global collective memory. Since public memories are subjective, selective and often contested and shaped by ideological systems that serve particular interests, the question of the source of the frames used to define the situation should be raised. This leads us to one more feature of the 9/11 events, namely an ambiguity.

Ambiguity and a terror of image

On September 11, 2001 there was no statement, no message attached to the event, and no one actually claimed responsibility for the acts right after the event. Since the perpetrators had not revealed their identities, responsibility had been attributed rather than claimed (Gupta 2002). Blondheim and Liebes (2003) argued that it was precisely this reticence in disclosing identity that added tremendous power and unique dimensions to the inevitable terrorist act and posited that anonymity was a crucial aspect shaping television coverage of the attacks on the WTC.

Furthermore, once the cameras were ready to record and the TV reporters were ready to spread the image immediately around the globe, the event turned out to be developing. The visual impact of the second attack on the WTC was increased by a shared time and space of a reporter and a viewer, and the "you are there" type of reporting.

Once pushed to open-ended live coverage, the journalists discovered that they had no script and no routine that might have been employed. This resulted in the extraordinary style of news reporting by professional journalists: bewildered by the dreadful scenes, reporters joined their audience in the search for terms and interpretations. To emphasize the significance of that situation, let us borrow Francis Debrix's (2004) term of a "moment of terror of the image," meaning a "silence, misunderstanding and moment of trauma experienced in the media and by those who are caught in it." According to Debrix (2004), what traumatizes and is sometimes expressed as the "interruption of the real" is "the silence of the media and their unexpected lack of explanation."

Having not even a general idea what had happened, the TV editors could only hypnotize viewers by recycling and repeating images of the airplane crashing into the tower and then the collapse of the towers of the WTC, while viewers "stopped simply watching television in order to stare transfixed" (Doane 2005).

At the same time, a desperate struggle over the meaning of the event took place, although indirectly, between the perpetrators and the U.S. government. The former attempted to spread the message about the vulnerability of the superpower. The latter immediately introduced a frame of war that defined a conflict in terms of a radical polarization between "us" and "them." Hence, the media found themselves under tremendous pressure since the journalists were charged with the responsibility of contributing to the establishment of a worldwide discourse, while being trapped into broadcasting images of terror (McChesney 2002).

The element of surprise combined with a high level of deviance and social significance (proximity and relevance) of the event resulted in a breach in the basic rules of reporting. On September 11, 2001, despite the common assumption that audience attention is best held by a diversity of elements (story mixture–subject, balance–graphic, balance–demographic, balance–

212

political balance), all the major U.S. TV channels focused exclusively on the attack and its aftermath for three days (Greenberg 2002), while the coverage and framing were strongly affected by a sudden wave of patriotism (Mogensen et al. 2002; Zelizer and Allan 2002).

It is worth mentioning that although journalists around the globe used the familiar local and domestic context to integrate the foreign events and to connect the events to their readers (Volkmer 2002; Pludowski 2007), on the day of attacks and in their immediate aftermath the U.S. news providers served as a coordinating source for international coverage on the details regarding the attacks and the investigation.

For example, as the results of my study showed (Stepinska 2007), about 90 percent of the items presented on Polish TV channels and newspapers on September 11 and 12, 2001 were provided by the CNN and the Associated Press, while the content of special editions of magazines was based almost exclusively on the images provided by the news agency mentioned above. In addition, the results of the study of cover stories of 28 websites of foreign newspapers and magazines on September 11, 2001 indicated that more than 50 percent of the stories framed the events as "terrorist attacks." However, in about 40 percent of stories the frame of "war" was used by introducing the following terms into the event's description: allies, enemy, coalition, declaration of war, battlefield, and so on (Stepinska 2007).

Nevertheless, in the following days one could observe how the consensus caused by the shock began to crumble as journalists, politicians, and societies fell back to their old positions. While the Americans still vowed for war, some of the Middle Eastern and Latin American countries revealed their anti-U.S. attitudes, and in many European countries, including Germany and France, the idea of a "crusade against terrorism" was strongly criticized and the concept of 9/11 as a "clash of civilizations" denied (Volkmer 2002; Pludowski 2007). Hence, it became evident that despite a moment of unity, *We cannot all be Americans*, as Portes (2007) suggested in the title of the paper on the French media reception of the 9/11 events.

Conclusions

Today, any single event can be transformed into a domestic news item covered by the national media, while being immediately spread all around the world as foreign news, and vice versa. The analyses of the media coverage of the 9/11 event clearly showed both directions of the information flow mentioned above. On the one hand, the U.S. TV channels seemed to play a role as crucial sources of images and frames for the media in other regions of the globe (see Pludowski 2007). On the other hand, one could observe a tendency for a domestication of foreign news, a contextualization of the terror attacks in the U.S. with the national conflicts, and an interpretation of the same information accordingly to the national advantage (Volkmer 2002; Pludowski 2007).

Interestingly, the analysis of the 9/11 attacks in terms of disruptive media events leads us to similar conclusions. Receiving unprecedented global live media attention and total coverage, the 9/11 events became a common, mass-mediated experience of millions of people around the world. The political character of the event, however, resulted in a variety of media representations, as well as in differences in audiences' perceptions. Thus, political media events, whether ritual or disruptive, while broadcast globally, will never have a global framing, interpretation, and understanding. Consequently, media organizations could be perceived as centers emotionally integrating the audiences (even on the global scale), but more by providing dreadful images and spreading anxiety or sympathy, than by delivering a commonly accepted interpretation of the event.

Acknowledgment

The author was supported in the years 2008 to 2011 by The Ministry of Science and Higher Education, Poland, grant No. N N116 113534.

References

Blondheim, M. and Liebes T. (2003) "From Disaster Marathon to Media Event: Live Television's Performance on September 11, 2001 and September 11, 2002", in A.M. Noll (ed.) *Crisis Communications. Lessons from September 11*, Oxford: Rowman & Littlefield, 185–98.

Bouvier, G. (2007) " 'Breaking News': The First Hours of BBC Coverage of 9/11 as a Media Event", in T. Pludowski (ed.) *How the World's News Media Reacted to 9/11. Essays From the Around the Globe*, Spokane: Marquette Books, 51–83.

Brown, W.J., Bocarnea, M., and Basil, M. (2002) "Fear, Grief and Sympathy Responses to the Attacks", in B.S. Greenberg (ed.) *Communication and Terrorism. Public and Media Responses to 9/11*, Cresskill, NJ: Hampton Press, 245–60.

Carey, J. (2002) "American Journalism On, Before and After September 11", in B. Zelizer and S. Allan (eds) *Journalism After September 11*, London: Routledge, 71–90.

Dayan, D. and Katz, E. (1992) *Media Events: The Live Broadcasting of History*, Cambridge, MA: Harvard University Press.

Debatin, B. (2002) "Plane Wreck with Spectators: Terrorism and Media Attention", in B.S. Greenberg (ed.) *Communication and Terrorism. Public and Media Responses to 9/11*, Cresskill, NJ: Hampton Press, 163–74.

Debrix, F. (2004) "The Terror of the Image: International Relations and the Global Image Circuitry", in M. Semati (ed.) *New Frontiers in International Communication Theory*, Lanham, MD: Rowman & Littlefield.

De Fleur, M. (1966) *Theories of Mass Communication*, New York: David McKay Company.

Doane, M.A. (2005) "Information, Crisis, Catastrophe", in W. Hui Kyong Chung and T. Keenan (eds) *New Media. Old Media. A History and Theory Reader*, London: Routledge, 251–64.

Galtung, J. and Ruge, M.H. (1965) "The Structure of Foreign News", *Journal of Peace Research*, 2: 64–90.

Gans, H.J. (2004) *Deciding What's News. A Study of CBS Evening News, NBC Nightly News, Newsweek, and Time*, Evanston: Northwestern University Press.

Greenberg, B.S. (ed.) (2002) *Communication and Terrorism: Public and Media Responses to 9/11*, Crosskill, NJ: Hampton Press.

Gupta, S. (2002) *The Replication of Violence: Thoughts on International Terrorism after September 11th 2001*, London: Pluto Press.

Haes, J.W. (2003) "September 11 in Germany and the United States: Reporting, Reception and Interpretation", in A.M. Noll (ed.) *Crisis Communication. Lessons from September 11*, Oxford: Rowman & Littlefield, 125–32.

Katz, E. and Liebes, T. (2007) " 'No More Peace!': How Disaster, Terror and War Have Upstaged Media Events", *International Journal of Communication*, 1: 157–66.

Kellner, D. (2004) "9/11, Spectacles of Terror, and Media Manipulation: A Critique of Jihadist and Bush Media Politics", *Critical Discourse Studies*, 1, 1: 41–64. Available HTTP: <http://www.gseis.ucla.edu/faculty/kellner/essays/911terror spectaclemedia.pdf > (accessed December 1, 2008).

La Porte Alfaro, M.T. and Sadaba, T. (2007) "September 11 in the Spanish Press: War or Terrorism Frame?", in T. Pludowski (ed.) *How the World's News Media Reacted to 9/11. Essays From the Around the Globe*, Spokane: Marquette Books, 104–21.

McChesney, R. (2002) "September 11 and the Structural Limitations of US Journalism", in B. Zelizer and S. Allan (eds) *Journalism After September 11*, London: Routledge, 91–100.

McNair, B. (2007) "UK Media Coverage of September 11", in T. Pludowski (ed.) *How the World's News Media Reacted to 9/11. Essays From the Around the Globe*, Spokane: Marquette Books, 29–37.

Miller, A.H. (ed.) (1982) *Terrorism, the Media and the Law*, New York: Transnational Publishers.

Mogensen, K., Lindsay, L.X., Perkins, J. and Beardsley, M. (2002) "How TV News Covered the Crisis: The Content of CNN, CBS, ABC, NBC and Fox", in B.S. Greenberg (ed.) *Communication and Terrorism. Public and Media Responses to 9/11*, Cresskill, NJ: Hampton Press, 101–20.

Nacos, B.L. (1994) *Terrorism and the Media. From the Iran Hostage Crisis to the World Trade Center Bombing*, New York: Columbia University Press.

—— (2002) *Mass-mediated Terrorism*, New York: Rowman & Littlefield.

Noll, A.M. (ed.) (2003) *Crisis Communications. Lessons from September 11*, Oxford: Rowman & Littlefield.

Paletz, D.L. and Schmid, A.P. (eds) (1992) *Terrorism and the Media*, Newbury Park: Sage.

Pludowski, T. (ed.) (2007) *How the World's News Media Reacted to 9/11. Essays From Around the Globe*, Spokane: Marquette Books.

Portes, J. (2007) " 'We cannot all be Americans': French Media Reception of 9/11", in T. Pludowski (ed.) *How the World's News Media Reacted to 9/11. Essays From Around the Globe*, Spokane: Marquette Books, 84–103.

Pukniel, A. (2001) "Amerykanska mobilizacja" [American Mobilization], *Press*, 10: 29–30.

Robins, K. (1994) "Forces of Consumption: From the Symbolic to the Psychotic", *Media, Culture and Society*, 16, 3: 449–68.

Schmid, A.P. and de Graaf, J. (1982) *Violence as Communication. Insurgent Terrorism and the Western News Media*, London: Sage.

Shoemaker, P.J. and Cohen, A.A. (2006) *News Around the World. Content, Practitioners, and the Public*, London: Routledge.

Silverstone, R. (1994) *Television and Everyday Life*, London: Sage

Sreberny, A. (2002) "Trauma Talk: Reconfiguring the Inside and Outside", in B. Zelizer and S. Allan (eds) *Journalism After September 11*, London: Routledge, 220–34.

Stepinska, A. (2005) "The Global Flow of Information and Propaganda. Terrorist Attacks on the USA, September 11, 2001 as a Media Event", in S. Wojciechowski (ed.) *Terrorism as a Timeless Actor on the International Stage*, Poznan: Wydawnictwo Instytutu Nauk Politycznych i Dziennikarstwa UAM, 51–62.

—— (2007) "Media and terrorism: new phenomena, new relations", paper presented at the ICA pre-conference on Methodologies of Comparative Research in a Global Sphere: Paradigms–Critique–Methods in San Francisco, May.

Tuchman, G. (1978) *Making News: A Study in The Construction of Reality*, New York: Free Press.

Volkmer, I. (2002) "Journalism and Political Rises in the Global Network Society", in B. Zelizer and S. Allan (eds) *Journalism After September 11*, London: Routledge, 235–46.

Wark, M. (2005) "The Weird Global Media Event and the Tactical Intellectual [version 3.0]", in W. Hui Kyong Chung and T. Keenan (eds) *New Media. Old Media. A History and Theory Reader*, London: Routledge, 265–75.

Weimann, G. and Winn, C. (1994) *The Theater of Terror. Mass Media and International Terrorism*, New York: Longman.

Zelizer, B. and Allan, S. (eds) (2002) *Journalism After September 11*, London: Routledge.

15

EVENTSPHERES AS DISCURSIVE FORMS

(Re-)Negotiating the "mediated center" in new network cultures

Ingrid Volkmer and Florian Deffner

Introduction

Media events are like "holidays" that "halt everyday routines" and "transform the daily life into something special" – as Daniel Dayan and Elihu Katz famously argued more than a decade ago (Dayan and Katz 1992: 5). The authors claim that mass media events constitute "interruptions of routine; they intervene in the normal flow of broadcasting" simply by "mediating"[1] forms of collective experience (Dayan and Katz 1992: 5). In their definition, media events are preplanned and viewers "actively *celebrate*" (Dayan and Katz 1992: 13, emphasis in original) the mediation of epic moments of politics, sports, and popular culture. Over more than a decade, Dayan and Katz' work has contributed to a conceptual differentiation of media events as "contests, conquests, and coronations" which create powerful ritual representations of national moments of "unity" within one nation – or in the "entire world" (1992: 12).

Indeed, many aspects of Dayan and Katz's concept seem to be still important for the understanding of the role of ritual symbolic forms in today's complex and multi-layered transnational media culture. However, contemporary global and multi-directional network structures have replaced the predominantly national "mass" media culture of the late 1980s, and have formed constant streams of supra- and subnational content "flows" via satellite and Internet where "breaking" news constitutes no longer the "exceptional" but the norm. These transnational (and transcultural) event publics construct new forms of ritual symbolic communication, constituting collective experiences of moments of "unity" across a global discourse terrain. Furthermore, communicative networks, from television, newspaper to interactive sites, alter the way in which media events are not only selected and framed but also – for lack of a better word – "contextualized." This is in particular relevant for political media events which are our sole focus in this chapter. For example, national political media events, such as the 2008 election crisis in Kenya and the 2009 demonstrations in Iran, summits taking place in Africa, Asia, Europe, and elsewhere as well as even minor conflicts, are no longer framed in relation to one nation but are increasingly contextualized from a transnational angle. These – depending on the geographical, cultural or political perspective – macro and micro media events are no longer staged but shape moments of "world" experience among an otherwise constant stream of content. These event forms are no longer distributed through "mass" media, reaching the majority of a national audience and thus constituting a moment of national "unity." Instead, media events have become a communicative ritual, a sometimes short, sometimes extended moment of, in many cases, transnational public discourse and – depending on the nature of the event – even transnational deliberation. This communicative ritual affects public debate in new ways. The coverage of events via satellite television or Internet creates – as argued elsewhere – a "power of immediacy" (Volkmer 2004) by encouraging "live" responses from government and other officials to unfolding events. This power of immediacy, which has characterized the satellite era of the late twentieth century and has coined the terms "media diplomacy" (e.g. Seib 1997) and "CNN effect" (Robinson 2002), has gathered pace in the network structure of today's global public spheres. Photographs taken on a mobile phone, and posted – not necessarily in mainstream media but straight to interactive sites – have the power of not only setting the agenda of transnational news outlets, but of creating transnational political events.

Communicative mediation

Over the past decade, various academic debates have refined Dayan and Katz's approach and have identified important additional conceptual nuances. For example, Douglas Kellner argues that not only "scandals" but the "the world of spectacle" has affected almost all media forms, "from politics to entertainment" (Kellner 2003: 5). Simon Cottle defines in particular political "events" as "mediatized conflicts" (Cottle 2006, 2008; Couldry and Rothenbuhler 2007). In his view, processes of media-centered mediatization are shaped by a "media sphere where different flows and networks . . . reciprocally inform each other" (Cottle 2006: 51). Others, such as Jerry Landay (1993) and Paddy Scannell (1996), consider Dayan and Katz's model as being too narrow and suggest incorporating "the unplanned," i.e. events which often "shock the world." Elihu Katz and Tamar Liebes (2007) have recently proposed a more integrative model of "ceremonial" but also "live" events, signifying also political conflicts and crises as "events," such as September 11 in 2001 and the London Bombings in 2005, military conflicts (e.g. the Iraq War in 2003), but also natural disasters (e.g. Hurricane Katrina in 2005; Boxing Day Tsunami in 2004). "Immediacy" being mediated and constructed through breaking news narratives constitutes the crucial element in these spontaneous event categories. They are the key difference between the original concepts of mass media events, featuring the intentional staging and dramatic coverage of preplanned symbolic moments in history, and unintentional events, such as humanitarian disaster, war and terror. For example, Blondheim and Liebes (2002: 272) highlight with regard to the September 11 attacks that the series of repetitious acts ensured that the event gained an exclusive long-term presence on television screens around the world. The coverage of September 11 serves again as a prime example, delivered continuously "live." Liebes (1998) has described these broadcasts as "disaster marathons" involving the endless repetition of images from the scene, portrayals of rescue workers and interviews with victims, creating a new form of ritualized 24/7 conflict coverage. Other concepts address mediation as "eventization" – as new forms of thematic transnational spectacles, such as the Olympics (Price and Dayan 2008), having an influence on new forms of international relations (Crack 2008; Gilboa 2002). Strictly speaking, processes of "eventization" have also shaped new international TV formats, such as *Big Brother, Who Wants to be a Millionaire* or *American Idol* as well as "popular media events" like award shows (e.g. *MTV Music Awards; Academy Awards Show*) and large-scale concerts (e.g. *Live Earth*) to the point of event-driven announcements of blockbuster movies. These approaches reconceptualize not so much the phenomenon of a "media event" *as such* but rather varying degrees of mediation of this ritual form shaping media events within an advanced global digital landscape.

However, mediation does not only refer to "representation" and "eventization" as discussed above but to processes of negotiation; in other words, to a "communicative," and (not or) "discursive" form. Dayan and Katz only vaguely touch on these aspects. They claim that "viewers seat different selves in front of the set" – referring to the television set – and that events take on the role of a "family holiday" (Dayan and Katz 1992: 134, 204). Douglas Kellner clearly highlights what we might call the "reciprocal" process of mediation when he argues that "experience and everyday life are shaped and mediated by the spectacles of media culture and consumer society" (Kellner 2003: 2) and Silverstone et al. state – building on Giddens' notion of "ontological security" (Giddens 1990: 278) – that everyday media practice is re-constructed as a "semantic universe":

> Objects and meanings, in their objectification and incorporation within the spaces and practices of domestic life, define a particular semantic universe for the household in relation to that offered in the public world of commodities and ephemeral and instrumental relationships.
>
> (Silverstone et al. 1992: 19)

Such "semantic universe" is also deeply embedded in the lifeworld, for example, in the phenomenological sociology of Alfred Schutz and Thomas Luckmann as the everyday reality experienced by ordinary people: "the lifeworld is the quintessence of a reality that is lived, experience, and endured" (Schutz and Luckmann 1989: 1). Therefore, then, "[t]he world of everyday life is . . . man's fundamental and paramount reality" (Schutz and Luckmann 1974: 3). In its "natural attitude" it is taken for granted and "self-evidently 'real' " (Schutz and Luckmann 1974: 4). The media world, being immanent to our lifeworld, is taken for granted in their ordinariness as well. As such, it encompasses the everyday reality experienced through "mediated transitions." This is probably the main reason why media are constitutive parts of our wider social world: they broaden our horizons of experience by showing close and distant, expected and unexpected, familiar and unfamiliar, interesting and uninteresting events – all conveyed by a media infrastructure that is global in its reach and multi-perspective in its output. Especially under the conditions of the thematic lifeworld "relevance" (Schutz and Luckmann 1974: 186) one might claim that "event" experiences are not only "holidays" (Dayan and Katz 1992) but symbolically intrude and extend lifeworlds at the same time: on the one hand they "colonize" (Habermas 1987) the lifeworld and on the other, engage with a "wider world" – ironically often through "colonizing" structures. In a way these experience structures constitute what Gadamer meant by *Erlebnis*, the experience of being "alive," quite similar to Heidegger's notion of *Dasein* as the ultimative subjective world experience, and *Erfahrung* as a socially constructed (world) experience (Gadamer 1993). These processes of *Erlebnis* and *Erfahrung* are not passive world experiences. Gadamer's term *Erlebnis* "signifies not only the process of acquisition, moreover, but also the residual content of what is so acquired – that is both the immediacy of the origin of an experience and its lasting significance" (Weinsheimer 1985: 87), whereas *Erfahrung* relates to "knowledge that can be gathered from others" (Weinsheimer 1985: 87). It seems that Gadamer's notion of *Erlebnis* could help to conceptualize the experience of events as "reciprocal" processes of mediation where the meaning of "experienced" events is reconstructed, producing a "lasting significance." The experience of such an *Erlebnis*, however, becomes even more complex through network structures of digitalization, reconceptualizing the "semantic universe" (Silverstone et al. 1992: 19) through a collective *Erlebnis* moment across transnational communities.

The lifeworld "eventsphere"

It seems that forms of what we call "communicative" mediation (i.e. the subjective de- and reconstruction of media events within lifeworld parameters) had already gained some relevance in the time of national "mass" media where media events were "staged" and "distributed" from "a" to "b," strictly from "sender" to "receiver" in an almost Chomskyian sphere of "manufacturing consent" (Herman and Chomsky 2002) within a national public sphere. Results of our international study, which aimed to compare media memories from people's youth across three generations in nine countries, suggest that media events are recalled in re-mediated forms, using media images. This is in particular the case in the "middle" generation of our study, born between 1954 and 1959 as well as in the "young" generation, born between 1978 and 1984. Whereas the "oldest" generation (born between 1935 and 1945) recall media events as strictly lifeworld events, reconstructing, re-mediating the event strictly within (place-based) lifeworld experiences, the characteristics of the reconstruction of media events in the middle generation involved in this study reflect the first transnational mass (space-based) media culture in the sense that the *same* events are remembered across nations involved in this study in quite similar ways.

In the study members of three generations were interviewed employing the method of focus group discussion. The objective of these interviews in nine countries, including Australia, Austria, Czech Republic, Germany, Japan, India, South Africa, and Mexico, was to recall media memories throughout youth years in each of these three generations (Volkmer 2006). Members of the "radio" generation involved in this study, born between 1924 and 1929 and living through their youth years in the 1930s, recall media events in all nine countries through a quite different "local" re-mediation of lifeworld experiences. Events, such as sport events and major war reports, were re-mediated through social communication in the "place" of social forms of interaction. In contrast, responses of the generation who were raised in the first mass media culture of the 1960s show that a number of events are communicatively re-mediated not through "place"-based lifeworld experience (as in the older generation) but through other media forms – processes that are subsequently reconfiguring the lifeworld as "communicatively" (not discursively) stretching across a transnational "space." Whereas Dayan and Katz argue that events are "framed," we claim that re-mediation is a process of engaging communicatively with media texts, and indeed, with frames, which becomes in particular apparent when events are being recalled. However, focus group members of the "Black and White Television" generation, born between 1954 and 1959, for example, in the Czech Republic and Australia, re-mediate the Vietnam War already in a similar and most interestingly media-centered way. As Jan Jirak notes, the

> Vietnam War was recalled second after the Prague Spring in terms of richness of media experience. . . . The first image participants recalled was the photo of the running girl (after the napalm attack). The topic of Vietnam was closely associated with napalm: "The word *napalm* appeared in my head immediately, but I cannot see any other images from television, nothing like that."
>
> (Jirak 2006: 65, emphasis in original)

Responses were very similar in Australia, as the following interview sequence shows:

A: "I can remember quite a few from the Vietnam War, but not only the war but also the anti-war protests in North America, the Kent State University things. These images are very strong."

Interviewer: "Can you remember the context of that memory, I mean, where you saw them?"

A: "– the napalm"

B: "the napalm"

Unidentified: "Yeah, the napalm kid. Yeah."

(Slade 2006: 26).

The visual image of the "napalm kid" has become the angle of re-mediating the event for these groups. Members of the young generation, for example, in South Africa, born between 1978 and 1984, recall the historical moment of the fall of the Berlin Wall vaguely but remember that they watched "that" on CNN, i.e. communicatively engaging more with the mediated form and less with the event as such as tended to be the case in media memories of the oldest generation.

B: "I remember like a wall in Germany or something."

J: "The wall separated East Germany and West Germany."

M: "And they broke it down."

D: "Lots of wire and that sort of thing."

J: "There's a piece of the wall in Cape Town."

M: "Wasn't that the unification of Germany or something like that?"

D: "Just like the First World War."

S: "No the Second World War."

K: "1990."

M: "I remember watching that on CNN."

(Teer-Tomaselli 2006: 172)

Recalling the "eyewitnessing" of the mediation (for example, through CNN) and less of the event seems to be similar to the memories of the first Gulf War where mainly visual images (quite congruent with news media's video footage) are recalled and re-mediate the Gulf War even in memory as a visual almost iconographic *Erlebnis* among the young focus group in India. "The Gulf War reminds me of tanks burning and other stuff. Seeing every day the jets firing, the missiles launched, and the petrol on fire" (Kumar 2006: 113).

Another response shows how respondents reflect events through media-centered reconstruction:

International events? Especially I remember Vietnam, Watergate, of course, but not much, but then I had followed it up later on the BBC, when they telecast it just before the Clinton scandal; they had carried a series of shows on TV, as to how Watergate took place, how he was trying to bug all information of all opposition members, and then finally how he had been asked to resign. This I followed up much later, but not when it did (happen, IV).

(Kumar 2006: 105)

These three focus group responses reveal different forms of communicative mediation where events are repositioned and reconstructed by integrating media forms.

It seems that mediation and re-mediation processes of events in networked media de- and re-center the relevance and meaning of (for example) mainstream news coverage of events. It could be argued that the global network media space in its totality seems to be at the center of varying or oscillating networked spheres, enabling direct re-mediating discourse across national and cultural boundaries. The multi-layered – or in media terms multi-channeled – structure of such a discourse could be conceptualized through emerging networked processes of negotiation. This is mainly due to the fact that the "great globalization debate' " (Held and McGrew 2003) is replete with metaphors of "networks" (e.g. Castells 1996; Holton 2008), "flows" (e.g. Castells 1996) and "connectivity" (e.g. Tomlinson 1999; Hepp et al. 2008) all pointing toward a substantially increased globally mediated experience which not only mediates events transnationally but also creates a new form of proximity.

Transcultural formation of discursive eventspheres

As the above interview sequences show, communicative re-mediation renegotiates an event and constructs a "lifeworld eventsphere." In the case of the interview sequences, CNN and BBC have served as a platform for this process. However, communicative re-mediation remained within the boundaries of the lifeworld. The globalization of communication as well as the diversification of network communication profoundly altered the cultural form not only of media events but eventspheres. Examples of these processes are YouTube clips, posted by soldiers in Iraq which provide lifeworld insight and a re-mediation of a major news event, delivered on mainstream media through subjective comments. Furthermore, these subjective accounts of media events are not only internationally accessible from news platforms but shape a subjective transnational discourse, reflecting what is – in many cases – a transnational event *Erlebnis*. In this sense, a media event is not only "mediated" in many different cultural forms but is discursively re-mediated through individual sites, blogs, and comments on digital platforms. In this sense, events create not only communicative re-mediation *within* lifeworlds, but increasingly discursive "moments" *across* transnational lifeworlds as they establish a transnational accessible discursive "eventsphere" which re-mediates the event in extended transnational debates. It is this discursive re-mediation which not only becomes an interesting component of new mediated spheres but constitutes also a powerful space for a transnational public. Furthermore, the digital media environment as well as the emergence of a globalized "public" space transform traditional conceptual frameworks of media events. Media events are no longer mediated within national contexts, providing a powerful national collective "mass media" experience, but are delivered in a multi-platform environment, and are renegotiated and repositioned in a transnational sphere. These new forms of events are no longer primarily selected and "scripted" as a national collective experience but are shaping "eventspheres." These new forms are instead continuously debated, renegotiated and repositioned in a transnational context from macro events, such as the crisis between Georgia and Russia, to micro events, such as incidents of Hillary Clinton's campaign. On Facebook in September 2007, the "Stop Hillary Clinton" group outpaced with more than 418,000 members any other group for or against a presidential candidate (Cullen 2007). It seems that events are characterized by new types of – for lack of a better word – event "rhetoric" which involves conceptual and structural elements: the conceptual integration instantaneously delivered details of event developments by so-called citizen journalists through "live" images taken by mobile phones (Volkmer and Heinrich 2008) and a structural component as events accelerate and gain symbolic power through "speed" (Hassan 2008).

In today's network culture key moments of events are frozen in time on sites such as YouTube and could theoretically be accessed from anywhere in the world at any time. However, globalized network structures also allow not only the posting but discursive interaction about these (key) event moments. Naim calls this the "double echo chamber," where the first "echo" "is produced when content first posted on the Web is re-aired by mainstream TV networks. The second occurs when television moments, even the most fleeting, gain a permanent presence thanks to bloggers or activists who redistribute them through websites like YouTube" (Naim 2007: 1) – phenomena which could be described as discursive re-mediation. Given this spatial "network" eventsphere, not only can key moments be continuously viewed but it seems that the meaning of these moments might change over time. An example of this is the events of September 11 which could be watched continuously; however, the process of reconstructing the tragedy has clearly shifted. In particular the construction and mediation of conflict-related events have been "transformed by network technologies in conjunction with an advanced process of globalization of 'public' discourse" (Volkmer 2008: 93).

It seems that forms of transnational discursive re-mediation first appeared in the context of the U.S. invasion of Afghanistan. Besides the coverage of national Western mainstream media who attempted to build up the "event" of the war, other voices, such as Al Jazeera, counterbalanced the global (in particular CNN's) framing of the event. Whereas some Western mainstream news media began to critically reflect their "frames" of war coverage, forms of discursive re-mediation created new types of debate in a new transnational public space. In particular Al Jazeera's website showed critical footage which attracted individual comments; for example, from the U.S., to which Al Jazeera reacted by posting responding content over the course of several weeks, occasionally interrupted by a radicalization of this process: whenever Al Jazeera posted photographs of civilian victims, the site was hijacked and these images were replaced by varying U.S. images, such as a U.S. flag and the phrase "Let the freedom bell ring" (Volkmer 2004).

Advanced forms not only of a globalized media infrastructure have shaped new *Erlebnis* experiences of transnational events which even influence national events such as the Catholic World Youth Day (see Hepp and Krönert, Chapter 18, this volume). Furthermore, the digital media environment as well as the emergence of a globalized "public" space transforms traditional conceptual frameworks of media events. The coverage of the Tibet crisis could serve as an example where mainstream media coverage was discursively re-mediated, which has, in response, transformed the framing of mainstream media. For example, about 30,000 comments discuss the video clip which blames Western media coverage for misrepresenting the Tibet conflict. This discursive re-mediation of the Tibet event reflects not only the political background but subjective experiences and viewpoints.

Another example for the creation of an eventsphere is John McCain's television ad which sarcastically compares the celebrity status of Barak Obama to Paris Hilton and Britney Spears. This television ad has not only triggered responses from mainstream media in various countries, but Paris Hilton has posted her response to McCain on YouTube and has re-mediated the original meaning. In her satirical clip she refers to McCain as "that wrinkly white haired guy" and the "oldest celebrity in the world." This remediation of the original "event" posted shortly after the television ad was aired in the U.S. triggered a transnational discussion which generated about 300 comments within just a few days.

Nick Couldry argues in his book *Media Rituals* (2003) that media rituals are often associated with a form of a powerful societal center. He claims that media events "are privileged moments, not because they reveal society's underlying solidarity, but because they reveal the mythical construction of the mediated centre at its most intense" (Couldry 2003: 56). This center is not only depositioned but the role of media powerfully defining this center is being renegotiated in an emerging transnational eventsphere. It seems that processes of transnational discursive remediation crisscross the mediated center and establish their own eventspheres, often far beyond the original "mediated center." The transnational debate about the so-called Danish Cartoon case has revealed this phenomenon where many participants in these debates were not even part of the original mediated event "moment." Phenomena which might be considered "hybrid forms of ritualization" emerging between the "ordinary" and the "extraordinary," which "challenges the outstanding status of events, and pushes them to a paradoxical in-between position, neither routine, nor extraordinary, open to various conflicting interpretations regarding their collective relevance" (Csigo 2007: 13). However, this "myth of the center" relates to a "second myth that 'the media' has a privileged relationship to that 'centre', as a highly centralized system of symbolic production whose 'natural' role is to represent or frame that 'centre'. Call this the myth of the mediated centre." (Couldry 2003: 45).

We agree with Couldry in his notion that the ritual and in particular media rituals are stretched across "multiple sites" and create their own social space (Couldry 2003: 13). However, given today's global communication space, multiple "mediated centers" are created and renegotiated in the discursive eventsphere. Examples are the diverse "framing" of Tibet in 2008 in video clips posted on websites, debalancing not only the mainstream coverage of mainstream news media through the highlighting of diverse "authentic" details but also different forms of re-mediation from Chinese diaspora in Europe, the U.S. and Canada – a quite distinct positioning of "mediated centers" within one eventsphere.

When we aim to understand the negotiation of the "mediated centre" (Couldry 2003) in "new network cultures," the Internet – or more precisely different facets of mediation enabled by the technological framework of the Internet – lie at the heart of analysis. This is not to say that "display media" (Schoenbach 2007) (i.e. television, newspapers) become meaningless in the process of negotiating/consuming media content. Traditional forms of media are coexisting alongside "new" information and communication tech-nologies. Moreover, as touched upon above, they are to a substantial degree also reproduced online. Looking beyond the technological side of things, traditional media will continue to maintain their main content-related unifying function. As Klaus Schoenbach argues: "unrequested, display media inform us about what *the* others or what, at least, *others* find important, what one should be concerned about in one's community or country, or in the world." (Schoenbach 2007: 347, emphasis in original). Thus it is the eminent quality of display media to convey a sense of "being" in a wider world, regardless of those bits of news and information that are personally interest-ing to us. In the specific example of media events in Dayan and Katz's (1992) classic sense, the symbolic power of television creates this feeling of belonging by enthralling very large audiences within nations or across the globe in front of their TV screens, jointly getting excited about the event (Dayan and Katz 1992: 12). The same goes for "war, conflict, and terror" covered in "breaking news" as they also televise an event in the moment of its being.

It seems that mainstream media have lost this role of constituting *Erlebnis* moments as symbolic spaces of national and transnational "unity." Instead, "places" in the space of transnational network communication structures not only symbolically relate to each other but rather shape transnational discourse which creates proximity. A proximity which "describes a common conscious *appearance* of the world as intimate, more compressed, more part of everyday reckoning – [as] for example in our . . . mundane use of media technologies to bring distant images into our most intimate local spaces" (Tomlinson 1999: 3, emphasis in original).

Along the same lines, Anthony Giddens (1991: 187) notes that "[a]lthough everyone lives a local life phenomenological worlds are for the most part truly global." In creating structures of approximation of diverse phenomenological worlds and conveying a feeling of belonging to a global or "world society" (Beck 2000), large-scale events like the first moon landing, the Olympic Games or September 11, to name just a few among many other examples, are most obvious "mediatized" epiphanies of moments of togetherness and create a "world consciousness," for example, among generations (see media generation examples above).

The fundamental difference, obviously, lies in today's technological possibilities of news distribution. The immediacy of breaking news in international and national news channels and the interactivity of the worldwide web re-charts/renegotiates the "mediated center" of a global society and unfolds its whole complexity. With an infinite number of players, events are decentered and delivered through a variety of platforms (Volkmer 2008: 95). This decentralization of "event-perspectives" not only takes place in various national and transnational television channels, but also through "personal websites" (blogs), mobile phone communication as in the case of London Bombings via Google, YouTube, debates on myspace.com, or Ohmynews, a so-called citizen journalism news platform in Korea. Interestingly, events are based on an interplay between mainstream/traditional/mass/public service/corporate media and "nonmarket actors" (Benkler 2006: 220). Whether and under what circumstances these transnational discursive eventspheres create new forms of cosmopolitanism has yet to be discussed. Ulrich Beck has recently identified "reflexive cosmopolitanism" (Beck 2006: 94) as a form of *Dasein* in the transnational space. However, it seems that this consciousness of not only a global/local but also a transnational/national *Erlebnis* is most vivid in subjective reflection, as a young Danish expatriate living in Australia claims:

> a big event would be the upcoming presidential elections in the US. . . . For that, I would easily try to reach some American news about that. I would probably even – I will and I have already – see some news sections on YouTube, because the good thing there is I

227

don't need to actually stream American TV and wait for them until they say something interesting. The interesting ten minutes, they are on YouTube. So I definitely do that, but I also use Danish news. Maybe Australian news if they cover that in an interesting way.[2]

In this sense, larger approaches to discuss "mediated globalization" (Rantanen 2005) would be too narrow if they only related to perceptions of "distance" and "proximity" of media events. However, a phenomenological concept of "mediated globalization" should address different angles of the positioning of events in the center of lifeworlds in a transnational context in order to identify ways in which events delivered to mobile devices and laptops create a momentum of reflection and possibly contemplation in an otherwise constant stream of content. It might be useful to conceptualize these angles of not so much ritual as symbolic positioning of "events" in lifeworld centers as communicative and discursive mediation, since these processes take on a new relevance within the contemporary globalized media culture. This is important, as these cultural specific forms of lifeworld constructions affect discourse competence within the emerging transnational public sphere.

Notes

1 In doing so, they identify a phenomenon that transcends Daniel Boorstin's (1969) critical assessment of (mass) mediated events as "pseudo-events."
2 This interview was conducted in October 2007 by Florian Deffner as part of his PhD thesis.

References

Beck, U. (2000) *What is Globalization?*, Malden: Polity Press.
—— (2006) *The Cosmopolitan Vision*, Malden: Polity Press.
Benkler, Y. (2006) *The Wealth of Networks. How Social Production Transforms Markets and Freedom*, New Haven, CT: Yale University Press.
Blondheim, M. and Liebes, T. (2002) "Live Television's Disaster's Marathon of September 11 and its Subversive Potential", *Prometheus*, 20, 3: 271–6.
Boorstin, D. (1969) *The Image: A Guide to Pseudo-events in America*, New York: Harper Colophon.
Castells, M. (1996) *The Rise of the Network Society, The Information Age: Economy, Society and Culture, Vol. 1*, Oxford: Blackwell.
Cottle, S. (2006) *Mediatized Conflict*, Maidenhead: Open University Press.
—— (2008) " 'Mediatized Rituals': A Reply to Couldry and Rothenbuhler", *Media, Culture and Society*, 30, 1: 135–40.
Couldry, N. (2003) *Media Rituals: A Critical Approach*, London: Routledge.
Couldry, N. and Rothenbuhler, E.W. (2007) "Simon Cottle on Mediatized Rituals: A Response", *Media, Culture and Society*, 29, 4: 691–5.
Crack, A.M. (2008) *Global Communication and Transnational Public Spheres*, New York: Palgrave Macmillan.

Csigo, P. (2007) "Ritualizing and Mediating 'Ordinary' Reality in the Era of 'Event Television' ", paper presented at the conference on Media Events, Globalization, and Culture Change at the University of Bremen, Germany, July 5–7.

Cullen, R.T. (2007) "Anti-Hillary Facebook Site tops Obama", *politico*, September 25. Available HTTP: <http://www.politico.com/news/stories/0907/5989.html> (accessed 4 July 2008).

Dayan, D. and Katz, E. (1992) *Media Events: The Live Broadcasting of History*, Cambridge, MA: Harvard University Press.

Gadamer, H-G. (1993) *Wahrheit und Methode. Ergaenzungen, Register*, Tuebingen: Mohr Siebeck.

Giddens, A. (1990) *The Consequences of Modernity*, Stanford, CA: Stanford University Press.

—— (1991) *Modernity and Self-Identity*, Cambridge: Polity Press.

Gilboa, E. (2002) "Media Diplomacy in the Arab–Israeli Conflict", in E. Gilboa (ed.) *Media and Conflict: Framing Issues, Making Policy, Shaping Opinion*, Ardsley Park: Transnational Publishers, 193–212.

Habermas, J. (1987) *Theory of Communicative Action*, Vol. II, Boston, MA: Beacon Press.

Hassan, R. (2008) *The Information Society. Cyber Dreams and Digital Nightmares*, Cambridge: Polity Press.

Held, D. and McGrew, A. (2003) "The Great Globalization Debate: An Introduction", in D. Held and A. McGrew (eds) *The Global Transformation Reader*, Cambridge: Polity Press, 1–50.

Hepp, A., Krotz, F., Moores, S. and Winter, C. (eds) (2008) *Connectivity, Networks and Flows. Conceptualizing Contemporary Communications*, Cresskill, NJ: Hampton Press.

Herman, E.S. and Chomsky, N. (2002) *Manufacturing Consent: The Political Economy of Mass Media*, New York: Pantheon Books.

Holton, R.J. (2008) *Global Networks*, New York: Palgrave MacMillan.

Jirak, J. (2006) "Czech Republic", in I. Volkmer (ed.) *News in Public Memory: An International Study of Media Memories across Generations*, New York: Peter Lang, 53–68.

Katz, E. and Liebes, T. (2007) " 'No More Peace!': How Disaster, Terror and War Have Upstaged Media Events", *International Journal of Communication*, 1: 157–66.

Kellner, D. (2003) *Media Spectacle*, London: Routledge.

Kumar, K.J. (2006) "India", in I. Volkmer (ed.) *News in Public Memory: An International Study of Media Memories across Generations*, New York: Peter Lang, 95–118.

Landay, J.M. (1993) "Review Work: Media Events: The Live Broadcasting of History by Daniel Dayan & Elihu Katz", *Film Quarterly*, 46, 4: 45–6.

Liebes, T. (1998) "Television's Disaster Marathons: A Danger for Democratic Processes?", in T. Liebes and J. Curran (eds) *Media, Ritual and Identity*, London: Routledge, 71–84.

Naim, M. (2007) "The YouTube Effect", *Foreign Policy*, January/February 2007. Available HTTP: <http://www.foreignpolicy.com/story/cms.php?story_id=3676> (accessed 3 December 2008).

Price, M.E. and Dayan, D. (eds) (2008) *Owning the Olympics: Narratives of the New China*, Ann Arbor, MI: University of Michigan Press.

Rantanen, T. (2005) *The Media and Globalization*, Thousand Oaks, CA: Sage.

Robinson, P. (2002) *The CNN Effect: The Myth of News, Foreign Policy and Intervention*, London: Routledge.

Scannell, P. (1996) *Radio, Television and Modern Life*, Cambridge: Blackwell.

Schoenbach, K. (2007) " 'The Own in the Foreign': Reliable Surprise – An Important Function of the Media?", *Media, Culture and Society*, 29, 2: 344–53.

Schutz, A. and Luckmann, T. (1974) *The Structures of the Life-world*, London: Heinemann.

—— (1989) *The Structures of the Life-world, Vol. II*, Evanston: Northwestern University Press.

Seib, P. (1997) *Headline Diplomacy. How News Coverage Affects Foreign Policy*, Westport, CT: Praeger.

Silverstone, R., Hirsch, E. and Morley, D. (1992) "Information and Communication Technologies and the Moral Economy of the Household", in R. Silverstone and E. Hirsch (eds) *Consuming Technologies. Media and Information in Domestic Spaces*, London: Routledge, 15–31.

Slade, C. (2006) "Australia", in I. Volkmer (ed.) *News in Public Memory: An International Study of Media Memories across Generations*, New York: Peter Lang, 27–34.

Teer-Tomaselli, R. (2006) "South Africa", in I. Volkmer (ed.) *News in Public Memory: An International Study of Media Memories across Generations*, New York: Peter Lang, 159–76.

Tomlinson, J.B. (1999) *Globalization and Culture*, Chicago, IL: University of Chicago Press.

Volkmer, I. (2004) "The Globalization of Media: From CNN to Al Jazeera and Beyond", paper presented at the conference "Globalization, Identity, Diversity", *Forum Barcelona*, July 26–29.

—— (ed.) (2006) *News in Public Memory*, New York: Peter Lang.

—— (2008) "Conflict-related Media Events and Cultures of Proximity", *Media, War and Conflict*, 1, 1: 93–101.

Volkmer, I. and Heinrich, A. (2008) "CNN and Beyond: Journalism in a Globalized Network Sphere", in J. Chapman and M. Kinsey (eds) *Broadcast Journalism: A Critical Introduction*, London: Routledge.

Weinsheimer, J.C. (1985) *Gadamer's Hermeneutics: A Reading of Truth and Method*, New Haven, CT: Yale University Press.

Part VI

MEDIA EVENTS AND CULTURAL CONTEXTS

16

SPORTS EVENTS

The Olympics in Greece

Roy Panagiotopoulou

Introduction

It is widely acknowledged that television has transformed the nature, the scope and the resources of some major sport events in general and the Olympic Games in particular (Wenner 1998; Real 1998; Maguire 1999; Roche 2000: 159). The opening ceremonies of the Olympic Games (OG), although they have nothing to do with sports, have become an indispensable part in the organization of this event and function as a special media event. Their success constitutes a decisive element in the overall success of the organization, as the OG have become the most watchable TV program nowadays.[1] It is therefore evident that each city/country which is hosting the OG pays great attention to the production and the broadcasting of the best possible television program in relation to the competition and also to the opening and closing ceremonies, which are especially designed for television viewing (Moragas et al. 2003: 282–3).

This chapter will focus on the Opening Ceremony of the Athens 2004 OG and its narrative approach to the presentation of the nations to the world. Prior to the analysis of the ceremony a brief description of the relationship between sport and media as well as a theoretical review of the opening ceremonies as media event will be provided. Furthermore, this chapter discusses the use of this type of mega event for promoting the national image of Greece as demonstrated in the example of the Athens 2004 Games.

The relationship between sport and media

Global sport in general and the Olympics in particular constitute one of the biggest mediated phenomena and a popular culture expression of our time. "Ignoring MediaSport[2] today would be like ignoring the role of the church in the Middle Ages or ignoring the role of art in the Renaissance" (Real 1998: 15). The interdependency between sport and the global media sport complex has multiple levels. Sporting organizations, politics, entrepreneurial interests, international and national communication flows, cultural heritage, technological advances in media coverage, new media information reception and new journalistic practices, altogether constitute a complex relationship with multifaceted impacts.

While people's interest in global sport competitions has increased, the number of sport printed and electronic media in both traditional and new media has risen as well. Furthermore, the broadcasting right fees for international competitions and especially the Olympics have reached very high levels, and the increasing interest in sponsoring sports organizations, athletes and competitions demonstrates the growing global significance of sport for the media. Sporting events which were once mostly local or national events have nowadays become global media spectacles (Maguire 1999: 144).

Gradually, the globalization of sport has become synonymous with commercialization of the events. These new conditions have made sport competitions one of the most popular broadcasting genres, and some of them (e.g. the Olympic Games or the World Soccer Cup) have become mega media events.[3]

The Olympic Games are more than a game (Guttmann 2002). They draw their ideological background from a long-lasting cultural and civilization legacy starting from antiquity and continuing through to nineteenth-century liberalism. Nowadays, their most important cultural impact derives from the late twentieth-century developments when the Olympics turned into a global televised event. Their present social context is that of a "global village" in which people feel they gain a new cosmopolitan identity of "citizen of the world" (Maguire 1999: 144; Roche 2006: 28; Barnard et al. 2006). The main bulk of the large audiences of the Games follow the discourse about the Olympic ideals which tend to promote universalistic values of peace, equality, brotherhood, fair play, and harmony between body and mind. At the same time, these audiences participate in a unique cultural space that promotes messages of global community and culture. Opening ceremonies function as an "introduction" to the event and the Olympic ideals trying to gain the attention not only of sport fans but of all citizens.

Olympic games and opening ceremonies: theoretical approaches

The examination and interpretation of the role of Olympic ceremonies (opening, closing, and medals) has become a research issue for many scholars. We can recognize three major approaches to the interpretation of the ceremonies: the interpretation of the initiators of the International Olympic Committee (IOC), the anthropological-sociological approach of the ceremonies as rituals, and the media event approach as the mediated form of the ceremonies.

Initiators' approach

The initiators of the Olympic Movement have tried to point out the symbolism, meanings, and ritual character of Olympic ceremonies and the opening ceremony especially. According to the founder of the modern Olympic Games Pierre de Coubertin, the purpose of the opening ceremony is for purely pedagogical reasons: that is, to unite all nations[4] in a parade "classified by nations and their flags" (Coubertin 1931). Another vision was expressed by Liselotte Diem, who stated that the "Ceremony gives form to an event, it sets the emphasis, it builds up climaxes, it carries the audience along in sympathy, reflection, repose and final harmony" (Diem 1964; quoted in Carrard 1996: 24). It is obvious that ceremonies were initially designed to strengthen the cohesion among the nations and athletes participating in the biggest international sport competition of their time, a cohesion sustained by a broader educational and humanitarian ideology.

Anthropological-sociological approach

The anthropological-sociological approach became the leading approach among Olympic scholars. The work of John MacAloon examined the history and culture of the Olympic Movement and the richly textured rituals which respect cultural differences, give a dramatic essence to the festival and offer a set of common, universal values that unite participants and global audiences. He analyzed the modern Olympic Games as a complex cultural form that is composed of four distinct genres simultaneously, namely "spectacle," "festival," "ritual," and "game" (or sport competition) (MacAloon 1984: 242).[5] MacAloon emphasized the ritual character of the ceremonies that provides them with a "transcendental ground," that of humankind-ness, universality, and brotherhood (MacAloon 1984: 251). Following the arguments of Arnold van Gennep and Victor Turner,[6] MacAloon deems that rituals are organized around the schema of rites of passage (separation from "ordinary life"), and remarks that the "opening ceremonies are rites of separation from 'ordinary life', initiating a period of public liminality and stress the juxtaposition of national symbols and the symbols of the transnational 'human' community" (MacAloon 1984: 252). National (e.g. flags, anthems) as well as transnational symbols (e.g. Olympic flag, anthem, arrival of "sacred" flame) represent the unity of the world and the noble competition.[7]

Michael Real's approach focuses on the impact of commercialism and technology in the relationship between media and sport. He argues:

> No force has played a more central role in MediaSport complex than commercial television and its value system – profit-seeking, sponsorship, expanded markets, commodification and competition. The example of steady change in modern Olympic Games during the

past one hundred years illustrates the shift from the "modernist" tradition to the "postmodern" condition.

(Real 1998: 17)

Further, he analyzes the importance of Olympic TV to construct ritual and mythic events and shape the preferences of the audience. He emphasizes the behavior patterns of TV viewers who by watching the Olympic competitions participate, as sports fans or otherwise, both adopting a patterned behavior and being receptive in a culturally differentiated way to meanings and symbols communicated by the broadcasters. Commercialization of the Olympics and the respective TV program offer an intense mixture of images and messages in a fragmented way which leads to an information "overload" and "overdose" in sports coverage and in Olympic ideals (Real 1996).

Undoubtedly, the Olympic Games are nowadays seen as media events owing to the development of the media and foremost that of television. A number of scholars take Dayan and Katz's (1992) theoretical approach of media event (discussed below) as a starting point but they stress the more sociological-anthropological factors than the impact of the new television genre. Some anthropological studies published in the book edited by Klausen (1999) regarded the OG as public events which focus on a multicultural perspective, emphasizing culture as an artistic or aesthetic expression and as an element of group identity (Klausen 1999: 2).

Maurice Roche follows a political sociological approach to analyze the contemporary role and impact of mega events, especially the Olympics and expos, using a set of three sociological characteristics (modern/non-modern, national/non-national and local/non-local) (Roche 2000: 11). Mega events are seen as important elements in the orientation of national societies to international or global society and in the theory and practice of public culture.

Global events contribute to establishing an international public culture which provides, first, public images of diverse subordinate nationalities, ethnicities or religious groups; second, national, public images and attitudes to "other nations"; third, images of international society and transnational universalistic principles and practices, and fourth, foreign policies of inter-governmental organizations (e.g. IOC) that operate with respect to all accepted cultural and communication premises (Roche 2000: 21). In this sense mega events like the Olympics serve to establish an "official" version of international culture and parallel versions of collective identities and an international "ranking" of nations to the Western world cultural prototype.

Examining the contemporary role of mega events in modernity, Roche uses the imagery of "networks," "flow," and "hubs," and remarks that mega events may be conceived as "temporary cultural and physical bridges between these two forms of social space [global and local], between elites and the people" (Roche 2000: 234). He perceives event-as-hub (or as switching center) that provides an opportunity for event producer groups and their associated political, economic, and cultural networks to meet and consume the event together (and thus create shared cultural memories and cultural capital). Moreover, masses of people are temporarily mobilized to become active members of an intercultural movement.

Media event approach

In their seminal study about media events Dayan and Katz wrote about the festive viewing of television that "includes epic contests of politics and sports, charismatic missions, and rites of passage of the great Contests, Conquests and Coronations" (Dayan and Katz 1992: 1). They proposed a new television narrative genre of media events that are defined by certain main characteristics and effects.[8]

The Olympic Games were seen as a typical example of a global ceremony, preplanned and widely advertised in advance, broadcast live, occurring periodically in limited time and space, attended by large numbers of audiences around the world.[9] The authors categorize them in their typology of media events into that of Contest (Dayan and Katz 1992: 33–4), bearing mostly in mind the competition part of the Games. However, the Olympic Games are a complex spectacle not easily fitting just one kind of event. Therefore, Olympic ceremonies do not belong to the Contest category of media event but rather to the Coronation metaphor which seems more adequate (Puijk 2000: 311), because they are distanced from reality by keeping the symbols, time, and place of the ceremony "pure," reminding societies of their cultural heritage, providing at the same time reassurance of cultural continuity and inviting the public to take part in the constructed narration of the myth.

The impacts of this analysis led to many publications reinforcing or rejecting the media event criteria (Couldry 2003: 59–74; Hepp 2004: 326–40). After 15 years Dayan revisited several aspects of his approach, taking into account the changes in broadcasting media events and the new landscape emerging from the use of ICT. Using the example of broadcasting the Olympic Games, he characterizes them as a "repertory" event "of discontinuous existence made of long intervals and of episodic reenactments" (Dayan 2008: 391) with two dimensions: religious (doctrine of Olympic "spirit") and legalistic (contracts ensure a franchised format that guarantees successful reproduction) (Dayan 2008: 391).

In the last decades not only ceremonial events but also conflict situations (disasters, terror attacks, armed conflicts) or special live broadcasting programs (e.g. *Big Brother, Eurovision*) have covered some of the characteristics of media events and urged scholars to modify the criteria either to incorporate a wider rage of events in the category of media events or to specify a series of new dimensions covering new media practices. By slightly rephrasing some of the old criteria, Dayan insists on the concept of media events.

The new version of media events' criteria contains the following major features: (1) insistence and emphasis (omnipresence of the broadcast event, length of schedule, live transmission, and repetition of certain shots), (2) explicit performative dimension (reports are not objective, not balanced, use pompous language), (3) loyalty to the event's self-definition (accepting the definition as proposed by the organizers), and (4) access to a shared viewing experience (narrative continuity, visual proximity, and shared temporality) (Dayan 2008: 394).

Nevertheless, changes in media practices such as individualized reception by the new media, cynical behavior, and creation of disbelief may threaten the broadcasting of the Olympics by "semantics of conflictualization," "syntactics of banalization," and "pragmatics of disenchantment" (Dayan 2008: 395).

Under the new broadcasting conditions emphasis is given to conflict, stigmatization, and shame (e.g. doping), to merging news and media events causing a banalization of the format and the information flow. It further emphasizes new media that gather and multiply information from different sources and agents, fragmenting individual reception possibilities and, by doing so, reinforcing the disenchantment with the event which leads to a gradual loosening of the collective "we."

Regarding the Olympics as media event Dayan remarks that they are at a risk of experiencing certain disenchantment because the dimension of spectacle becomes predominant, leaving aside the ideological dimension of Olympic values and ideals. Consequently, the changes in media practices do not affect so much the ideological framework but rather each new version of the ceremony and the frame in which it is presented.

Opening ceremonies: organization and narrative approaches

Olympic ceremonies' rituals follow strict formalization patterns with a prevailing theatrical character and intense symbolic meanings. During the staging of the Games the Olympic stadium becomes a "diplomatic territory" and a de facto "sacred site" (Roche 2000: 98) but at the same time a television studio, where spectators can experience a dazzling array of cameras shooting and giant screens displaying the event (Moragas et al. 1995: 118, 122). The protocol that must be followed by the organization of the opening ceremony consists of two main parts:

- The compulsory program containing a number of Olympic rituals listed in Rule 58 of the Olympic Charter.[10]
- The artistic, cultural program designed by the host organizers and approved by the IOC. This part consists of selected segments presenting

the historical continuity of the host nation using simple, easy-to-understand symbols and connotations and an aestheticized version of the country's tradition.

The dimension of spectacle gained priority over the other genres when the ceremonies became media events, and the spectators in the stadium as the TV viewers at home were expected to be awestruck at the scale, narrative and postmodern grandeur rhetoric of the opening ceremony's elements (Roche 2000: 165). This has become more evident since the Los Angeles 1984 Games where more sophisticated broadcasting techniques have been used and a Hollywood style spectacle was incorporated into the opening ceremonies. Regarding the concept of the ceremony themes, they were presented in a comprehensive language of popular entertainment and symbolism addressing the majority of Western audiences in an all-embracing naiveté concerning the messages of Olympic ideals and of the host city/country (Tomlinson 1996: 590–3). These new showbiz elements set the guidelines that each new host nation tried to follow or even to surpass by giving its own interpretation of the event.

In trying to conceptualize the complexity of the organization and production of the ceremonies, MacAloon (1996: 36–7) distinguishes three organizational models:

- The *impresario model*: A well-known impresario from the entertainment industry in collaboration with showbiz experts gets the general authority to prepare the spectacle (e.g. Los Angeles 1984; Barcelona 1992; Atlanta 1996; Sydney 2000).
- The *cultural experts' model*: An intercultural group of experts and intellectuals assume the responsibility of designing the main segments of the ceremony and when the scenario is completed a group of artists and showbiz specialists carry out the work (Seoul 1988).
- The *auteur model*: A well-known single, creative young artist provides the scenario for others to realize (Albertville 1992; Athens 2004; Beijing 2008).

Another research tradition focuses on journalists' commentaries and the invented narrative approach in which three different perceptions are distinguished (Moragas et al. 1995: 104–11):

- A *historical event*. The broadcasters tend to emphasize the unique historical event taking place at that moment which forms part of a historical chain in the Olympic myth. The importance of Olympic rituals, their repetition, and symbolism are predominant and the host nation gives its own interpretation.

- A *celebration*. The opening ceremony is a celebration paying attention to the cultural elements and the exceptional character of the spectacle.
- An *entertainment*. The opening ceremonies are evaluated as an entertainment prior to the "real" excitement, which is the sports competition.

The opening ceremonies are designed to celebrate universalism through the national perspective of the host city. These ideological premises offer the necessary framework to construct the national narrative in a variety of artistic forms. In many cases, the host nations give to the compulsory program a specific national interpretation, presenting these universalistic rituals as a display of national character, pride, power, and progress.

The narrative of a nation

"Nowadays, nations are more than geopolitical entities, they are discursively constructed 'imagined communities'" (Anderson 1983). That is a shared sense of the character, culture and historical trajectory of a people" (Hogan 2003: 101–2). In the globalized discourse about a nation, we encounter a set of stories, images, landscapes, historical events, national symbols, and rituals that stand for the shared experiences which give meaning to a nation (Hall 1992: 293). Apart from the media, such discourses are found in museum exhibitions, tourism pamphlets, television advertisements, and so on. These agents provide the main sources from which the majority of people construct its perception, stereotypic opinions, or even prejudices about a foreign nation.

All individuals, collective entities, institutions, and nations need a connection to their past, although this past is rarely connected with what is revealed by academic historical research. In the majority of cases people or nations construct a discourse such as "what is good for us" or "for our country" (Hobsbawm 1998: 228–9, 324).[11]

Olympic opening ceremonies provide a nation with the opportunity to present its narrative and to demonstrate its past in an idealized rather than a realistic way. Due to the gigantic commercialization of the OG, this narrative serves not only as an affirmation of national identity but also as an extended advertisement for the host nation offering an opportunity to promote tourism, international corporate investment, trade, to improve bargaining position in international negotiations, impede a political ideology controlling domestic social inequalities, and strengthen cultural diplomacy (Hogan 2003: 102). Due to these characteristics, we used the approach of the presentation of a nation as the core of our interpretation.

Athens has a long-lasting and close relationship with the Olympic Games. Therefore, the selection of Athens to host the 28th Olympic Games in 2004 was from the very beginning linked with the history of the OG and with the revival of Olympic Movement values, rejuvenated in an ethical discourse with strong references to the narratives of antiquity (Panagiotopoulou 2003).

The Athens opening ceremony aimed to fulfill two major tasks: one was to revive the "tired" Olympic narrative, which had been called into question owing to prior organization scandals (Burbank et al. 2001: 2–4; Guttmann 2002: 176–7), intensive commercialization and gigantism, by referring at the same time to ancient values and ideals. The other was to present the history of a nation, closely related to the event and at the same time making it popular, understandable, and interesting for foreigners without making it trivial for nationals, which would risk offending their national pride. Historical sources and texts form a kind of "frame of reference" and serve as legitimation of national identity.

The opening ceremony of Athens 2004

The concept for the creation of the opening ceremony following the typology of MacAloon was that of the auteur.[12] The main idea of the creator was to present an "allegory," drawing from the fact that the OG were returning home to the country where they were born and revived. The opening ceremony visualized a journey through time and history giving a primordial position to ancient Greek civilization – mostly that of the classical era – as we recognize it through globally well-known artworks.

In the words of the artistic director the message of the ceremony as well as the way of communicating it was:

> The Opening Ceremony is a unique opportunity for modern Greece to share its joy in and pride of the centuries of its history; a history that gave birth to ideals, values and principles which still enlighten us all today. Democracy, Philosophy, Theater, Sport itself, the Olympic Games – all were born in Greece. We use images to tell our story. Images derived from the rich history and diversity of Greek Art. . . . All the artists that have worked for this ceremony believe that above symbolism lies fascination, beauty and the emotional intensity of images that unfold in the stadium.
>
> (D. Papaioannou, in *Opening Ceremony Media Guide* 2004: 20)

According to the *Opening Ceremony Media Guide* (2004: 24–70), the parts of the Athens 2004 Ceremony comprised the following: Countdown, Welcome, the Raising of the Greek flag and introduction of officials, Allegory (three iconic periods of Greek sculpture symbolizing the evolution of Greek civilization), Clepsydra, The book of life (DNA strand symbolized the common stuff of all human beings), The olive tree (a powerful symbol of Greece, Olympic winners and peace), The athletes of the world (a parade and assembly of the national teams), Oceania (song), Olympic cities tribute (a reminder of the modern history of the Olympic Games), and the Compulsory part (opening of the Games, raising of the Olympic flag, the Olympic anthem, oaths), Journey of the torch (presentation of the torch's journey around the world), Lighting of the cauldron (torchbearers with the flame enter the stadium, the last torchbearer ignites the cauldron), and the Finale (fireworks).

There were two parts in the opening ceremony where the nation was presented to the world: "Allegory" and "Clepsydra." The time continuum and the selected presentation of certain moments in Greek history was an idealized and simplified narrative of a nation, presented by the ATHOC.

In the part called "Allegory,"[13] the journey in time had one purpose: that is, the presentation of the three most revealed periods of Greek sculpture through a dreamlike atmosphere, symbolizing the evolution of the ancient Greek civilization (*The Official Report of the 28th Olympiad* 2005, Vol. 2: 170). The particular references to Geometry and Philosophy were direct references to the commitment of the ancient Greek civilization to the development of a sound scientific thought and logic, a contribution to the understanding of the world. For Greek thought art was its guide and a form of expressing its wonders and conquests. In addition, the ancient Greek thought was presented through the values of science, politics, and philosophy, which in turn constituted the foundations of Western civilization.

"Clepsydra"[14] was a chronological colorful parade of 11 floats depicting stylized figures from Greek frescos, mosaics, sculptures, and paintings from prehistoric to modern times. "Clepsydra" is an effective reference to time, its volatility, but also to historical continuity. The narrative of the history had to fit into the logic of the spectacle for the needs of an international disparate audience. Thus, the approach of history through art was the highest moment of the ceremony, good enough to avoid an ideological load and at the same time presenting an understandable but also an attractive picture to the average spectator and viewer. In order to achieve these results, techniques of the advertising industry were used more or less. The narrative of history was free of a scholarly approach, but full of aesthetics that followed the technique of a clip or the narrative of a visualized fairytale.

It is a very complex process to understand the connection that Greeks have with their history. The weight that ancient history carries always tips the scales in favor of the past. National histories are the result of a dialogue with various conceptions and involved agencies. Greek historians are anxious to demonstrate the continuity of Greek history, the value of neglected post-classical periods (e.g. Byzantium), the contribution of these periods to European history and their kinship to Hellenism (Liakos 2007: 222). In the European concept of universal history, the Greek classical past is seen as a Western past. In contrast, the past in the Greek imagination was their ancestral past and Greek historians claimed their own interpretation of it (Liakos 2007: 221).

The concept of the opening ceremony surpassed in a very delicate and cosmopolitan way this contradiction by showing the art masterpieces rather than an interpretation of the historical past. Hellenism was always at the roots of universal history and that was the main message of the opening ceremony. However, history can often be used as an instrument for the imposition of power over others. Modern Greek national identity has emerged from constant strife between the present and the past in a love-and-hate relationship. In the Clepsydra introduction, the one-sided approach to the past is obvious from the fact that the presentation of ancient Greece forms a big part of the program.[15]

In general, the concept of Clepsydra did not appeal only to the Greek audience, but also to the audience of the Western world which could easily identify the different art forms, the starting points of the Western world civilization and its basic moral values.[16] Although broadcasters tend to reproduce standardized representations of national identity and stereotypes (Kenneth and Moragas 2008: 262), Clepsydra contributed to the positive image of the country through the construction of attractive visuals which could be decoded easily and consumed with no particular effort from the general viewing public.

However, this rather simplified apolitical choice of the better-known and familiar images of Greek history through sport and culture has become for certain elite groups the vehicle for new approaches to nationalism, a fact that was first presented in the Athens opening ceremony. The Greek media imposed a new interpretation of the past and sustained a new feeling of national continuity and pride free of fights, wars, death, and sorrow. It is the beauty of artistic masterpieces that represents what is nationally important and worthy to be promoted or what should stay in the dark. It is not a coincidence that the organizers named the respective segments of the ceremony "Allegory" and "Clepsydra." With allegories – that is, imagined – symbolic acts, you cannot explain historical facts and come to the causalities of socio-political and economic relationships that shape the past of all nations and serve as fundaments for their future.

Epilogue

It is acknowledged that the Opening Ceremony which fascinated 70,000 spectators in the Olympic stadium and millions of viewers around the world received exceptionally positive reviews in the Greek and international Press.[17] The reason for this may be attributed to some degree to the following facts:

- It presented a politically "correct view" of the ancient Olympic ideals. This narrative of antiquity was a way to save the Olympic movement from the scandal-ridden Olympic establishment and the worn-out Olympic values and ideals.
- It contributed to the improvement of the country's image, which was not always positive due to delays in the preparation works for the games and to the uncertainty as to whether Greece could organize a safe Games.

- It reinforced national pride and presented a new version of Greek history resulting in the construction of new national identifications.
- It brought substantial economic benefits owing to advertising revenues and contributed to a better and positive image of the country.
- It contributed to the breakdown of the stereotypical views about certain Greek national characteristics.

However, the presentation of a nation with such a long history in such a "Disneyfied" way (Tomlinson 2004) can have negative future consequences, because it can cause misunderstandings, misconceptions or even controversies in relations with other countries and domestic social groups. A sanitized version of history that smoothed injustices and inequalities based on the historical development of the country can only serve for a small local power elite and the global media that in cases of celebration avoid conflict and diversification. In addition, it can even create confrontation among the supporters and non-supporters of such a version of history.

The organization of the Olympic Games in Athens in 2004 was unquestionably a landmark for Greece's economic, social, and cultural development (Panagiotopoulou 2006). Countries like Greece that do not have a strong international position regarding economic and political relations try to promote a new favorable international image expecting to add to its global appeal. The OG provide national and international publics with the experience of something unique, dramatic, and extraordinary, and they promise to put a city/country as a well-known destination on the world map (Roche 2000: 7). Therefore, the expectations concerning the post-Olympic impacts may be overestimated. The eagerness of domestic elites to acknowledge new global roles can lead to exaggerations such as the willingness to promote a new interpretation of national history with a global appeal. This usually comes out as a new expression of nationalism deriving from a new national imagery of unity imposed by a media sporting spectacle.

The Opening Ceremony of the Olympic Games of Athens 2004 was one more event in the glorious Olympic opening ceremonies chain. In the well-known ceremonial postmodern jargon of the media commentators (Moragas et al. 1995) it was characterized as an unforgettable dream trip in history. It managed to time travel the spectators and viewers through sports, culture, and the arts and it gave them the opportunity to rethink all those things that unite the world and comprise the basic ideals and values of Western civilization and the Olympic Movement. In this sense it fulfilled all the requirements to present a politically correct narration.

Notes

1 The broadcasting data of the Athens 2004 Olympic Games are remarkable. According to statements by Jacques Rogge, President of the IOC and the Athens

Olympic Broadcasting (AOB) data, the Athens Olympics were transmitted by more than 300 television stations in 220 countries throughout the world. With 3.9 billion TV viewers, they have put a new benchmark on this "race" and surpassed all expectations (Rogge 2004: 2). A total of 44,000 hours of dedicated coverage were broadcast. This established the Athens 2004 Games as the most covered in their history (Rogge 2004: 1; Exarchos 2006).

2 The relationship and interdependence between media sport and the related institutions such as sports organizations, global conglomerates (which in many cases hold sport organizations and media enterprises), entertainment, and leisure industry is defined either as media-sport complex (Maguire 1999) or MediaSport complex (Real 1998; Wenner 1998). Both concepts adopt more or less the same criteria.

3 In the Athens 2004 Olympics 10,500 athletes from 202 countries participated in 28 different sports. In addition, 21,500 journalists (twice the number of athletes!) worked for broadcasting and transmitting the event, which was broadcast by 300 television stations worldwide. A total of 35,000 hours of programming were transmitted, i.e. approximately 2,000 hours per day (Exarchos 2006).

4 In the value system of Coubertin the nation-state was the most important unit of modern social organization. The rituals incorporated into the Olympic ceremonies sustained the structural identities of individuals that are: the self, the nation, and humankind (MacAloon 1984: 252).

5 Further, he observed that these four genres "do by no means exhaust the roster of performance types in an Olympic Game. But they are semantically and functionally the most significant" (MacAloon 1984: 242).

6 The theories of the two anthropologists have also influenced the approach to media events by Dayan and Katz. As Couldry (2003: 21–35) analyzed in his book, the term *ritual* has three basic senses: as habitual action, as formalized action, and as an action associated with transcendent values (religious or secular). Rituals operate within a certain context and stand in for wider values and frameworks of understanding. "The actions comprising rituals are structured around certain categories and/or boundaries. Those categories suggest, or stand in for, an underlying value. This 'value' captures our sense that the social is at stake in the ritual" (Couldry 2003: 26).

7 MacAloon epitomizes the ritual character of the ceremonies by stating:

> The Olympic Ceremonies' intellectually challenging, emotionally moving, and politically mobilizing linkages of bodily practice and social identity, human feeling and technological power, civil society and state authority, cultural history and commercial struggle, popular interest and world system structure into a single performative composition have contributed to making the Olympic Ceremony – from the standpoint of raw attention, and for better or worse – into the closest approximation to a truly global ritual of humanity that our species has yet managed to devise.
>
> (MacAloon 1996: 34).

8 The characteristics are mentioned only briefly because they are more extensively discussed in other parts of this volume. They break routine, intervene in the broadcasting flow, are happening live, the events are preplanned, announced,

245

and advertised in advance, organized outside the media, presented with reverence, respect, even awe, celebrate reconciliation and omit conflict, and finally electrify very large audiences (Dayan and Katz 1992: 3–9). For a detailed presentation of Dayan and Katz's media events analysis and a critique of the typology and dimensions of the genre see Couldry (2003: 55–67); Hepp (2006: 232–43).

9 According to Real (1989: 240), "Olympic media coverage provides a single event in which seemingly everyone in the world can share. The super media Olympics is the international tribal fire around which we gather to celebrate events and values." Further, the Games provide an integrative function and offer information about other people and nations, and make different people from different nations work together. It is well known that audiences in different countries experience different access to the event and decode cultural messages in a different way (Moragas et al. 1995).

10 These elements are: raising the host nation flag to the accompaniment of the national anthem, the introduction of the Presidents of OCOG and the IOC, the athletes' parade, official speeches, and declaration of the opening of the Games by the head of the hosting state. Moreover, it contains the raising of the Olympic flag to the accompaniment of the Olympic anthem, the oaths of the athletes and judges, the release of doves, the end of the torch relay, and finally the lighting of the cauldron.

11 The classical example of a culture for constructing identity that is based on the past using myths veiled in history is nationalism. Oblivion or even forgery of history constitutes a decisive factor of the constitution of a nation (Hobsbawm 1998: 324–5). The recognized historiographers of a nation usually select carefully, shape, reshape, or even falsify the decisive "events" in order to construct the "narrative of the nation" (Hall 1992: 293).

12 The concept creator and artistic director was a young choreographer Dimitris Papaioannou and the production of the event was undertaken by the British enterprise Jack Morton Public Events. See *Opening Ceremony Media Guide, Games of the XXVIII Olympiad*, 13 August 2004, Athens: Athens Organizing Committee for the Olympic Games (ATHOC).

13 Allegory is a literary expression form or narration that uses symbolic acts of imagined characters to promote a message and to emphasize its meaning to the public.

14 Clepsydra was an ancient clock, which used the constant flow of water or sand to count time units but not the hour.

15 It should be noted that out of a total of eleven floats, seven referred to the Athens classical civilization and the rest to Byzantine and modern Greece culture (*Opening Ceremony Media Guide* 2004: 37–47).

16 For an exhaustive report on the positive comments and impressions of the Opening Ceremony in the international press see Demertzis et al. (2004: 165–70) and *Ta Nea*, August 27, 2004 (cf. N.N.).

17 The opening ceremony was seen by 2,431,000 million Greek viewers (81 percent of TV market share) (AGB Hellas, September 8, 2004). Similar levels of viewership were recorded in Germany where more that 14 million viewers watched the event (Preuβ 2007: 272), in the U.S.A. 56 million, and in the U.K. 10.2 million (AGB Hellas, August 26, 2004). In their empirical research on the

image of Greece in the international press during the pre-Games and Games period [October 2003 to September 2004], Demertzis et al. (2004: 165–70) reported that the great majority of international press (including the EU countries, the U.S.A., Russia, and Australia) commented very positively on the opening ceremony.

References

AGB Hellas (2004) "High Television Viewership of the Athens 2004 Olympic Games", press release, September 8. Available HTTP: <http://www.agb.gr/> (accessed December 8, 2008).

Anderson, B. (1983) *Imagined Communities*, London: Verso.

Barnard, S., Butler, K., Golding, P. and Maguire, J. (2006) " 'Making the News.' The 2004 Athens Olympics and Competing Ideologies?", *Olympika*, 15, 1: 35–56.

Burbank, M.J., Andranovich, G.D. and Heying, C.H. (2001) *Olympic Dreams. The Impact of Mega-events on Local Politics*, London: Lynne Rienner.

Carrard, F. (1996) "The Olympic Message in the Ceremonies. The Vision of the IOC", in M. de Moragas, J. MacAloon and M. Llines (eds) *Olympic Ceremonies: Historical Continuity and Cultural Exchange*, Lausanne: International Olympic Committee, 23–9.

Coubertin, P. de (1931) "La valeur pédagogique du cérémonial olympique", *Bulletin du Bureau International de Pédagogie Sportive*, 7: 3–5.

Couldry, N. (2003) *Media Rituals: A Critical Approach*, London: Routledge.

Dayan, D. (2008) "Beyond Media Events: Disenchantment, Derailment, Disruption", in D. Dayan and M.E. Price (eds) *Owning the Olympics: Narratives of the New China*, Ann Arbor, MI: Michigan University Press, 391–401.

Dayan, D. and Katz, E. (1992) *Media Events: The Live Broadcasting of History*, Cambridge, MA: Harvard University Press.

Demertzis, N. et al. (2004) *The Image of Greece in the International Press during Preparation and Staging the Olympic Games (October 2003 – September 2004)*, final report, Athens: University of Athens [in Greek].

Diem, L. (1964) *The Ceremonies. A Contribution to the Modern Olympic Games*, Ancient Olympia: International Olympic Academy.

Exarchos G. (2006) "Olympic Games and Television. The Global Image and the Greek Heritage", in R. Panagiotopoulou (ed.) *Athens 2004: Post-Olympic Considerations*, Athens: General Secretariat of Information, 63–75 [in Greek].

Gennep, A. van (1977) [1908] *The Rites of Passage*, London: Routledge.

Guttmann, A. (2002) [1992] *The Olympics. A History of the Modern Games*, second edn, Urbana: University of Illinois Press.

Hepp, A. (2004) *Netzwerke der Medien. Medienkulturen und Globalisierung*, Wiesbaden: VS.

—— (2006) *Transkulturelle Kommunikation*, Konstanz: UVK (UTB).

Hall, S. (1992) "The Question of Cultural Identity", in S. Hall, D. Held and T. McGrow (eds) *Modernity and its Future*, Cambridge: Polity Press, 273–326.

—— (2006) *Transkulturelle Kommunikation*, Konstanz: UTB.

Hobsbawm, E. (1998) *On History*, Athens: Themelio [in Greek].

Hogan, J. (2003) "Staging the Nation", *Journal of Sport and Social Issues*, 27, 2: 100–22.

Kenneth, C. and Moragas, M. de (2008) "From Athens to Beijing: The Closing

Ceremony and Olympic Television Broadcast Narratives", in D. Dayan and M.E. Price (eds) *Owning the Olympics: Narratives of the New China*, Ann Arbor, MI: Michigan University Press, 260–83.

Klausen, A.M. (ed.) (1999) *Olympic Games as Performance and Public Event*, New York: Berghahn Books.

Liakos, A. (2007) "Historical Time and National Space in Modern Greece", in T. Hayashi and F. Hiroshi (eds) *Regions in Central and Eastern Europe: Past and Present*, Hokkaido: Hokkaido University, 205–27. Available HTTP: <src-h.slav. hokudai.ac.jp/coe21/publish/no15_ses/11_liakos.pdf> (accessed December 9, 2008).

MacAloon, J. (1982) *Report of the IOA 1982*, Ancient Olympia: International Olympic Academy.

—— (1984) "Olympic Games and the Theory of Spectacle", in J. MacAloon (ed.) *Rite, Drama, Festival, Spectacle. Rehearsals Towards a Theory of Cultural Performance*, Philadelphia, PA: Institute for the Study of Human Issues, 241–79.

—— (1996) "Olympic Ceremonies as a Setting of Intercultural Exchange", in M. de Moragas, J. MacAloon and M. Llines (eds) *Olympic Ceremonies: Historical Continuity and Cultural Exchange*, Lausanne: International Olympic Committee, 29–43.

Maguire, J. (1999) *Global Sport, Identities, Societies, Civilizations*, London: Polity Press.

Moragas, M. de, Rivenburgh, N.K. and Larson, J.F. (1995) *Television in the Olympics*, London: John Libbey.

Moragas, M. de, Belen Moreno, A. and Kennett, C. (2003) "The Legacy of the Symbols: Communication and the Olympic Games", in M. de Moragas, A. Belen Moreno and N. Puig (eds) *The Legacy of the Olympic Games: 1984–2000*, Lausanne: IOC, 279–88.

N.N. (2004) "Millions have seen the Opening Ceremony in 11 Countries", *Ta Nea*, 27 August.

Official Report of the 28th Olympiad (2005), vol. 1 and 2, Athens.

Opening Ceremony Media Guide, Games of the XXVIII Olympiad, August 13, 2004, Athens: Athens Organizing Committee for the Olympic Games (ATHOC).

Panagiotopoulou, R. (2003) "'Join us in Welcoming them Home.' The Impact of the Ancient Olympic Games Legacy in the Promotion Campaign of the Athens 2004 Olympic Games", in M. de Moragas, A. Belen Moreno and N. Puig (eds) *The Legacy of the Olympic Games: 1984–2000*, Lausanne: IOC, 346–52.

—— (ed.) (2006) "Introduction", in *Athens 2004: Post-Olympic Considerations*, Athens: General Secretariat of Information, 1–7 [in Greek].

Preuβ, H. (2007) "Ökonomische Aspekte des Sports im Fernsehen", in N. Müller and D. Voigt (eds) *Gesellschaft und Sport als Feld wissenschaftlichen Handelns*, Festschrift für Manfred Messing, Niederhausen: Schors Verlag, 269–85.

Puijk, R. (2000) "A Global Media Event?", *International Review for the Sociology of Sport*, 35, 3: 309–30.

Real, M. (1989) *Super Media: A Cultural Studies Approach*, London and Thousand Oaks, CA: Sage.

Real, M. (1996) "The (Post) Modern Olympics. Technology and the Commodification of the Olympic Movement", *Quest*, 48: 9–24.

—— (1998) "MediaSport: Technology and the Commodification of Postmodern Sport", in L.A. Wenner (ed.) *MediaSport*, London: Routledge, 14–26.

Roche, M. (2000) *Mega-events and Modernity: Olympics and Expos in the Growth of Global Culture*, London: Routledge.

—— (2006) "Mega-events and Modernity Revisited: Globalization and the Case of the Olympics", *The Sociological Review*, 54, 2: 25–40.

Rogge, J. (2004) "Global TV Viewing of Athens 2004 Olympic Games Breaks Records", 12 October. Available HTTP: <www.olympic.org/uk/news/olympic_news/full_story_uk.asp?id=1117> (accessed December 10, 2008).

Rothenbuhler, E.W. ((1989) "Values and Symbols in Public Orientations to the Olympic Media Event", *Critical Studies in Mass Communication*, 6, 2: 138–57.

Tomlinson, A. (1996) "Olympic Spectacle: Opening Ceremonies and Some Paradoxes of Globalization", *Media, Culture and Society*, 18, 4: 583–602.

—— (2004) "The Disneyfication of the Olympics? Theme Parks and Freak-shows of the Body", in J. Bale and M.K. Christensen (eds) *Post-Olympism? Questioning Sport in the Twenty-first Century*, Oxford: Berg, 147–63.

Turner, V. (1977) *The Ritual Process*, Cornell, NY: Cornell University Press.

Wenner, L.A. (ed.) (1998) *MediaSport*, London: Routledge.

17

PERFORMING
GLOBAL "NEWS"
Indigenizing WTO as media event

Lisa Leung

In spite of its proclaimed status as "Asia's international city," Hong Kong has seldom played host to international events, such that news reporting in the area is more often concerned with the local/parochial. But when the WTO conference was staged in the territory in December 2005, the Hong Kong news media (both Chinese and English language) was caught up, along with journalists worldwide, in the coverage of such an international event.

This chapter interrogates the discursive production of a "media event" involved in the news coverage of a "global" event, such as the WTO conference(s). It examines the "mediatized space" that results when the local news media frame global events for local interests, and in so doing sensationalize the near-local, as well as alienate what is deemed "global." The process of "mediatizing" the WTO, however, has not been straightforward. By "performing" the WTO protesters as violent, irrational, and disorganized, the reporters were encountered by experienced Korean protesters who forced them to disrupt the ritualistic representation of the whole event. As such, this is one of the problems facing the local news media, as they are also caught up in the interplay between the local/global, mainstream/alternative in the coverage of the WTO event.

From "mediation" to "mediatization": rethinking "events"

I am referring to Dayan and Katz's foremost definition of "media events" as "pre-planned, non-routine, live transmission of events" (Couldry 2003: 61). To them, media events possess the power of being able to attract the largest audience worldwide, realizing the full potential of electronic media technology, and declaring civil holidays. With the significance of the media, events are uprooted, from its "truer" reality, to a mediated one. As such, Dayan and

Katz are well aware that this mediated reality is liable to become the product of hegemonic abuse by relevant parties, who are only too eager to turn events into political spectacles (Dayan and Katz 1992: 14–19).

Borrowing from the Durkheimian notion of "rituals," Couldry complicates the discussion of media events by the notion of "media rituals," which he defines as "formalized actions organized around media-related categories and boundaries." The result of the media "construction" of the event was to bring about the "social togetherness" that televised media creates for the audience (Couldry 2003: 61). On top of Dayan and Katz's notion of media event, Couldry argued that media rituals should include those that "exacerbate social conflict, or which do not achieve a stable hegemonic interpretation against the intentions of their producers" (Couldry 2003: 60). Fiske, on the other hand, articulated the discursive nature of mediated event as it serves the media's interest to maximize the "visibility and [maximum turbulence] that demonstrations exude" (Fiske 1994: 7). Under this rubric, Kellner's notion of "media spectacle" goes beyond a critique of implosion of media images as commodities. Expanding Debord's idea of "society of spectacle," he critiques the "entertainmentization of economy as necessary development of capitalist expansion" (Kellner 2003: 2). More recent media critics have asserted that the level of representation of events by the media is such that the mediated event acquires a separate reality from their original event (Cottle 2006b: 59). Cottle even termed mediated events as "mediatized rituals" to demonstrate the extent of "intensified media performance" of current news coverage of demonstrations/protests as events. Quoting from Kellner, he argued that the news media, in covering demonstrations, tend to work through the medium of "public spectacle," turning protests into vehicles of entertainment (Cottle 2006b: 420). For Cottle, the coining of the term "mediatized" was, on the one hand, to graphicize the escalation of this "media-tion"; on the other, to alert the politics/contestation among the actors involved in this "mediation process." In response to Rothenbuhler and Couldry's critique, Cottle emphasized the "performative agency" of media in "staging, enacting and propelling certain events and processes forward," to the effect of "sustain[ing] and/or mobiliz[ing] collective sentiments and solidarities" (Cottle 2008: 139). In the context of protest reporting, the "highly partisan" news media could lend itself to becoming the authority's mouthpiece and voice for political elites, as it relies on government sources for information (Cottle 2006b: 36, 49).

While "mediatized ritual" may well elucidate the discursiveness of news framing and is especially applicable in the context of WTO reporting, the implications of "ritual(s)" needs further deciphering in the critical reflection of the multiple and complex forces that are at play in today's mediated events. Rothenbuhler and Couldry reminded us of the mythical meanings derived from rituals as "formalized actions" (Couldry and Rothenbuhler 2007: 692). This is especially applicable in the case of covering demonstrations and protests, which involves different levels of "ritual." Protesters, whose prime objective was to enhance the visibility of opposition against an organization or the ideologies they represent, would too readily employ tactics (including violent ones) to invoke the "transcendental human experience" through collective formalized actions to advance their cause (Couldry and Rothenbuhler 2007: 137). In this chapter, I will examine how the convergence of demonstrations as rituals ('the ritual that the media reports') and media rituals ('rituals that are themselves ritualized') may reveal the complex contestations (or cooptation) between media, politics, and civil society. In addition, in deciphering the impact of this "double ritualization," I will argue how the coverage of a "global" event might complicate the formation of a "global ritual space of the media" where global protesters interact with local government as well as the local audience.

The "local" and "global" of media event

Drawing on Dayan and Katz's notion of media events, Lee et al. examined the reporting of the Hong Kong handover in 1997 by international media. Comparing news coverage of the handover by selected media across eight areas,[1] they contend that despite the efforts of globalization, news reporting by some so-called international media, such as CNN and CBS, remains inherently ethnocentric, nationalistic, and even state-centered (Lee et al. 2003: 178–82). As such, global news assumes above all national significance, which necessitates news reporting to be essentially indigenized to suit an imagined home audience, but more importantly to cushion national ideological interests. Lee et al.'s contribution to the debate of the relationship between local news media and events is that indigenization seems to be the *raison d'être* for news agencies, local or international, when covering a local or international news event, regardless of their positioning relative to the event. They went further to imply that the local news media serve as state apparatuses to adapt events to serve dominant national ideologies. The point of contention here is that they assumed that the domestic media and the event both *originate from the same context/locale*. For Western and even mainland Chinese media, covering the Hong Kong handover is likened to foreign/global news media globalizing (presenting to the international stage) a pseudo-international event (at best) in a foreign locale (as Hong Kong). For the Hong Kong news media, their role would be straightforward, namely presenting a local event to its home audience.

The WTO conference departs from these earlier definitions of media events, by the nature and scope of the event itself, as well as the scale by which the events have been mediated. Unlike national events such as the Queen's Coronation (which inspired Dayan and Katz's critique of "events"), the WTO's international membership renders the conference "global" in nature and not rooted in any given national jurisdiction. It is also "global" in multiple senses:

a global (supranational) organization hosting the event, drawing delegates worldwide to discuss global issues such as world trade that affect economies and livelihoods especially in developing nations. The fact that successive conferences have been held in different countries across different continents serves to emphasize the WTO's supranational/global governance. The migratory nature of WTO conferences also renders the event(s) continuous and episodic, challenging earlier notions of events as "one-off" and geographically entrenched. From a temporal point of view, each particular conference tends to inherit a lot from previous "episodes," from the outstanding issues, the conference participants, as well as the entourage surrounding the conferences, including journalists and protesters. The representation of these events is thus bound to be similarly hereditary and lineal. However, from a spatial point of view, the migratory nature of the conference(s) enables each successive event to acquire a (unique) flavor from the context of different locales. As such, the coverage of the WTO as global event(s) presents a dynamic space where media representation stages contests between the global/local, the continuous and discrete, that warrant new conceptualizations of what constitute "events." The conferences also depart from Lee's contention in that the Hong Kong news media find themselves reporting a global event situated in the locality. While there is an immediate domestic relevance of the event, "indigenization" of the event by the local news media may not come about as uncontested. In addition, although the scale of the event between the Hong Kong handover and the WTO varies depending on whether it is received by local or international audiences, the latter demonstrates a wider and deeper sense of "globality." Given the variance in the nature and scale of the event, and the locale that situates the event, they are bound to cause different resonances and interplays between the event, locale and the media, local and international alike.

Protests and/as WTO "event"

The WTO Ministerial Conference, started in 1996, was held with an aim "to contribute to a better understanding of development and environment concerns in the context of international trade."[2] Over the years, however, the conference has gained media fame (or notoriety), not so much through the achievements that have been made at the conference tables, but by the anti-globalization demonstrations it has courted ever since the session was held in Seattle in 1999. In fact, the conferences as well as the protests have become inseparable thereafter. Nacos gave an account of how the Seattle round of the conference, now better known as the "Battle of Seattle," has seen the emergence of a bunch of extremists in the multifaceted anti-globalization, anti-capitalist movement and their amateurish recruits by staging violence on the streets of Seattle: "a relatively small number of protesters in fatigues and black jackets retrieved hammers, M-80 firecrackers, and spray paint from their knapsacks and vandalized brand name stores such as Starbucks, Nike, FAO Schwarz, and Old Navy." Dubbing the loose alliance of anti-globalization "terrorists," an "amateur traveling circus," Nacos is highly critical of the heavy slant of the mass media toward covering the violence rather than the conference itself. She concluded that it was the anti-globalization protesters who "exploited the mass media at the end of the twentieth century" (Nacos 2003: 70). Since the Seattle conference in 1999, the WTO has become a "serialized media event." Public/worldwide imaginary on the WTO has been deeply entrenched in images of anti-globalization protesters wearing colorful clothes and headbands, beating drums, smashing windows, and burning tires. The demonstrations would soon evolve into local police spraying water mains, firing tear gas, finishing off with several policemen overpowering an angry protester as the latter is sent kicking and screaming all the way to the police cars.

In the following sections I will first demonstrate, through textual analysis of news reporting of the WTO conference from December 13–18, 2005, how the Hong Kong media oscillate between constructing the event with the advantage of being the "home" media, but having to replicate the assumed imaginary of the WTO. The Hong Kong newspapers I focused on are, namely, two circulation-oriented presses, the *Apple Daily* and *Oriental Daily*, and one, more middle-class based newspaper, *Ming Pao*. More importantly, I wish to intervene to focus on the position of local reporters, who as cultural intermediaries have to translate the global event for local readers' consumption, as well as negotiate between the different parties involved: the conference itself, the multicultural anti-globalization protesters, as well as the local (national) government.

Setting the stage of the "WTO imaginary"

The first news about WTO appeared as early as six months previously, as newspapers were making predictions about the imminent global event by drawing from the experience of the London Bombing. A few prominent newspapers were reporting about how the Hong Kong government was expecting "terrorist attacks" during the WTO conference.[3] Quoting from organizations preparing for the WTO conference, newspapers reported that "they cannot guarantee that the violent clashes that occurred during the G8 summit will not appear in Hong Kong." It was also predicted that up to 12,000 protesters would threaten the territory. The protesters, the news said, "would include the groups that participated in the WTO conference held in Cancun, in which a Korean farmer set fire to himself." Korean farmers already became the imagined enemies to be "invading Hong Kong" (*Ming Pao*, July 11, 2005). *Oriental Daily*, for example, had already painted an apocalyptic picture of the WTO conference as "feared to be out of control." By August, the WTO had already been imagined as beset by "terrorist attacks" as newspapers depicted weapons used by some protesters such as spears in earlier WTO conferences, in reports about police briefings (*Sing Pao*, July 20, 2005).

With the London Bombing, the G8 as well as previous WTO conferences (including the one in Seattle) in mind, the government began to announce a series of measures to prepare for the presumed "battle" that the WTO conference would incur. The idea was to instill an image that the government was swift and efficient toward presumed attacks, to "restore order and minimize the turbulence on daily life." News reports in August and September concentrated on the wide range of government measures that were designed to combat protests, from deploying more police to the area, freeing up prison spaces for house-arrested protesters/instigators, designing the protest zone, and demanding nearby schools to cancel classes. The news reports also detailed strategies to combat the imagined "terrorist tactics" of the protesters: "police would employ shields instead of teargas, because the latter would only be used in more authoritarian and poverty-stricken countries" (*Oriental Daily*, August 10, 2005). These articles paralleled reports of government officials justifying why such a global event should be staged in Hong Kong. As reports grew about the amount of government resources needed to organize the conference in Hong Kong, there were mounting doubts about why the territory should bother doing it in the first place.

While one of the foremost tasks for journalism is "whistle-blowing," news reporting at this stage successfully set the stage for the WTO conference. These reports served multifaceted purposes: to induce the risk as well as pleasure among audiences by heralding the danger and scale of violence, which also helped to justify the over-the-top measures that the government employed, including the nuisance those measures imposed on the public. More importantly, they served to label the WTO as a mega (violent) event, with the protesters as terrorists, who looked set to wreak havoc. The binary characterization of protesters/government (police) legitimized local government hegemony in the name of law, order, and public safety.

Covering the WTO, "demonizing" Korean farmers

From this trajectory, it may be seen that the focus of the reports on the conference was on the protests outside the WTO conference. A survey showed that *Ming Pao*, a newspaper with a middle-class readership (hence boasting a more educated and objective image) carried 30 articles on the WTO conference during that week, but less than six were devoted to the conference proceedings. Another general interest (majority appeal) newspaper, *Apple Daily*, devoted 23 articles to the protests, but fewer than 10 were about the conference itself. When the first day of the conference (December 13) quickly developed into the first protest (the first-ever WTO protest held in Hong Kong), stories about the protests filled all the Chinese (and English) dailies the following day. Huge headlines read: "Protests with strange strategies broke out the first wave of protest" (*Ming Pao*). The more influential English daily, the *South China Morning Post*, on the other hand, heralded the start of the conference with a carnival touch to the first day of protest, with "A swim, a burning coffin and a scuffle – Koreans pitch in" as its headlines. The same newspaper was also the only one that had the first day of the conference ("Curtain rises on summit with call for unity") as the lead story. *Apple Daily* filled its pages with larger-than-life photos of the clash between protesters and armed police. The headline read: "Combat – opening of WTO" as "[Korean] protesters seized 14 police shields" (*Apple Daily*, December 14, 2005). As may be seen, while most newspapers captured the violence at the first row on either side of the protesters/police, the angle taken was from the side of the police. As such, the agitated faces of the (unarmed) protesters are clearly depicted. Such a perspective was important in reinforcing the "defensiveness" of the heavy numbers of well-protected policemen. Caught on camera, their use of pepper sprays on the protesters was legitimized as a last-ditch measure to maintain public order and ensure the safety of the delegates in the conventional hall. To substantiate this logic, *Apple Daily* even included a series of photographs depicting how the Hong Kong policemen were desperate for respite, with captions such as "Police having a hard time." In another small piece, the newspaper explained the police use of pepper spray as "using the least possible force to quell violence." One of the subtitles even read: "[once sprayed, protesters] will lose their activity in 12 seconds," and readers seemed to be expected to applaud the effectiveness of the pepper spray.

Villainizing Korean farmers

Korean farmers were singled out as the face of the protest. *Ming Pao* had already signaled to readers that Korean farmers were to be "the lead in the entire protest party," with a photo showing the Korean face to look out for. In fact, the so-called 4,500 protesters represented "a cross-section of interests but with a common aim" (*SCMP*, December 14, cover page), including Indian fishermen, NGOs from Indonesia, the Philippines, Thailand, as well as migrant labor organizations from Hong Kong. It was *SCMP* which came closest to including in their coverage the diverse groups within the protest.

The focus on Korean farmers confirmed a violence-hungry mode of (local) reporting. Besides the history of violence of Korean farmers in previous WTO experience, cultural stereotypes fuel the characterization of these farmers as militant. *Apple Daily* detailed the Korean protesters as highly action-oriented, as "the Koreans carefully formed into rows, pushing back the police with their bodies, kicking hard at their shields." In a second round, the front line of attackers, "who seemed even more organized, jumped up and kicked at the shields repeatedly, while hurling bamboo poles and empty bottles at the police. As the battle drums snarled faster, the offence gained momentum" (*Apple Daily*, December 14, cover page). The behavior of the Korean protesters, though militant, was far from being like a mob, as the newspaper presented them as protest savvy and cunning:

> [a] woman protester, when noticing how the Hong Kong police had to beat their shields to boost collective morale, grinned and shouted at the police, "calm down, calm down". One other Korean farmer spokesperson, when interviewed, was quoted that the day's action was actually "very civilized, and aimed at warming up and testing police strength".
>
> (*Apple Daily*, December 14, supplement p.1)

The turn – from villain to victim

In the early days of the demonstration, it became apparent that the focus on Korean farmers as the single protesters, and then framing them as violence-prone "villains," highlighted the ritualized practice of Hong Kong mainstream news media. The commercial news media have been critiqued as simplifying events for general readership. The combative Korean protesters, then, provided an easy target as well as scope for the news media to sensationalize their "violent" moves for readers' entertainment. This ritual, however, took a sharp turn on December 16, when, the day before, a group of farmers adopted a different strategy which became known as "three steps and one bow." Groups of farmers dressed in white traditional Korean costume knelt and took a deep bow with every three steps along the way. Earlier on, the press and the Hong Kong public had been impressed by the highly organized, hugely disciplined and deeply structured mode of procession that the Korean protesters adopted. Dubbing the action "three steps and one bow," the media glossed over the fact that this stylized action was itself steeped in the history of Korean demonstration, which was borrowed from a Buddhist ceremonial practice.[4] *Ming Pao* used the headline "Thousand farmers using three steps and a bow, earning tears and applause." The news also recorded the instant impact of the process on the Hong Kongers, who could not turn a blind eye to the suffering that plagued the Korean farmers. The sympathetic crowd was reported to have offered flowers and food to the Korean protesters. Some Hong Kong youth even followed suit to join the kowtowing ritual (*Apple Daily*, December 16: A2). The headlines were substantiated with melodramatic description of the spontaneous and sweet friendship formed between Korean protesters and their Hong Kong onlookers, as the latter joined in the slow and painstaking protest to show their support to the farmers, and their anti-globalization cause.

The swift transformation of the Korean farmers from "villains" to "victims" was also due to a popular Korean TV drama. Female Korean protesters, dressed in their national costumes, started chanting the theme song of *Daejanggeum*.[5] When it was broadcast in Hong Kong in 2005, *Daejanggeum* created a sensation among Hong Kong viewers, scoring ratings as high as 48 points, one of the highest in recent Hong Kong TV history. The singing not only captured the hearts of the Hong Kong public, but made such an impact on Hong Kong reporters that the tone of the news coverage changed overnight. *Ming Pao* included a photo of some jovial-looking woman (Korean) protesters smiling in front of the camera, with captions that read "these woman protesters fully demonstrated the spirit of *Daejanggeum* with their drum beating and performance during the protest" (*Ming Pao*, December 17: A1). *SCMP* drew the relevance of the Korean wave to the public perception of Korean protesters in a straightforward manner by contending that the popularity of Korean TV dramas and films created a group of fans who were ready to embrace other aspects of Korean culture. When the Korean farmers went out of their way to bow in front of the Hong Kong audience (and indeed the rest of the world), the unwary Hong Kong public fell prey once again to the (melo)drama they have long associated with Korean dramas – only this time it was acted right before their eyes.

Terrorizing the climax – the "siege of Wanchai"

The overpowering sympathy for Korean protesters, however, was not meant to last. Indeed, when the poised protesters suddenly went wild on the evening of December 17, breaking through the rails that marked the boundaries of the protest area, the news media went all the way to cover what was seen as the "most violent riot to have occurred in Hong Kong since 1967" (*Ming Pao*, December 18: A1). On December 18, both Chinese and English newspapers filled their cover pages with the story of how the police sealed off the entire Wanchai, fired tear gas to quell the protesters, and eventually detained up to 900 people inside the sealed territory, including many Hong Kong supporters. Headlines would label the incident as "riots," with the magnitude of "siege" (*SCMP*), "Wanchai fallen" (*Ming Pao*), "Longest night," and "Wanchai rendered ghost town." In the inset of the *Apple Daily* supplement, the newspaper headlined how protesters "with careful scheming, took Wanchai within minutes" (*Apple Daily*, December 18, supplement inset).

News photos best captured the "violence" involved in the evening's commotion. *Sing Tao*'s front page fulfilled readers' long-awaited image of "violence": with smoke obscuring most of the imagined action, the only visible human beings were the photographers trying to capture the spur of the moment. The accompanying headline was to spark off controversy and heated debate later on: "Mega-riot in Wanchai" (*Sing Tao*, December 18, supplement front page). The term "riot" was to justify the level of police force (aka tear gas) to stave off the protest once and for all. *Ming Pao*, again taking its position from the police, captured the glaring fire from the tear gas in the center of the cover photo. The police were also shown clearly in the foreground, while protesters were obscured by the tear gas being fired at them; as if to further binarize their roles as "goodies" and "baddies" there was a sharp contrast between the clear image of police and blurred image of protesters. With an accompanying lengthy narrative, the newspapers all launched into graphicizing the tumultuous and violent state of the "riot" as it unfurled. *Apple Daily* detailed how the barricade that had protected the conference delegates for the past week gave way to the unrelenting attacks by the frenzied protesters.

Reproducing the WTO event – which ritual? whose ritual?

Nacos, in her analysis of the coverage of WTO Seattle by international news media, argues that news reports (both in the U.S. and elsewhere) were heavily tilted in favor of the violence surrounding the summit. Protests were widely covered, where the "anarchists" were likened to terrorists and their politically motivated acts to "terrorism" (Nacos 2003: 71). Some reports, on the other hand, showed concern and a sympathetic stance toward the motives of the protesters, as well as the presence of diverse groups of protesters. But Nacos' analysis seemed to infer that this relationship between the reporters and protesters was not one of unilateral exploitation, but a *quid-pro quo* one, since the protesters were also mobilizing themselves to attract media attention to publicize their cause (Nacos 2003: 72). Nacos concluded that rather than "manufacturing" the WTO event, the news media were suffering from excessive coverage of the terrorist side of the event, and succumbing to the exploitation of the violent anti-globalization protesters (Nacos 2003: 82).

The disproportionate emphasis on the demonstrations at the WTO Hong Kong, on the other hand, may be seen as a means for the Hong Kong media to negotiate the local and the global, the continuous and the particular. The episodic and continuous nature of international conferences such as WTO enabled violence to become a media ritual: the presumed violence-induced risk as well as pleasure of the anticipated violence, while the emphasis on the protesters' use of violence justified the reciprocated violence from the police. The mediated violence has been perpetuated as the "WTO imaginary" which is destined to be passed on, fetishized and commodified. Second, especially for the local Chinese dailies, the singular focus on the protests (and the violence) is seen as a way to indigenize and domesticate the event. The ritualistic "violentizing" of WTO reporting may be habitual, but the "novelty" lies in the geographic locality in which the event took place. In addition, by focusing on the "violence" side of the event, the Hong Kong news media "hyper-proximate" the event for the Hong Kong public. Following Baudrillard's coining of media representation as "hyper-real," I argue here that the Hong Kong news media made the event so close and so large that the violence overwhelmed readers' attention. The "violentizing" of events, in fact, is not alien to Hong Kong news practice. For a small readership market in Hong Kong, cut-throat competition renders the news media obsessed with sensationalizing news to appeal to majority reader interest. Commodification of news ensures that violence exudes risk, pleasure, and entertainment which appeals to majority readers. The focus on violence not only simplifies the message but ensures risk, pleasure, and entertainment for the general reader. The result of this indigenization is that the Hong Kong news media "distanced" itself from the conference in favor of the protests, which were seen as more visible to the Hong Kong public. The proceedings of the WTO conference, on the other hand, were sidelined if not denied at the expense of balanced reporting, along with a fuller comprehension of the true meaning of the WTO conference for local readers.

The habitual representation of the WTO protesters, however, was turned overnight from violent villain into hapless victim, much to the protesters' advantage. Their strategic blending of the "three steps and a bow" tactic, with the chanting of a popular Korean TV theme song, was so powerful that it orchestrated this turn. The religious and popular cultural symbolisms fully epitomized the ritualization of demonstrations, which seemed to have to call upon spiritual, even mythical, aspects of "transcendental human experience" to achieve their cause. In this case, Korean protesters were successful, transforming not just the mood of the demonstrations, but also causing the media to surrender to the protesters' strategies and contradict their own ritualistic news narrative – flipping from "violentization" to "melodramatization."

Orchestrated ritualized performance

To the Hong Kong news reporters, reporting on the WTO conference fitted into what reporters think of as a mega event. Some newspapers even started preparing for the event six months in advance, but their early preparation focused more on procuring safety protection equipment such as gas masks and helmets. This WTO imaginary, on the other hand, was renewed and reconfirmed by the government briefings held as early as six months ahead of the conference. Reporters were often lectured on the elaborate measures that the government would adopt to tackle the prescribed violence by the "terrorists." Not only were the contents of the frequent government briefings faithfully transcribed into news reports, but the government's panic mentality, anti-terrorist approach in turn infected news producers. What they were not aware of was that their faithful reports of the (frequently held) government briefings turned them into an eager mouthpiece of the government. A few reporters also expressed their belief that the whole event was a performance, with Korean farmers very smart and strategized to employ theatrical skills to sensationalize and convey their message, the police exaggerating their defense, and, of course, the sensationalized reporting of the willing media.[6] Indeed, the forging of this deal would create a "win-win" situation where the parties involved (i.e. the government, the protesters, and the news media) would all benefit from this staged performance.

Conclusion: globalized ritualized violence, indigenized performance

Dayan and Katz, and indeed Couldry, attempt to interrogate the magnitude and power of the media, drawing on Durkheimian concepts of ritual and event. Still, the discursive formations of "rituals," and the social integrative powers of "mediatized events" need to be further re-examined. More importantly, such interrogation needs to be contextualized within the global–local nexus as events become more globalized. In the case of the WTO conference, this explicates a category of events that are intrinsically "global," but as they travel through physical space they are more closely entwined with the geographical local.

It is evident how the WTO imaginary/myth is reproduced and perpetuated with excessive and ritualized portrayal of violence. Here violence serves as the symbol of the WTO conference, to the point that news media in different locales seem to be compelled to reproduce similar images about the conference. But it also serves to domesticate the event, as the protests are seen as most "visible," and the part of the WTO conference that affects the local public most. From a market-driven point of view, mediatized violence is also a ritualistic practice of the sensationalism-ridden Hong Kong news media. However, the "turn to victimization" also epitomizes the fluidity and volatility of this global ritual space of mediatization, where violent, carnivalesque, melodramatic media elements can interplay to invoke fear, pleasure, sympathy, and excitement. This fluidity also allows the local news media to shift from one ritual (of villainizing the protesters) to victimization, which is the result of a change in demonstration rituals. In the case of the WTO conference, its global nature may pose a necessary distance for local news media, so that the latter find easy justification for concentrating their focus of the WTO conference on its visible local impact – violence. By "indigenizing" the event, the Hong Kong news media make the protest accessible to the local audience, but, in so doing, distance and alienate the conference from the local audience.

The discursive interplay between distantiation/proximation also operates at the level of the protesters. By focusing on Korean farmers as the singular violent/victimized protesters, the Hong Kong media "distantiated" or "foreign-ized" the South East Asian protesters (Filipino migrant laborers, Indonesian fishermen, etc.), some of whom hold concerns more proximate to local social reality.[7] This alienation may be strategic for the local media, which could further "foreign-ize" the WTO event, freeing themselves from any ties and responsibilities to be accountable to the conference. This may be of more interest to the local government, which would benefit from diverting local attention from domestic problems.

In an increasingly hyper-real mediatized world, (mainstream) news reporters are the shamans, the high priests(esses), who, along with the local chiefs, perform the sacrificial rites to ward off the foreign devils – the Korean farmers. The WTO conference becomes a site where these rites are repeated – the same "sacrificial lambs" but different sacred sites. But the perpetuation of the WTO myth, in this case, is not complete without the interplay of multi-layered rituals, orchestrated by the protesters, the media, and even the local government. While the government was eager to influence the new media to "violentize" the Korean protesters, the protesters uncannily reverted this ritual by strategically adopting spiritual and popular cultural symbols (as rituals). The enemies were actually playing on the same logic of media rituals, and more importantly the same set of "social truths" of what Beck (1992) terms as "risk society" – security and moral panic. Cottle challenges us to rethink the concept of rituals, that performativity of rituals necessitates the "doing" of spectators as well as that of the media producers (Cottle 2006a: 428). In the case of the WTO conference in Hong Kong, the performativity of mediatized rituals also involves the willing participation of the protesters, as well as that of the local government, in the hegemonic production of the ritual(ized) violence). If journalistic professionalism is about performing, constructing an imaginary, we have to ask what and who *is not* included in this ritualized process: the "other" foreign protesters (but their status as "other" was itself produced) such as South Asian fishermen, Filipino migrant workers, as well as the ethics of objectivity and balanced reporting.

Notes

1 The eight areas are: PRC (China), U.S.A., Britain, Hong Kong, Taiwan, Japan, Australia and Canada (Lee et al. 2003: 10–11).
2 Please refer to the organization's website: http://www.ictsd.org/ministerial/index.htm.
3 Please refer to *Hong Kong Economic Daily, Oriental Daily* and *Ming Pao* (July 10, 2005).
4 The ritual is steeped in Buddhist tradition, as was reported, which signified a way of praying for salvation to the grief-stricken farmers.
5 *Daejanggeum* is an epic drama which tells the story of the first woman doctor in the Chosun dynasty called Janggeum. The female lead, Lee Young Ae, became an international Korean icon after starring in the drama. *Daejanggeum* was not only popular in Asia, but in North America, Europe and even in some Middle Eastern countries. See Leung 2004, 2008.
6 It was rumored that long before the conference, government and police reps had flown to Korea to talk to the Korean farmer groups who would be staging their

protest in Hong Kong, striking a deal that they would have to behave themselves if the local government in principle gave them access to express their demands.

7 The Filipino migrant laborers, especially, are closer to the social life of Hong Kong, as Filipinos constitute the biggest foreign working population in Hong Kong.

References

Beck, U. (1992) *Risk Society: Towards a New Modernity*, London: Sage.

Cottle, S. (2006a) "Mediatized Rituals: Beyond Manufacturing Consent", *Media, Culture and Society*, 28, 3: 411–32.

—— (2006b) *Mediatized Conflict*, Maidenhead: Open University Press.

—— (2008) " 'Mediatized Rituals': A Reply to Couldry and Rothenbuhler", *Media, Culture and Society*, 30, 1: 135–40.

Couldry, N. (2003) *Media Rituals: A Critical Approach*, London: Routledge.

Couldry, N. and Rothenbuhler, E.W. (2007) "Simon Cottle on Mediatized Rituals: A Response", *Media, Culture and Society*, 29, 4: 691–5.

Dayan, D. and Katz, E. (1992) *Media Events: The Live Broadcasting of History*, Cambridge, MA: Harvard University Press.

Fiske, J. (1994) *Media Matters. Everyday Culture and Political Change*, Minneapolis: Minnesota University Press.

Kellner, D. (2003) *Media Spectacle*, London: Routledge.

Lee, C.C., Chan, J.M., Pan, Z.D. and So, C.Y.K. (2003) *Global Media Spectacle: News War over Hong Kong*, New York: State University of New York Press.

Leung Yuk-ming. L. (2004) " 'Ganbaru' and its trans-cultural audience: imaginary and reality in Japanese TV dramas", in Koichi Iwabuchi (ed.) *Feeling Asian Modernities: Transnational Consumption of Japanese TV dramas*, Hong Kong: Hong Kong University Press, 89–106.

Leung Yuk-ming, L. (2008) "Mediating nationalism and modernity: The transnationalization of Korean dramas on Chinese satellite TV", in Chua Beng Huat and Koichi Iwabuchi (eds) *East Asian Pop Culture: Analysing the Korean Wave*, Homg Kong: HKU Press, 53–70.

Nacos, B. (2003) *Mass-mediated Terrorism: The Central Role of the Media in Terrorism and Counterterrorism*, New York: Rowman & Littlefield.

Other sources

Burgis, T. and Watts, J. (2005) "Global Trade Riots Rock Hong Kong", *Guardian Unlimited*. Available HTTP: <http://www.guardian.co.uk/china/story/0,,1670082,00.html> (accessed December 18, 2005).

Castle, S. (2007) "Trade Deal Ends EU Farm Export Subsidies", *The Independent*, June 20.

Cheng, J. (2005) "WTO puts Hong Kong on Edge; How Globalization Foes are Handled will carry High Stakes", *Wall Street Journal*, Eastern edn, New York, September 1: A9.

Harney, A. (2005) "How it All Ended in Teargas for Hong Kong", *Financial Times*, London, December 19: 6.

Khor, M. (2005) "Tumultous Week as WTO Meets in Hong Kong", *Global Trends*.

Available HTTP: <http://www.twnside.org.sg/title2/gtrends84.htm> (accessed December 19, 2005).

Leahy, C. (2006) "What Does Hong Kong Inc Get Out of the WTO Jamboree?", *Euromoney*, London, January: 1 (source: *ProQuest*).

Wikipedia: WTO Ministerial Conference of 2005. Available HTTP: <http://en.wikipedia.org/wiki/Hong_Kong_issues> (accessed December 10, 2008).

Williams, F. (2005) "Thorny 'New Issues' Set to Dominate Debate", *Financial Times*, London, December 9: 6.

Various Chinese daily newspapers in Hong Kong: *Ming Pao, Apple Daily, South China Morning Post* and *Sing Tao*, on specified dates.

18

RELIGIOUS MEDIA EVENTS

The Catholic "World Youth Day" as an example of the mediatization and individualization of religion

Andreas Hepp and Veronika Krönert

Media events and religion

From the outset, the discussion surrounding media events bore a certain relation to questions of religion. Daniel Dayan and Elihu Katz (1992: 16) see a deep link between media events and religion when they argue that the latter "play a part in the civil religion": "Like religious holidays" media events "mean an interruption of routine, days off from work, norms of participation in ceremony and ritual . . . and of integration with a cultural center" (Dayan and Katz 1992: 16). This becomes concrete as a consequence of media events being "presented with *ceremonial reverence*, in tones that express sacrality and awe" (Dayan and Katz 1992: 12). Moreover, in other research on media events we find a common reference to religion. Just to take two examples: Eric Rothenbuhler (1988: 78) in his early work on media events considers the Olympics as a ritual media event with a quasi-religious dimension, like Knut Lundby (1997: 161), who researches "sacralized moments" in the opening of the Winter Olympics.

In this chapter we want to continue this discussion and move it in a new direction. So far the theorization of media events and religion has had a tendency to argue for the "quasi-religious" function of what we want to call "ritual media events," that is, media events in the sense of Daniel Dayan and Elihu Katz: today media events would have the transformative role in relation to social forms and functions that sacred religious celebrations had before. While this argument is still important, we have to focus *in addition* on the increase of religious celebrations that are intentionally staged as media events. Examples of this are exceptional mass-mediated celebrations of televangelism, mediated church congresses, or the Catholic World Youth Day. Our argument is that if we want to understand these religious media events in an appropriate way it is not enough to conceptualize them simply as a further form of "ritual media events." They are hybrid phenomena at least in a double sense. On the one hand, they include moments of traditional religious celebrations (liturgy, for example, or prayer), which are "mediatized"; that is, transformed in a process of staging them as a "ritual media event." On the other hand, they contain aspects of what we want to call "popular media events," being more marked by consumer culture, for example, outstanding music festivals, reality TV events like *Big Brother*, and so on (see also Hepp and Couldry, Chapter 1, this volume). In a global age, this is staged not nationally, but with a focus on the "deterritorial" character of religious communities in mind – that is, belief communities for whose "thickening" (Löfgren 2001; Hepp and Couldry 2009) the reference to (national-) territorial belonging is of little relevance. An understanding of religious media events in the present era makes it necessary to analyze their hybrid character.

This core argument will be developed by concentrating on one specific religious media event under consideration; the Catholic Church's World Youth Day. This goes back to the year 1985, when it was initiated by Pope John Paul II as part of the United Nation's International Youth Year. Since then it is celebrated every second or third year not only as a local event with more than a million participants, but also as a media event in the hosting country as well as countries with a majority of Catholic inhabitants. There the World Youth Day opens the Catholic Church to a media presence it normally has only at Christmas or Easter. While this media event is considered by the Catholic Church as a chance to get in touch with Catholic youth, critics consider it to be a "sell-out" of Catholicism. These different evaluations again indicate the hybrid character of the event.

In a collaborative research project we investigated in detail the Catholic World Youth Day 2005 in Cologne, not only as an organized local event, but also as a media event (cf. Forschungskonsortium WJT 2007; Hepp and Krönert 2009). While it is not possible in this chapter to discuss our research in total, we want to present some prominent results to make our already mentioned approach to the hybrid character of religious media events comprehensible. First, we will contextualize our investigation of religious media events in general processes of religious change, namely of individualization and mediatization. Second, having taken these reflections as a starting point, we intend to discuss empirically the hybrid character of the World Youth Day as a media event. Third, we wish to make some concluding remarks on researching religious media events.

In all, the empirical base of our argument takes the form of interviews with Catholic representatives responsible for the cultural production of the World Youth Day and interviews with journalists. In addition, we conducted quantitative and qualitative content analyses of World Youth Day media coverage in both print and TV media in Germany and Italy. We also interviewed groups of young Catholics in Germany and Italy about their appropriation of World Youth Day media coverage, and analyzed the feedback left in a participatory communication booth at the venue in Cologne. Throughout, our research has a "transcultural perspective" (Hepp 2009a; Hepp and Couldry 2009): while it is clear that certain aspects of Catholicism differ across national cultures, we analyzed World Youth Day across Germany and Italy in its transcultural character as a media event related to the deterritorial belief community of Catholicism as a whole.

Religion between individualization and mediatization

If we want to discuss the character of religious media events in detail, some incipient but cursory remarks on the present transformation of religion are necessary. During the 1980s and 1990s in social sciences and cultural studies the "secularization thesis" was quite common, arguing for a loss of relevance of religion in "(post)modern consumer societies." Correspondingly, religion was not considered to be a truly important aspect of present media communication. While this argument has for a long time come in for criticism for the U.S. (Hoover 1997) and Latin America (Martín-Barbero 1997), we have begun to realize that also within Europe religion, despite its changing public role in the last decades, never disappeared completely. So while the thesis of the "re-emergence of religion" in Europe seems to be wrong, as it is a mirror-inversion of the "secularization thesis" (cf. Graf 2007: 20), we are witnessing new ways of "re-articulating" ever-present different forms of religion.

To research this rearticulation of religion, Ulrich Beck recently proposed discussing this in the frame of individualization theory (cf. Beck and Beck-Gernsheim 2001). Generally speaking, individualization does not mean an increasing "isolation" or "atomization" of the individual; the personal (however unequally shared) responsibility and necessity to make a selection becomes a dominant cultural pattern in many contexts of the present. This may also be said for religion. Relating to earlier thoughts by Peter L. Berger (1980), religious individualization means that "the individual builds out of his or her religious experiences an own individual religious roofing, a religious 'canopy' " (Beck 2008: 31 [own translation]). Therefore, religious individualization means the necessity to appropriate a certain belief as one's "own god," a reflexive process that is driven by the decision of the individual, and not primarily by social origin and/or religious organization. This process does not mean the end of religion, but the entrance into a new, contradictory narration of the "secular religiousness" (Beck 2008: 31 [own translation]) one has to decipher.

When we focus on religious media events, the remarkable point is how Ulrich Beck brings the media into his reflections: Beck diagnoses a "mass mediatization" (Beck 2008: 55) of religion as part of its individualization; that is, an increasing staging of religious institutions and their main representatives in the mass media. Examples he quotes are especially media events like the funeral of John Paul II, the election of Benedict XVI or the so-called "Danish Cartoon Crisis." While these events do not fill churches, they offer the chance for a deterritorial staging of religiosity by a media which is itself globalized. The present individualization of religion is in a certain sense related to its mediatization, as media are the main "mediators" of highly different faith offers *across* different territories and traditions. Nowadays, "the world religions having been historically separated from each other are forced to compete and communicate with each other in the boundless space of a mass-mediatised public sphere" (Beck 2008: 169 [own translation]).

In considerations like these we find again the already mentioned argument that "the media" are a central "mediator" of "faith" in the present. But while these considerations are suggestive when discussing individualized religion in present societies, we have to reflect further what "mediatization" in detail means in relation to religion.

In his book *Religion in the Media Age* Stewart Hoover develops a highly interesting argument on this. He argues that "in the relation between 'religion' and 'the media', the latter are, in many ways, in the driver's seat" (Hoover 2006: 284). This metaphorical formulation refers to what the concept of "mediatization" tries to theorize and what Beck and others coming from sociology and religious studies do not reflect on further, i.e. that the "adoption" of "the media" by religious institutions is not a neutral act, but rather a reaction to the way in which these institutions are articulated.

Used here, the concept of "mediatization" (cf. Thompson 1995; Krotz 2008; Hepp 2009b) enables us to clarify what Hoover captures in the metaphor of the "driver's seat": if we understand "mediatization" as the process of an increasing spreading of "technical communication media" in different social and cultural spheres, there is indeed a need to differentiate this concept further. Doing this, we can argue that the process of mediatization has a quantitative aspect (more and more media are accessible at more and more times, in more and more locations, and so on) and a qualitative aspect (this increase is related to the change of our forms of communication and further sociocultural contexts).

Both aspects of mediatization are a challenge for religious institutions, since in "the media age" they can no longer situate themselves outside of mediatization. If we share with Nick Couldry (2003) the assumption that the main aspect of "the media age" – or maybe more concrete: of "media cultures"[1] – is that media are successfully staged as the "unquestioned centre of society"; this refers to the relevance mediatization also has for religion: any form of religion and spirituality that wants to be in the "center" of societies has to be staged in "the media," and media events are a prominent way of doing this.

This argument can be substantiated by the spiritual movements within traditional churches and beyond them. If we think of the New Age, the Pentecostal Church or the spiritual aspects of the present Wellness movement, they all share, as Hubert Knoblauch (1999: 101–4) has shown, a communication focus on electronic media. The media offer a kind of "sense market" (Winter and Eckert 1990: 151) that is itself presented as the "center" of society, which with the globalization of media becomes increasingly fragmented and deterritorialized. Religion and spirituality are part of this. They have to present themselves in the media if they want to be considered as relevant "faith offers," either as a resource within a certain individualized belief community or as an offer for personal, again individualized, beliefs.

But the way in which certain religious or spiritual communities "use" the media is not "neutral." The media as a "technology and cultural form" (Williams 1990) exert certain "pressures" on the way religion and spirituality are communicated – both become "mediatized": television implies the need to communicate religion and spirituality visually, based on appealing symbols and practices; the Internet puts religious or spiritual statements in a further discourse of different, increasingly individualized "believers" and "non-believers," and so on.

In this perspective, we can understand "branding" as *one* dominant pattern of mediatization of religion. As Mara Einstein (2007: 35) argues, at the moment when people are free to choose religion "the market place of religious practice has changed"; that is, churches and belief communities have to "brand" their religious offers. In the same way Lynn Schofield Clark speaks of a "religious lifestyle branding" (Schofield Clark 2007: 27) that she understands as characteristic of the present "spiritual marketplace." Basically, "branding" describes a communicative process in which – based on a so-called "core brand" that is the fundamental area of competence and the central offer of a benefit or a product – a brand is positioned with the aim of differing in an appropriate way from competing products and being taken into the "relevance set" of consumers (cf. Siegert 2000: 75). This idea is that when religion is communicated in the media as a "faith offer" it has to present itself in such a way.

For sure, this transfer of the marketing concept of branding to religion might have problematic aspects if one overestimates the similarities,[2] but nevertheless it offers the chance to capture two main aspects of the mediatization of religion (and spirituality):

1 First, mediatization implies a pressure on different religions to communicate themselves across different media. Only when a "religious offer" is spread across the different media does it have a chance to present itself "in the center" of media cultures. So the "core meaning" of its "brand" has to be communicated widely on TV, radio, print, the Internet, and so on. This is the point where aspects of the "ritual media event" emerge as a prominent way of staging this center.
2 Second, mediatization means that religious contents do lose their "sacred space" of communication, their "exclusive space" as we can understand churches. The public of the media is at present increasingly a

commercialized space of product competition; therefore, branding refers to the necessity of a self-presentation in the commercialized space of the present media. This is the point where aspects of "popular media events" enter the argument.

But – and this is the point where a one-to-one transfer of the marketing concept of branding falls short – the "branding of religion" is distinctive because the "brand" of religion itself is special. Until the present, the core of religion – also in the media – is its "transcendent" or "sacred" claim (cf. Lundby 2006; Sumiala-Seppänen 2006); so "branding religion" means on the one hand presenting religion in the "profane" space of mostly commercialized media, without losing on the other hand the "sacred" aspect of the religious offer. How far these more general processes concretize in certain religious media events becomes more understandable if we focus on the Catholic World Youth Day as an example.

The World Youth Day as religious hybrid media event

As argued above, if we designate the World Youth Day as a religious media event, we should begin by pointing out that such a phenomenon may be seen as comprising aspects of "ritual media events" and of commercialized and entertainment-orientated "popular media events." In this hybridity we can understand it as a manifestation of the present individualization and mediatization of religion. This becomes more obvious when we focus on the example given in Figure 18.1.

What you can see here is a poster of Pope Benedict XVI, published during World Youth Day on August 17, 2005 in *BRAVO* (issue 34/06), the largest German youth magazine with sales of more than 600,000 copies per week at this time (first quarter of 2006). On the one hand, it is obviously a religious image with many sacred implications: the Pope in front of a deep blue sky with white clouds, lifting a hand – half in greeting, half in blessing. His sacred position is emphasized by the glittering signet ring on his finger and the shiny crucifix around his neck. On the other hand, the poster clearly comes within the framework of popular culture, since it is arguably the style of poster normally associated with the promotion of popular music or TV. Underlined with an informal nickname "Bravo, Bene!" the poster signals a personal relation to the "religious star" Benedict XVI. The Pope as a kind of "brand" for the Catholic Church seems to be able to symbolize both the extraordinary-holy (or sacred) associated with religion and the everyday-popular associated with present-day youth.

This tension between the sacred and the popular, brought into conjunction by the Pope as a "brand" symbol of Catholicism, is also evident in the way in which World Youth Day is articulated as a hybrid religious media event.

Figure 18.1 Poster of Pope Benedict XVI, published on August 17, 2005 in *BRAVO*.

Producing the media event: controlling
the "sacred" and losing the "popular"

We can argue this at the level of the media event's production. Based on the interviews we conducted with the press spokesman of the World Youth Day organization office, with the priest responsible for liturgical planning, and also with different media journalists, one can demonstrate that the Catholic Church has different focal points which alternate between the "sacred" and the "popular" aspects of the media event.

All things within the sphere of the sacred are produced with a high mindfulness and under the significant control of the Catholic Church. The opening service; the arrival of the Pope in Cologne; his visit in the synagogue; the vigil; and finally the Pope's service at the Mary-Field were all sacred in character and therefore prepared in great detail. The focus of this cultural production was on the sacred dimension of Catholicism, which moves with World Youth Day into an "open field." The Catholic Church invested much of its knowledge in the pursuit of making the event seem like something "mysterious." To quote the priest whose responsibility was liturgy planning: "If the people get the impression that everything has been said here, then we have missed the essential, because it should also stay mysterious; . . . if the last person thinks he has fully understood, that isn't religion."

In detail, such a cultural production of the sacred consists of three factors:

1 *Access:* The access of journalists to sacred ceremonies of World Youth Day was controlled by the Catholic Church. Only a defined set of accredited journalists had the chance to take their own pictures of the events, quite often from predefined positions, such as specific stands.
2 *Focus:* The Catholic Church tried to stage the sacred ceremonies in the "right" focus, presenting faith as something extraordinary which cannot be completely understood and which remains mystical.
3 *Spaces:* There are no spaces for the journalist to influence the progression of sacred ceremonies. They are preplanned with media coverage (especially television) in mind. For example, the way the TV cameras were positioned was decided by the organizers in advance, and there was no opportunity for journalists to influence the progression of the sacred ceremonies to suit their own coverage.

Within the field of the sacred, host broadcaster WDR (West German Broadcasting Company), together with its print media partner the *Bild-Zeitung*, have an outstanding but predefined role.

By contrast, within the field of the popular there is a great deal more space for autonomous media coverage – and this is therefore the area where the "preplanning" of the media event becomes impossible. For example, the streets of Cologne and the Rhine's riverbanks are felt to be important but nevertheless uncontrollable by Catholic Church representatives. Access to these public spaces is not controlled by the Catholic Church, which means they are consequently available for use by anyone, including journalists. Here the Catholic Church itself takes a background role, especially since public spaces and popular scenery are places where journalists traditionally find "their own" stories and their own "take" on proceedings. And these are often stories of jolly celebrations or condom use; that is, stories about what the young Catholic people do on the streets and beyond religious celebrations.

Representing the media event: Catholicism as deterritorial religious community

In order to grasp the complexity of the media event of World Youth Day – which in reality is the progression of a number of different events – the Catholic Church (like the journalists) use the Pope as a linking "brand symbol": on one hand, the sacred ceremonies – at least the ones which were important in the media – are widely staged as the program of the Pope during World Youth Day. On the other hand, the uncontrolled public spaces become integrated into the cultural production of World Youth Day as the Pope himself moves through them.

In fact, the media coverage itself is marked by the triad structure of the sacred, the popular, and the Pope (Figure 18.2). We can locate the media coverage which focuses on World Youth Day, its organization, background, and sustainability in the core of the scheme which comprises the main themes of the topic. Yet around this, media coverage focuses on the sacred, the popular, or the Pope.

First, the sacred aspects of World Youth Day as represented in the media include the spiritual arrangement of World Youth Day, belief practices, and traditions. These aspects are brought into focus in reports about the ceremonial events of World Youth Day.

Second, there is the popular: the young people, as "pilgrims" in Cologne, take part in a program that is not wholly sacred and ceremonial but which also consists, for example, of pop concerts. The atmosphere is especially one of popular celebration, peaceful but unceremonious, taking place in the streets until late in the evening. In addition, World Youth Day is also a commercialized event, which has led to the appearance of merchandised material represented in media images of the event.

Third, within media coverage, World Youth Day was communicated principally as a "Pope event." The different media in Germany and Italy articulated World Youth Day as a "visit" by the Pope, as part of his program. Again the Pope was constructed as a kind of "brand," a "figure" linking both the sacred and the popular: the sacred arrangement was an arrangement focusing on Pope-related aspects, with belief practices and traditions discussed in relation to the rather conservative position of the Pope. Meanwhile, the

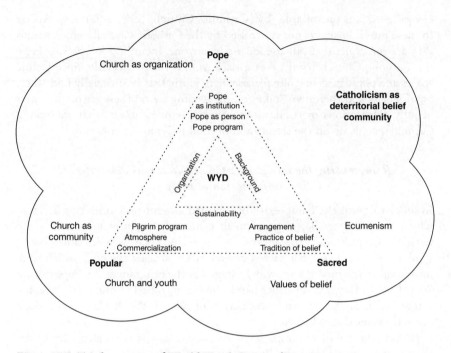

Figure 18.2 Triad structure of World Youth Day media coverage.

connection between the popular and the Pope came about as a result of the way in which aspects such as atmosphere, a "pilgrim" program, and merchandising had been focused on the Pope as well.

In a nutshell we can say that World Youth Day was a *hybrid* media event, because we find both ritual celebration and popular outbreak prominently within it: the sacredness of holy media rituals and the popular of a consumer culture. That both aspects can so easily form part of the same media event is thanks to the Pope, who acts as a linking brand symbol.

However, we must understand the religious hybrid media event World Youth Day in its global context. To make this point clearer, one can argue that it is only possible to understand this event by acknowledging the Catholic Church as being not merely national in character but rather as a transcultural institution with a long history beyond the national territorial frame. It is therefore helpful to look at this media event against a "meaning horizon" of Catholicism as a "deterritorial religious community" (Figure 18.3).[3]

This becomes clearer when we discuss five topic fields within World Youth Day media coverage: the ecumenism, which is present in all coverage focusing on questions of the relation between Catholicism and other Christian and non-Christian denominations (and, in our definition, other more general religious communities); values of belief, which form media coverage focusing on questions of Catholic values; media reports on the relation between the

274

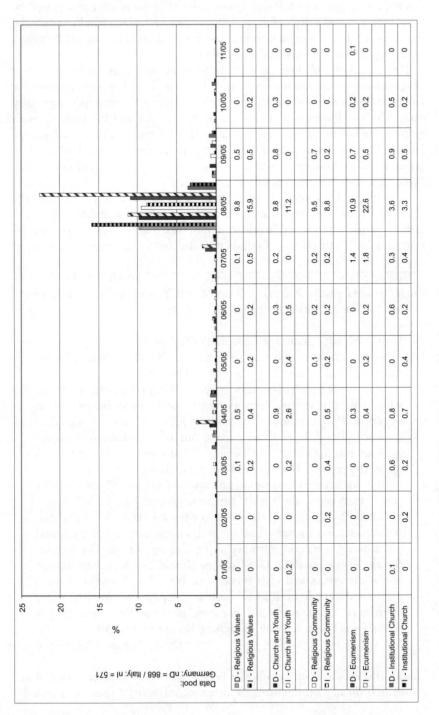

Figure 18.3 World Youth Day media coverage of Catholicism as a belief community.

Church and youth, which also indicates a deterritorial youth culture; and the Church as a community defining itself per se in a transcultural deterritorial frame, as it acts as an organization across national borders (this finally points to the topic field of an institutional church).

The importance of these topic fields becomes evident as we focus on their progression through the media event. What is striking here – comparing the German and Italian media coverage – is the relevance of ecumenism, especially caused by the Pope's visit to a German synagogue and his meeting with members of Islamic religious groups and other Protestant Christian churches. However, more interesting for us is the topic field of the Church as a community. By looking at media coverage, we can begin to understand how this community is articulated through the media.

In many articles and TV programs which focus on these factors, the religious community of Catholicism is represented in a global range: it is named "world church" or "world religion," with references to its "nation-transgressing connections." Catholicism is considered almost as a kind of "socialist Internationale."

Characteristic of this kind of coverage is an article in the German *Frankfurter Allgemeine Zeitung*, calling World Youth Day a meeting of the United Nations under the Cathedral of Cologne:

> United Nations under the Cathedral of Cologne
> Souvenir hunters and God seekers from all over the world / notes from the World Youth Day / by Daniel Deckers
> A crowd of hundreds of thousands of young men from across the whole world, who have been moving towards the shrine for several days now, are welcomed by the smile of Johannes Paul II – who died in April – as a huge mosaic made out of thousands of passport photographs high above their heads. "Thank you JP II" can be read under the picture. His successor's name is Benedict XVI, and he too rules if one believes the speaking choirs formed by divisions of young people from across the world: "Esta es la juventud del Papa."
> Certainly the whole of the world is here. For days, the newly constructed station square – like the stairs from here to the Cathedral – is a mobile general conference of the United Nations. On average, the age of the guests in Old-Cologne should be lower than the age of the diplomats and civil servants in New York. And it is more joyous and more loud. Brazilian samba groups are the most harmless occurrence. . . . It gets more complex resisting the dynamic of a polonaise of South Koreans ploughing the stations square.
> (*FAZ*, August 20, 2005: 3)

Taking this article as an example, it becomes easier to comprehend how the representation of Catholicism as a deterritorial belief community actually works: young people from different parts of the world playing regional music, waving flags and singing symbolize in a peaceful way the reach of Catholicism across the world. Such a scenario was, of course, evoked by the name of the event itself – World Youth Day – and it is therefore apparent why such images are used in the media to articulate the Catholic Church as a community. In the German and Italian media, the (mediated) events at World Youth Day in Cologne function as local evidence of the deterritorial pretension of Catholicism.

Appropriating the media event: individualized ways of believing

With everyday (religious) life in mind, one has to ask the question of how such an event is appropriated (cf. Hoover 2006: 113–46). In order to discuss this, we researched two forms of appropriating the media event; first, the participation opportunity of the "Talk-to-him" box at the World Youth Day in Cologne as a form of mediatization *in situ*; second, the appropriation of the media event at home by selected German and Italian youth.

Taking the "Talk-to-him" box as our first example, the West German Broadcasting Company (WDR) assembled a "vox-pop" booth in which any visitor to World Youth Day could speak his or her personal message to "him" – the meaning of "him," whether it be God or the Pope, was to be the personal choice of the participant (Figure 18.4). A selection of these messages was broadcast each day on the radio. All in all, about 800 takes were made within this box, from which we analyzed 689.

These takes offer a deep insight into how far Catholicism as a deterritorial belief community is individualized among the youth participating in World Youth Day and how far they take the offer to communicate this via the media into the "center of societies." To quote one "vox-pop":

> I am from Canada, from the district of Quebec. I am 31 years old and
> I am asked what I believe. First of all I believe in me, and although I
> trust in God, before anything else I believe in humankind.

Within this "individualized Catholicism" different Catholic groups become important as reference points in the articulation of religious identity. Examples taken from the booth include different fraternities, the Schoenstatt-movement, Opus Dei, and more often local groups. While these groups undoubtedly provide their own points of religious orientation, and do affect the personal beliefs of their members, it is striking how far members of such groups declare differing views compared to their group's official position. For example, one Franciscan monk declares that in most religions "God" is written in German spelling with four letters, meaning that there is no significant difference between all the religious variants of "God." In another example, a

Figure 18.4 "Talk-to-him" box.

young 14-year-old girl who is a member of Opus Dei, and who initially came to the booth with her friend, later returned to declare that although she has been told a lot about vocation, she now admits that she does not love God to the extent that she wants to give Him her life. Rather she would like to find a "prince" and marry him instead. In addition, the focus on people from conservative groups such as Opus Dei also led to the opening up of new and diverse possibilities and ways of believing.

In addition, we would say that within the booth very different religious values are articulated. On the one side, there are people sharing conservative sexual values akin to the position espoused by the Vatican; on the other, there are Catholics who are gay or lesbian. On the one side, there are people with a conservative understanding of the role of women in the family; on the other, there are self-confident and open-minded women demanding a stronger position for women in the Catholic Church.

However, as far as there is a wide variety of believed Catholicism and religious orientations, the different youth share a certain focus on the Pope on whom World Youth Day is centered. In spite of rejecting many of the moral and religious positions taken up by the Pope, they share an enthusiasm for him as a figure who has the power to center religiosity in the present plurality of their societies – mainly through the media.

Comparable processes of individualization may also be observed in the 27 interviews we conducted with youth audiences of the media event in Germany and Italy. Across these young people – understanding themselves in a wide sense as Catholic – we can typify two patterns of articulating religiosity; one we call "me-religiosity" and another we can call "group-religiosity" (cf. Hepp and Krönert 2009). Among youth with me-religious orientation the appropriation of religion is related more to a personal self-discovery, while among youth with a "group-orientation" the shared appropriation within the local group dominates. However, in both cases Catholicism is understood as a possible faith offer that has to be appropriated personally and therefore is individualized.

Referring to World Youth Day as a media event, the interesting point is that young Catholics in general appropriate the media event not as something that can offer answers to their religious questions, but as a representation of the lively and blissful but nevertheless plural form of religion in contrast to the official religion presented in local institutions such as churches.

Based on this, the status of the media event differs slightly between me- and group-orientated young Catholics: while for me-orientated it is just a perceived religious happening in the flow of general media offers, group-orientated youth Catholics not only track the live broadcast of the media event but discuss it in their groups as a main "faith impulse." But again, across both types of religiosity the main focus is related to the Pope: While the Pope's positions are refused, he remains widely accepted as a moral figure symbolizing Catholicism.

Overall, these few examples show how far "faith" is individualized among the youth who define themselves as Catholic. With these appropriations of Catholicism in mind, it becomes clear how religious media events like World Youth Day are important in the articulation of Catholicism as a deterritorial religious community: While they do not "integrate" a "religious community of shared values" they offer a resource in the "mediated center" for individualized beliefs.

Researching religious media events

We began our chapter with the argument that it is not sufficient to investigate media events and religion only in the frame of the question of how "ritual media events" overtake certain forms of religion. We also have to bear in mind that in the present era religions *themselves* are staged in media events and that these media events have a hybrid character, transforming on the one hand religious festiveness into media coverage, but on the other hand taking forms of popular consumer culture into the field of religion. This can be related to more general questions of religious change, i.e. an increasing individualization and mediatization of religion.

Within this frame, the case of Catholic World Youth Day demonstrates a good example how such a hybrid character of religious media events becomes concrete. On the one hand we have the highly controlled religious celebrations in the media, as rituals symbolizing the sacred dimension of Catholicism. On the other hand we have the popular in the form of youth celebrating uncontrolled in the streets and being represented in this way by the media. In the media coverage, this diversity is held together by a focus on the Pope, acting not only as a representative but as a "brand symbol" of Catholicism. The "marketing" of Catholicism linked to him is not far away from other forms of branding. All this is related to a deterritorial belief community, marked by a high transcultural plurality of values and orientations, but in the media event sharing a certain orientation towards the Pope in his role as brand symbol.

Such an analysis has important general implications for researching media events in the global age. In our perspective it is not sufficient just to take the typifications that Daniel Dayan and Elihu Katz have outlined in their groundbreaking work on media events. Moreover, it seems to us helpful to understand this work as an intervention that makes clear the central role outstanding events have as forms of media communication. This is a strong argument, as it makes us look not just for the "average" of media communication (as so often in media research) but also for the "incisive" and the "singular." This argument is sustained by the increasing relevance media events have in different social fields like religion. However, we have to conduct research on these media events in various social fields differently to capture their specificity, making it not only possible to understand their outstanding character in their particular social setting but also elsewhere. We hope this chapter has demonstrated some aspects of this for the field of religion.

Notes

1 By "media culture" we characterize all cultures whose main cultural resources are communicated by technical media (cf. for a comparable approach Kellner 1995; Real 1996; Bignell 2000). Such a perspective does not imply that these cultures in total are a "simulacrum" (Baudrillard 1994), as ideas of French postmodernism imply. Rather this understanding refers to the idea that "the media" are articulated in a certain sense as the "center" of these cultures (cf. for comparable arguments Couldry 2003).
2 Cf. Ballardini (2000) for a stimulating essay that nevertheless tends to get lost in the metaphorical logic of describing (and criticizing) the Catholic Church in the language of marketing.
3 For a discussion of the concept of deterritorialization cf. García Canclini 1995; Tomlinson 1999.

References

Ballardini, B. (2000) *Gesù lava più bianco*, Rome: Edition minimun fax.
Baudrillard, J. (1994) *Simulacra and Simulation*, Ann Arbor, MI: Michigan University Press.

Beck, U. (2008) *Der eigene Gott: Von der Friedensfähigkeit und dem Gewaltpotential der Religionen*, Leipzig: Insel Verlag.

Beck, U. and Beck-Gernsheim, E. (eds) (2001) *Individualization: Institutionalized Individualism and its Social and Political Consequences,* London: Sage.

Berger, P.L. (1980) *Heretical Imperative: Contemporary Possibilities of Religious Affirmation*, New York: Doubleday.

Bignell, J. (2000) *Postmodern Media Cultures*, Edinburgh: Edinburgh University Press.

Couldry, N. (2003) *Media Rituals: A Critical Approach*, London: Routledge.

Dayan, D. and Katz, E. (1992) *Media Events: The Live Broadcasting of History*, Cambridge, MA: Harvard University Press.

Einstein, M. (2007) *Brands of Faith: Marketing Religion in a Commercial Age*, London: Routledge.

Forschungskonsortium WJT (2007) *Weltjugendtag 2005: Megaparty Glaubensfest. Erlebnis, Medien, Organisation*, Wiesbaden: VS.

García Canclini, N. (1995) *Hybrid Cultures. Strategies for Entering and Leaving Modernity*, Minneapolis: Minnesota University Press.

Graf, F.W. (2007) *Die Wiederkehr der Götter: Religion in der modernen Kultur*, München: Beck.

Hepp, A. (2009a) "Transculturality as a Perspective: Researching Media Cultures Comparatively", *Qualitative Social Research (FQS)*, 10. Available HTTP: <http://www.qualitative-research.net/>.

—— (2009b) "Differentiation: Mediatization and Cultural Change", in K. Lundby (ed.) *Mediatization: Concept, Changes, Consequences*, New York: Peter Lang, 135–54.

Hepp, A. and Couldry, N. (2009) "What Should Comparative Media Research be Comparing? Towards a Transcultural Approach to 'Media Cultures' ", in D.K. Thussu (ed.) *Globalising Media Studies*, London: Routledge, 32–47.

Hepp, A. and Krönert, V. (2009) *Medien, Event und Religion: Der Weltjugendtag als religiöses Medienevent*, Wiesbaden: VS.

Hoover, S. (1997) "Media and the Construction of the Religious Public Sphere", in S. Hoover and K. Lundby (eds) *Rethinking Media, Religion and Culture,* New Delhi: Sage, 3–14.

—— (2006) *Religion in the Media Age*, London: Routledge.

Kellner, D. (1995) *Media Culture. Cultural Studies, Identity and Politics between the Modern and the Postmodern*, London: Routledge.

Knoblauch, H. (1999) *Religionssoziologie*, Berlin: Gruyter.

Krotz, F. (2008) "Media Connectivity. Concepts, Conditions, and Consequences", in A. Hepp, F. Krotz, S. Moores and C. Winter (eds) *Network, Connectivity and Flow. Conceptualising Contemporary Communications,* New York: Hampton Press, 13–31.

Löfgren, O. (2001) "The Nation as Home or Motel? Metaphors of Media and Belonging", *Sosiologisk Årbok*, 1–34.

Lundby, K. (1997) "The Web of Collective Representations", in S.M. Hoover and K. Lundby (eds) *Rethinking Media, Religion and Culture,* New Delhi: Sage, 146–64.

—— (2006) "Contested Communication. Mediating the Sacred", in J. Sumiala-Seppänen, K. Lundby and R. Salokangas (eds) *Implications of the Sacred in (Post)Modern Media,* Göteborg: Nordicom, 43–62.

Martín-Barbero, J. (1997) "Mass Media as a Site of Resacralization of Contemporary

Cultures", in S. Hoover and K. Lundby (eds) *Rethinking Media, Religion and Culture,* New Delhi: Sage, 102–16.

Real, M. (1996) *Exploring Media Culture: A Guide,* Thousand Oaks, CA: Sage.

Rothenbuhler, E.W. (1988) "The Living Room Celebration of the Olympic Games", *Journal of Communication,* 38, 3: 61–81.

Schofield Clark, L. (2007) "Identity, Belonging and Religious Lifestyle Branding", in L. Schofield Clark (ed.) *Religion, Media, and the Marketplace,* New Brunswick: Rutgers University Press, 1–33.

Siegert, G. (2000) "Branding – Medienstrategie für globale Märkte?", in H.-B. Brosius (ed.) *Kommunikation über Grenzen und Kulturen,* Kostanz: UVK, 75–91.

Sumiala-Seppänen, J. (2006) "Implications of the Sacred in Media Studies", in J. Sumiala-Seppänen, K. Lundby and R. Salokangas (eds) *Implications of the Sacred in (Post)Modern Media,* Göteborg: Nordicom, 11–29.

Thompson, J.B. (1995) *The Media and Modernity. A Social Theory of the Media,* Cambridge: Cambridge University Press.

Tomlinson, J. (1999) *Globalization and Culture,* Oxford: Polity Press.

Williams, R. (1990) *Television: Technology and Cultural Form,* London: Routledge.

Winter, R. and Eckert, R. (1990) *Mediengeschichte und kulturelle Differenzierung,* Opladen: Leske + Budrich.

19

CONCLUSION

The media events debate: moving to the next stage

Stewart M. Hoover

Much has changed in the ways we think about media and mass communication in the half-century since the emergence of the household screen media. To an extent, this change has resulted from increasing frustration with the limitations of the early positivist–empiricist paradigm that determined most media scholarship. Of equal importance has been a growing sense that the media and processes of mediation – regardless of the aspirations of the institutions and industries that produce them – could be seen as having larger implications than their effects on discrete audiences and behaviors. Among these implications, those which brought the *contexts of mediation* to the fore have been both among the most complex, most interesting, and most significant.

What we are now coming to call theories of "media events" have been both promising and vexing. From the early groundbreaking work of Dayan and Katz (1992), the role and status of unique and particular mediated events have been under spirited discussion. Two important dimensions have been particularly intriguing in the scholarly discourse: how such events relate to the received category of *ritual,* and their relation to certain fundamental ideas about *religion* and/or *"civil"* or *"civic"* religion. There is obviously a relationship between these questions, rooted most notably in the thought of Emile Durkheim, who linked ritual and ideas of the public, religion, and society in a complex that is at least implied by modern moments and events of public mediation. Dayan and Katz's approach to this was to assess modern mediated events in relation to an imputed Durkheimian function of social stability and an application to whole cultures. Other ways of looking at the potential ritual implication of media events (Rothenbuhler 1988) also focused on such questions, though in relation to contexts across varying scales.

It is illustrative of the challenge here to point to James Carey's (1989) seemingly very different invocation of the term "ritual" in relation to media and mediations. Carey suggested that traditional ways of thinking about media suffered from an instrumentalism that saw media only in terms of

283

whether they succeeded in producing the outcomes implicit in their production. Instead, he argued for what he called a "ritual" view that saw media in terms of their integration into the cultural context of the lived worlds of audiences. There is a difference in scale and perspective between the aspirations of the emergent "events" literature and those of Carey. However, we can now see this difference as a deepening and an enrichment rather than as a contradiction. Thinking about everyday media consumption in ritual terms points to the context of audience practice and meaning-making as significant, thus opening up a wide range of mediations and moments of consumption to interpretation and analysis. Further, such a view also points to the ways in which media function culturally to define the extents and limits of geographies of the imagination, to refer to Anderson (1991).

This volume's project

Such complexities of concept, context, and construction are what make this volume a major watershed in our understanding of media events. The chapters here function both to illustrate the range of ways that such mediations happen and to substantively build our scholarly understanding of their theoretical, social, and cultural implications. The agenda is laid out by Hepp and Couldry in their introduction (Chapter 1). As they quite rightly point out, Dayan and Katz's work must be seen for what it was: a paradigm-shifting definition of an entirely new ground on which to understand the role of the media and of mediation.

Hepp and Couldry (Chapter 1) provide both an account and a critique of the trajectory of thought in the area of media events that is worth reviewing here as we move to an assessment of what this volume has accomplished. They lay out a critique in three areas: the assumptions of the ritual perspective approach to media events; the assumed genres of their representation; and the narrowness of the categories of event that have been identified. As they point out, the literature of media events begins with a rather large and totalizing aspiration: the understanding of how processes of mediation might relate to the constitution or maintenance of whole cultures. The form and structure of these events suggests this, as the spread of television and then digital media during the latter half of the twentieth century gradually broadened to include majorities of households, at least in the industrialized West, and as some of the twentieth century's signal events came to the attention of publics worldwide through these media. It was thus logical for Dayan and Katz to assume that the implication of these phenomena would be wide, even culture- or society-wide, and that for an appropriate theoretical framework we should look to Durkheim.

Taking media events to be equivalent to the determinative religious rituals in Durkheim's theory implied that they should be seen to occupy a kind of sacred center of society. There was much about the events analyzed by Katz and Dayan that appeared to assume such a place. These were large, obvious, and specific "contests," "conquests," and "coronations." They fixed the attention of large national and even global publics. They invoked and represented widely shared common symbols, values, and ideas. There were important ways that these events served processes of cohesion and social integration. There were interesting commonalities in the ways they were consumed as well as the ways in which they provided the cultural languages of interaction and social identity. Thus, Dayan and Katz presented much evidence that these various "media events" seem at least to approximate the centering function of traditional Durkheimian ritual.

Hepp and Couldry point out that scholarship followed Dayan and Katz with some important critiques that began a rethinking of what Couldry (2003) calls their "neo-Durkheimian" approach. Rothenbuhler's work on the Los Angeles Olympic Games showed that that event's consumption was not universal or consistent, but rather took place in a variety of ways across various contexts. Zelizer's work on the Kennedy Assassination foregrounded the role of the media in such events, with media performance thus becoming an important dimension of analysis. These and other subsequent studies and reflections on events served to substantially broaden the range of locations and practices under analysis. For much earlier thought, the very centrality, unity, and generality of such events necessarily implied Durkheimian functions. The broadened perspective that has followed has not necessarily dismissed the idea that the public media might be involved in social maintenance (Carey, for instance, saw such functions to be at the very center of his "ritual" theory), but suggests that we must look beyond large, central, universal, and universalizing phenomena for examples of this. Further, much of this thought also points to the role that the media play in constituting – not just representing – these moments, locations, and performances.

This book's substantive contribution to thought about media takes a number of directions, but the most significant is probably its rethinking of the form and content of what we call "media events." We can think of this as a kind of "denaturing" (and then a "renaturing") of the formalism and structuralism that have been attached to theorizations of media rituals and media events. There are really two dimensions to this. First is the question of the *contexts* within which media rituals or media events (leaving aside for the moment the question of the difference between these two categories) may be seen to function or have their meaning or effect. Second is the question of the actual *form* or *constitution* of the phenomenon itself, its elements, its extents, and its limits. This process of rethinking or denaturing responds to emerging and evolving thinking along these lines. The overall project is the recovery of a generic definition of "media events" that elides received issues such as tacit, totalizing implications or functions, the questions of context, and of the diversity of locations where such events may be seen to be taking place.

Globalization

This book also aspires to place its discussions in a larger framework, one that has been only dimly represented in much prior work: that of *globalization*. As is obvious in many of the works here, media events are today largely deterritorialized; they are consumed globally or are at least accessible well outside their geographies and nations of origin. The most obvious question becomes a more profound challenge to the neo-Durkheimian project: whether such globally experienced events *can* be integrative (or be a "center") in any real sense. The obvious consequence is that the generic definition I have spoken of also needs to be tensile enough to account for the integrative or other consequences of a given event across a range of contexts or levels. Or, to be more correct, it needs to be a definition that allows events to find their footing in the complex and layered cultural geographies of globalized modernity.

Dayan and Katz have taken important steps in this process of rethinking in their own chapters in this volume (Katz is joined here by Tamar Liebes). In these, they recover from their earlier work essential elements that can contribute to a more elegant, more nuanced, and ultimately more descriptive framework for understanding the constitution of rituals and events. In Chapter 2, Dayan, for example, applies an anthropologist's framing to the deconstruction of the essentialist model that has bedeviled prior research and theory-building, moving away from the formalism that has defined some earlier work. He proposes four categories of the event "object." These are "emphasis," which stands in for the centering claims, tropes, and symbols of the event, "performativity," which describes the specifics of the event's constitution in space and time, "loyalty," which concerns the constitution of publics, communities, and audiences, and "shared experience," which concerns the broader performance and constitution of the event in those publics, communities, and audiences. This is a major contribution to the part of this book's project that concerns the nature of the events themselves. In Chapter 3, Katz and Liebes underscore the necessity of such a rethinking of the event as cultural "object," by exploring the emergence of new categories of disruptive events that necessarily undermine earlier assumptions about structures and their formalistic relationship to mediations.

In Chapter 1, Hepp and Couldry extend and further deconstruct Dayan's argument, using his framework to elaborate a new concept for the description and understanding of events in light of the interactive and interrelated contexts of geography and culture in an era of globalization. They argue that any concept of culture in such a time must radically account for the deterritorializing effects of modernity, and must recognize a kind of cross-national reflexivity regarding cultural products and practices. Rather than being coterminous with geographic, political, or social spaces, cultures are seen today to float more freely. Their origins, intentions, loyalties, and

286

circulations are in a certain sense transparent, and are thus accessible in both their central constitution and in their deployment and consumption in broader contexts and communities. This also means that cultures are significant beyond their constitution of particular or specific social or geographic spaces, that they can have form and meaning beyond those spaces.

Rethinking cultures and events

Hepp and Couldry, both in this volume and elsewhere (Hepp and Couldry 2009), describe culture as a "thickening" of ongoing articulations of meaning across social and – more importantly – geographic spaces and times. Whereas we might once have looked for cultural meaning exchange and representation as finding its footing in formally structured locations, and thus as defined by those locations, we must now look for the ways, places, and times that these exchanges become *systematic* in some sense. When and where do logics and truth claims and collective or shared receptions, interpretations, and meanings come together in significant ways? These are the points and places of "thickening" that Hepp and Couldry theorize, and that the contributions to this volume identify in a variety of places. Thinking of culture in this way opens up a new perspective on the two major axes I raised earlier: (1) the nature and constitution of media events, and (2) the contexts or frames in which these events are seen to have form, meaning, and (perhaps) effect or function. We might once have essentialized the category of "media event" by looking for inductively ascribed characteristics of their existence and functioning. The neo-Durkheimian approach to media ritual is an example of this. The works in this volume establish that to do so misses the broader sweep of ways in which media events are active. Our calculus thus needs to shift from what is *ascribed* in meaningful media events to what is *achieved* by and through them. And, essential to this achievement is that they find their sources, claims, loyalties, and practices across a wide range of levels, contexts, geographies, and cultures, with consequently complex depths and breadths of significance for a range of publics, audiences, and communities.

In their introduction (Chapter 1), Hepp and Couldry provide a definition of media events that articulates his new perspective:

> media events are certain situated, thickened, centering performances
> of mediated communication that are focused on a specific thematic
> core, cross different media products and reach a wide and diverse
> multiplicity of audiences and participants.
>
> (Hepp and Couldry, Chapter 1, this volume: 12)

This provides us with a definition that recognizes the specific and particular things we might call "media events." At the same time, this definition recognizes some of the boundaries and issues relevant to the purpose of

287

extending the traditional understanding to new areas. Its main value, in the end, is the way this approach can account for some of the specific and concrete instances of mediation or media events in relation to globalization. They also account for media events that transcend the most typical model, that of public, more or less consensual, shared experiences. Hepp and Couldry argue that the category of "media event" must also extend to two phenomena that have become common in media experience, and which clamor for attention. The first of these is "conflictual media events," or those that do not conform to generalized senses of cohesion or commonality, but stress difference and conflict (see also Katz and Liebes, Chapter 3, this volume). Second, they suggest that much of what goes on in the world of celebrity culture also justifies consideration under the rubric of media events. Each of these presses itself into our considerations as each has become more and more prominent in the global experience of mediated cultures. These also interact with the kinds of media events that scholars have typically looked at. In addition to its invitation to rethink the form and contexts of media events, this book makes a third important contribution. Its chapters provide a rich and varied geography of the public mediation of cultures and of cultural meanings. Over against received and determinative (perhaps even "neo-Durkheimian") ideas about the nature and meaning of large, shared, mediated experiences, we see here a provocative array of phenomena that demand to be interpreted under shared scholarly rubrics, thus challenging us to a deepened and enriched understanding of what these things are and what they mean.

What are these phenomena? They range across the three domains introduced by Hepp and Couldry: mediations of shared social purpose and solidarity; mediations of conflict; and mediations of charisma and celebrity. In these pages, we have seen substantive analyses of the Olympic Games, one of the most significant, central events of modern public life (Dayan, Chapter 2; Panagiotopoulou, Chapter 16). Katz and Liebes give an account of how terror and terrorism are defined and deployed within modern media. Major phenomena in the natural world also provide powerful moments of centering and shared attention. Wilke (Chapter 4) compares the mediation of the Lisbon earthquake of 1755 and the Boxing Day Tsunami of 2006. Arguably the most important example of a conflictual media event in the twentieth century is the terror attacks on September 11, 2001. They are considered here by Stepinska in Chapter 14. Also focusing on the level of states and nations, Krotz (Chapter 7) considers the meaning construction that accompanied the epochal reunification of the "two Germanys" following the collapse of the Soviet Union. Two chapters focus much more on the domain of entertainment and celebrity cultures. Bolin (Chapter 9) analyzes the Eurovision Song Contest as a media event, and Wildermuth (Chapter 11) looks at the beauty pageant through which Indian contestants are selected as part of the Miss World event. Hepp and Krönert (Chapter 18) consider a ritual of rising popularity, Catholic World Youth Day, which was held in Germany in 2005.

This introduces a cultural dimension – religion – that is invoked and implied in much of the thought on media rituals and media events, but which has been rather in the background of much theory-building, a matter I will turn to later.

The very diversity of levels, locations, and contexts here illustrates the challenges of developing a general theory of media events. At the same time, there are important commonalities between these examples, not least the extent to which the media are active in their construction, representation, consumption, and shared experience. Each of them, for example, centers attention around shared ideas and values. Each involves the representation of important social, cultural, and political values and symbols. In each, a kind of reflexive engagement may be seen to function as producers, presenters, artists, audiences, and communities share a common understanding of the moment and its concomitant practices, whether or not they choose to invest their loyalties. In each, there is at the same time at least a contestation of values, symbols, and practices. Thus in none of them do we see the kind of cultural definition or determination that instrumentalist theories of the media have proposed. Each represents the kind of "thickening" of which Hepp and Couldry speak.

Globalization

The works in this volume explicitly address the implications of globalization for media events. The Dayan and Hepp/Couldry approaches to "de-natured" theories of events introduce a kind of fungability and flexibility to the category, accommodating theory to the most fundamental reality of globalization. Globalization, particularly in relation to cultures, is at its base a function of the media, mediation, and mediatization. It is typified by a historical moment where the technologies, practices, structures, and institutions of the media have fundamentally changed cultures. Simply put, they have made it impossible to have a private conversation anymore. Something that in the past might have been a phenomenon limited to a specific geographic or historical-cultural context is today accessible well beyond those boundaries. Important recent examples of this include the so-called "cartoon controversy" of 2006, where the publication of supposed images of the Prophet Muhammad in the Danish newspapers became known to large populations in the Muslim world, leading to demonstrations, riots, violence, and even deaths. In a similar vein, in 2007 the U.S. American actor Richard Gere publicly kissed the Indian film star Shilpa Shetty during an AIDS fundraising event. As in the cartoon incident, news of this spread quickly, via the media, across the world, resulting in protests and demonstrations by conservative Hindus.

This dimension of globalization was also at the root of the sex scandals that have rocked the Catholic Church over the past decade. Whereas in the past it might have been possible for such a powerful religious institution to control access to its internal matters, that is no longer the case. The implications of this for institutional power and authority (of religion, but also of other leading institutions) are obvious. Such institutions have lost control over both the meanings of their symbols in a time when the media are more and more definitive of social and cultural meanings, and over the ways and places that those symbols, ideas, values, and claims are circulated and understood. It is this latter fact that is most important to our considerations here. In addition, it is this fact that has most fundamentally confronted traditional, neo-Durkheimian, "whole culture" views of media events. We simply can no longer assume that the circulation of media events is technologically limited to their cultures and locations of origin. All of them potentially become the property of cultural contexts outside their "home" contexts.

Technological change has been an important driver of these changes, of course. The "screen" media are no longer limited to terrestrial distribution through broadcasts or film exhibition. In addition, they are further loosened and unconstrained in the digital age (see Ingrid Volkmer and Florian Deffner, Chapter 15), where their accessibility is becoming limited only by political control in contexts such as the People's Republic of China, and by issues of economic "threshholds" elsewhere. The role of the digital age also signals another dimension that is obvious in many of the works in this book: the role of the audience and its reflexive engagement in media events (see Peter Csigo, Chapter 10). To refer to Dayan's categories for a moment, we are in an age where audiences can position their own "loyalty" in relation to the events they wish to experience. This kind of participation in meaning construction is a hallmark of the new so-called "social media" of Web 2.0, and is an important source of the momentum that repositions and reconstructs media events, producing the flexible "thickenings" that define them.

Cultural authority

As an important milestone in the development of scholarly ideas around the category of media rituals, this book invites a rethinking of categories of culture and cultural practice that are implicated in these processes. Lurking behind much of this work and interest in it is an interest in authority. That is, who, or where, or which forces are (or wish to see themselves as) positioned to take advantage of these processes? There are actors, institutions, and discursive truth claims circulating in and around each of the cases presented in these pages. These forces and interests are addressed both explicitly and implicitly by these authors. There are a wide range of ways to think about the relation of ideology to such processes and contexts, but a prior question is the positionality of authority here. Where is it obvious? What are its prospects? And, most important, perhaps, is the question of whether media events, as redefined in these pages, constitute a *mediatization* of authority? That is, has the interaction of the technologies, routines, social practices, and consumption of media events produced something entirely new in the way that authority must function?

The question of authority is in some ways more obvious when we return to the early models of media events and most particularly of media rituals. In those considerations, a rather traditional view of the working of these mediations was on the agenda, and the invocation of Durkheim, in particular, brought to the fore the central function of social maintenance and the centralizing, regulatory, maintenance function of *religion* in traditional society. It may be argued that religion was insufficiently theorized in much of this work, aside from reference to the germinal contribution of ideas of "civil religion" to understandings of these ideas as processes of modernity. And, of course, there is little cause here to necessarily introduce some more formal or determinative role for religion in social contexts which have been so extensively secularized (in the consensually accepted definition of that term). At the same time, there is a way in which the question of religious authority can be a powerful heuristic device for understanding the way that authority as a category might be seen to function or be implied in the kinds of "de-natured" theory-building present here. Religion does, in fact, play a formal role in certain of these cases (and in others we could describe). In others, a kind of "implicit" religion, worthy of further theorization, may be seen to be involved. I will return to the issue of religion *qua* religion at the end of this chapter, but for now, let us consider the question of authority, recognizing that in some ways religion provides a central illustrative case relevant to our considerations and thus lurks behind some of what I will focus on here.

As I said, the meanings and prerogatives of authority are clearly "in play" here. It presents itself in a formal and particularized way in the Olympics, and in Catholic World Youth days. At the same time it is contested in those contexts, but is clearly confronted on the one hand and supported on the other in the cases of representations of terror. Authority is appealed to in representations of nationalism and national or ethnic identity, seen here in formal terms in German reunification, and in the contexts of entertainment culture in the Eurovision Song Contest and the Miss World Pageant. Political authority and its abilities to provide the legitimated definition of the situation is present in a number of the chapters here.

But it is more importantly "in play" in the sense that its ability to pursue and secure its goals is made problematic by the conditions of mediation. We can begin to see the outlines of a re-theorization of authority in relation to media events in at least the following categories.

First, authority is put "in play" through the mediation and mediatization[1] of its symbols. The media sphere has become the definitive context for the articulation, representation, and circulation of cultural symbolism, and it is in the media that symbols increasingly find their definitive meanings and referents. The case of formal religion is illustrative here. Madonna's use and manipulation of Christian symbolism unleashed a new trajectory of meanings and associations for those symbols quite outside the control and purview of institutional religious authority, much to the chagrin of religious leaders. Even seemingly pious and well-intended efforts such as Mel Gibson's 2004 *The Passion of the Christ* provide novel and autonomous invocations of important symbolism outside the control of formal authority. Similarly, Muslim theologians have objected to the (largely mediated) circulation of new interpretations of the terms "*fatwa*" and "*jihad*."

Second, authority is put "in play" due to the cultural autonomy of the media sphere, an autonomy that is made nearly absolute by virtue of its political economy. There are, of course, very real ways in which "the media" are subject to political, economic, and cultural control. At the same time, though, they benefit from a structural independence and autonomy that is rooted in their location in markets. The evolution of printing in early modern Europe was also an evolution of processes of mediation as products of a commodity marketplace. As the historian of printing Elizabeth Eisenstein demonstrated two decades ago, a major impact of the printing revolution was the evolution of the publisher as a new, potentially independent (and thus threatening-to-authority) cultural force. The modern media sphere has continued to develop along these lines. The commodification of culture and of cultural symbolism has been subject to much cultural criticism from both Leavesite and cultural-critical directions. At the same time, it is this commodification that is at the root of its cultural power and signifi-cance in relation to existing centers of power and authority. To a great extent, "media events" and their various constituent elements are among these commodities, and their social and political implications need to be seen in that light.

Media commodities need also to be seen in relation to Hepp and Couldry's notion of cultures as locations of "thickening" in globalized modernity. Such commodities are deployed by their own logics, are invoked, imbricated, reconstructed, and redeployed along chains of meaning construction and transmission, becoming important symbols and tropes in these "thickenings." That they can flow through these systems following economic logics rather than the logics of traditional authority or social function is an important element of, and challenge to, analysis and interpretation.

Third, authority is put "in play" by the practices of audiences and their own cultural autonomy. We will need to leave aside for the moment the question of agency versus determination in audience practice, but we can say that the lodgment of these processes in a cultural marketplace of supply that is also an economic marketplace suggests a certain repertoire of consumption practices for audiences that positions them actively in the process. To refer to Dayan's categories in this volume, audiences are made active in practices of "loyalty" and "performativity" that are systematically connected with markets of cultural exchange, and thus are autonomous from the conditioning aspirations of other centers of authority. Audiences are conditionally free to participate in rituals of attention, representation, exchange, and imbrication of symbols, tropes, truth claims, and values embedded in moments of mediated "event." These can even be seen to develop into novel and unique imbrications of ritual and performativity such as in the ways in which audiences and communities of shared experience may be seen to function in relation to the media events discussed here. Indeed, one of the important objectives and achievements of a de-natured approach to theorizing media events is to allow both for the cultural-practical flexibility of consuming communities and for those practices to find a systematic form outside the bounds of ascriptive cultural authority.

Fourth, cultural authority is put in play by the achievement through media events of new contexts and practices of what has been called "civil religion." Across a variety of cultural and political contexts, we have seen in modernity the evolution of large public rituals that function in quite the way Durkheim prescribed. The State Opening of Parliament, the inaguration of the U.S. American president, the coronations, contests, and commemorations that Dayan and Katz described, each of these is an example of the public, central, and in a way totalizing performance of rituals of social and political solidarity and maintenance. Media events, as understood in these pages, displace the centrality of such rituals both by their unique and autonomous imbrication of symbols and performance and by their autonomous existence across time and space. This latter temporal contradiction is in many of the cases described here invoked by circumstance (i.e., many conflicts and crises just "happen") but in other cases it evolves according to its own cultural or performance logics.

This is not to say that the autonomy I am highlighting is absolute. We can see in the area of public performances and rituals of solidarity that loyalty and performance are actually at the same time both *autonomous* and *contingent*. Their autonomy needs to be seen in relation to their invocation of received and widely shared interpretations. These are at some times accorded loyalty, while at other times they are contested. In fact, it is probably most descriptive to say that the practices of loyalty and performativity of audiences and communities in relation to media events are typified by unique combinations of the received and the contested. This is particularly obvious in the case of digital and Web 2.0 "communities" where the ability to position identity in relation to a unique critique of received symbols and truth claims is often a central logic of participation and loyalty.

A fifth way in which authority is put "in play" follows on from this notion that the contexts and constitution of events are important because of that authority's relationship to structure. New, unique, and (to an extent, autonomous) constitutions of community, civic space, and civil society are invoked, pointed to, or even created through the kinds of media events encompassed by the frame of "media event" introduced in these pages. These cultural "thickenings" are important and meaningful to the extent that they are constitutive. They allow practices of circulation, articulation, and reception to aggregate common interests, and to re-center attention publics. A very important and provocative line of research would follow these constitutions with inquiries into the realm of actual politics. Certainly the earlier chapters begin this project, but much more remains to be done, and it is of great importance. I will, in fact, end with an example of this frame.

In many of the examples given in this volume, and indeed in most things we would call "media events," there is a very particular and centered role for authority; that is, for the authority of the interests that may have organized or initiated the event. In Chapter 7, Krotz helpfully theorizes this, suggesting that we think of it along the lines of an investment of (referring to Bourdieu) "symbolic capital." The effectivity of the event then becomes a question of the "fit" of the aspirations of such authority to the sensibilities and aspirations of the implied and affected audiences or communities of interpretation, which are, as I have suggested, invested with a certain autonomy to attend to these events and invest them with loyalty and performance. The situation is made additionally complex by the fact that such cultural investments and loyalties around media events can be interrogated for the "fit" of the whole complex (the mediatized articulations in particular – the "story" that is being told or celebrated) and the real situation to which it refers. Krotz, for example, notes that the ostensible story of the October 3 event was the unification of Germany, but that the real story was order and authority under a regime of "symbolic violence." It seems obvious to point out that a particular constitution of authority, power, intention, loyalty, and performance could, in fact, invest modern "media events" with precisely the kind of centralizing ritual function envisioned by Durkheim. However, in light of the important theory-building and critical engagement called for here, we must now see that, to the extent they exist, such constitutions must be seen as conditional, not formal. They emerge from a particular constellation of conditions and practices. Their normative status is not found in their form, genre, or content, but in a complex and layered set of conditions and interactions.

The "mediated center"

Incidents of conflict and crisis are experienced as media events and it is perhaps too easy to suggest that in these cases, the system works to connect the symbolic capital of various political interests to the loyalties and performances of audiences – to become again what Couldry (2003) has called the "mediated center." It will always be the impulse to see things in this way, particularly in such cases. Hepp and Couldry caution us not to confuse the intentions and aspirations of power and authority with their actual functionings. To put it in the terms of their arguments here, they want to contest the determinative power of the "emphasis" category:

Exactly this appropriation can also be a "bypassing" or "reinterpretation" of the centering. Therefore, in the case of media events too, the construction of a "mediated center" remains an uncertain and contested process, however totalizing the claims that construction involves.

(Hepp and Couldry, Chapter 1, this volume: 12–13)

This is fully consistent with, and flows from, their overall arguments here, but it is also necessary to look to and theorize particular cases. Cases such as large social or political crises and conflicts press the edge of the envelope, bringing substantial cultural, practical, and political forces to bear on systems of signification and even – for a time – creating various kinds of cultural "centers." The stream of thought represented here would urge us to think of these kinds of cases as particularly focused examples within an overall framework that understands the conditional and contested nature of events as cultural "thickenings," not as the normative examples of formally constituted "media events" to which all other moments of "event" compare as weak and imperfect variations.

We must return here to the complexities of this situation that are introduced by the conditions of globalized late modernity. As has been widely argued, we can no longer assume any singular public sphere within which media events may be articulated. Instead, there are multiple public spheres, even within what we once thought of as particular, bounded cultural or national contexts. Different races, genders, ethnicities, generations, religions, and other identities see and articulate culture very differently. Their "thickenings" can be particular and unique, and the cultural resources they attend to and cultural capital they accumulate and exchange are relevant to those multiple spheres. At the same time, they are reflexively engaged across those same spheres, and can attend to meaningful "thickenings" across a variety of geographies, contexts, and levels. It goes without saying that the media encourage this. It is one of the fundamental conditions of life today.

This also means that reflexivity is engaged as global audiences contemplate and consider the meaning of "the national," "the regional," "the global," and indeed other large categories. The media and processes of mediation provide audiences with a perspective that enables them to in a sense stand outside of, and look back on, these definitions and categories at the same time that they are subject to them. Increasingly, the whole complex of mediated cultures, including entertainment and popular culture as well as news, provides symbolic resources and a contextual perspective that makes received categories problematic. Borders, boundaries, and senses of nation, ethnicity and identity become fungible, negotiable, and seemingly conditional at the same time that the claims and demands of political, economic, and cultural power can become large and portentous.

The case of religion

As a systematic source of cultural emphases that seek to deploy repertoires of practice and loyalty, and through them to produce shared experience, religion remains always nearby as we think about media events as a category of practice that aspires to cultural centrality. What Warner (1993) has called the "ascriptive" view of religion – that is, to interpret it in terms of its own claims to this kind of authority or in terms of formalist historicism – seems to map well on to media events as cultural projects that aspire to "centering" status. This also makes religion easy to dismiss as a dominant or formative cultural category in late modernity, at least in the secularizing industrialized West.

There are, however, reasons why religion cannot be ignored in these considerations. The first among these I raised earlier: religion provides important, even determinative ways of understanding cultural practice. It is, as I said, a powerful heuristic for more general processes of cultural meaning production, even if invoked only metaphorically. Second, religion cannot be ignored here because of the very framework of globalization that must necessarily define the contexts of this theory-building. The global context is not, after all, defined by the industrialized West. It is a context of interactions and trajectories of meaning that link the West with a world that is far from secularized, and where the manifestly "religious" makes much more of a difference. Indeed, many of the crises of modernity that have presented as "media events" are crises defined by continuing struggles over the claims of religions. A third way that religion cannot be ignored is far more significant to the emerging theoretical direction argued in these pages. Following Warner's argument for new ways of understanding religion, shifting our focus away from religion "as ascribed" to religion "as achieved" opens up considerations here to a complex and layered set of registers within which symbols and meanings that are either "religious" or that bear a family resemblance to it can be expressed in the "cultural thickenings" of media events. In many of the cases represented here, and in a wide range of other examples of such events (the whole genre of reality television comes to mind), the tropes and symbols through which these thickenings are articulated can and do involve the appropriation, imbrication, and deployment of received symbols and tropes of religion. Many of them will also demonstrate in their embedded contexts of participation a reflexive contemplation of the religious "object."

Even on a formal and structural level, a kind of persistence or re-emergence of religion, for example, is present in the controversy over the so-called "Christian roots" of Europe in debates surrounding the European constitution and in the Pope's recent claims regarding the normative status of Christian identity in the European context. Examples from the United States abound. So there is reason to argue that "the religious" will continue to contest the public space of media rituals and events. Traditional centers of authority will

296

continue to have some kinds of power or at least wish to wield some kinds of power, and religion is one of these.

A media event of the global age

At the time of writing, the United States has just elected its first African-American president. I am reluctant to be seen to fall into a discourse of "American exceptionalism," but there are ways in which the Obama election presents itself as the kind of media event that our theorizing here is intended to contemplate, interpret, and understand. It was, after all, an election in the United States, so we might argue that it should be seen as limited to that context and that whatever determinism or "centering" it might have achieved should be seen only there. It was extensively mediated, even "mediatized." The Obama campaign is widely credited with inventing a new kind of politics that integrated social and viral media in unprecedented ways. It has been called the first "internet campaign." This mediatization necessarily made it accessible well beyond the boundaries of its polity. Screen media, journalism, and digital media circulated its images, routines, and events to a global audience.

It was a postmodern and global election in the sense of the real, concrete politics involved – global publics had been galvanized to an unprecedented extent by the excesses of the Bush foreign policy[2] – where publics attended to a political process in which they had a real interest even though they themselves lacked a vote. Thus, a global context of consumption connected with this mediation of politics. There is a kind of unprecedented "thickening" in the viral digital mediation of the Obama campaign in its natural political context (the United States). This bounded context of "emphasis" and "loyalty" may be seen as a straightforward example that demonstrates the utility of the new, de-natured approach to "event" laid out in these pages.

But the Obama election also *problematized* the dimension of globalization that is so important to these considerations. To what extent might we say that it had the capacity to weave together a specific and systematic "thickening," to become a global "media event?" Certainly it was such an event on a more superficial level, but how might it also represent the hailing of global publics into a systematic process of meaning-making, invoking more or less authentic and grounded loyalties to more central "emphases?" Such an emphasis surfaced around normative notions of justice and a seemingly globally shared commitment to humanistic values of egalitarianism.

Mediations of this surfaced in journalistic accounts of the consumption and circulation of the election in non U.S. contexts. I noticed this in November, 2008 radio reports (National Public Radio 2008a, 2008b). In these stories, the symbolic "thickening" around the symbolism of the Obama election was expressed in the question of *when* a given country might – to paraphrase – "elect our own Barack Obama."

In the light of our evolving theories here, such discourses may be argued to represent just the kind of "thickening" Hepp and Couldry have in mind. They are moments of cultural construction where a shared "emphasis" has been circulated by means of a mediated event, and is then attended to and invested with loyalty through a practice of self-reflection and grounding in specific geographic and political contexts. Curious as to how widespread (that is, how "global") this thickening might have become in relation to this event, I conducted an online search using the U.S. American Lexis/Nexis service, looking for the terms "our own Obama." This resulted in over 130 "hits." A review of these found this question being raised about specific, grounded, ethnic and racial politics by journalists and cultural authorities in the following countries: The United Kingdom, France, India, Nigeria, Canada, Australia, Singapore, and Malaysia.[3] It is hard to escape the sense that in the Obama election event we were witnessing a particularly important example of the phenomenon at the center of the concerns of this book. It clearly presented a kind of consistent "emphasis" across a range of national contexts, and invoked culturally constructive processes of meaning-making in those contexts. Regardless of the actual implication of the event for real politics, real racial relations (even in its own national context), and real social progress, it represented a moment of cultural difference that was mediated and global.

A more complete analysis of the Obama election in these or other terms is beyond the scope of my project here. At this turn, it is enough to point to it as a critical test and a crucial example of the theory-building present in this volume. A broader analysis in these terms begs to be done. But my superficial review of only this one dimension of the event demonstrates both the utility of the project here and its potential to make a provocative contribution to our knowledge of cultural processes in globalized, mediated modernity. And, it provides a persuasive argument for the flexible, de-natured approach to media events and media rituals represented in these pages. A whole category of media practice is opened up by the theory-building we have seen here. An exciting future of scholarship awaits.

Notes

1 I use this term, and the distinction between "mediation" and "mediatization," in the sense argued by Hjarvard (2008).
2 I am of course not overlooking the long-standing problematic nature of U.S. foreign policy, only that it achieved a new level during the Bush years.
3 These resulted from my review of only the first *half* of the "hits."

References

Anderson, B. (1991) *Imagined Communities: Reflections on the Origin and Spread of Natonalism*, London: Verso.

Carey, J. (1989) *Communication as Culture: Essays on Media and Society*, Boston, MA: Unwin Hyman.

Couldry, N. (2003) *Media Rituals: A Critical Approach*, London: Routledge.

Dayan, D. and Katz, E. (1992) *Media Events: The Live Broadcasting of History*, Cambridge, MA: Harvard University Press.

Hepp, A. and Couldry, N. (2009) "What Should Comparative Media Research be Comparing? Towards a Transcultural Approach to 'Media Cultures' ", in D.K. Thussu (ed.) *Globalising Media Studies*, London: Routledge.

Hjarvard, S. (2008) "The Mediatization of Religion: A Theory of the Media as Agents of Religious Change", *Northern Lights*, 6: 9–26.

National Public Radio (U.S.) (2008a) "Soccer Match Reopens Ethnic Tension Wounds", *Morning Edition* (Eleanor Beardsley, reporting), November 28.

National Public Radio (U.S.) (2008b) " 'The Obama Effect' prompts Europeans to Confront Racism", *Tell Me More* (Michele Martin, host), November 20.

Rothenbuhler, E.W. (1988) "The living room celebration of the Olympic games", *Journal of Communication*, 38: 61–81.

—— (1998) *Ritual Communication: From Everyday Conversation to Mediated Ceremony*, Thousand Oaks, CA: Sage.

Warner, R.S. (1993) "Work in Progress Toward a New Paradigm for the Sociological Study of Religion in the United States", *American Journal of Sociology*, 98, 5: 1044–93.

INDEX

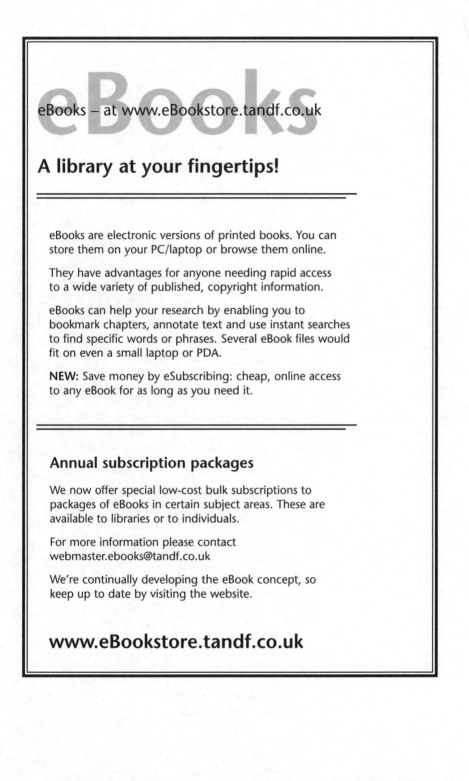